TRIED BY FIRE

TRIED BY FIRE

THE STORY OF CHRISTIANITY'S
FIRST THOUSAND YEARS

WILLIAM J. BENNETT

Nelson Books

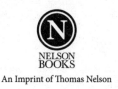

NELSON
BOOKS

An Imprint of Thomas Nelson

Published in Nashville, Tennessee, by Nelson Books, an imprint of Thomas Nelson. Nelson Books and Thomas Nelson are registered trademarks of HarperCollins Christian Publishing, Inc.

Thomas Nelson titles may be purchased in bulk for educational, business, fund-raising, or sales promotional use. For information, please e-mail SpecialMarkets@ThomasNelson.com.

Unless otherwise noted, Scripture quotations are taken from the Holy Bible, New International Version®, NIV®. Copyright © 1973, 1978, 1984, 2011 by Biblica, Inc.® Used by permission of Zondervan. All rights reserved worldwide. www.zondervan.com. The "NIV" and "New International Version" are trademarks registered in the United States Patent and Trademark Office by Biblica, Inc.®

Scripture quotations marked DRB are from the Douay-Rheims Bible (public domain).

Scripture quotations marked ESV are from the ESV® Bible (The Holy Bible, English Standard Version®). Copyright © 2001 by Crossway, a publishing ministry of Good News Publishers. Used by permission. All rights reserved.

Scripture quotations marked NASB are from New American Standard Bible®. Copyright © 1960, 1962, 1963, 1968, 1971, 1972, 1973, 1975, 1977, 1995 by The Lockman Foundation. Used by permission. (www.Lockman.org)

Any Internet addresses, phone numbers, or company or product information printed in this book are offered as a resource and are not intended in any way to be or to imply an endorsement by Thomas Nelson, nor does Thomas Nelson vouch for the existence, content, or services of these sites, phone numbers, companies, or products beyond the life of this book.

ISBN 978-0-7180-1871-9 (eBook)

Library of Congress Cataloging-in-Publication Data

Bennett, William J. (William John), 1943-
    Tried by fire : the story of Christianity's first thousand years / William J. Bennett.
        pages cm
    Includes bibliographical references and index.
    ISBN 978-0-7180-1870-2
    1. Church history--Primitive and early church, ca. 30-600. 2. Church history--Middle Ages, 600-1500. I. Title.
    BR162.3.B465 2016
    270--dc23
                                                        2015033527
Printed in the United States of America

16 17 18 19 20   RRD   10 9 8 7 6 5 4 3 2 1

To those Christians around the world who are still tried by fire and who have given everything for their faith.

Contents

INTRODUCTION

Christians in North America and Europe have always looked forward to celebrating Christmas. The sense of anticipation surrounding the holiday is an indication of what it offers: rejoicing in the Savior's birth, chances to celebrate traditions with family, the exchange of gifts, time off work, and so much more. But Christians around the world don't always have that same sense of anticipation. For some, the approach of the day can be clouded with dread. Let's examine some events of the season that took place around the globe to see why:

- In Somalia, fourteen peacekeepers were killed by Islamist militants as they celebrated Christmas.
- In Iran, seven Christians were hung at dawn on Christmas Day.
- In Kenya, thirty-six Christians in a work camp near the Somali border were either shot or beheaded by Islamist gunmen.
- In Pakistan, a twenty-eight-year-old woman, already the mother of four children and pregnant with another, was forced to walk naked through town and beaten with pipes by her employers. She miscarried. The charge against her? Being a Christian.[1]

And the story of persecution and martyrdom continues; there is more Christian persecution now around the world than at any time in history. Pope Francis made headlines when he suggested as much in 2014.[2] In the same year, the Pew Research Center confirmed: Christians are the world's most persecuted religious group.[3] One needs only to follow the reports coming out of Islamic State–occupied territories to get a sense of how bad the violence against Christians can get. In February 2015, twenty-one Egyptians were beheaded by the Islamic State as they cried out to Christ.[4]

The persecution of Christians is a dismal reality. And yet to Christians it is nothing new. The reignition of persecution of Christians around the world—in Iraq and Syria, Nigeria and Somalia, Pakistan and India—recalls the first few centuries after Christ, when devastation of the church was normal in places that are relatively tolerant today, like Italy, France, and Spain.

This book is the story of that early church, and predominantly its endurance through persecution. The burnings, beheadings, and other tortures of the first few centuries AD did not quash the ability of Christians everywhere to persist in belief. On the contrary, it is clear from the sources from the era that the ravages visited upon the church actually *strengthened* it. As the third-century writer Tertullian declared, "The blood of the martyrs is the seed of the church."[5] Such a phenomenon is so counterintuitive and so supernatural that it deserves new attention here. Most aspects of the growth and theology of the early Christian church are explored here, but special focus is given to how it endured centuries as a target of violence. Stories of Maximus the Confessor, whose tongue was cut out, or Perpetua, who was gored by a bull before being stabbed to death, still cry out to us and remind us of our spiritual roots.

Biography is one of the most excellent ways of teaching history. Consequently, *Tried by Fire* also has a heavily biographical focus. Great weight is given to the accomplishments, inner conflicts, and vital details of scholars (Augustine, Jerome), preachers (John Chrysostom, Gregory

Nazianzus), missionaries (Pope Gregory, Saint Boniface), kings (Constantine, Justinian), and eccentrics (Simeon the Stylite, who lived atop a pillar in the desert; and Origen, who castrated himself). Their stories help illustrate the remarkable nature of their lives and times, and show how the extraordinary depth of their convictions shaped the world. Many of them are very graphic, and I warn the reader ahead of time of some disturbing material.

One of the difficulties in writing a book on the church is that there are so many definitions of what a Christian is. In the centuries since Christ founded his church, divisions over matters great and small have split the church into different sects, with the main divisions being Catholic, Protestant, and Orthodox. The theological framework I employ in this book tries to encompass the most basic points of belief shared among all three. I acknowledge that each group will have, according to its own theological rubric, very different interpretations of the same historical events. The intent of *Tried by Fire* is not so much to declare what turns of history were right or wrong (except in the most obvious cases, such as the Arian denial of the divinity of Christ or the perversions of the tenth-century papacy), but to describe the causes and effects of various events in the first thousand years of the church.

There are already many excellent books on the Christian church. Men have, in fact, been writing histories of the church since the book of Acts. In recent decades, books like Robert Wilken's *The First Thousand Years* and Justo González's *The Story of Christianity* have told the story more than adequately. For clarification, you will notice many factual claims common to church historians that are not accompanied by footnotes. This decision not to cite every fact was made purely out of a consideration of added time to completion of the book and the length of the manuscript, and not a desire to obfuscate my sources. I am indebted to those books and others for much of the research for this book, but it is time to tell more fully this bloody part of the church's story.

In the mid-first century, the apostle Peter wrote to a church suffering persecution. He wanted them to understand that it was not for nothing. He urged that "the trial of your faith (much more precious than gold which is tried by the fire) may be found unto praise and glory and honour at the appearing of Jesus Christ" (1 Peter 1:7 DRB). I hope that your faith will be strengthened by reading the accounts of those who have come, thought, written, and suffered before us.

WILLIAM J. BENNETT
SPRING 2016

ONE

SCATTERED SHEEP

Paul in Rome, the Appeal of Christianity,
Missionary Journeys, and Deaths of the Apostles

O n the night of July 18, AD 64, a great fire erupted in the south-
eastern end of the Circus Maximus, a popular area in the city of
Rome for commerce and entertainment. It quickly swept through the
city, incinerating three districts and severely damaging seven others. Our
idea today of ancient Rome is very often a city of concrete lustered with
marble. In reality, most structures were made of wood or brick, which
offered virtually no protection against fire. This particular blaze raged
for six days before it was extinguished. The Roman historian Tacitus
vividly described the damage the fire inflicted on the city and the panic
experienced by its inhabitants as they tried to save one another:

> Added to this were the wailings of terror-stricken women, the feeble-
> ness of age, the helpless inexperience of childhood, the crowds who
> sought to save themselves or others, dragging out the infirm or wait-
> ing for them, and by their hurry in the one case, by their delay in
> the other, aggravating the confusion. Often, while they looked behind
> them, they were intercepted by flames on their side or in their face.[1]

The emperor at the time was a twenty-seven-year-old descended from a wealthy and powerful line of emperors: Nero Claudius Caesar Augustus Germanicus, or, as he is more commonly known to us, Nero. According to the Roman historian Suetonius, Nero was known for his insatiable lust, avarice, and brutality. His rise to power began with matricide. For fun, he would have innocent men and women bound to a stake. Nero himself, clad in the skin of some wild animal, then would spring forth from a cage and attack their private areas. On this night, claimed Suetonius, Nero dressed in stage costume and sang a popular song about the burning of the mythical city of Troy.

In the aftermath, Nero decided to build a palace, the Domus Aurea (Golden House), on the site where the fire began. Rumors began to spread around Rome: Had Nero himself engineered such carnage, all to build a palace for himself?[2]

We don't know how exactly the inferno began, or what Nero's role was in engineering it. But we do know that Nero, to deflect attention from the rumors that labeled him an arsonist, quickly looked for

A bust of the Emperor Nero in the Pushkin State Museum, Moscow.

a scapegoat. His sinister gaze would soon fall on a group that had nothing to do with it, a group that Suetonius described as "a class of men given to a new and mischievous superstition."[3]

Nero had targeted the nascent Christian community in Rome. His vindictive purge was the first state-sponsored persecution of Christians in history. In the words of Eusebius of Caesaria, a historian from the fourth century AD who is often called "the Father of Church History," Nero "began to plunge into unholy pursuits, and armed himself even against the religion of the God of the universe."[4] Tacitus paints a sickening portrait of the Neronian persecutions. Christians were arrested and forced to confess under threat of death. Many were then sentenced to death, not so much for setting the fire, but for hatred against mankind. Their deaths were humiliating and excruciating:

> Mockery of every sort was added to their deaths. Covered with the skins of beasts, they were torn by dogs and perished, or were nailed to crosses, or were doomed to the flames and burnt, to serve as a nightly illumination, when daylight had expired. Nero offered his gardens for the spectacle, and was exhibiting a show in the circus, while he mingled with the people in the dress of a charioteer.[5]

But even such violence did not—could not—stamp out the Christians. Tertullian, writing in the third century, managed to praise the Neronian persecution as evidence that the Christian life was something worth living: "We glory in having such a man as the leader in our punishment. For whoever knows him can understand that nothing was condemned by Nero unless it was something of great excellence."[6]

Few Roman citizens loudly objected to the persecutions. But Nero's outrageous and unjust administration eventually incited a rebellion and earned him the title of public enemy. As his enemies closed in on his hideout in 68, he ordered one of his attendants to stab him to death. Nero's famous dying words were *"Qualis artifex pereo,"* which translates into English as "What an artist dies in me!" To his last breath, Nero was a man who gloried in his own violence, lust, and narcissism. His self-conception was the very opposite of his most famous victim's, to whom we now turn our attention.

PAUL IN ROME

From the mid-30s AD onward, the man born Saul of Tarsus had devoted himself to telling the Mediterranean world about Jesus, a Jewish carpenter from the small town of Nazareth in the Roman province of Judea. Initially, Saul himself was a member of the Sanhedrin, the Jewish religious teaching class; he had been a zealous persecutor of those who adhered to Jesus' teachings. "Saul began to destroy the church," says the book of Acts. "Going from house to house, he dragged off both men and women and put them in prison" (8:3). One day in probably the year 33 or 34, Saul set out for Damascus, in Syria, to find any Jews there who were members of "the Way" (Acts 9:2) so that they might be imprisoned in Jerusalem for violating Jewish religious law. But while on the road there, he was blinded with a bright light and fell on his face. A voice accompanied the light: "Saul, Saul, why do you persecute me?" "Who are you, Lord?" Saul asked. "I am Jesus, whom you are persecuting," the voice replied (vv. 4–5). Saul eventually reached Damascus and lay blinded for three days, until a Damascene Christian named Ananias came and healed him. Ananias was afraid to approach Saul, knowing how intensely he hated Christians. And he must have been puzzled by God's own words describing how he planned

to use Saul: "Go! This man is my chosen instrument to proclaim my name to the Gentiles and their kings and to the people of Israel. I will show him how much he must suffer for my name" (vv. 15–16). Ananias laid hands on Saul, and the next day Saul went to the Jewish synagogue in Damascus, where he preached "fearlessly" that Jesus was the Son of God (v. 27).

Caravaggio, *The Conversion of St. Paul*, ca. 1600.

Saul then traveled to meet the other disciples in Jerusalem. Initially, they were fearful of him, not believing he was really a disciple because of his reputation as a destroyer of Christians. But he was soon accepted on the basis of his preaching. He took the name Paul, choosing to adapt the Gentile (meaning non-Jewish) way of pronouncing his name in order to ingratiate himself to them. Paul began visiting synagogues, teaching to the Jewish congregations that the life, death, and resurrection of Jesus Christ was the fulfillment of messianic prophecies found in the Hebrew Old Testament. (In English, the word *Christ* comes from the Greek word *Christos*, which means "anointed one." This was a transliteration of the Hebrew word *Messiah*, which means the same.) Paul's reputation as a persecutor preceded him, and his conversion confounded his audiences. As the book of Acts says, "All those who heard him were astonished and asked, 'Isn't he the man who raised havoc in Jerusalem among those who call on this name? And hasn't he come here to take them as prisoners to the chief priests?'" (9:21). But Paul kept declaring to them that Jesus was the Christ.

In time, Paul became an itinerant evangelist, crisscrossing the Mediterranean world, telling the gospel of Jesus Christ to Jews and Gentiles. At Athens, Paul confronted Stoic and Epicurean philosophers with the gospel. On the island of Cyprus, he temporarily blinded a false prophet (Acts 13:4–12). At Ephesus, a city in the ancient world famous for its shrine to the Greek goddess Artemis, Paul fled a mob of craftsmen that had been angered by his insistence that their gods of silver and gold were not real gods (19:23–41). It wasn't out of piety that these craftsmen chased him down; the Ephesian economy was dependent on visitors to the shrine. At times, as God had told Ananias would happen, Paul suffered an incredible amount of physical persecution for following Christ. As Paul recounted in 2 Corinthians,

> Five times I received from the Jews the forty lashes minus one. Three times I was beaten with rods, once I was pelted with stones, three times I was shipwrecked, I spent a night and a day in the open sea, I have been constantly on the move. I have been in danger from rivers, in danger from bandits, in danger from my fellow Jews, in danger from Gentiles; in danger in the city, in danger in the country, in danger at sea; and in danger from false believers. I have labored and toiled and have often

gone without sleep; I have known hunger and thirst and have often gone without food; I have been cold and naked. Besides everything else, I face daily the pressure of my concern for all the churches. (11:24–28)

But none of it deterred Paul. He planted multiple churches across the Mediterranean world and won many converts. Now, in AD 67, Paul was in Rome, and his faith would again be tested. Nero's persecution was raging. Although we have no contemporaneous written record of Paul's last days or martyrdom, and there is still a healthy amount of scholarly debate on the topic, early church tradition claims that Paul was beheaded at Rome during the Neronian persecution.

A letter by Clement of Rome, written in about AD 90, comments on Paul's attitude in facing death: "After that he had been seven times in bonds, had been driven into exile, had been stoned, had preached in the East and in the West, he won the noble renown which was the reward of his faith . . . he departed from the world and went unto the holy place, having been found a notable pattern of patient endurance."[7]

In 2002, the Vatican commissioned an excavation of a tomb in the Basilica of Saint Paul Outside-the-Walls in Rome, a church near the Vatican that for two millennia has been thought to contain the remains of the apostle. In 2009, the pope released the results of the excavation. He noted that a white marble sarcophagus had been found containing bone fragments that were carbon-dated to the first or second century AD. In addition to the bone fragments, the archaeologists also found "some grains of incense, a 'precious' piece of purple linen with gold sequins, and a blue fabric with linen filaments." A slab of cracked marble with the Latin words for *"Paul apostle martyr"* was also found set in the floor above the tomb. "This seems to confirm the unanimous and uncontested tradition that they are the mortal remains of the Apostle Paul," declared Pope Benedict.[8] What motivated Paul to embrace suffering and death? Certainly being a Christian brought him no earthly rewards, like money, social acceptance, or a life of comfort. To answer the question, we look now at how the earliest iterations of Christianity contrasted with the paganism of the ancient world.

THE APPEAL OF CHRISTIANITY TO THE CLASSICAL WORLD

To its first-century (and modern) practitioners, the Christian hope of eternal deliverance from eternal punishment and earthly misery was so attractive that Paul could write to the Philippians that, for him, "to die is gain" (Phil. 1:21). Under the rubric of Jesus' and Paul's teachings, the first Christians understood Christ's righteousness to be their own. The virtue was not obtained through one's nature, habits, power of reason, or intelligence, but through the grace of God. This was a huge change from the classical notion that virtue was mostly a cultivated trait. The Christian faith also put no intellectual, ethnic, racial, gender, or class restriction on who could be a member. This ministry on earth presaged the unity that Jesus intended for the future church in his absence. As Paul had written in his epistle to the Galatians, "There is neither Jew nor Gentile, neither slave nor free, nor is there male and female, for you are all one in Christ Jesus" (Gal. 3:28). Jesus as he appears in the Gospels is also radical for his associations with the sinful, poor, infirm, and ignorant. This concern for the lowest stratum of society revealed a valuation of human life that was vastly more empathetic than Greco-Roman notions. To the Christian, every human being, having been made in the image of God, is precious in the sight of the Almighty. In time, this attitude would permeate Western thinking on all kinds of issues; in the early Middle Ages, for example, it was the Christian ethic that ended slavery in the Roman world. Christianity, and in particular its approach to sexual morality and gender norms, also improved enormously the condition of women, a topic to be explored in a later chapter.

Values derived from Christianity have largely been responsible for the relative economic, personal, and political freedoms enjoyed in the West. Although Western civilization has, especially in the past century, drifted from its Christian roots on issues like the sanctity of life, the importance of work, the formation of the family, and the centrality of faith in public life, our culture is still more derivative of Christianity than of any other world religion. Even amid the rise of secularism, the average Western man or woman has a concern for the inherent dignity of the individual, the condition of the poor, and the right to religious expression. And countries around the world have taken note of what has allowed Western civilization to distinguish itself. Harvard professor Niall Ferguson's 2011 book, *Civilization*, carried a remarkable quote from a member of the Chinese Academy of Social Sciences, which had recently conducted a study that attempted to identify the dominant factor that made Western civilization so successful compared to other civilizations:

> We were asked to look into what accounted for the . . . pre-eminence of the West all over the world . . .
>
> We studied everything we could from the historical, political, economic, and cultural perspective. At first, we thought it was because you had more powerful guns than we had.
>
> Then we thought it was because you had the best political system. Next we focused on your economic system. But in the past twenty years, we have realized that the heart of your culture is your religion: Christianity. That is why the West has been so powerful. The Christian moral foundation of social and cultural life was what made possible the emergence of capitalism and then the successful transition to democratic politics. We don't have any doubt about this.[9]

The societal benefits of Christianity may seem obvious to some of us now. But it took centuries before ideas that had their origin in the gospel would become permanently knit into the cultural fabric. This is evident as we examine some of the struggles of the apostolic age of the church.

MISSIONARY ACTIVITY AND PERSECUTION OF THE DISCIPLES

The traditional view of the origin of the Christian church is that it began at Pentecost. Pentecost fell on a feast day in ancient Israel that celebrated Moses' receipt of the Law on Mount Sinai. On this day in AD 33, it happened to occur within a few days of Jesus' ascension into heaven, when 120 or so believers were gathered together to pray and ponder their next steps. On that day, the Holy Spirit, "like the blowing of a violent wind," swooped down from heaven and enabled all of the assembled to understand one another in a common language, despite the fact that they all were speaking their native tongues: Cappadocians, Cretans, Elamites, Egyptians, Galileans, Jews, Judeans, Medes, Mesopotamians, Pamphylians, Parthians, Pontians, Phrygians, and Romans (Acts 2:2–10). Some observers who heard the commotion were bemused by the sight and suggested that they were all drunk. But the apostle Peter stood up in response and delivered the first sermon of the Christian church: "Therefore let all Israel be assured of this: God has made this Jesus, whom you crucified, both Lord and Messiah" (v. 36). The preaching must have been powerful; the book of Acts reports that "about three thousand were added to their number that day" (2:41).

The significance of Peter rising to preach should not be overlooked. In Matthew 16, Jesus told his disciple Simon, "And I tell you that you are Peter, and on this rock I will build my church, and the gates of Hades will not overcome it. I will give you the keys of the kingdom of heaven; whatever you bind on earth will be bound in heaven, and whatever you loose on earth will be loosed in heaven" (vv. 18–19). Catholics have interpreted these words to establish that Christ appointed Peter to be the head of the Christian church, and one to whom the other disciples

9

would defer in matters of doctrine and ecclesiastical dispute. Among other sects of Christianity, there is a great diversity of opinion as to what exactly Jesus meant by this. Whatever one thinks about the question, the Gospels' depiction of Peter as one of the disciples to whom Jesus was closest, along with Peter's preeminence in Acts, establishes him as one of the leaders of the New Testament church.

The book of Acts captures in detail Peter's ministry in the time of the New Testament church. He was uncompromisingly brave in the face of legal and physical retribution. Peter and John, "unschooled, ordinary men," were thrown in jail before being tried by the Jewish ruling council (Acts 4:13). As punishment, the council declared they would have to stop preaching in public. But Peter and John could not be deterred. "We cannot help speaking about what we have seen and heard," they declared (v. 20). When Peter arrived at a house in which a young woman had died, the woman's friends were there, crying and holding out the pieces of clothing that she once made. With the words "Tabitha, get up," Peter raised her from the dead (9:40). When Peter was put in prison, an angel freed him, an event that went unnoticed by sixteen Roman guards. After "no small commotion," the sixteen were executed for their dereliction (12:18–19).

The apostles' work would not be impeded by the martyrdom of one of their own. The first martyr of the Christian church was Stephen, as documented in the book of Acts. Stephen was stoned to death by a mob of angry Jewish leaders, who were incensed by Stephen's accusation: "You always resist the Holy Spirit . . . you who have received the law that was given through angels but have not obeyed it" (7:51, 53). Acts tells us that in Stephen's final moments he saw the heavens open, with

Paolo Uccello, *The Stoning of St. Stephen*, ca. 1435.

Jesus standing at the right hand of God. His final words were, "Lord, do not hold this sin against them" (v. 60).

The first of the apostles to die for the faith, and the second known martyrdom of the Christian church, was James, the brother of John, who died in AD 44, approximately ten years after Stephen. James was beheaded, the book of Acts says, as Herod Agrippa I, the grandson of King Herod, laid "violent hands" on members of the church (12:1 ESV). Perhaps James was singled out for his passion; he and his brother John were nicknamed the "sons of thunder" by Jesus on account of their temper (Mark 3:17). A story told by Clement of Alexandria holds that as James was being led to his execution, one of the soldiers guarding him was so moved by his courage in the face of death that he himself made a sudden profession of faith in Christ. This sudden change of heart came with a price: both James and the soldier were executed that day.[10] Soon after the death of James, however, Herod was struck dead during a speech "because Herod did not give praise to God." His body, the writer of Acts told us, was eaten by worms (12:23).

Herod Agrippa's reasons for persecuting Christians are not clear. Perhaps he felt a duty to defend the Jewish order, or perhaps he was acting at the behest of his Roman masters. Many Romans were suspicious of Christians for their close-knit communities, and accused them of incest (Christians called one another "brother" and "sister") and cannibalism (a gross misunderstanding of the Lord's Supper). The Romans also looked with scorn on the Christian practice of declining to acknowledge the Roman emperor as a god. In their minds, such atheism had potential to disturb the social order and anger the traditional Roman gods, who would exact vengeance on Rome.

In the decades after the formation of the church in AD 33, the apostles devoted themselves exclusively to missionary activity in Judea and around the world. Save for a few of them, their lives all culminated in martyrdom. Most of the sources that mention Matthew ("the Evangelist") describe a connection to the areas south of the Caspian Sea, though some suggest he traveled to Ethiopia. Some traditions also say he was beheaded around

AD 60 with a halberd, a type of ax with a sharp pike extending through the top. Andrew (derived from the Greek word *andros*: "manly, brave") traveled to regions around the Black Sea—what we today would recognize as Istanbul, Bulgaria, and even as far as Ukraine. He is said to have been crucified on an X-shaped cross in either Greece or Turkey. This style of cross is known today as Saint Andrew's Cross.

The apostle Philip was sent out to the regions of Lydia and Phrygia, which today are parts of modern-day Turkey. After Philip healed and preached to the wife of the Roman governor there, the governor became enraged and had Philip, his sister, Mariamne, and Bartholomew strip-searched, scourged, and crucified. A crowd that assembled begged that the proconsul release them from their crosses. They took Bartholomew and Miriamne down, but Philip refused to be taken down, and in his last breath prayed that the Lord would deliver him from evil: "Let not their dark air cover me, that I may pass the waters of fire and all the abyss. Clothe me in thy glorious robe and thy seal of light that ever shineth."[11] His dying instructions to the crowd that had gathered were supposedly, "Build a church in the place where I die."[12] In 2012, after more than fifty-five years of multigenerational efforts, an Italian archaeological team discovered what they believed to be the tomb of Philip in Hierapolis (modern-day Denizli, Turkey). The tomb was located in the center of a once magnificently adorned church.[13] One of the key pieces of evidence that was discovered was a metallic seal four inches in diameter, with the words "Saint Philip" on one side. The archaeologists believe that this seal was impressed into freshly baked bread distributed to pilgrims to the church, so that they could know it was a special bread to be kept with devotion.[14]

James, said to be by many the brother of Jesus and the author of the book of James in the Bible (also called James "the Just" or "the Great"), is considered by many Protestants to have been the leader of the church at Jerusalem for nearly thirty years after the death and resurrection of Christ. Jerome, quoting the first-century Christian chronicler Hegesippus, said he "drank neither wine nor strong drink, ate no flesh, never shaved or anointed himself with ointment or bathed."[15] Sometime probably in AD 62, James was arrested and brought before the Sanhedrin and stoned. Eusebius's account holds that James was thrown from the pinnacle of Solomon's temple and then given a deadly blow to the head from a fuller's club, a tool used for wringing out garments after they had been dyed.[16]

Peter's own death had been foretold by Jesus in the book of John: "When you are old you will stretch out your hands, and someone else will dress you and lead you where you do not want to go" (John 21:18). Tertullian and Origen, scholars in the third century, report that Peter, believing himself unworthy to die the same death as his master, was crucified upside down in Rome. One modern historian has placed Peter's death as occurring three months after Nero's great fire in AD 64. The famous phrase "*Quo vadis?*" (in English, "Where are you going?") is said to have been what Jesus asked Peter in a vision Peter had as he was fleeing persecution in Rome. Convicted by this visitation, the legend goes, Peter turned around and faced his foretold end.

One of the most interesting apostolic stories is that of Thomas. Thomas is reputed to have traveled as far as India on his missionary journeys, a claim that has substantial evidence to its credit. One of the legends associated with Thomas is that an Indian king, Gondophares, needed a palace built, and that Thomas, though not an architect, showed up and volunteered to do it. When the king discovered that Thomas was giving money earmarked for the palace to the poor, Gondophares had him thrown in prison. But then the king's brother Gad was thought to have died. When Gad's "death" turned out to be a temporary lack of consciousness and he was revived, he said he had seen a marvelous heavenly palace that Thomas was building with the king's money. The king and his brother were then converted and baptized. The story of Gondophares as told above seems unlikely. But there is substantial evidence to suggest that Thomas really did visit India and that there really was a King Gondophares with a brother named Gad. In the middle of the nineteenth century, an inscription dated to about AD 46 was found mentioning the name King Gondophares, as well as many coins bearing his name that were minted no later than the end of the first century AD.[17] The poems of Ephrem the Syrian, composed in the middle of the fourth century, also attest to Thomas's presence in India:

> The One-Begotten his Apostles chose,
> Among them Thomas, who he sent
> To baptize peoples perverse, in darkness steeped
> A dark night then India's land enveloped
> Like the sun's ray Thomas did dart forth
> There he dawned, and her illuminated.[18]

In the Western church, Jerome, Ambrose, Isadore of Seville, Gregory of Tours, and the Venerable Bede all attest to Thomas's travels to India. The most popular tradition states that Thomas was speared to death by a group of soldiers, while other traditions say he died a natural death. In the case of Thomas and the other apostolic accounts, many of the historical sources that we have about the lives and works of the apostles are of questionable reliability, and sometimes obvious unreliability. In general, hagiography, the written accounts of saints' lives, is characterized by embellishment and half-truths. Often the goal of hagiographers, even through the Middle Ages, was to depict the character of their subjects through fictional (or semifictional) episodes. Therefore, varying degrees of credence should be given to much of the extrabiblical information that we have about the lives and deaths of the apostles. At best, many of the accounts that we believe today are the culmination of tradition, whether accurate or not. Regardless, as church historian Justo González noted, "It is significant that from a relatively early date there was a church in India, and that this church has repeatedly claimed Thomas as its founder."[19]

Antagonists of Christianity often claim that Christianity was merely a tool that the wealthy and powerful used to control and oppress the helpless. But the lives of the apostles after Christ reveal them to be men who were nothing if not rejected and hated. If these men conspired to start a religion, what did it profit them to live a life of modest material gain, remove themselves from family and friends, endure the hardships of travel, and die violent deaths? Their motivation was something that transcended their immediate comfort and reputation, and they had no guarantees that their message of the Way would make their faith famous to future generations. But even as the apostolic generation died out, mostly in the AD 60s and 70s, it was clear to anyone who traveled across the ancient world that their work of planting churches and making disciples had not been in vain, and that a new generation of pastors and writers was ready to make sure it would continue.

TWO

The First Saints

*The Domitianic Persecutions, Christian
Communities as Seen in Clement and
Ignatius, and the Martyrdom of Polycarp*

B y the time the last apostle died, Christianity had established a foothold in the Roman world and beyond. Churches had sprouted up
in both important and lesser cities across the Mediterranean—including
Rome, Corinth, Jerusalem, Ephesus, and more. But the Christian
church's relative lack of prominence did nothing to assuage the ire that
its mere existence incited. The second great wave of persecution of the
Christian church (the first was Nero's) occurred under Domitian, the
Roman emperor from AD 81 to 96. Domitian had a number of bizarre
personality traits, one of which was enjoying extreme periods of isolation.
Suetonius, the historian of the first Caesars, noted, "At the beginning of
his reign he used to spend hours in seclusion every day, doing nothing
but catch flies and stab them with a keenly sharpened stylus."[1] Although
Domitian's appetites for food, women, and entertainment were (compared to his predecessors') relatively restrained, Domitian was also
capable of enormous cruelty. He once put to death an apprentice actor for
a performance too similar to his master's, as well as a historian—along

with his slaves—who wrote some inelegant prose. Domitian thought he could produce loyalty in his subjects by creating a personality cult in his image, and he micromanaged every piece of imperial administration, while believing himself to be a god. By the end of his reign, Suetonius noted, "he had become an object of terror and hatred to all."[2] A letter to the Corinthian church written by the leader of the church at Rome, Clement, around AD 96 describes "our recent series of unexpected misfortunes and set-backs."[3] This is sometimes thought to be a reference to Domitian's persecution.

Domitian's fanaticism for the traditional Roman gods (this included himself) meant that he could not abide the religious practices of the Christians. As such, he undertook a strident campaign of persecution, known as the Second Persecution. It is possible that the apostle John was one of his victims. One tradition holds that John was apprehended and cast into a pot of boiling oil in the middle of the Colosseum, only to escape unscathed by divine intervention.[4] We do know for certain that John was exiled for his faith to Patmos, a tiny and barren island off the coast of Turkey, where he served as a slave in the island's salt mines. John received his revelation and recorded it sometime in the latter half of the first century AD, in most scholars' views. It is most likely that he died around AD 98 in Ephesus; he was one of the few apostles who was not killed for his faith. John was also the last apostle to die, his life having spanned nearly the entire century.

Another biblical figure who was martyred in this time was Timothy, the younger companion of the apostle Paul. In the New Testament, Timothy had proved his endurance as a Christian. He was jailed at least once, and Paul, no stranger to suffering, wrote to the Philippians, "I have no one else like him" (Phil. 2:20). Tradition in the Orthodox Church holds that Timothy was killed in Ephesus in AD 93 at the age of eighty. Timothy at that time was the leader of the church of Ephesus, and one day saw some of the Ephesians celebrating a pagan festival by carrying idols through the streets and singing hymns to them. Devastated by the worship of false gods, Timothy decided to preach the gospel to them, and was rewarded by being beaten with clubs, dragged through the streets, and stoned to death.[5]

Around the time of the Domitianic persecutions, the first major theological controversies surrounding the Christian faith began to develop. The Council of Jerusalem, held around AD 50, as recounted in the book of Acts, attempted to remedy the very first substantial theological disagreement among Christians: some of the disciples were divided as to whether Gentile converts should be obligated to keep some elements of the old Jewish law, including circumcision.[6] But the parties in that disagreement had all been Christians who agreed on the essential elements of the faith. Now greater threats were at hand. Jesus previously warned in Matthew that there would be false teachers who "come to you in sheep's clothing, but inwardly they are ferocious wolves" (7:15). Paul's and Peter's epistles also warned of the same and condemned false teachers who preyed on the first Christian churches. But around the beginning of the second century, individuals who challenged accepted doctrine were gaining a bigger following than ever. A man named Cerinthus, evidently operating in the same area as John, was teaching that some power other than God created the world, that Jesus was the product of a union between Joseph and Mary, and that Jesus was not the Christ until his baptism. Cerinthus also thought that adherence to the Jewish law was absolutely necessary for salvation. This false teaching, some scholars speculate, was John's motivation to write the epistle now known in the New Testament as 1 John. Irenaeus, writing at the end of the second century, reported that when John went to the bathhouse at Ephesus and saw Cerinthus inside, he rushed out without bathing, exclaiming, "Let us fly, lest even the bath-house fall down, because Cerinthus, the enemy of the truth, is within."[7] Fortunately, the currency of Cerinthus's teachings was limited, and over time the false teachings, which taught that the application of Jewish law was necessary for salvation, died out. Still, the early church would be forced to confront many contentious theological questions in the years ahead. Thankfully, the generation of church leaders at the end of the first and beginning of the second century helped rightly define the theology of Christianity, the structure of the church, and how Christians should live.

CLEMENT HELPS GUIDE THE CHURCH

At the end of the first century, the Christian church was a loose association of congregations that were not yet under the authority of the church at Rome. These congregations (many of which are written to in the New Testament) were usually led by a council of elders (in Greek: *presbyteroi*) or overseers (*episcopoi*). This first generation of leaders to come after the disciples were probably either appointed by the disciples themselves or chosen by the congregation according to the standards for eldership prescribed in the New Testament.[8] In time, however, the eldership model (still practiced in many Protestant churches today) gained less popularity, and each city, often containing multiple churches, came under the authority of a single leader called a bishop (also from Greek *episcopos*, from which our English word *episcopal* comes, and one can hear clearly the transformation from *ePISCOPos* in Greek to *BISHOP* in English). There were a few reasons for this change: many came to believe that a single bishop more clearly represented the unity of the church, could be an unencumbered source of authority, and also served as an unmistakable public figurehead. We will read later how these independent bishops became subject to the bishop of Rome.

The most important theologian and churchman of the Western church at the end of the first century was Clement of Rome, who would later be remembered as Pope Clement I. Just as his papal predecessors Peter and Linus are mentioned in the New Testament, Clement is probably the Clement referred to in Philippians 4:3. His only surviving piece of writing (known as First Clement) is an epistle to the Corinthian church, which at the time was apparently suffering a crisis of leadership. Younger men in the church, motivated by pride and jealousy, were expelling older, more faithful leaders from their leadership posts. Although First Clement was written around AD 96, a complete manuscript of this work wasn't rediscovered until 1628, when a Bible presented to King Charles I was found to have some additional writings in the back of it. Clement's work is studied consideration of the doctrine that was handed down from the apostles: the certainty of the resurrection of Christ, rules governing the administration of the Eucharist, the preaching of the gospel, and so on. But the most significant aspect of the letter is his commentary on how churches are to respect the authority of those who lead them:

> Similarly, our Apostles knew, through our Lord Jesus Christ, that there would be dissensions over the title of bishop. In their full knowledge of this, therefore, they proceeded to appoint the ministers I spoke of, and they went on to add an instruction that if these should fall asleep, other accredited persons might succeed them in their office. In view of this, we cannot think it right for these men now to be ejected from their ministry, when, after being commissioned by the Apostles (or by other reputable persons at a later date) with the full consent of the Church, they have since been serving Christ's flock in a humble, peaceable, and disinterested way, and earning everybody's approval over so long a period of time.[9]

Clement's letter shows how the first church leaders wrote to give each other a dose of encouragement against a hostile world. In time, however, later interpreters would cite Clement's letter to the Corinthians as an example of the authority that the Roman church had over others, since that authority (they claimed) was granted by the apostles themselves to the bishop at Rome. Clement's epistle is also important for its references to Scripture. Clement directly quotes from numerous books in the New Testament, including 1 Corinthians, Ephesians, and Hebrews, and from the Old Testament books of (at least) the Psalms, Isaiah, and Jeremiah. The significance of this should not be overlooked. Clement's citation of these books in a letter that was itself subsequently circulated meant that the church was beginning to gain an understanding of which books were to be considered inspired by the Holy Spirit. Clement's references to the Old Testament showed that the early church acknowledged a theological continuity between the New and Old Testaments. Although the practices of Judaism had fallen away, Clement, like Paul, recognized that the Jewish Scriptures too were useful for teaching the Christian faith (Jesus, of course, often quoted the Old Testament also). Clement took a high view of Scripture, emphasizing that the Scriptures are authoritative statements of Christian belief: "By all means be pugnacious and hot-headed, my brothers, but about things that will lead to salvation. Just take a look at the sacred scriptures; they are the authentic voice of the Holy Spirit, and you know that they contain nothing that is contrary to justice, nor nothing in them falsified. You are not going to find men of piety evicting the righteous there."[10]

Clement died during the reign of the emperor Trajan, probably as a martyr. But the sources for Clement's death are no younger than the fourth century, making it difficult to verify an accurate account of how he died. The traditional story goes that during the reign of the emperor Trajan, Clement was arrested for being a Christian and banished to the Black Sea. When he arrived at the penal colony, the other prisoners were suffering from thirst. Clement knelt down to pray, and when he looked up, he saw a lamb standing on the spot where he should find water. He struck the spot, and a geyser of water burst forth. Upon seeing this, hundreds of the other prisoners converted to Christianity. The incensed overseer of the camp put Clement to death by throwing him in the sea with an anchor around his neck. To this day, one of the symbols associated with Saint Clement is an anchor. Probably because of his association with the Black Sea region, which later would come under the jurisdiction of the Orthodox Church, Saint Clement is the only Roman pope to be honored in the Russian Orthodox Church with a church in his name. But Clement's most meaningful legacy was his views on church leadership and his definition of the canon of Scripture.

IGNATIUS OF ANTIOCH

At roughly the same time, on the other end of the Roman world in Syria, Ignatius, the bishop of Antioch, was considering and writing about the same topics as Clement. Ignatius had been a disciple of John, and tradition in the Eastern Orthodox Church holds that Ignatius was personally appointed by Peter to be the bishop of Antioch.[11] Like Clement, Ignatius's concern for orthodoxy dominates his writings. Many of the most recognizable features of Christianity are described therein. Ignatius functioned as the most prolific link between the apostles and the early church, and om the words of one scholar, "his testimony must necessarily carry with it the greatest weight and demand the most serious consideration."[12]

All of Ignatius's surviving letters were written on a journey to Rome, where he would meet death by being torn to pieces by lions. Consequently, his letters to the churches around the Roman world are wrought with a desperate love and concern for his brothers and sisters. One of Ignatius's main themes is a pleading that the churches would reject the heresies that were creeping into the church. "I entreat you . . . not to nourish yourselves on anything but Christian fare, and have no truck with the alien herbs of heresy," he wrote.[13] Rejection of heresy included shunning those who claimed to be Christians but adhered to false teaching: "You must keep away from these men as you would from a pack of savage animals; they are rabid curs who snap at peoples unawares, and you need to be on guard against their bites, because they are by no means easy to heal."[14] Ignatius also emphasized the importance of the Eucharist (the Lord's Supper), declaring it the "medicine of immortality."[15] As one who was personally instructed by at least one of the apostles, he was equipped to say much on the subject.

In matters of ecclesiology (the study of the church), Ignatius, like Clement, emphasized the line of apostolic succession and the obedience of each church to its leadership: "[N]obody's conscience can be clean if he is acting without the authority of his bishop, clergy, and deacons."[16] Ignatius also insisted that Christians routinely gather together as a bulwark against sin: "When you meet frequently, the powers of Satan are confounded, and in the face of your corporate faith his maleficence crumbles."[17] The spiritual consequences of removing oneself from the body of Christ are grave: "Anyone who absents himself from the congregation convicts himself at once of arrogance and becomes self-excommunicate."[18] At the root, Ignatius's pronouncements reflect a desire for unity; in fact, his epistle to the church in Smyrna contains the first recorded usage of the Greek word *katholikos* ("catholic, universal") in an ecclesiastical sense: "Where the bishop is to be seen, there let all his people be; just as wherever Jesus Christ is present, we have the world-wide (*katholikos*) church."[19] Ignatius's use of the word indicates that he hoped the church would be a worldwide body, bonded together in the spirit of Christ.

Sometime in the early first century, the emperor Trajan sought to make recently conquered areas in the East bend more submissively to Roman rule by ordering that only religions that worshipped the Roman gods would be allowed in those areas. Anyone who disobeyed this law would be persecuted. Ignatius began to preach the gospel with more fervency than ever before. Of course, this led to his arrest and conviction. The emperor Trajan happened to be visiting Antioch, and when Ignatius was summoned before him, Ignatius fearlessly proclaimed the truth of Jesus Christ to his face. Trajan, unmoved, ordered him to be bound in chains and taken to Rome, where he would be food for wild beasts. Around AD 107, Ignatius was transported to Rome via ship. His vessel made multiple stops along the way, and Christians from various communities, who were aware of his impending execution, came out to offer support to him. To these churches he wrote a number of letters, encouraging them to persist in the faith and embrace sound doctrine. While others grieved the old man's impending death, Ignatius zealously desired his own martyrdom. His epistle to the Romans is a profoundly personal exultation of the heavenly crown that awaits the martyr, and he even urges the Christians at Rome not to prevent him from meeting his desired end:

> For my part, I am writing to all the churches and assuring them that I am truly in earnest about dying for God—if only you yourself put no obstacles in the way. I must implore you to do me no such untimely kindness; pray leave me to be a meal for the beasts, for it is they who can provide my way to God. I am His wheat, ground fine by the lions' teeth to be made purest bread for Christ. Better still, incite the creatures to become a sepulchre for me; let them not leave the smallest scrap of my flesh, so that I need not be a burden to anyone after I fall asleep. When there is no trace of my body left for the world to see, then I shall truly be Jesus Christ's disciple.

The martyrdom of Ignatius of Antioch as depicted in an eleventh-century Byzantine illuminated manuscript.

> So intercede with Him for me, that by their instrumentality I may be made a sacrifice to God . . . How I look forward to the real lions that have been got ready for me! All I pray is that I may find them swift. I am going to make overtures to them, so that, unlike some other wretches whom they have been too spiritless to touch, they may devour me with all speed . . . Fire, cross, beast-fighting, hacking and quartering, splintering of bone and mangling

of limb, even the pulverizing of my entire body—let every horrid and diabolical torment come upon me, provided only that I can win my way to Christ![20]

Later in that year, Ignatius was fed to the lions in the Flavian amphitheater in Rome. His loving yet firm instruction to other congregations and his eagerness for martyrdom illustrate the depth of his faith conviction. To the end, "he proves himself in every sense a true pastor of souls, the good shepherd that lays down his life for his sheep."[21]

RESURFACING OF PERSECUTION IN THE LATE-FIRST AND EARLY-SECOND CENTURIES

Instances of martyrdom like the ones recounted above might suggest that Roman persecution of Christians, wherever they were, was official imperial policy in the late-first and early-second centuries. But in the first few centuries of the Christian era, the campaigns of persecution that made victims of Clement and Ignatius were generally localized and sporadic affairs, more organized by governors of the provinces than by the emperors at Rome. The lack of an official imperial procedure on legal prosecution is evident from a surviving correspondence between Pliny the Younger, a governor of a Roman province in what is now Turkey, and the emperor Trajan himself. Pliny wrote to Trajan asking for official guidance on how to handle the prosecution of Christians. Having not received any previous instruction on how to manage these cases, Pliny did what seemed best to him at the time:

> In the meanwhile, the method I have observed towards those who have been brought before me as Christians is this: I asked them whether they were Christians; if they admitted it, I repeated the question twice, and

threatened them with punishment; if they persisted, I ordered them to be at once punished: for I was persuaded, whatever the nature of their opinions might be, a contumacious and inflexible obstinacy certainly deserved correction.[22]

Pliny questioned the Christians who appeared before him, demanding to know what their religious practices were. They told him that they assembled before dawn, prayed, and took the Lord's Supper together. But Pliny didn't believe them at first, and tortured two deaconesses to identify what they were really up to:

> After receiving this account, I judged it so much the more necessary to endeavor to extort the real truth, by putting two female slaves to the torture, who were said to officiate in their religious rites: but all I could discover was evidence of an absurd and extravagant superstition. I deemed it expedient, therefore, to adjourn all further proceedings.[23]

Pliny worried about what would happen to the traditional Roman religion if he granted clemency to the Christians, since the spread of their "contagious superstition" threatened not just the cities but the villages and countryside too. But he also feared being too zealous in punishing them, since many enjoyed the legal rights of Roman citizens.[24] Trajan's reply acknowledged the complexity of administering justice against believers: "It is not possible to lay down any general rule for all such cases . . . Do not go out of your way to look for them."[25] Still, Trajan insisted that those who declared themselves Christians but would not renounce their faith should be punished. Many of the accounts of persecution in the time of the reign of Trajan (AD 98–117) are fleeting. Phocas, the bishop of Sinope, is said to have been thrown into a hot lime kiln on Trajan's order and then enclosed in a hot bath. Simeon, the bishop of Jerusalem, was the target of pagans who infiltrated Christian circles, and after being tortured for many days, he was crucified at an old age. The situation mostly remained the same under the emperor

Hadrian, who ruled as emperor from 117 to 138, although he did give the church a concession in that Christians had to be given a trial before they could be punished.

THE MARTYRDOM OF POLYCARP

The first absolutely verifiable eyewitness account of early Christian martyrdom is the death of Polycarp, the bishop of Smyrna, on the Aegean coast. Polycarp (in Greek, "much fruit") died probably in 155, at the age of eighty-six, and other writers of the early church say that he, like Ignatius, was a disciple of John, who probably personally appointed him bishop. Though the account of his martyrdom depicts him chiefly as a kind and saintly old man, he was also a tough guardian of orthodoxy, in one instance telling the heretic Marcion to his face that he was "the first-born of Satan" for his denial of the Old Testament as Scripture.[26] This uncompromising adherence to the truth is evident in a spellbinding account of Polycarp's death, about which the church at Smyrna wrote to a neighboring church as an encouragement.

The scene begins amid a violent persecution of the Smyrnean church. Polycarp's friends begged him to leave the city, but instead he remained holed up in a farmhouse not far from the city, "doing nothing else day and night but praying for us all, and for churches all over the world, as it was his usual habit to do." Three days before his arrest, he had a vision and said, "I must be going to be burnt alive."[27] At the end of the three days, a search party came for him and tortured one of the houseboys to learn Polycarp's whereabouts. When they came to the house to arrest Polycarp, they found him in bed in an attic, refusing to be hustled away. The old man came downstairs as he heard them arrive, and "everyone there was struck by his age and his calmness, and surprised that the arrest of such an old man could be so urgent."[28] He ordered that his captors be given food and drink, and in return all he asked for was an hour in prayer. He ended up praying out loud for two hours, and "all who heard him were struck with awe, and many of them began to regret this expedition against a man so old and saintly."[29]

Finally Polycarp was placed on top of a donkey and marched into the city. The police commissioner and his father came out to meet him; they put him in their carriage and began to reason with Polycarp so that he might renounce his faith. "Come now," they said, "where is the harm in just saying 'Caesar is Lord,' and offering the incense,[30] and so forth, when it will save your life?"[31] But their pleas fell on deaf ears, and eventually they threw him out of the carriage as it moved, breaking his shins. Polycarp was led into the town arena, where a deafening cry for blood was rising among the spectators. There he faced the governor, who also urged Polycarp to recant: "'Have some respect for your years . . . Swear an oath 'By the Luck of Caesar'—Own yourself in the wrong, and say, 'Down with the infidels!'"[32] Polycarp indicated with a sweep of his hands the assembled crowd around him and growled, "Down with the infidels!" The governor's patience was at an end, and he pressed him once

more: "Take the oath, and I will let you go," he told him. "Revile your Christ." But Polycarp would not relent: "Eighty and six years I have served Him, and He has done me no wrong. How then can I blaspheme my King and my Savior?"[33]

Polycarp Burnt.

A pen and ink drawing of the burning of Polycarp of Smyrna.

The governor continued threatening him with devourment by wild beasts and then being burned at the stake. But Polycarp was steadfast: "The fire you threaten me with cannot go on burning for very long; after a while it goes out. But what you are unaware of are the flames of future judgment and everlasting torment which are in store for the ungodly."[34] The writer relates that Polycarp's disposition the whole time was "overflowing with courage and joy, and his whole countenance was beaming with grace."[35] The crowd cried out for Polycarp to be burned alive and supplied the kindling, which they had brought along for the purpose. The chains that bound Polycarp to the stake were fastened, and the guards tried to nail him in place as well. But Polycarp insisted that wasn't necessary: "Let me be; He who gives me strength to endure the flames will give me strength not to flinch at the stake, without your making sure of it with nails."[36] With his final breath, he cast his eyes up to heaven and said, "For this, and for all else besides, I praise thee, I bless thee, I glorify thee; through our eternal High Priest in heaven, thy beloved Son Jesus Christ, by whom and with whom be glory to thee and the Holy Ghost, now and for all ages to come. Amen." The flames went up, and Polycarp was of this earth no longer.[37]

THREE

DEFINING DOCTRINE

*Irenaeus and the Valentinians; Justin Martyr
and Apologetic; Marcion and Early Definitions of
Doctrine, Scripture, and Church Governance*

I t is one of the awe-inspiring paradoxes of Christianity that the church
experiences some of its most significant growth in times of the worst
persecution. In 2013, a bishop in the country of Nigeria, which has in
the last few years been the site of terrible bloodletting, said:

> The fact that we've gone through several persecutions, religious tur-
> bulences and provocations and deprivations has not quenched the light
> of the church. Solidly, we're there because you can destroy a church
> building but you can't destroy the church itself. You can kill people but
> you can't kill the church.[1]

This outlook was as true in the second century as it is today. In spite
of Trajan's and Hadrian's onslaughts, by the middle of the second century, Christianity was slowly growing.

But even more threatening to the church was the emergence of various heresies that were rooted in a spiritual worldview called Gnosticism.
Each of the strains of Gnosticism (from the Greek word for "knowledge")

that the church confronted in subsequent centuries claimed its own peculiar possession of secret knowledge as the basis for a relationship with God. The Gnostics claimed that their knowledge, whether found in philosophical learning, the natural world, or sacred rituals, was transmitted via a secret oral tradition initiated by Jesus himself. Taking some cues from the Greek philosopher Plato, Gnostics despised the material world, believing that all physical matter was corrupted and evil, while the spiritual world was pure and good. Gnosticism was an unorganized phenomenon, existing both inside and outside of the church. Consequently, practices varied widely from sect to sect and were infused with unchristian strains of mysticism. One sect insisted that its members refrain from any sexual activity, even within the bond of marriage!

One of the most destructive strains of Gnosticism in the early second century was the teaching of Valentinus, who cultivated a popular following in the first half of the second century. Valentinus was educated in Alexandria, a city famous for its scholarly community since the time of the ancient Greeks. A gifted speaker, Valentinus later went to Rome, which was slowly becoming the ecclesiastical headquarters of the Christian world. The Christian writer Tertullian claimed that when Valentinus was denied a bishopric (bishop's appointment), it was then that "he applied himself with all his might to exterminate the truth; and finding the clue of a certain old opinion, he marked out a path for himself with the subtlety of a serpent."[2] Another church father, Epiphanius, claimed that Valentinus was driven to madness after a shipwreck. Whatever the case, Valentinus claimed that he had received a secret teaching handed down through Theudas, a follower of Paul. This secret knowledge proffered a highly esoteric conception of the physical nature of the universe and the spiritual nature of Christ. Aside from what was itself a bizarre theology, rife with ideas that Jesus and the apostles never taught, the Valentinians contorted the Scriptures to fit their own highly idiosyncratic ideas. Valentinus himself died around 160, but his ideas were adapted by others and lived on well into the third century. One sect in Turkey derived from Valentinus's ideas was led by a man named

Marcus, who used obscure magic rites in his practices, which apparently his own converts didn't completely understand:

> For some of them prepare a nuptial couch[3] and perform a mystic rite with certain forms of expression addressed to those who are being initiated, and they say that it is a spiritual marriage which is celebrated by them . . . But others lead them to water, and while they baptize them they repeat the following words: "Into the name of the unknown father of the universe, into truth, the mother of all things, into the one that descended upon Jesus." Others repeat Hebrew names in order the better to confound those who are being initiated.[4]

MARCION OF SINOPE

The Valentinians enjoyed no small amount of popularity. But the most infamous heretic of the first centuries of the Christian faith was Marcion (85–160), who at one point was the bishop of the town of Sinope, in modern-day Turkey. Marcion was supposedly a wealthy man by way of his career as a seafaring merchant, and had at one point donated two hundred thousand sesterces (by a very rough estimate, hundreds of thousands of dollars in today's money) to the church. Whether through cunning or wealth, he eventually rose to become the bishop of Sinope and began to deceive many. He was referred to as "the wolf of Pontus"[5] by some of the church fathers, since his false teaching led astray some "lambs" from the flock of Christ. Marcion taught that the vengeful God of the Old Testament, being radically different in nature from the merciful God of the New Testament, was not the Father of the Lord Jesus Christ. Rather, Jesus was the Son of a different father-god entirely. Additionally, Marcion, being similar to the Gnostics, who conceived of the material world as evil, also denied the physical birth, death, and resurrection of Jesus Christ.

The natural consequence of Marcion's teaching was his discarding of the Old Testament and all of the Gospels except Luke,[6] and even parts of that were cut out. In AD 144, Marcion went to Rome, which (as will be explained shortly) was emerging as the center of the Christian world, whose bishop was becoming an arbiter in intra-faith disputes. The church at Rome quickly realized that Marcion's teaching conflicted with Christian orthodoxy, and he was excommunicated. In response, Marcion founded his own church, which spread to other locations across the Roman world and lasted for several more centuries. Marcion's church used as their scriptures an edited version of Luke and ten of Paul's letters. Marcion's church, therefore, had in many ways the outward appearances of Christianity but in its essence denied many of its core truths. The theology that the church embraced to respond to these heresies would have major reverberations through the ages.

IRENAEUS AND JUSTIN CONFRONT THE PAGANS

Two great teachers of the church who lived during the middle of the second century took up the task of refuting both Valentinus and Marcion. Irenaeus, the bishop of Lyon (in modern-day France) and Justin Martyr, a Christian philosopher at Rome, were the two most indispensable Christian thinkers of their age. Irenaeus (d. 202) was brought up in a Christian family in Smyrna and likely was a disciple of Polycarp. For reasons unknown, Irenaeus migrated to Lyon, where he became a presbyter (pastor). From his writings, it is evident that his chief concern was instructing his flock in correct doctrine. A later writer described Irenaeus's tenacity in fighting for orthodoxy: "The same Irenæus unfolds with the greatest vigor the unfathomable abyss of Valentinus' errors in regard to matter, and reveals his wickedness, secret and hidden like a serpent lurking in its nest."[7] Irenaeus contended for the faith most famously in his lengthy polemic titled *Against Heresies*. Irenaeus insisted that the one true God of the Old and New Testaments formed the world, "like a wise architect, and a most powerful monarch."[8] But the Gnostics, said Irenaeus,

> believe that angels, or some power separate from God, and who was ignorant of Him, formed this universe. By this course, therefore, not yielding credit to the truth, but wallowing in falsehood, they have lost the bread of true life, and have fallen into vacuity and an abyss of shadow. They are like the dog of Aesop, which dropped the bread, and made an attempt at seizing its shadow, thus losing the real food.[9]

But Irenaeus needed a greater reference point for proving his points than Aesop's Fables. He needed the Bible.

SETTLING SCRIPTURE

The church's settlement of what books were to be included in the New Testament canon proved to be one of the most powerful instruments for refuting heresy. The canon consists of those books of what we now call the Bible that, although written by men, are considered inspired by the Holy Spirit. The very first Christians, following Jesus, accepted the Old Testament as canonical; in the book of Acts, Paul is depicted teaching from the Old Testament in the Jewish synagogues. As the Gospels and other books of the New Testament began to circulate as the revealed Word of God during the era of the apostles, churches often read from these books in church services and instructed congregants from them. But even in the middle of the second century, there was not yet a uniform agreement among all churches as to which books were definitively the Word of God.

One of the most hotly contested books of the day was the book of Revelation, which had entered the corpus of the New Testament decades after the other books of the New Testament were written and was thus often suspected of being inauthentic. Revelation is a difficult book to interpret; even modern scholars are divided on what material is to be taken as allegorical and what should be understood as literal. For this reason, one Dionysius suspected that the heretic Cerinthus had authored it in order to serve his own twisted theology:

> [He] dreamed that [God's] kingdom would consist in those things which he desired, namely, in the delights of the belly and of sexual passion; that is to say, in eating and drinking and marrying, and in festivals and sacrifices and the slaying of victims, under the guise of which he thought he could indulge his appetites with a better grace.[10]

But after some deliberation, Dionysius decided that the complexity of the book did not invalidate its divinely inspired nature: "I do not measure and judge them by my own reason, but leaving the more to faith I regard them as too high for me to grasp. And I do not reject what I cannot comprehend, but rather wonder because I do not understand it."[11] Dionysius's word did not settle the argument, but it does reflect the attitude of many churchmen of his day. Revelation eventually gained universal acceptance in the church as a holy book.

Irenaeus was perhaps the most influential voice of his time in helping define what ought to be considered Scripture. As a student of Polycarp, a man who "related all things in harmony with the Scriptures,"[12] Irenaeus took a high view of the Scripture, and he was alarmed at the Valentinians' misuse of the Scriptures to justify their errors: "By transferring passages, and dressing them up anew, and making one thing out of another, they succeed in deluding many through their wickedness and in adapting the oracles of the Lord to their opinions."[13] Additionally, Irenaeus and others realized the threat that Marcion's homemade

André Thevet, *Irenaeus of Lyon*, 1584.

canon posed to the church. If Christian theology was not defined by what the Scriptures said, what was to stop breakaway sects from whimsically making up doctrine, or wrongly including or excluding books of the New Testament? Around AD 180, Irenaeus was the first known Christian author to use the terms *Old Testament* and *New Testament* in reference to the two broad divisions of Scripture.[14] He insisted that only Matthew, Mark, Luke, and John be considered true Gospels. His writings also show a substantial familiarity with all books of the New Testament except for Philemon, 3 John, and Jude.

IRENAEUS'S THEOLOGY

Two additional points of Irenaeus's theology were profoundly influential on the development of the church. First, Irenaeus declared that the church alone was to be the expositor of Scripture. In his view, the bishops (Protestants might say elders) of the various churches around the world were all part of a line of succession that originated with the apostles. Because Jesus had directly conferred upon the apostles the powers to preach the Word of God, subsequent bishops in the churches founded by the apostles were the stewards of orthodoxy, able to interpret the Scriptures in the ways that God intended. This viewpoint was a useful corrective to Marcion, who by nature of his excommunication was not bestowed with an authority to teach the Scriptures. Irenaeus was also the first known theologian to defend in writing the idea of the primacy of Rome over other churches. Like his view of who was fit to interpret the Scriptures, Irenaeus's concept of who was suitable to lead the churches depended on his theory of the apostolic line of succession. Irenaeus claimed that the church at Rome enjoyed a special kind of authority over others, since it was founded by the apostles Peter and Paul:

> We do put to confusion all those who . . . assemble in unauthorized meetings . . . by indicating that tradition derived from the apostles,

of the very great, the very ancient, and universally known Church founded and organized at Rome by the two most glorious apostles, Peter and Paul; as also [by pointing out] the faith preached to men, which comes down to our time by means of the successions of the bishops. For it is a matter of necessity that every Church should agree with this Church, on account of its preeminent authority, that is, the faithful everywhere, inasmuch as the tradition has been preserved continuously by those [faithful men] who exist everywhere.[15]

Irenaeus's words have served as a major point of controversy between different sects and denominations for centuries. In essence, Irenaeus indicated that Rome was to have authority over other churches. He continued in his treatise to list the first twelve men to hold the "inheritance of the episcopate" at Rome. In later generations, these bishops of Rome would be regarded as the first popes. Yet the bishop of Rome in Irenaeus's day did not wield the same powers as his successors: he had no formal authority over other churches until the middle of the fourth century. Still, from the second century onward, the bishop of Rome began to be consulted as an authority in settling ecclesiastical and doctrinal disputes, a precedent that had roots in Jesus' statement to Peter that he would have the keys to the kingdom of heaven, and in Clement of Rome's prescriptive letter to the Corinthians (discussed in chapter 2). But as a result of Irenaeus's efforts to combat heresies, the Roman bishopric occupied a special place in the ecclesiastical world of the second century.

JUSTIN MARTYR

Around the same time as Irenaeus, another writer was gaining distinction for his contentions on behalf of the faith. In time, Justin Martyr (ca. 100–ca. 165) would become, after Paul, the most original and influential Christian thinker of the first few centuries of the church. Justin was born in Judea to a Christian family. From a young age, he was exceptionally curious—"the contemplation of ideas furnished my mind with wings"[16]—and he investigated multiple schools of philosophy to determine which one offered the best way to live. Yet Justin remained spiritually unsatisfied with every branch he studied.

One day, while walking on a remote part of the seashore, Justin chanced upon an old man who was also learned in philosophy. They entered into a dialogue about God, and the old man shared with him the truth about the prophets and the Holy Spirit. Justin's response was unlike anything he had experienced before: "straightway a flame was kindled in my soul; and a love of the prophets, and of those men who are friends of Christ, possessed me; and whilst revolving his words in my mind, I found this philosophy alone to be safe and profitable."[17]

André Thevet, *Justin Martyr*, 1584.

Justin began to devote his life to studying the Bible, evangelizing, and making written arguments in explanation and defense of the faith. One of his works is the *Dialogue with Trypho*, a Christian replication of the ancient dialogues of Plato, in which Justin, the Christian, attempts to prove to Trypho, a Jew, the superiority of Christianity over Judaism. The *Dialogue* shows Justin's exceptional skill in interpreting the Old Testament, and he was especially fond of invoking the book of Isaiah to show how figures and prophecies in the Old Testament prefigured the coming of Christ and the Gentile participation in the new covenant. Justin, for instance, interpreted Noah and the flood as a foreshadowing of Christ's work of salvation. Just as Noah survived the flood by believing God's command to build an ark that would save him from the flood, "by water, faith, and wood, those who are afore-prepared, and who repent of the sins which they have committed, shall escape from the impending judgment of God."[18] To Justin, faith in Christ, baptism by water, and the wood of the cross would deliver the Christian from God's judgment. His unqualified embrace of the Old Testament was also a useful corrective to the heresy of Marcionism, which he virulently opposed:

> And there is a certain Marcion of Pontus, who is even now still teaching his followers to think that there is some other God greater than the creator. And by the aid of the demons he has persuaded many of every race of men to utter blasphemy, and to deny that the maker of this universe is the father of Christ, and to confess that some other, greater than he, was the creator. And all who followed them are, as we have said, called Christians, just as the name of philosophy is given to philosophers, although they may have no doctrines in common.[19]

In time, Justin made his way to Rome, where he wore the popular fashion of the day for philosophers, a cloak called a *pallium*. This was a signal to the world that Christianity could be understood as a religious *and* philosophical system. At Rome, Justin composed his most famous work, his *First Apology*, to the emperor Antoninus Pius. The *First Apology* is a bold missive, declaring to the emperor that Christians ought not to be punished in civil courts merely for being Christians:

> [W]e demand that the charges against the Christians be investigated, and that, if these be substantiated, they be punished as they deserve . . . But if no one can convict us of anything, true reason forbids you, for the sake of a wicked rumour, to wrong blameless men.[20]

In addition to a lengthy explanation of Christianity and its superiority over the Roman religion, there are parts of Justin's *First Apology* that also explain Christian ethics. Justin referred to Jesus' teaching in Matthew[21] to support his claim that Christians are to exercise civil obedience and submission to the government, insofar as they do not violate their religious conscience in the process. It must have been striking for the emperor to read that the Christians prayed for him: "to God alone we render worship, but in other things we gladly serve you, acknowledging you as kings and rulers of men, and praying that with your kingly power you be found to possess also sound judgment."[22] Justin condemned the practice of exposing children (abandoning newborns), since most of the exposed babies were found and sold into child prostitution.[23] But as in the *Dialogue*, Justin's chief aim was setting out an explanation of Christianity and indicating to the emperor that the kingdom Christians were striving for was not of this world:

> For if we looked for a human kingdom, we should also deny our Christ,
> that we might not be slain; and we should strive to escape detection,
> that we might obtain what we expect. But since our thoughts are not
> fixed on the present, we are not concerned when men cut us off; since
> also death is a debt which must at all events be paid.[24]

Justin's writings are rife with the claim that Christians do not fear death, and the publication of Justin's next work, his *Second Apology*, would be an opportunity for him to prove it. The *Second Apology* was addressed to the Roman Senate, and Justin can barely contain his ire that Christians were, once again, being unjustly punished. Justin wrote about the event that motivated him to criticize the public authorities. A certain husband and wife spent their lives in debauchery, but when the woman repented of her sins and converted to Christianity, the husband was incensed and asked the prefect of Rome, Urbicus, to punish her pastor, Ptolemæus. Ptolemæus was led into prison and interrogated. When he confessed that he was a Christian, the prefect ordered him to be taken away for execution. A fellow Christian who had witnessed the proceedings, Lucius, objected to such an action:

> What is the ground of this judgment? Why have you punished this
> man, not as an adulterer, nor fornicator, nor murderer, nor thief, nor
> robber, nor convicted of any crime at all, but who has only confessed
> that he is called by the name of Christian? This judgment of yours, O

41

Urbicus, does not become the Emperor Pius, nor the philosopher, the son of Cæsar, nor the sacred senate.[25]

The prefect observed that Lucius too seemed to be a Christian. When Lucius answered, "Most certainly I am," the prefect had him taken away for execution also. Justin records the man's fearless reaction to his own death sentence: "he professed his thanks, knowing that he was delivered from such wicked rulers, and was going to the Father and King of the heavens."[26] As he observed such a cavalier administration of justice, Justin suspected that martyrdom was soon to befall him. He wrote specifically about a rival philosopher, Crescens, who verbally attacked Christians to obtain the favor of the masses:

> I too, therefore, expect to be plotted against and fixed to the stake, by some of those I have named, or perhaps by Crescens, that lover of bravado and boasting; for the man is not worthy of the name of philosopher who publicly bears witness against us in matters which he does not understand, saying that the Christians are atheists and impious, and doing so to win favour with the deluded mob, and to please them.[27]

Justin's inklings about his own death proved to be right. Crescens somehow devised a plot that resulted in Justin and six other Christians being brought before the Roman prefect, Rusticus, on charges of atheism. The dialogue between Rusticus and Justin has been preserved:

> RUSTICUS: You are a Christian, then?
> JUSTIN: Yes, I am a Christian.
> RUSTICUS: You are called a learned man and think that you know what is true teaching. Listen: if you were scourged and beheaded, are you convinced that you would go up to heaven?
> JUSTIN: I hope that I shall enter God's house if I suffer that way.
> RUSTICUS: Do you have an idea that you will go up into heaven to receive some suitable rewards?

JUSTIN: It is not an idea that I have, it is something I know
    well and hold to be most certain.

RUSTICUS: Now let us come to the point at issue, which is
    necessary and urgent. Gather round then and with one
    accord offer sacrifice to the gods.

JUSTIN: No one who is right thinking stoops from true
    worship to false worship.

RUSTICUS: If you do not do as you are commanded you will be
    tortured without mercy.

JUSTIN: We hope to suffer torment for the sake of our Lord
    Jesus Christ, and so be saved. For this will bring us
    salvation and confidence as we stand before the more
    terrible and universal judgment-seat of our Lord and
    Savior.

RUSTICUS: Let those who have refused to sacrifice to the gods
    and to obey the command of the emperor be scourged and
    led away to suffer capital punishment according to the
    ruling of the laws.[28]

With that, Justin and his comrades were beheaded. Justin won the crown of martyrdom he so desired and is today known as Justin Martyr. Although distinguished by his death, his contributions to Christian philosophy and the interpretive tradition of Scripture are enormous, and his life was a passionate fight to explain systematically the truth and glory of God to anyone who would listen.

CHRISTIAN COMMUNITIES IN THE SECOND CENTURY

Justin's writings also give us some sense of how Christian communities were organizing and worshipping in the mid-second century. His description of a Christian worship service looks remarkably similar to how many churches today conduct their gatherings. Believers entered into an assembly (usually located in someone's modest residence) and offered up prayers. The head of the church and deacons distributed the elements for the Eucharist (Lord's Supper), allowing some members of the church to take the elements home to those who were absent. The head of the assembly also taught from the Scriptures:

> And on the day called Sunday, all who live in cities or in the country gather together to one place, and the memoirs of the apostles or the writings of the prophets are read, as long as time permits; then, when the reader has ceased, the president [pastor] verbally instructs, and exhorts to the imitation of these good things.[29]

Another document from the mid-to-late-first century, the *Didache* (in Greek, "Teaching"), also offered prescriptions for how Christians were to live: assembling on Sundays, saying the Lord's Prayer three times per day, supporting ministers out of their own generosity. The early Christians took seriously the ordinance of the Eucharist; unbelievers were forbidden to take it and were sometimes put out of church services before the distribution of the elements. Only baptized members of a church could receive it. At this time, most Christians were not members of the upper classes but were ordinary people, without money, influence, or often Roman citizenship. Hence, most converts were won by personal evangelism in the streets, shops, and workplaces; it wasn't until the fifth and sixth centuries that individuals launched major missionary campaigns to targeted ethnic groups.[30]

The celebration of Easter—the day of Jesus' resurrection—became common, and Easter was also the day when new converts were baptized (completely naked, men separated from women). Scholars are still divided on whether the early church baptized infants in the first two centuries. The similarity of Justin's corporate experiences to the *Didache* and other documents of the time shows a general uniformity of practice that was unenforced by any higher ecclesiastical authority. That most churches demonstrated relative homogeneity is remarkable, considering that Christianity was still technically illegal throughout all of the second century.

MARTYRDOM IN THE AGE OF MARCUS AURELIUS

Although the church could take comfort from the intimacy and unity of worship, it still continued to endure vicious persecution in the time of the emperor Marcus Aurelius (d. 180) and his son Commodus (d. 192). Marcus Aurelius was a man of intense contemplation; his masterpiece of philosophy, the *Meditations*, is an unusually thoughtful set of writings for a military man in the ancient world. But Marcus Aurelius was also given to great superstitions. When a series of natural disasters, wars, and plagues beset the empire at the beginning of his reign, he ordered mandatory sacrifices to the gods. As a consequence, regional authorities, perhaps believing that the Christian refusal to worship the Roman deities was leading the gods to afflict the Roman Empire, saw an opportunity to punish the Christians.

The signature episode of persecution during the reign of Marcus Aurelius occurred in Gaul in the year 177. A letter from the church at Lyon to the churches in Asia Minor (Turkey) describes the harrowing ordeal. First, Christians were barred from entering public buildings, like the baths and the city's forum (town square). Their homes were vandalized, and they were subject to mocking, beatings, draggings, robberies, stonings, imprisonment, and "all things

A bust of the emperor Marcus Aurelius. The presence of the beard is a conscious attempt to appear like a Greek philosopher.

45

which an infuriated mob delight in inflicting on enemies and adversaries." Household slaves accused the Christians of being practitioners of incest and cannibalism. Roman soldiers brought them to the forum to be questioned by the local mob. When they admitted to being Christians, they were imprisoned until the governor arrived to conduct a trial and mete out punishment. The governor treated them with "the utmost cruelty." Some were put in the stocks and stretched out until death. Many were confined to the darkest and foulest cells of the local prison, where they died of suffocation and disease.[31]

Sanctus was a new but passionate convert, and in response to every torture inflicted upon him, he merely stated, in Latin, "I am a Christian." Exasperated, the governor affixed red-hot brass plates to the most sensitive areas of his body. Sanctus's body "externally lost the human shape," but the tortures were nothing compared to his love of Christ; the writer of the letter says, "He was an example to the others that there is nothing fearful where there is the Father's love, and nothing painful where there is Christ's glory."[32]

Another woman, Blandina, experienced so much punishment that her own torturers became weary from it all. But she would not recant her testimony, saying merely, "I am a Christian, and there is no evil done among us." Pothinus, the bishop of Lyon, was over ninety years old, had trouble breathing, and was "worn out by age and disease." Yet he was reinvigorated by the opportunity to be a witness for Christ before the governor. When the governor asked who the God of the Christians was, he said, "If thou art worthy, thou shalt know." In retaliation for offending their gods, the mob punched and kicked him with such force that they "thought they would sin greatly if they omitted any abuse in their insulting treatment of him." Pothinus died in prison two days later. Sanctus and another martyr, Maturus, were dragged into the amphitheater, whipped, and then tied to wild beasts to be dragged around and mauled. Lastly, they were tied to an iron chair with flames underneath. The crowd was especially hungry to see them suffer. Says the letter, "Instead of all the variety which usually takes place in gladiatorial shows, they alone were the spectacle to the world throughout that day."[33]

Further prosecution would be stayed for a time; the governor had written to Marcus Aurelius to determine what should happen to the rest of them, some of whom were Roman citizens. When the emperor confirmed that prosecution could go forward against those who confessed, the governor finished what he started. At the opening of the public festival, he brought the Christians back from prison to the amphitheater and repeated the interrogation process as a spectacle for the crowd. Romans citizens who confessed were beheaded; noncitizens who admitted their faith were thrown to the wild beasts. One man who survived the beasts, Attalus, was given the iron chair. As his flesh smoldered and smoked, the governor asked what the name of God was. He replied, "God has not a name as men have." Two of the last ones to die were Ponticus, a fifteen-year-old boy, and his sister, the aforementioned Blandina. Blandina rejoiced in her death to such an extent that it was "as if she were called to a marriage supper rather than cast to wild beasts." Blandina was whipped, tossed to the beasts, and given the iron chair. She finally died when she was enclosed in a net and trampled by a wild bull. Even the heathens, claimed the account, had never seen a woman endure so much torture.[34]

In the aftermath, the persecutors did not even treat the corpses of the afflicted with dignity. The bodies of those who had suffocated in prison were fed to dogs. Other bodies that had been burned and mangled in the arena, along with various limbs and heads, were kept under guard so that nobody could properly bury them. Many mocked the piles of remains, saying, "Where now is their God? What good have they got from that religion which they chose in preference to their life?" The guard was maintained in spite of protestations, and finally, the bodies were burned and the ashes were thrown into the river. The authorities did this thinking it would prevent the promised heavenly resurrection that Christians believe in. Seemingly, this entire sequence of events would be disastrous to the remnants of the church at Lyon. But the account speaks repeatedly of how the Christians could muster faith in the face of suffering by clinging to their expectation of heaven: "They humbled themselves, under the powerful hand by which they are now highly exalted."[35]

Stories preserved in other sources also describe the carnage at Lyon. One man was buried in the ground up to his waist and left there for three days until he died. Epipodius, a Greek, was asked by the governor to participate in some pagan rituals. He declined, saying, "Your pretended tenderness is actually cruelty, and the agreeable life you describe is replete with everlasting death . . . Your pleasures lead to eternal death, and our pains to perpetual happiness."[36] The governor erupted, and Epipodius was stretched out on the torture racks and sharp hooks were put in his flesh. Finally, he was taken from the rack and beheaded. In total, forty-eight Christians were martyred for their faith at Lyon.

Persecution continued under Marcus Aurelius's son, a bloodthirsty megalomaniac named Commodus. In one episode, a man named Apollonius, who was "renowned among the faithful for learning and philosophy"[37] and who may have been a Roman senator, was given up by one of his servants and brought up on the charge of being a Christian who would not worship Commodus as the Greek god Hercules. His legs were immediately broken, and he was asked by the judge, Perennis, to recant.[38] He refused and was brought before the Senate to stand trial. He made a lengthy apology for the faith over the course of several days. "Are you bent on dying?" asked Perennis. "No," said Apollonius, "I enjoy life; but love of life does not make me afraid to die. There is waiting for me something better: eternal life, given to the person who has lived well on earth."[39]

The abundance of reliable manuscripts attesting to the bloody first centuries of the Christian experience should refute scholars like Candida Moss, who have recently claimed that Christians have for centuries wrongly used stories of questionable veracity as social and political propaganda.[40] Moss claims that the early Christians developed a persecution complex that helped inspire later, dangerous pathologies, like domestic abuse and American political conservatism. In claiming this, she ignores not only centuries of church history and historical theology (not to mention common sense), but also the purpose of the early martyrdom stories. Writers of these narratives wanted to bear witness to how God strengthens his people in times of trial and to show that accepting persecution for Christ displays evidence of being transformed by him. Of course, not every single Christian who was faced with persecution held firm; as we will see in the next chapter, the division between those who held fast and those who did not often produced deep divisions within the church. Many of the historical narratives cited here are not the model of perfect objectivity, but prefer to emphasize the moral example of steadfastness as an example to other Christians. As the second century drew to a close and the emperor Septimius Severus obtained the throne in 192, the church would enter a period of prolonged suffering and get a chance to prove how deep its well of faith really was.

FOUR

BRUTAL OPPOSITION

*Perpetua and Felicity, Tertullian, the Influence
of Early Christian Women, Montanist and
Paschal Controversies, the Persecutions of Decius
and Valerian, Cyprian and the Lapsed*

When the emperor Commodus died in 192, a power struggle broke
out at Rome. Emerging from the strife as emperor was Septimius
Severus, a career functionary in the Roman civil service who had quickly
ascended through the ranks to become the commander of the legions
on Rome's northwest border, in modern-day Hungary. Severus is distinguished for his successful military career during his reign, waging
successful campaigns in Asia Minor and in Britain before his death in
211. The arch of Septimius Severus, a hulking marble structure com-
memorating his victories in the East, still stands today amid the ruins
of the Roman forum. But the struggle of five different men competing for power had wounded the empire. In response, Severus thought to
cultivate political unity by subordinating all the philosophical and religious traditions of the empire to the worship of one god—*Sol Invictus*,
the Unconquered Sun.[1] Other gods could be worshipped, as long as the
adherents acknowledged that the Unconquered Sun was above all others.
Naturally, Severus's dictum was incompatible with Christianity.

At first, Severus adopted a tolerant attitude toward the faith, but around 202 he changed his mind and issued an edict that outlawed new conversions. Although Severus did not initiate a formal, empire-wide campaign of torment, his edict had the effect of intensifying the kind of sporadic persecution that Roman governors in the province were so fond of, so much so that the historian Eusebius wrote that Christians everywhere, and especially in Egypt, "won crowns from God through their great patience under many tortures and every mode of death."[2] Elsewhere, Eusebius said that the persecution was so great that at least one theologian believed these torments were a surefire sign that the appearance of the antichrist predicted in the Bible was imminent.[3]

PERPETUA AND FELICITY

The most famous persecution account from this time is the story of Perpetua and Felicity. Perpetua was a married mother from Northern Africa, about twenty-two years old, whose father persistently hurled insults at her for being a Christian. She pointed out to him that just as a water pitcher could not be called by any other name, so she could only be called a Christian. This enraged him, and he lunged at Perpetua to rip out her eyes. She managed to fight him off, but apparently her father had some influence with the local authorities, because she was put into the local prison, a place known for its darkness, heat (because of the mass of people inside), and cruel treatment from the guards. Additionally, Perpetua was concerned for who was looking after her children, one of whom was still an infant. Two deacons from the local church visited her in prison and paid some money to have her let out of the dungeon for a little bit so that she might breast-feed her child. As is the feeling common to almost any new mother, Perpetua decided she would rather stay in prison with her child than be apart from the baby. So the infant stayed, and, as Perpetua says, "the prison was made a palace for me."[4]

After a few days Perpetua learned she would be tried. Her father, grieving at the prospect, came and visited her in prison. But he was more concerned for his own image; he didn't want to be humiliated for having a daughter who was a Christian—and one who endured martyrdom at that. He promised never to insult her faith again if she recanted, but she would not: "That shall be done at this tribunal, whatsoever God shall please; for know that we are not established in our own power, but in God's. And he [the father] went from me very sorrowful."[5]

One day Perpetua and several other Christians were suddenly taken away from their meal and brought to the forum for their trial before the procurator (and agent of the emperor) Hilarian. Hilarian and Perpetua's father both begged her to perform a sacrifice on behalf of the prosperity of the emperor, thus sparing her child the misery of being without a mother. She answered, "I am a Christian." When her father begged again that she perform the sacrifice, the emperor ordered him beaten with a rod and Perpetua taken away—without her child—to be fed to wild beasts. A few days afterward, before the public spectacle began, her father reappeared at the prison with the same plea, swearing and ripping out the hairs of his beard to emphasize his point. But Perpetua still did not relent, and experienced a vision that she would confront not only wild beasts in the arena but also the devil himself. Still, she wrote, "I knew that mine was the victory."[6]

At this point in the story a new figure emerges: a young woman named Felicity, who was eight months pregnant. Felicity was upset that she might be spared torment, for Roman law forbade torture of pregnant women. She and her fellow prisoners prayed that she might give birth before the appointed day of execution, since they too did not want to leave behind "their fellow-traveller on the road of the same hope." Three days later, she gave birth to a daughter. A guard mocked Felicity's labor pains and sarcastically wondered, if she thought she was suffering now, what she would feel when fed to wild animals: "You that thus make complaint now, what wilt you do when you are thrown to the beasts, which you didst condemn when you would not sacrifice?"[7]

53

When the day of the public games arrived and the captives were led into the amphitheater, they showed no fear. On the contrary, "if they trembled at all, it was for joy, not for fear." A martyr named Saturninus was the first victim, given first to a leopard and later a bear. Another, named Saturus, was mauled by the leopard; there was so much blood that the writer of the narrative called it his "second baptism." A wild bull was unleashed on the women, and as all were dying from these

A mosaic of Perpetua, from ca. 1280.

injuries, they were lined up to have their throats cut. They, including Felicity, were killed first and died quickly. But the executioner, desiring that Perpetua might have some taste of pain, pierced her with a sword in her side. She shrieked out; and when the swordsman's hand couldn't find the right place to strike (for he was a novice), she herself plunged it into her own neck.[8]

TERTULLIAN

The persecution under Severus was at the time perhaps the worst since Nero's. And yet, as we have seen before, Christianity was in no danger of vanishing because of tribulation. One Christian writer in the early third century who took note of the growth of the faith amid persecution was Tertullian, a shrewd and systematic thinker from Carthage, in North Africa, who probably had a background as a lawyer and certainly some as an orator. "The blood of the martyrs," he noted, "is the seed of the church."[9] When Christians are put into prison, he wrote, they should consider it a place for spiritual growth: "Meanwhile let us compare the life of the world and of the prison, and see if the spirit does not gain more in the prison than the flesh loses . . . Let us drop the name

of prison; let us call it a place of retirement."[10]
Compared to his predecessors, like Ignatius,
Irenaeus, and Justin Martyr, a huge amount of
his work survives—thirty-one different works
in all. Tertullian's writing is filled with cutting
sarcasm in service of his points. In his *Apology*,
a lengthy refutation of false charges that
pagans levied against Christianity, he wryly
observed, "Oh how great the glory of the ruler

A portrait of Tertullian.

who should bring to light some Christian who
had devoured one hundred infants!"[11] In another place, he poked fun
at those quick to torment the Christians: "If the Tiber rises too high or
the Nile too low, the cry is 'The Christians to the lion.' All of them to a
single lion?"[12]

Yet the seriousness and force of Tertullian's arguments for the faith
reflect the fact that the intellectual circles of ancient Rome had to confront the claims of Christianity. Its purpose was serious, and its outlook
eternal. It was Tertullian's mission to poke holes in the presuppositions
and practices of the pagan religion and expose the inconsistencies within
it. Tertullian succinctly encapsulated his arguments by writing, "We do
not worship your gods, because we know that there are no such beings."[13]
Tertullian also undermined the idea that the Roman Empire had
attained such heights of power because of its piety before false gods: "But
how utterly foolish it is to attribute the greatness of the Roman name to
religious merits, since it was after Rome became an empire, or call it still
a kingdom, that the religion she professes made its chief progress!"[14] In
another work, Tertullian dismissed outright the notions that the philosophical traditions of thinkers like Socrates, Plato, and Aristotle should
shape the theology of Christianity, writing famously, "What has Athens
to do with Jerusalem?"[15] But Tertullian, probably following 1 Timothy
2, still admitted in his *Apology* that it was the Christian's duty to pray for
the emperor and the stability and security of the empire.[16] Not only did
Tertullian desire the personal salvation of the unbelieving authorities,

but he also recognized that the Roman Empire was established by God to be a bulwark of civilization, order, and peace in a world ringed by violent and politically primitive barbarian tribes.

EARLY CHRISTIAN WOMEN

The fact that intellectuals like Tertullian were taking Christianity seriously indicated that more and more inhabitants of the Roman Empire were now paying close attention to what the Christians had to say—and believing it. This period of growth began during the reign of Commodus; Eusebius noted in his *Church History* that in that time "our condition became more favorable, and through the grace of God the churches throughout the entire world enjoyed peace, and the word of salvation was leading every soul, from every race of man to the devout worship of the God of the universe."[17] Tertullian summarized the Roman anxiety over the growing number of conversions: "The outcry is that the State is filled with Christians—that they are in the fields, in the citadels, in the islands: they make lamentation, as for some calamity, that both sexes, every age and condition, even high rank, are passing over to the profession of the Christian faith."[18] And all this despite intermittant periods of persecution! Some of the most prolific (and unlikeliest) exponents of the faith in the early third century were upper-class women. From the outset, Christianity was for women a much more attractive alternative to the traditional Roman order. Christians affirmed that human beings were made in the image of God, and thus everyone should be treated with a supreme amount of relational and physical dignity. In the New Testament, Jesus and Paul taught about the exclusive and immutable bond of marriage to which Christians are called, as well as the husband's role in caring for his wife through practical service and marital faithfulness. This teaching was a radical break from the sexual norms that middle- and upper-class Roman men often enjoyed. Although men were expected to marry, adultery was a practice that was generally acceptable for Roman men to indulge in. Additionally, the New Testament records in several places that women occupied various positions of leadership,[19] an unheard-of idea in Roman culture apart from some of the priestesses of the mystery cults. The book of James made explicit the church's responsibility to care for widows. Christians were also distinguished for their opposition to the lawful status of prostitution, child sex, and abortion. As Tertullian wrote, "In our case, murder being once for all forbidden, we may not destroy even the fetus in the womb . . . To hinder a birth is merely a speedier man-killing; nor does it matter whether you take away a life that is born, or destroy one that is coming to the birth."[20] Based on Tertullian's writings, we see a sharpening of the intellectual conflicts between Christian and pagan.

But Tertullian is also known for his intricate theological reasoning. He was the first commentator to explicate in detail the doctrine of the *trinitas*, "the threeness" or "Trinity." Tertullian's motivation for clarifying the three distinct yet unified aspects of God (Father, Son, and Holy Spirit) was partly due to the persistence of Marcion of Pontus's form of the Gnostic heresy (see chapter 3), which stipulated that there were two distinct beings who could be called God. Tertullian wrote extensively and furiously against this error, exposing Marcion's poor theology: "The heretic of Pontus introduces two Gods . . . One whom it was impossible to deny, i.e. our Creator; and one whom he will never be able to prove, i.e. his own god."[21] Tertullian also went after Marcion in personal terms, saying, "What Pontic mouse ever had such gnawing powers as he who has gnawed the Gospels to pieces?"[22]

Like Irenaeus, Tertullian defended the apostolic line of succession as the principle for determining true Christian doctrine, claiming that only those churches that were founded and perpetuated in the apostolic lineage were teaching the truth: "all doctrine must be prejudged as false which savours of contrariety to the truth of the churches and apostles of Christ and God."[23] To Tertullian, the church at Rome, having been founded directly by two apostles, was also imbued with a special ability to preserve the correct doctrine:

How happy is its church, on which apostles poured forth all their doctrine along with their blood! Where Peter endures a passion like his Lord's! Where Paul wins his crown in a death like John's where the Apostle John was first plunged, unhurt, into boiling oil, and thence remitted to his island-exile! See what she has learned, what taught, what fellowship has had with even (our) churches in Africa! One Lord God does she acknowledge, the Creator of the universe, and Christ Jesus (born) of the Virgin Mary, the Son of God the Creator; and the Resurrection of the flesh; the law and the prophets she unites in one volume with the writings of evangelists and apostles, from which she drinks in her faith.[24]

By Tertullian's time, the catholic (universal) church was recognized as a collection of any churches that had an affection for each other based on a shared theology passed down from apostolic times. In that sphere, said Tertullian and others, was the true teaching of Christ preserved. It is therefore a great paradox that Tertullian would in time abandon his own prescriptions.

THREE CONTROVERSIES

For unknown reasons, Tertullian converted late in life to Montanism, also called the "New Prophecy," which grew up in Asia Minor in the late second century. The Montanists claimed that they were receiving direct revelation, or prophecy, from the Holy Spirit, and that this was their inspiration for a set of exacting views on certain matters of spiritual concern. Tertullian, for instance, declared that second marriages (when one's spouse had died) were sinful, and also stipulated the exact length of veils to be worn by women. In their severity, the Montanists also desired martyrdom: "Do not desire to depart this life in beds, in miscarriages, in soft fevers, but in martyrdoms, that He who suffered for you may be glorified," wrote Tertullian.[25] When receiving the prophecy, Montanists spoke in frenzied, sometimes incomprehensible utterances. Eusebius quoted an eyewitness of Montanus himself:

> [A] recent convert, Montanus by name, through his unquenchable desire for leadership, gave the adversary opportunity against him. And he became beside himself, and being suddenly in a sort of frenzy and ecstasy, he raved, and began to babble and utter strange things, prophesying in a manner contrary to the constant custom of the Church handed down by tradition from the beginning.[26]

Many began to question whether these prophecies were genuine revelation,[27] and around 177, the churches of Asia Minor called together a synod—a council of churches in which questions of ecclesiastical importance are settled. Churches had met to settle questions before, but this is believed to be the first such synod in Christian history with churches of a whole region represented. The synod excommunicated the Montanists, meaning that they considered the Montantists heretical and that their practice had no place in the true church founded by Jesus Christ. At the instigation of the churches in Gaul, the bishop of Rome also eventually excommunicated the Montanists. While Montanism did not claim a secret knowledge of God, as Gnosticism did, its practices were substantially different enough to warrant a disaffiliation. The excommunication reflects the development of the church as an institution that was prioritizing unity even while admitting that some traditions in individual churches could differ. But these differences could only extend to the point that they did not defy the essential elements of the faith. Each church was communicating with one another to define doctrine and often looking to Rome to confirm their decisions. While the Bible was the definitive reference point for settling questions of doctrine and practice, questions not clearly settled by Scripture that were of theological importance were numerous (and difficult), and churches could not always look to precedents in church history as a guide.

The difficulty of resolving disputes is evident in an even more serious controversy from the late second century. This was the Paschal controversy, one, said the thorough Eusebius, "of no small importance."[28] This controversy was so named from *Pasah,* a Hebrew word (with no easy English translation) that referred to the events, celebration, and remembrance of the Hebrew Exodus and Passover. The Paschal controversy hinged on the disagreement between Eastern and Western churches as to when Easter should be celebrated. Churches in Asia Minor had been, since the time of the apostles, celebrating the holiday at sundown on the fourteenth day of the Jewish month of Nisan, the annual date of the Jewish passover. Churches in the West, however, which were predominantly Gentile, had developed a custom of celebrating Easter on the Sunday following the Passover day. This was seemingly a minor quibble, but the fact that the celebration centered on the resurrection of Christ, the indispensable event of the Christian faith, imbued the dispute with special significance. In probably 198, multiple bishops from East and West gathered at different synods, in places like Gaul, Corinth, Palestine, and Mesopotamia, to sort out the issue, and they reached agreement that the resurrection would be celebrated on the Sabbath following Passover. But the Quartodecimans ("the fourteeners," so called because they insisted on celebrating on the fourteenth of Nisan) refused to comply with the decisions. Polycrates, the leader of the churches in Asia, sent a letter to the bishop of Rome, Victor I, saying that his churches would continue to celebrate in their own way, as the apostles Philip and John and the eminent Polycarp did. If such distinguished fathers of the faith had done things this way, that was good enough reason for him to extend the tradition.[29]

In response, Victor "immediately attempted to cut off from the common unity the parishes of all Asia, with the churches that agreed with them . . . and he wrote letters and declared all the brethren there wholly excommunicate."[30] To the other bishops, excommunication seemed extreme, and not a step toward the unity to which the New Testament calls believers. One of the concerned bishops was Irenaeus of Lyon, now an old man, but still hungry to defend what he believed was right. Irenaeus adopted a peacemaker's role in the controversy, serving as an intermediary between the churches.[31] He suggested to Victor that he consider decisions of previous bishops of Rome, and urged him to remember that when Polycarp visited Rome and quarreled with Victor's predecessor on the same topic, he still received the Eucharist, and both men "parted from each other in peace . . . maintaining the peace of the whole church."[32] But Victor did not relent. Nor did other bishops who had considered the matter. They said that "those who easily deceive their souls" should not continue to celebrate Easter in their own way.[33] While some churches rejoined the Catholic Church on the issue, others continued to keep their tradition into the fourth century, even after the Council of Nicaea in AD 325 confirmed that Easter should be honored on the Sunday after Passover. The legacy of the Paschal controversy showed the increasing, though not total, authority of the bishop of Rome. It marked the beginning of divergent theological traditions between East and West, despite a unity on cardinal issues of faith. Over the course of the next millennium, these differences would eventually become too great to reconcile. Curiously, the Quartodeciman controversy also occurred during a time of relative freedom of persecution in the church.

The last great dispute of the era was a heavily theological affair between Hippolytus, one of the most influential theologians at Rome, and Callistus, the bishop of that city. Around 217, Hippolytus accused Callistus of believing that God the Father and Jesus were just two names for the same person. Just as Irenaeus and Justin Martyr had done, Hippolytus emphasized that God the Father and Jesus were in fact two distinct yet unified, coequal persons of the Godhead. On the other hand,

Callistus accused Hippolytus of believing in two separate gods. More troubling for Hippolytus (and perhaps unchristian of him) was his anger at the bishop Callistus's forgiveness of Christians who had committed sexual sins, as well as Callistus's decision to consider as morally acceptable monogamous sexual relations between unmarried adults. To Hippolytus, this was a flagrant disregard of unrepentant sin. What was more, many of these women, he said, were using abortion-inducing drugs. Hippolytus raged at Callistus: "Behold, into how great impiety that lawless one has proceeded, by inculcating adultery and murder at the same time! And withal, after such audacious acts, they, lost to all shame, attempt to call themselves a Catholic Church!"[34] Lastly, Callistus granted church membership to individuals from breakaway sects who desired to be part of the Catholic Church but had not performed penance first. This was too much for Hippolytus; he decided to withdraw his church from the authority of the bishop of Rome, and for this he is sometimes considered the first antipope. In 235, as one of the highest-profile Christians in the city, he was exiled to the mines on the island of Sardinia as part of an imperial effort to stamp out Christianity. But Hippolytus later returned to Rome, where scholars believe that he was reconciled to the church before his death. Hippolytus's refusal to admit those who committed fornication and adultery (considered especially grave sins) back into fellowship presaged another controversy over the reception of believers into the church (one discussed at the end of this chapter).

THE PERSECUTIONS OF THE THIRD CENTURY

After the death of Septimius Severus in 211, the early third century was a relatively peaceful one for the church. Although there were intermittent spates of violence in the provinces, it wasn't until the emperor Maximinus's reign in 235 that widespread suffering resurfaced.

Foxe's Book of Martyrs, a sixteenth-century history of persecution, claims that during this period "numberless Christians were slain without trial, and buried indiscriminately in heaps, sometimes fifty or sixty being cast into a pit together, without the least decency."[35] One church historian a few centuries later reported that one of Maximinus's chief motivations for instigating persecution was his disgust at the prevalence of Christianity within the previous emperor's own household. On the whole, we know little of the specifics of Maximinus's persecution campaigns. The tradition holds that Hippolytus was torn in half by wild horses at this time, as was Martina, "a noble and beautiful" young woman.[36] A presbyter named Calepodius was drowned in the Tiber.[37]

By the time of Maximinus, the empire was undoubtedly creeping toward crisis. It had experienced a line of emperors who were either ineffectual or died quickly (usually both). Most transfers of power were by coup d'état, and Maximinus had never even visited Rome when he became emperor, an unthinkable occurrence only a few decades before. Two traditionalist emperors attempted to reverse the course of things. The reign of the emperors Decius (emperor from 249 to 251) and Valerian (253–260) instigated persecutions that were extraordinarily bloody, much more so than Severus's. Like Maximinus, Decius hated the prevalence of Christianity in the emperor's own home (he even suspected the previous emperor, Philip, of being a Christian). Decius, like Severus, was also fueled by the desire to recover the traditional Roman religious order.

In 250, Decius required that all citizens of the empire must perform a public sacrifice to the emperor. This sacrifice had to be performed with a Roman magistrate as an eyewitness, and a certificate (a *libellus*) that the task was done had to be issued as well. This edict was not decreed explicitly with the intent of persecuting Christians, but it wound up being the most direct challenge yet to the faith of many. Naturally, many refused to make the sacrifice and were put to death for it. Fabian, the bishop of Rome, was decapitated. Julian, a Christian in Cilicia, in Turkey, was stuffed into a leather bag with a number of serpents and scorpions and then thrown into the ocean. A young man named Peter refused to perform a sacrifice to Venus, the Roman goddess of love, saying only, "I am astonished you should sacrifice to an infamous woman, whose debaucheries even your own historians record, and whose life consisted of such actions as your laws would punish—no, I shall offer the true God the acceptable sacrifices of praises and prayers."[38] The enraged proconsul who heard this ordered him stretched on a wheel, by which all his bones were broken, and then beheaded. Trypho and Respicius, two eminent men of the town of Nice, were taken prisoner for the faith. After their feet were pierced with nails, they were dragged through the streets, scourged, torn with iron hooks, burned with torches, and then, finally, perhaps mercifully, beheaded. Seven Roman young men (or perhaps soldiers) who had converted to Christianity were ordered to make a sacrifice to a pagan god at Ephesus. They refused, but Decius gave them time to think it over. Fearing for their lives, they fled into a cave to escape punishment. But they were discovered and sealed inside, where they died of starvation. This episode is known as the story of the "Seven Sleepers."

Two of the most remarkable stories from the age belong to two women. One was a Sicilian woman named Agatha, a Christian possessing remarkable physical beauty. When the governor of Sicily, Quintian, became enamored of her and made advances, she repeatedly refused him. Quintian hired a prostitute named Aphrodica (surely not her real name, but a derivative of the name Aphrodite, the Greek goddess of love) to attempt to instruct Agatha in her prurient arts. But still Agatha would not abandon her God. Frustrated that he could not have what he wanted, Quintian channeled his lust into rage. Agatha was scourged, burned with irons, and shredded with sharp hooks before being made to lie naked on a mixture of glass and hot coals. From this she died in prison.[39]

The second famous heroine from the period was a woman named Theodora, from Antioch, who was sentenced to imprisonment in a brothel for her refusal to sacrifice. A Christian named Didymus heard about what had happened and, disguised as a Roman soldier, went there to free her. He entered her chamber and told her to escape wearing the soldier's clothes. When Didymus was discovered in the brothel instead of Theodora, he was brought before the local magistrate, where he professed himself a Christian and was sentenced to death. When Theodora heard about this, she ran to the court and threw herself before the judge, begging that she be the one punished. The judge decided to punish both of them, and they were beheaded, their corpses burned.[40]

Though Decius's persecution was torturous for many, it did not last long. He only ruled a few years, and in 251, he was killed in battle, an occurrence that at the time must have seemed to the church to be an instance of divine justice. But one of his successors, Valerian (253–260), was no less brutal. Valerian spent an abundance of his time fighting to protect the empire's eastern provinces, whether driving off Goths in Asia Minor or Persians in Syria. But he did manage to make several pronouncements regarding Christianity. The first was that all Christian clergy had to perform sacrifices to the Roman gods. The next year he ordered that bishops and other high-ranking church officials were to be executed and that Roman senators and knights who were Christians were to be stripped of their titles and their property. Accordingly, many prominent members of the Christian community suffered.

Saturninus, the bishop of Toulouse, in Spain, had his feet tied to the rear legs of a bull who had been marched to the top of a very high temple staircase. The bull was then whipped, and it rushed down the staircase with Saturninus in tow, smashing his head to pieces. Laurentius of Rome, more commonly known as Saint Lawrence, illustrated one of the more captivating displays of heroism in the time of Valerian. Saint Lawrence was born in Spain, but later came to Rome, where he served as a deacon in the Roman church, in charge of distributing alms to the poor. According to a law of the day, Christians were forced to suffer the confiscation of their property. When a prefect of Rome demanded Lawrence produce the church's wealth, he begged to be given three days to round up the offering. At the end of the third day, he approached the prefect, bidding him to come to a church to see a great heap of the church's treasure. The prefect happily agreed. When he got to the church, Lawrence presented to him scores of blind, invalid, destitute, leprous, and orphaned human beings, saying, "What are you displeased at? The gold that you so eagerly desire is a vile metal, and serves to incite men to all manner of crimes. The light of heaven is the true gold, which these poor objects enjoy." The prefect was furious at Lawrence's ploy and proclaimed death: "Do you thus mock me? Is it thus that the axes and the fasces, the sacred ensigns of the Roman power, are insulted?? I know that you desire to die; that is your [frenzy] and vanity: but you shall not die immediately, as you imagine. I will protract your tortures, that your death may be the more bitter as it shall be slower. You shall die by inches." He ordered Lawrence whipped and then broiled alive over an iron grid. Legend has it that the saint managed to find some humor in his hour of death. After some time being roasted on one side, he casually remarked to the prefect, "Let my body be now turned, one side is broiled enough!"[41] Some of the details of Lawrence's martyrdom were probably embellished over the centuries, but his name and basic biographical details are well attested to in early church sources.[42] The traditional date for Lawrence's martyrdom, August 10, coincides with the Perseid meteor shower, and for this reason the shower is sometimes referred to as "the tears of Saint Lawrence."

Herbert Schmalz, *Faithful Unto Death*, 1897.

CYPRIAN AND THE LAPSED

For every story that is recounted here of martyrs bearing unthinkable punishment with equanimity and courage, there are many unrecorded stories of those who capitulated when cast into the crucible and who denied that they were Christians. This often had a disheartening effect on members of the church; the author of the account of the great persecution at Lyon in the second century said that about one in ten of the accused did not hold fast, "causing us great grief and sorrow beyond measure, and impairing the zeal of the others who had not yet been seized."[43] Hence, one of the deepest theological controversies of the third century was the question of whether the church should reaccept into membership those who had faltered in their faith at such a moment. Tertullian thought that no one should ever flee from persecution, since everything is from God, and "in no way will it be our duty to flee from what has God as its author."[44] Those who did not weaken in the face of trial and were tortured but not martyred were called "confessors." Those who had evaded persecution entirely were called the "lapsed." Of course, there were varying degrees of faithlessness—some of the lapsed had purchased fake certificates of sacrifice, others made sacrifice and repented, and some had immediately sacrificed and not repented for it at all. Some thought that the confessors should be the arbitrators of whether, and how, to restore the lapsed back into communion with the church. Others believed that the authority to make that decision should rest with the bishops.

Sometime during the persecutions of Decius and Valerian, Cyprian, the bishop of Carthage, had fled from the city. Cyprian kept up his oversight of the Carthaginian church by means of extensive correspondence with a deacon. But other church leaders took umbrage at this, believing his flight to be a cowardly act. Cyprian responded by saying that this was a necessary precaution for a pastor of the flock. To resolve the situation, Cyprian called a synod of bishops. It was decided (unsurprisingly) that the bishops, and not the confessors, would have discretion over whom to admit back into fellowship. Those who had sacrificed and never repented of it would never be allowed back into the church, while those who had sacrificed but repented would be given an opportunity to be readmitted. In the end, Cyprian seems to have proved that his flight from Carthage had not been motivated by fear: he was martyred in 258.

A similar situation prevailed between the bishop of Rome, Cornelius, and a presbyter named Novatian, who was later described as one "who has sundered the Church and drawn some of the brethren into impiety and blasphemy, and has introduced impious teaching concerning God, and has calumniated our most compassionate Lord Jesus Christ as unmerciful."[45] At the end of the Decian persecution, Novatian had desired to be elected bishop of Rome, a position that had been unfilled for over a year because of persecution. A man named Cornelius, who advocated for receiving the lapsed back into fellowship, was elected instead. Novatian was incensed that one could be elected bishop who treated so loosely the receipt of the lapsed into the church. In response, Novatian had himself elected bishop by three other bishops, and thus became the second antipope. As another author has noted, "the issue was whether purity or forgiving love should be the characteristic note of the church."[46] Cornelius and sixty other bishops, at Cyprian's urging, sided with purity, and Novatian was excommunicated before suffering martyrdom in the same year as Cyprian, 258.

The first part of the third century had been a hard one for the church in terms of persecution. But this was always the expectation for the Christian; even in the middle of the first century, Paul wrote to Timothy that "everyone who wants to live a godly life in Christ Jesus will be persecuted" (2 Tim. 3:12). The worst of Severus, Decius, and Valerian could not frustrate the growth of the church. Undoubtedly, a martyr's acceptance of (and sometimes eagerness for) death suggested to the pagan that the Christian possessed something much more valuable than his own life. And as the writings of Tertullian show, pagan Rome had to confront its own religious superstitions against the backdrop of a superior moral framework and a crumbling empire. Like Tertullian, the greatest and most controversial theologian of the third century, Augustine, was also a North African. And just as the third century had opened with an emperor bent on restoring Roman values through the attrition of the church, so, as we will see, it also closed with one.

FIVE

EGYPT AND THE GREAT PERSECUTION

The Importance of Egypt, Clement of Alexandria and Origen, the Codex, the Persecution of Diocletian

We have seen that most of the important theological developments of the third century took place at Rome. But outside the Eternal City, Christianity was growing in other areas as well, and often adopting aspects of the local philosophical culture into its practice. A prime example of this was the Roman province of Egypt. Egypt itself was absolutely critical as the supplier of grain to all parts of the empire; and its port capital, Alexandria, was probably the second most important city of the empire. It was home to a mix of native Egyptians, Greeks, Romans, and Jews. Since the time of its founding by Alexander the Great, it was renowned for its intellectual culture and especially its library, which was considered the preeminent center of learning in the ancient world. Eusebius claimed that Saint Mark introduced Christianity into Egypt,[1] and against this multiethnic backdrop Alexandria served as a unique incubator for the exploration of theological questions. By the second century, a school of thought known as Neoplatonism, which was heavily influenced by the Greek philosopher Plato, was emerging in Egyptian Christianity. Although not pure Neoplatonists, the two most famous Christian theologians linked to this school of thinking were two church fathers from the city on the Nile: Clement of Alexandria and his pupil, Origen.

CLEMENT OF ALEXANDRIA

Similar to another Easterner, Justin Martyr, Clement of Alexandria (ca. 150–ca. 215) wandered the Mediterranean for years, studying different philosophies before settling in Egypt to study with an unknown master. Under this man's tutelage Clement began to spend all his time "gathering the spoil of the flowers of the prophetic and apostolic meadow."[2] Unlike Tertullian, who scoffed at the pagans and wondered, *What hath Athens to do with Jerusalem?*, Clement's writing is heavily colored with the language of Greek philosophy, and Plato in particular. This was not a mere affectation of intellectualism. Rather, Clement's motivation was to affirm Christianity as a philosophical system and a religion in hopes of winning pagans to the faith. Clement's most important work in this regard is the *Protrepticus*, or *Exhortation to the Heathen*. Demonstrating an extraordinary familiarity with Greek mysteries, myths, and legends, Clement, like Tertullian, attacked pagan religion on its own merits and cited examples in which the wisdom of ancient literature overlapped with Scripture. In urging his audience to turn away from the worship of the Greco-Roman gods, he offered a quotation from Homer's *Odyssey* to illustrate his point that the Christian must flee from illicit pleasures:

> She praises you, O mariner, and calls the illustrious; and the courtesan tries to win to herself the glory of the Greeks. Leave her to prey on the dead; a heavenly spirit comes to your help: pass by Pleasure, she beguiles:

Let not a woman with flowing train cheat you of your senses,
With her flattering prattle seeking your hurt.[3]

Another of Clement's works is the *Instructor*, a detailed exposition of the Christian's relationship to Jesus Christ. The *Instructor* establishes Jesus Christ as the *logos*, the Word, which is the ultimate, universal good. To fully understand the *logos*, Clement argued, the Scriptures must be interpreted not only literally but allegorically. Faith goes hand in hand with reason, and only he who understands it will obtain "true gnosis"[4] (by this he meant true understanding—"gnosis" here is not to be confused with the teachings of the heretical Gnostics). But Clement's emphasis on finding deeper meanings in the text (which may not be plain to the average interpreter) meant that his theology was sometimes more Platonic than scriptural. Clement believed that the soul went through an ongoing reeducation and purification process before entering heaven, and much of the doctrine of purgatory traces its roots to him.[5] His is a very esoteric theology, with suspect doctrines about the nature of Christ. Clement called Christians to be open to finding truth in philosophy, which over the centuries has made him at times unpopular in the Christian tradition. For instance, he is revered as a saint in Oriental Orthodox Christianity, Eastern Catholicism, and Anglicanism, but is little revered in the Eastern Orthodox Church and was decanonized from Catholic sainthood in the 1500s on account of questionable doctrine.

Apart from his ideas on Christ and the soul, Clement seems to have been a stern moralizer, and he left us a comprehensive commentary, some of it unwittingly humorous, on how one should conduct oneself with various social graces. It is not hard to see how these exhortations later became popular with Victorian audiences in the nineteenth century.

In consuming food, he encouraged moderation:

From all slavish habits and excess we must abstain, and touch what is set before us in a decorous way; keeping the hand and couch and chin free of stains; preserving the grace of the countenance undisturbed, and committing no indecorum in the act of swallowing; but stretching out the hand at intervals in an orderly manner.[6]

He condemned drunkenness:

You may see some of them, half-drunk, staggering, with crowns round their necks like wine jars, vomiting drink on one another in the name of good fellowship; and others, full of the effects of their debauch, dirty, pale in the face, livid, and still above yesterday's bout pouring another bout to last till next morning. It is well, my friends, it is well to make our acquaintance with this picture at the greatest possible distance from it, and to frame ourselves to what is better, dreading lest we also become a like spectacle and laughing-stock to others.[7]

And he even showed a concern for how to politely control sneezing and hiccups:

If any one is attacked with sneezing, just as in the case of hiccup, he must not startle those near him with the explosion, and so give proof of his bad breeding; but the hiccup is to be quietly transmitted with the expiration of the breath, the mouth being composed becomingly, and not gaping and yawning like the tragic masks.[8]

In modern terms, we might call Clement of Alexandria a "seeker"— one who is consistently on a quest for religious understanding. While he never became a bishop, Clement may have been a presbyter (a pastor or priest in modern church constructions) and was certainly the head of the Christian school at Alexandria. His theological understandings had lasting implications, as the distinction between faith and philosophy became at times blurred. To what extent these two areas complement each other is still a major point of contention between Protestants, Catholics, and Eastern Orthodox believers today.

ORIGEN

If Clement represented an important step in the absorption of philosophy into Christian theology, his star pupil, Origen, was antiquity's greatest proponent of the Alexandrian approach to interpreting the Bible (i.e., heavy on allegory and symbolism). Like Clement, Origen is remembered by posterity with contention: he is not recognized as a saint by either the Catholic or Orthodox churches. But he was absolutely the most prolific Christian writer of the ancient world; it is a pity that of his more than two thousand estimated works,[9] only a handful survive in their entirety. Origen was very widely known, read, and absorbed by his contemporaries. One commentator has written that of all the early church figures, Origen "exerted an influence on Christian thought, exceeded perhaps by no one except the apostle Paul himself."[10]

Before examining his theology, it is worth recounting the story of Origen's life. He was born into a Christian family in Alexandria, where his father, Leonides, gave him a thorough educational regimen of studying "the Greek sciences." But the Scriptures too were a subject "of no secondary importance." Memorization and recitation of the Bible was standard, but Origen hungered to understand Scripture intimately at an early age, and "sought for something more, and even at that age busied himself with deeper speculations, so that he puzzled his father with inquiries for the true meaning of the inspired Scriptures." When Origen was around seventeen, his father was martyred during the persecution of Severus. Though it may be the stuff of hagiography, Eusebius reported that young Origen too wanted to be martyred, and would have entered unto death, had not the pleas of his mother held him back. Yet Origen's desire for the martyr's crown still burned, and his mother had to resort to hiding his

André Thevet, *Origen of Alexandria*, 1584.

73

clothes so that he couldn't go out in public. Still, his father was dead, and his property had been confiscated, leaving Origen, his mother, and six younger brothers with no means of support. With so many mouths unable to be fed, it is likely either Origen set out on his own or some members of the Alexandrian church provided for his needs, for he was taken in by a wealthy woman as an adopted son. Although she treated him kindly, Origen's worldly learning soon made him noted around town, and he began to "earn a compensation amply sufficient for his needs at his age," probably through teaching literature and Scripture. In the wake of Severus's persecution, Alexandria was left with no one who was equipped to teach the faith. Origen recognized the deficit, and he first became the teacher of baptismal candidates, and later became the head of the Christian school in Alexandria, which had been vacated by Clement. He was only eighteen. Shortly thereafter, another round of persecution broke out. This round of violence apparently only targeted recent converts to Christianity, because Origen spent most of his time ministering to those who had been imprisoned, even going to join them in the jail himself, despite the threat of physical assault:

> For not only was he with them while in bonds, and until their final condemnation, but when the holy martyrs were led to death, he was very bold and went with them into danger. So that as he acted bravely, and with great boldness saluted the martyrs with a kiss, oftentimes the heathen multitude round about them became infuriated, and were on the point of rushing upon him.[11]

Origen's ministry was so passionate and fruitful at this time that the local authorities posted armed guards at his house to prevent him from going out and ministering. But he continued to sneak out, being driven from house to house because of the huge number of people who wanted to hear him preach and teach. Origen's life displayed a consistency of belief and action that is far too rare for many theologians; Eusebius wrote, "His manner of life was as his doctrine, and his doctrine as his life."[12]

But around this time, Origen was seized with the desire to stop teaching secular subjects, like grammar, rhetoric, literature, and philosophy, and he instead decided to focus exclusively on religious instruction. Origen did not mean that all other subjects were unchristian or unprofitable; rather, his call to ministry demanded he focus exclusively on studying and teaching the Scriptures. To pursue this, he sold off the entirety of his secular library, receiving an income of four *oboli* per day (which would have been the bare minimum one needed to live on).[13]

Origen's life at this time also became increasingly ascetic (deprived of physical pleasures). He would go through intense periods of fasting and sleep deprivation, and when he did sleep, it was never on a bed; the ground sufficed for him. He drank no wine, ate the most basic food, and did nothing else for his body, such that he was "in danger of breaking down and destroying his constitution."[14] He lived in "the very extreme of poverty," never wore shoes, and owned only a single cloak. Above all, he was devoted to incessant study of the Scriptures, immersing himself in them "for the greater part of the night."[15] But Origen's most signally bizarre act was "a deed . . . done by him which evidenced an immature and youthful mind, but at the same time gave the highest proof of faith and continence."[16] Evidently Origen took very literally Jesus' exhortation in Matthew 19:12: "For there are eunuchs who were born that way, and there are eunuchs who have been made eunuchs by others—and there are those who choose to live like eunuchs for the sake of the kingdom of heaven. The one who can accept this should accept it." Origen apparently felt that he could accept it and physically castrated himself![17] The intention behind his action was to deprive himself of any opportunity to act on sexual temptation, but even Eusebius said that Origen took the verse "in too literal and extreme a sense."[18] He intended to keep it a secret, but what he had done was soon discovered. He received praise from the bishop of Alexandria, Demetrius, and later, the praise of other bishops in the eastern regions of Caeserea and Palestine. Because of his outrageous action and his breadth of learning, Origen's fame spread abroad. By invitation of the prefect, he visited Arabia sometime around

214 to discourse on the faith. Later, two bishops in the East invited him to come and teach the Scriptures there.

Eventually Origen began to write, and the literary output of his entire career is believed to be around two thousand books (not the length of modern books, but sections of text equivalent to a chapter in a modern book). His commentaries on Scripture were extensive: Eusebius said he penned at least twenty-two books of a commentary on the book of John,[19] as well as twelve books on Genesis, twenty-five books on Ezekiel, thirty on Isaiah, and numerous others on the Psalms and other books. This kind of scholarly lifestyle required money, and Origen was financed by a wealthy Alexandrian friend named Ambrose, who provided funds for not only the expensive parchment, papyrus, or vellum (dried sheepskin) on which the books were copied, but also for the seven copyists to whom Origen dictated his thoughts, and a number of young girls with skilled handwriting who copied those copies.

Because of a theological conflict with his bishop, Origen eventually moved to Caesarea on the Mediterranean coast. He founded a school and started preaching three times a week before later preaching every day. Little is known about the last part of his life, although he was undoubtedly engrossed in thinking and writing about the Scriptures. His death came as a consequence of the persecution of Decius, during which time the "demon of evil marshaled all his forces" against the church. Origen had an iron collar placed around his neck and was thrown into a dungeon before being stretched out on a torture rack. The injuries did not cause instant death, but he was sufficiently old (almost seventy) that he died within a few years of his torture.[20] To the last, he proved that Christianity wasn't just an intellectual exercise, but something worth giving his life for.

Later interpreters through the centuries have had a difficult time knowing what to make of Origen's theology. The vast majority of his work conforms to what Irenaeus, Ignatius, and Justin Martyr had set down, but his illustrious career is clouded by elements of his theology that many have suggested stray from biblical orthodoxy. From the outset, Origen was not a Gnostic who believed in more than one divine being, or that there existed a secret tradition of Christian knowledge that only some believers could obtain. He believed in adhering to the tradition of the apostles, writing, "Nothing which is at variance with the tradition of apostles and of the church is to be accepted as true."[21] Origen also emphasized the necessity of interpreting Scripture literally and allegorically, but, like Clement, might have read his own ideas too strongly into the text (we might today accuse Origen of "confirmation bias"—favoring information that confirms his own preconceived beliefs).

Consequently, Origen developed two points of theology in particular that indicate a departure from what the church had traditionally taught. The first is his belief in the preexistence of souls, a point that may seem minor, but which contradicts the creation narrative told in the book of Genesis. The second was his speculative belief in an eternal cycle of spiritual rebellion and restoration, which culminated in an eventual universal salvation. In time, believed the eunuch, even Satan himself could be saved from judgment. This eternal cycle narrative had roots in the Platonic tradition, and later philosophers who rejected Christianity, but still respected the man as an intellectual power, attacked him for mixing Greek and Christian teachings: "in his life conducting himself as a Christian and contrary to the laws, but in his opinions of material things and of the Deity being like a Greek, and mingling Grecian teachings with foreign fables."[22]

In spite of some questionable elements of his theology, Origen made very important contributions to the discipline of textual criticism (the scholarly analysis of how texts are passed down from generation to generation). In his magnificent *Hexapla* (now only preserved in fragments), Origen compiled the entire Old Testament and laid out in six columns (a) the original Hebrew text of the Old Testament; (b) the Hebrew language redone phonetically in Greek, so that readers of Greek could better comprehend Hebrew sounds, even if they didn't read the language; and (c) four different translations of the Old Testament in Greek, including the Septuagint (the Greek translation of the Old Testament). The original work totaled nearly seven thousand pages and was recorded in fifteen volumes. Accompanying his Septuagint was a complicated series of symbols (in modern scholarly terms, an *apparatus criticus*) to indicate discrepancies in different manuscripts of the same text. Scholars still use Origen's basic idea of the *apparatus criticus* today to convey their ideas about a text. Origen used the principles of textual criticism and manuscript evaluation to help determine which books he considered holy Scripture. In a letter to a friend, he suggested that the absence of the History of Susanna and Bel and the Dragon stories from the earliest Hebrew manuscripts warranted their exclusion from the Christian Bible's Old Testament:

> I have to tell you what it behooves us to do in the cases not only of the History of Susanna, which is found in every Church of Christ in that Greek copy which the Greeks use, but is not in the Hebrew, or of the two other passages you mention at the end of the book containing the history of Bel and the Dragon, which likewise are not in the Hebrew copy of Daniel.[23]

For his prodigious learning and profound ideas on the interpretation and transmission of the Scriptures, Origen was widely read well into the Middle Ages, and the adoption of his theological ideas caused two separate controversies in future generations: (1) debates over the origin of souls and (2) their ultimate destinies. The church would not see a man of his scholastic brilliance again until Augustine of Hippo, who thrived about 150 years later.

THE CODEX

When discussing such a voluminous writer as Origen, it is appropriate to also address one of the more important but relatively quiet inventions in intellectual history. The rise of Christianity in the earliest centuries of the first millennium helped facilitate a critical development in the history of the printed word: the rise of the codex. Before the codex, texts of all kinds were kept on wax tablets, or on long scrolls, which had to be unrolled whenever one wanted to read them. This changed in the first century with the appearance of the codex: pieces of papyrus or, more frequently, parchment or vellum (sheepskin) were bound together by a single spine, much like a modern book. This organization made reading a much more convenient activity: both sides of the page could be used for writing, and the reader could open to any page he wanted instead of unfurling a long roll.

For reasons that are not definitively known, Christians became the first people to adopt the codex en masse. One theory suggests that it made for easier collection and transportation of multiple sets of scriptures—such as the Gospels or the letters of Paul—and that people who received them transmitted new copies in the same form as they received them. Additionally, the codex could distinguish a set of writings as Christian merely by its external appearance, when Jewish or pagan writings were still being put down on rolls. The largest codices were over several hundred pages, but it was rare that they ran over two hundred. In terms of size, the largest codices could be ten inches long and nine inches wide, and the smallest approximately one inch by one and a half inches (to fit into amulets worn around the neck). By the beginning of the fourth century, the codex rivaled the scroll as the dominant form of book preservation, and by the sixth century the codex alone was used.

One of the great surviving masterpieces of antiquity is the *Codex Sinaiticus* (the Sinai Codex), so named for its discovery during the nineteenth century in Saint Catherine's Monastery, located at the foot of Mount Sinai in Egypt. Owing to the dry climate of the Egyptian desert, the *Sinaiticus* is perhaps the best-preserved piece of early Christian writing in the whole world, dating to the early fourth century. It contains half the Old Testament (usually a codex had the whole thing) and the entire New Testament on about four hundred pages. It has been estimated that it took 360 animals to get enough vellum for it and cost about a lifetime of wages to produce.[24]

Some scholars believe that because of the richness of the manuscript, it must have been produced at Rome by an edict of Constantine, who ordered fifty copies of the Bible produced after his conversion in 313. The discovery and subsequent dispute over ownership of the manuscript is itself a remarkable story: A German scholar was visiting the monastery in the 1840s when he

A selection of Jesus' Sermon on the Mount in the Codex Sinaiticus.

noticed some pieces of paper sitting in a bin used for collecting fuel for the monastery's ovens. He examined the script and the content, and realized he was looking at a very rare style of handwriting that had recorded the Old Testament in ancient Greek. The scholar rescued the paper from the bin and tracked down the complete codex. For decades, different pieces of the manuscript changed hands, and it was housed in the Russian Imperial Library until it was sold to the British Museum in 1933 for the equivalent of 6 million British pounds (roughly 9 million dollars) in today's currency.

The entire codex has now been scanned and uploaded onto the Internet, with an extensive set of tools for examining it in detail, as well as an *apparatus criticus* to help the reader resolve thorny textual issues (many places in the codex are different from other manuscripts, largely because of the errors of unskilled copyists). The *Sinaiticus* contains the oldest surviving complete New Testament in the world, and for this reason alone it is extremely valuable. Despite some cosmetic copying errors, it is also considered more accurate in places than many other, later manuscripts. While probably not produced in Egypt, it is, without question, one of the greatest treasures the archaeologically rich sands of Egypt have ever bequeathed.

DIOCLETIAN AND THE GREAT PERSECUTION

The Roman Empire was struggling to remain a stable political structure in the middle part of the third century. This period of Roman history is usually referred to as the Crisis of the Third Century, so named because of major military, political, economic, and social turbulence. Beginning in 235, the empire had suffered through a quick succession of emperors, none of whom were effective (or lived long enough) to hold the empire together in the thick of civil strife and enemy incursions on the frontiers. The seat of political power moved to Milan in 286, and Rome became a kind of ornamental capital, although the Senate still took up their duty there. Some provinces formed their own mini-empires (although they were later restored).

This kind of disunity did little to rescue the empire from numerous barbarian invasions. Groups like the Goths (initially from Sweden via the Black Sea) and Vandals (southern Poland) were now assaulting the empire with greater frequency. In addition to stretching the military thin, these invasions had an adverse economic impact, as longstanding commercial and transportation networks disintegrated. Lastly, desperate efforts over the years to increase the size of the army had necessitated an increase in spending; the empire fell into the red, a new abundance of coinage resulted in a devaluation of the Roman currency, and long-distance trade ground to a halt. So it was nothing short of miraculous that when the emperor Diocletian took charge of the empire in 284, he instituted a series of reforms that spared the empire from total collapse. Diocletian was born in modern-day Croatia, where the beautiful ruins of his palace still exist in the city center of the town Split. He was a military man who was chosen by his army as co-emperor after the death of Numerian and later defeated Carinus, his rival for the throne, in battle.

Over the next twenty-one years, Diocletian implemented a number of reforms that reorganized and reinvigorated the empire. His most

81

important reform was to create two co-emperors and two junior emperors, so that an established plan of succession would be in place whenever crisis hit. This arrangement was known as the *tetrarchy*. Most of his other reforms incorporated an overhaul of institutions that concentrated power in imperial hands. This effort had mixed results: a reorganization of the military proved successful, although his economic policy was extremely centralized, and the Roman economy continued to languish under him. But the empire recovered its military footing, and it wasn't until a swarm of barbarian invasions one hundred years later that Rome could again be fairly described as being on the edge of collapse.

As turbulent as the third century was, the Christian church actually enjoyed a period of relative peace and growth between the death of the persecuting emperor Valerian (d. 260) and Diocletian's campaign of persecution, which began in 303. Paradoxically, however, this period of peace seems to have made the church less vigilant toward its manner of life, and laziness and friction began to plague it. Said Eusebius, "We fell into laxity and sloth, and envied and reviled each other, and were almost, as it were, taking up arms against one another, rulers assailing rulers with words like spears, and people forming parties against people, and monstrous hypocrisy and dissimulation rising to the greatest height of wickedness."[25] But despite the desultory and factious condition of the church, Christianity had grown enormously during this time. One contemporary scholar has suggested that the Christian population of the Roman Empire grew from about 1.1 million in the year 250 to about 6 million in the year 300.[26] But amid the explosion of the faith, pagan intellectuals were beginning to battle back against a changing culture. Many pagans didn't mind that the state had periodically cracked down on Christians. "To what sort of penalties might we not justly subject people," wondered the philosopher Porphyry of Tyre, "who are fugitives from their fathers' customs?"[27]

It was at this moment that Diocletian initiated the last and most brutal of all the ancient persecutions. Diocletian conceived of himself as the savior of the Roman Empire, and he demanded the kind of fealty that he believed suitable for such a great ruler: wearing of purple was forbidden to anyone but the emperor, he went around wearing a golden crown and jewels, and his subjects had to prostrate themselves in his presence; some were allowed to kiss the end of his robe. His image, enshrined in numerous sculptures and paintings, was constantly displayed to the people. Such an emphasis on imperial power also demanded that the old Roman value system be preserved. Diocletian saw himself as a type of Jupiter, and he worked to reinvigorate the worship of the imperial cult. In his mind, dispensing with the Roman deities was an inauspicious and dangerous decision.

The beginning of his rage came in 299, during a Roman religious ceremony in which the entrails of a slain animal were examined by a priest as a means of predicting the future. Diocletian sought an oracle from the entrails of a victim, but Christians observing the process (who considered animal sacrifice a form of witchcraft) made the sign of the cross as the interpretation was being given. The priest, unable to interpret the entrails, suggested that the Christians' gestures were thwarting his power. Diocletian was angry and demanded that anyone assisting in the ceremony, or even just living in the imperial palace at the time, be forced to perform a sacrifice to the emperor or be scourged. Additionally, anyone serving in the army was forced to make a sacrifice to the emperor or be discharged and lose his pension. Hence, we see a seed already implanted in Diocletian's mind that the Christians were detrimental to the success of the empire.

In 301, Diocletian received a letter from the proconsul of Africa that expressed agitation about the Manichaeans, a heretical Gnostic sect of Christians who "have set up new and hitherto unheard of sects in opposition to the older creeds so that they might cast out the doctrines vouchsafed to us in the past by divine favour. " He continued, "Our fear is that with the passage of time, they will endeavour . . . to infect . . . our whole empire . . . as with the poison of a malignant serpent."[28] Why Diocletian singled out just the Manichaeans isn't clear, but he continued his anti-Christian policies by ordering that lower-status Manichaeans in

Africa be burned alive, along with their books. The upper-class members were sent to work in the salt mines.

But it wasn't until about 302 that Diocletian adopted a sustained persecution of Christians as imperial policy. In that year, Galerius, one of the tetrarchs, suggested to Diocletian that an empire-wide punishment of Christians was necessary. Galerius himself was partly motivated to suggest this because of his mother's hatred of Christians; she couldn't stand the fact that Christian dining companions wouldn't eat food that had been sacrificed to the Roman gods (the apostle Paul addressed this very subject in 1 Corinthians 8).[29] But Galerius had already seen firsthand the threat that the Christians posed to the perpetuation of the Roman gods and, by extension, the empire. Diocletian initially demurred, saying that this would cause a headache for him; Christians sought death, and to institute a campaign of punishment would mean an empire-wide bloodbath. It was good enough for him if they were merely expelled from the imperial household and the army. To resolve the question, Diocletian consulted some of his advisers; most, whether because of their own anti-Christian sentiments or fear of Galerius, suggested he proceed with it. Lastly, Diocletian consulted the Oracle of Apollo at Miletus, a town on the coast of Turkey. The Oracle (who probably didn't appreciate the Christian competition for religious affection) told him to go ahead with the plan.

THE EDICT AGAINST THE CHRISTIANS

In 303, Diocletian issued his "Edict Against the Christians," which instituted an empire-wide assault against the faith. The persecution began the day after the Roman festival day known as the *Terminalia*, so named for Terminus, the Roman god of boundaries. The meaning here is unmistakable; Diocletian and his cohort wanted to terminate the Christians. Galerius had insisted that all Christians should be burnt alive, but Diocletian was content to let things proceed "without bloodshed."[30] The edict ordered the destruction of Christian writings and churches, which had grown beyond house churches by this point. Christians were forbidden to assemble for worship or to appear in the courts. Former slaves who had become Christians were reenslaved, and members of the Roman nobility and military who professed themselves Christians were stripped of their titles and the civil privileges that came with them. The first thrust in the anti-Christian offensive was a planned burning of the church in Nicomedia, a town in Turkey, an event that Diocletian and Galerius observed personally:

> [W]hile it was yet hardly light, the prefect, together with chief com-
> manders, tribunes, and officers of the treasury, came to the church
> in Nicomedia, and the gates having been forced open, they searched
> everywhere for an image of the Divinity. The books of the Holy
> Scriptures were found, and they were committed to the flames; the
> utensils and furniture of the church were abandoned to pillage: all was
> rapine, confusion, tumult.[31]

It was only Diocletian's fear of the city's total incineration that prevented the mob from setting the church on fire. Instead, the Praetorian Guard, the emperor's personal detachment, hacked away at the structure with swords and axes, leveling it in only a few hours. The next day the edict was published in town. A man named Eutius went and tore it down, saying, "These are the triumphs of Goths and Sarmatians!"[32] He was tortured and burned alive.

At first, Diocletian was content to let the campaign start out as a bloodless pursuit, but civil magistrates across the empire had the

The Christian Martyrs's Last Prayer, by Jean-Léon Gérôme, 1883.

85

authority to issue capital punishments in judicial cases, and many did just this because of longstanding prejudices. What seems to have pushed Diocletian to an insatiable rage was a fire that broke out in the imperial palace in 303. Lactantius, the best historical source for the Great Persecution, claimed (perhaps falsely) that Galerius himself secretly instigated it, and managed to convince Diocletian that the Christians had done it.[33] Whatever the case, Diocletian unleashed a tide of blood unknown to Christians in the history of the empire. Eusebius said, "It is impossible to relate how many and what sort of martyrs of God could be seen, among the inhabitants of all the cities and countries."[34] The next eight years resulted in thousands of slain Christians. Lactantius described how the madness began:

> Presbyters and other officers of the Church were seized, without evidence by witnesses or confession, condemned, and together with their families led to execution. In burning alive, no distinction of sex or age was regarded; and because of their great multitude, they were not burnt one after another, but a herd of them were encircled with the same fire; and servants, having millstones tied about their necks, were cast into the sea. Nor was the persecution less grievous on the rest of the people of God; for the judges, dispersed through all the temples, sought to compel every one to sacrifice. The prisons were crowded; tortures, hitherto unheard of, were invented; and lest justice should be inadvertently administered to a Christian, altars were placed in the courts of justice, hard by the tribunal, that every litigant might offer incense before his cause could be heard.[35]

Eusebius was eager to recount the martyrdom of one of the palace attendants who happened to be a Christian:

> A certain man was brought forward in the above-mentioned city, before the rulers of whom we have spoken. He was then commanded

to sacrifice, but as he refused, he was ordered to be stripped and raised on high and beaten with rods over his entire body, until, being conquered, he should, even against his will, do what was commanded.

But as he was unmoved by these sufferings, and his bones were already appearing, they mixed vinegar with salt and poured it upon the mangled parts of his body. As he scorned these agonies, a gridiron and fire were brought forward. And the remnants of his body, like flesh intended for eating, were placed on the fire, not at once, lest he should expire instantly, but a little at a time. And those who placed him on the pyre were not permitted to desist until, after such sufferings, he should assent to the things commanded.

But he held his purpose firmly, and victoriously gave up his life while the tortures were still going on. Such was the martyrdom of one of the servants of the palace, who was indeed well worthy of his name, for he was called Peter.[36]

The eastern portions of the empire—Palestine, Egypt, and Turkey— saw the worst persecutions. Eusebius described how hundreds of people were killed at one time, and the authorities sometimes disinterred the bodies of the slain and threw them into the sea, fearing that the survivors would worship them as gods.[37] Some were nailed to crosses, where they perished with hunger. Others had their bodies scraped with seashells until they died. Women were hung naked by one leg from tree trunks. Sometimes the Romans took the stoutest branches of two trees and bent them to the ground using siege machines. A Christian was tied in between the branches, and when the machines were released, the branches snapped back into their natural position, instantly ripping the Christian in two down the middle.

Others endured on their bowels and privy members shameful and inhuman and unmentionable torments, which the noble and law-observing judges, to show their severity, devised, as more honorable manifestations of wisdom. And new tortures were continually invented, as if they were endeavoring, by surpassing one another, to gain prizes in a contest.[38]

The most famous martyr of the era was Saint Sebastian. Sebastian was a Gaul who had been educated at Milan and later became part of the emperor's personal guard. Yet he remained a faithful Christian in this position, "untainted by evil examples, and uncontaminated by the hopes of preferment."[39] When persecution broke out, Sebastian refused to sacrifice to the emperor and was marched to the Campus Martius, a large field in Rome used for public activity. As punishment, he was shot through with arrows. Sebastian lay on the brink of death, but some Christians who had observed the torture, including Saint Irene of Rome, came to his aid and helped him recover. Later that day, Sebastian deliberately placed himself in Diocletian's path as he was going to the temple. Diocletian was stunned at the sight of his old guardsman, now bloody and near death from the arrowheads. Sebastian then "reprehended him for his various cruelties and unreasonable prejudices against Christianity."[40] But the emperor wasn't moved and ordered Sebastian beaten to death. To make sure that Christians wouldn't recover the body, he also commanded that his body be thrown into the sewer. Still, a woman named Lucina managed to get ahold of it, and his remains are stored today in the Basilica Apostolorum (Basilica of the Apostles) in Rome. He also remains a popular saint with soldiers.

The brutality of the age would be enough to dissuade anyone from becoming a Christian. Still, Eusebius reported, most Christians didn't wither when peering down into the canyon of death:

And we beheld the most wonderful ardor, and the truly divine energy and zeal of those who believed in the Christ of God. For as soon as sentence was pronounced against the first, one after another rushed to the judgment seat, and confessed themselves Christians. And regarding with indifference the terrible things and the multiform tortures, they declared themselves boldly and undauntedly for the religion of the God of the universe. And they received the final sentence of death with joy and laughter and cheerfulness; so that they sang and offered up hymns and thanksgivings to the God of the universe till their very last breath.[41]

Diocletian issued a second edict later in the year—all members of the clergy were to be arrested and imprisoned. The effect of this was an overcrowding of the prisons, and hardened criminals were turned out onto the streets to make room for the Christians. As a celebration of his twenty years in power, Diocletian issued a third edict, which released the clergy from prison, provided they sacrificed to the emperor. His fourth and final edict, in 304, compelled all men, women, and children to gather in a public space and make a collective sacrifice. Those who did not would be executed.

In 305, Galerius forced Diocletian, now in poor health, and his co-emperor, Maximian, to resign from power. Galerius now became emperor, with Constantius as co-emperor. This induced a great deal of chaos, as Galerius and a host of other rivals began to attempt to outmaneuver one another for total control of the empire. It was a bloody time for anyone involved in public life, and men of power suspected total strangers of being spies, torturing them to find out the truth: "the sea could not be navigated, nor could men sail from any port without being exposed to all kinds of outrages; being stretched on the rack and lacerated in their sides, that it might be ascertained through various tortures, whether they came from the enemy."[42] Sensing his own tenuous grip on power, Galerius petitioned Diocletian to help him restore order. But Diocletian, now enjoying the quiet repose of

The Martyrdom of St. Sebastian, Painting from Upper Bavaria, ca. 1475.

his estate in Croatia, would have none of it. He replied, "If you could show the cabbage that I planted with my own hands to your emperor, he definitely wouldn't dare suggest that I replace the peace and happiness of this place with the storms of a never-satisfied greed."[43] The factious nature of the empire led to a breakdown in the universal enforcement of the laws, and the persecution quieted in the West, although it persisted in the East, where Galerius reigned.

It had now been eight years since Diocletian's first edict in 303, and the persecution had not relented. But a very unlikely source soon commanded it to stop. Galerius fell ill in 311, and he perhaps attributed his sickness to divine judgment, for he issued a proclamation changing his policy only five days before he died. Said Eusebius:

> Wrestling with so many evils, he thought of the cruelties which he had committed against the pious. Turning, therefore, his thoughts toward himself, he first openly confessed to the God of the universe, and then summoning his attendants, he commanded that without delay they should stop the persecution of the Christians, and should by law and royal decree, urge them forward to build their churches and to perform their customary worship, offering prayers in behalf of the emperor. Immediately the deed followed the word.[44]

There should have been reason for the Christians to rejoice, but the tetrarch Maximinus, the successor to Galerius in Asia, continued his own round of persecution through the year 312. By imperial decree, Maximinus instituted a new round of forced worship:

> That all men, women, and children, even infants at the breast, should sacrifice and offer oblations; and that with diligence and care they should cause them to taste of the execrable offerings; and that the things for sale in the market should be polluted with libations from the sacrifices; and that guards should be stationed before the baths in

order to defile with the abominable sacrifices those who went to wash in them.[45]

Predictably, those who refused to cooperate were mutilated or slain. Egypt was the site of the worst bloodshed: many had their noses, ears, and eyes mangled or cut off; one woman was stripped naked and whipped to death as she was marched through the streets. It wasn't until 313 that Maximinus died, and the Great Persecution finally came to an end.

THE CONSEQUENCES OF DIOCLETIAN'S PERSECUTION

Such sustained violence had major repercussions for the church. As had happened in previous generations with the Novationists (see chapter 4), the church divided on the question of what should happen to those Christians who had denied the faith or sacrificed to the emperor under threat of death. Many others had simply fled to safer places, where the persecutory decrees were not as widely enforced. Some Christians accused those held in prison of being show-offs. The church in Alexandria underwent a schism on the issue of whether they should readmit the lapsed into the church. When the Christians there later found themselves jailed in the same prison cell, and neither side was willing to forgive the other, Peter of Alexandria, the bishop of the church there, who had fled persecution, put up a curtain in the prison cell to divide it in two. Such an action is almost reminiscent of two children fighting over their bedroom. The issue would be confronted in full in the next decade with the rise of Donatism (covered in the next chapter). But the church had still survived, and in retrospect, the era was a period of darkness before the dawn. In the aftermath of a century of civil war and decades of persecution, the church was about to receive as an ally the kind of man it never would have dreamed of having: the emperor.

SIX

CHURCH, STATE, AND EMPEROR

Constantine

As we saw in the last chapter, for nearly a decade in the late third century, the Great Persecution swept across the empire, leaving a trail of sorrow and ecclesiastical fragmentation in its wake. The church in the eastern areas of the empire—what we now call North Africa, Turkey, Egypt, Israel, Palestine, and Syria—had been especially devastated. But in the West, a few rising generals had decided that though they themselves did not profess to be Christians, persecution was a politically insensible policy. One of these generals was a young man born on the Danube frontier, Constantine. In time, Constantine would become the emperor of the Roman world and embrace Christianity in ways that seemed previously unthinkable for an emperor.

Constantine was the son of Constantius, a general who ruled part of the western portion of the empire as a Caesar, or a junior emperor. A legend, certainly false, goes that one night Constantius was staying at an inn and asked for some female company. The innkeeper relinquished to Constantius his beautiful daughter, Helena. During the night, Constantius looked up and saw wondrous celestial activity in the sky, which he took as an omen from Apollo. In the morning, he left behind a purple cloak as a token of gratitude. Years later, the legend continues, some soldiers were visiting the same inn and began teasing the young product of their union, not knowing it was Constantius's son Constantine. Helena snapped at them that they were teasing the son of an emperor, and when she produced the cloak to prove it, the soldiers hurried back to tell Constantius what they had seen. Constantius then rushed to invite Constantine and Helena to join him at his imperial court. This story is an exaggeration of the likely reality that Helena was of low birth and probably a courtesan for Constantius.[1]

What is known is that Constantine grew up as a kind of hostage in Diocletian's court, deliberately placed there by Constantius. This kind of arrangement was common in the ancient world, when rulers would send their children to live in rival or enemy households as a kind of insurance policy against unexpected power grabs. If the hostage's parent did something that displeased the caretaker, there was always the threat that the child could be killed. Thus, Constantine spent his youth in Diocletian's care, learning philosophy, Latin, and Greek at his court. When Diocletian died, and the hated Galerius assumed control of the eastern part of the empire, Constantine stayed there. Galerius apparently sensed Constantine's political ambitions, especially since his father held significant power in the West. Galerius subscribed to that old adage, "Keep your friends close, and your enemies closer." He refused to allow Constantine to travel westward when Constantius summoned him, instead devising plots to have him killed; at one point he even made Constantine fight wild beasts, under the pretense of getting him some exercise.

Finally, when Constantius was near death in 306, Galerius allowed Constantine to travel to him. But Constantine somehow discovered that Galerius intended to have him arrested and detained on a false charge while on the road there. Constantine sneaked out in the middle of the night, taking with him all the horses of the imperial stables. The next morning Galerius, who had waited in his bedchamber until noon anticipating the news of Constantine's arrest, discovered what had happened and demanded Constantine be hunted down and brought back. When his attendants announced that all the horses were missing, and thus nobody could chase him down, "he [Galerius] could hardly refrain from tears."[2] Constantine hurried at a breakneck pace to see his father, who was preparing an invasion of Britain. Constantius and his son fought together in the invasion, and before Constantius expired a few months later, he nominated Constantine to his soldiers as the next emperor. Constantius then died in peace and quiet, as he had wished. When news was brought to Galerius of what had happened, along with a portrait of Constantine in imperial dress, he was so mad he almost tossed the portrait into a fire. But his advisers dissuaded him from doing so; Constantine was popular with the troops in the East. Galerius begrudgingly sent him a purple robe as a sign of his acceptance of Constantine in the imperial order.[3]

CONSTANTINE CONSOLIDATES HIS POWER

One of Constantine's first moves as emperor in the West was to rescind Diocletian's persecution edicts. Wrote Lactantius, a member of Constantine's court, "Constantine Augustus, having assumed the government, made it his first care to restore the Christians to the exercise of their worship and to their God."[4] This annulment of the edicts probably had a political motivation; the persecutions of the past ten years had become unpopular with many citizens, particularly in the West, and Constantine may have seen a political constituency in the mass of the persecuted. But this annulment was most likely of increasingly little concern to Galerius and the other tetrarchs. The tetrarchy was in a perpetual state of simmering rivalry and backstabbing, and Constantine had to carefully choose with whom he would ally himself. In time, he picked Licinius, his co-emperor in the East, a decision that was solidified by Licinius's marriage to Constantine's sister, Constantia. Both

Licinius and Constantine also shared the same tolerant attitudes toward Christians. But this too would change in time.

Galerius died in 311, leaving power divided between Constantine (who controlled Gaul and Britain), Licinius, and two others: Maxentius at Rome and another ruler in the East, named Maximinus Daia, who continued the persecutions of Galerius (although Galerius died having rescinded the orders of persecution). Constantine unexpectedly marched on Rome in October 312 (perhaps motivated by a desire to liberate the city from the cruel Maxentius), and a showdown developed outside of Rome at the Milvian Bridge, one of the critical crossing points over the Tiber into Rome. One of the most famous episodes in the Constantinian story then took place. According to the historian Lactantius, Constantine had a dream in which he was commanded before battle to have his soldiers paint the Greek letters *chi* and *rho* (forming an insignia that represented Christ) on their shields.[5]

A chi rho symbol.

Eusebius had a different take, reporting that Constantine realized he needed something more powerful than his own army to defeat Maxentius, who (claimed Eusebius, perhaps falsely) practiced black magic.[6]

Constantine also considered that many emperors before him had been promised victory or success by different oracles, but failed just the same. Therefore, Constantine decided to "honor his father's God alone," evidence that perhaps Constantius too was a Christian.[7] The reality of Constantine's conversion is much more complex and is addressed later in this chapter. It is doubtful that he became a Christian at this time; for instance, we know he continued worshipping the Unconquered Sun after the Battle of Milvian Bridge. Whatever the case, the day before the battle, Constantine had a vision of a cross of light in the sky, on which were inscribed the words *By this sign you shall conquer* (in Latin, *in hoc signo vinces*). Constantine had a dream that night that confirmed the event in which Christ ordered him to make his army standards[8] in the form of a cross. Constantine did as he was ordered. The two armies clashed and displayed "the utmost exertions of valor."[9] Eventually Constantine gained the upper hand, and as Maxentius's forces pulled back onto the bridge, Maxentius was accidentally pushed into the river by a mass of fleeing troops. His body was pulled out of the river, and his head decapitated and paraded through the city. Constantine marched into Rome as a liberator, and his decisive victory at the Milvian Bridge established his power over the entire western part of the empire.

After the battle of the Milvian Bridge, Constantine and Licinius (one of the other tetrarchs) allied themselves even more closely by jointly issuing the Edict of Milan, so named for the city in which Constantine and Licinius forged the agreement. The edict declared a formal end to persecutions (although they continued in the East under the brutal Maximinus Daia even after this) and the restoration of property and assembly rights to Christians:

Giulio Romano, *The Battle of the Milvian Bridge*, 1520–1524.

When we, Constantine and Licinius, emperors, had an interview at Milan, and conferred together with respect to the good and security of the commonweal, it seemed to us that, amongst those things that are profitable to mankind in general, the reverence paid to the Divinity merited our first and chief attention, and that it was proper that the Christians and all others should have liberty to follow that mode of religion which to each of them appeared best; so that that God, who is seated in heaven, might be benign and propitious to us, and to every one under our government. And therefore we judged it a salutary measure, and one highly consonant to right reason, that no man should be denied leave of attaching himself to the rites of the Christians, or to whatever other religion his mind directed him, that thus the supreme Divinity, to whose worship we freely devote ourselves, might continue to vouchsafe His favour and beneficence to us. And accordingly we give you to know that, without regard to any provisos in our former orders to you concerning the Christians, all who choose that religion are to be permitted, freely and absolutely, to remain in it, and not to be disturbed any ways, or molested.[10]

Scholars have long debated the motives behind the edict. Some suggest that it was just an extension of the political calculus of the two men who believed that it was good politics to leave the Christians alone. In any case, it was the first wave of action in Constantine's program of religious toleration. The political arrangement now pitted Constantine and Licinius against Maximinus Daia in the East. Sensing that a conflict was inevitable, Daia struck first against the two in 313 but was quickly crushed at Byzantium, at that time a small town bestriding the waterway that separated modern-day Turkey from Europe.

Now the entire empire was divided between Licinius and Constantine, but neither man was ready to concede that he had enough territory already; both aspired to rule the entire empire. In 314, Constantine discovered an assassination attempt that Licinius had helped to orchestrate, and for the next six years, an uneasy truce persisted, with occasional military skirmishes between them. In 320, Constantine discovered that Licinius had gone back on the Edict of Milan and heard reports of persecutions against Christians, although nothing on the scale that had occurred under Diocletian, Galerius, and Maximinus Daia. Nonetheless, "Licinius did not renounce his wickedness, but rather increased his fury against the peoples that were subject to him, and there was left to the afflicted no hope of salvation, oppressed as they were by a savage beast."[11] Eusebius's reports (which are probably exaggerated to some degree) told of men and women forbidden to meet in the same church, bishops murdered, churches burned, and people who were cut to pieces and then thrown into the sea "as a food to fishes."[12] The true extent of Licinius's persecution is unknown, but something happened to induce Constantine to confront Licinius about the disrespecting of Christians' rights. It is more likely that Licinius used his imperial power to arbitrate disputes between Christians in ways that made him look heavy-handed, and Constantine, already irritated by Licinius's incursions into his territory, decided to intervene. Whether Constantine had sincere motivations for protecting Christians or merely saw an opportunity to appear as a political defender of Christianity is unknown, but he ultimately defeated Licinius in a series of battles in 324. Before the decisive battle, Licinius ordered his men not to look directly at Constantine's standards, which bore a cross on them. Constantine routed Licinius in battle, and with that was master of the entire empire. He then set about administering it in his way.

CONSTANTINE THE EMPEROR

Constantine is best remembered for the way he shaped Christendom, but his secular accomplishments deserve attention as well. By unifying the empire under one man, he did away with the tetrarchy, which had proved to be an unrealistic and violent arrangement. At his death, Constantine bequeathed different parts of the empire to his sons, establishing the principle of hereditary kingship that became the norm for Western government until the American Revolution. While the empire suffered runaway inflation during the Diocletian years, Constantine encouraged the minting of gold pieces—*solidi*—which stabilized the nation's currency. He reconquered provinces along the Danube River that had been lost to the Goths. By any account, he was a much more capable ruler than any of his recent predecessors.

Constantine was also an enormously skilled politician. From the outset, Constantine embarked on an ambitious plan of public construction projects that projected political power. Immediately after Constantine's defeat of Maxentius in 312, the Senate voted him a triumphal arch to celebrate the occasion. The arch still stands in the Roman forum today, bearing this inscription:

> To the Emperor Caesar Flavius Constantinus, the Greatest, *Pius*,[13] *Felix*,[14] Augustus: inspired by (a) divinity, in the greatness of his mind, he used his army to save the state by the just force of arms from a tyrant on the one hand and every kind of factionalism on the other; therefore the Senate and the People of Rome have dedicated this exceptional arch to his triumphs.[15]

Notable here is the phrase "inspired by (a) divinity." Knowing the reputation of Constantine, the words obviously imply a Christian coloration but do not distinguish exactly *which* divine being was responsible for the inspiration. A pagan reader of the fourth century might have taken it to mean *his* god was responsible. The ambiguity here would turn up in other ways during Constantine's reign: he sometimes consulted the Oracle of Apollo and referred to himself, as the pagan emperors had done, as the "High Priest" of Roman religion. These kinds of ceremonial trappings had the effect of making the emperor's decrees indicative of his Christian faith; but they also raise questions, to modern observers, as to whether he really was a Christian, or if he accommodated traditional pagan attitudes in ways that undermined his profession of faith.

Constantine's central mission was to preserve and strengthen the empire by means of Christianity. To attain this goal, he embarked on a campaign of culture shaping that pushed Christianity into the public sphere in ways that were previously unknown. One scholar has described Constantine as a man who "baptized public space."[16] And of course the most immediate effect of state-institutionalized Christianity was a cessation of state-organized physical persecution of Christians during his reign. Constantine had a theology to explain this intertwinement of faith and government; to him, a key purpose for adopting Christianity was the earthly blessings it afforded the state. We see this in a decree that clergymen be exempted from civic duties:

> Wherefore it is my will that those within the province entrusted to thee, in the catholic Church, over which Cæcilianus presides, who give their services to this holy religion, and who are commonly called clergymen, be entirely exempted from all public duties, that they may not by any error or sacrilegious negligence be drawn away from the service due to the Deity, but may devote themselves without any hindrance to their own law. For it seems that when they show greatest reverence to the Deity, the greatest benefits accrue to the state.[17]

In 321, Constantine declared that the first day of the week, already kept by Christians as the Sabbath, would be an official day of celebrating the Sun throughout the empire. This too had an ambiguity to it: pagans could retain their customs of worshipping the Unconquered Sun, while Christians could venerate their supreme God. Thus we can trace our tradition of calling the Sabbath day of rest a "Sun-day" to this period. Constantine compelled his troops to celebrate the day by reciting a prayer of his own crafting, and this prayer is colored in such a way that Christian or pagan might feel comfortable reciting it to his god:

> We acknowledge thee the only God: we own thee, as our King and implore thy succor. By thy favor have we gotten the victory: through thee are we mightier than our enemies. We render thanks for thy past benefits, and trust thee for future blessings. Together we pray to thee, and beseech thee long to preserve to us, safe and triumphant, our emperor Constantine and his pious sons.[18]

But in other ways, Constantine was much more generous to Christians than pagans. The emperor passed statutes celebrating Easter and feast days of martyrs and saints. Mystic rites, pagan sacrifices, gladiatorial games, and the worship of the Nile were banned. Pagan temples were destroyed. Clergy were exempt from taxes. An old Roman law that limited unmarried people twenty-five and older from making a will was repealed; Constantine considered it a hindrance to Christians devoting themselves to lifelong celibacy.[19]

Constantine was also very keen to represent himself as a Christian in the public arts. In the *Vita Constantini* (Life of Constantine), Eusebius remarked that Constantine had a series of coins minted depicting himself "in the posture of prayer to God": either with his eyes fixed up to heaven, or with his hands outstretched.[20] Many busts of Constantine are preserved today, and nearly all of them eschew the classical Greek style that was so popular with the pagans: painstaking replications of human physiology and debonair, confident gazes and poses. The surviving busts of Constantine, such as the gigantic one on display in the Capitoline Museum in Rome (pictured here), instead show a grave countenance and eyes fixed upward on the divine, a style more austere than classical precedents. The emperor's faith, the sculptures seem to say, imbues him with a sense of purpose and mission.

The most significant way in which Constantine conveyed a new linkage of politics and Christianity was the founding of Constantinople—"the city of Constantine." The site of the city, today called Istanbul, was previously occupied by a small town on the Bosphorus Strait called Byzantium— the same place that Constantine defeated

Bust of Constantine, Capitoline Museum, Rome. Note how the sculptor has fixed Constantine's gaze upward, as if toward heaven.

Licinius for control of the empire. Constantine had multiple reasons to pick Byzantium as the new capital of the Roman world. For one thing, it possessed a critical strategic advantage: any ships that wanted to travel in or out of the Black Sea had to pass through its narrow strait, which could be easily defended. Secondly, the western Roman Empire was constantly under assault from barbarian tribes, such as the Franks and the Gauls, and a new capital in the East provided a measure of security from their incursions. Lastly, the old aristocracy at Rome was still fairly pagan; by building a "New Rome" entirely, Constantine would not have to listen to their complaints that the new God had eclipsed the Unconquered Sun. So Constantine, "led by the hand of God," founded his eponymous city.[21]

Constantine spared no expense in building the New Rome, which, like the old one, became the crowning metropolis of the world. He populated it with transplants from Rome, some of whom were induced to move to the sparsely populated city with promises of free food and housing, and others who were coerced. To make it more livable, he built a hippodrome (racetrack), a replica Senate house, and lavish porticoes (covered outdoor walkways, usually attached to a building). The best pagan statues, portraits, jewels, and artisanal items were taken from their places across the empire and reappropriated for beautifying the city. Someone walking through it would have observed a previously unseen concentration of riches from across the Roman world; in later times, Jerome lamented that all the cities of the East had been despoiled of their best treasures for the purpose of adorning the emperor's New Rome.[22]

All throughout the metropolis, Constantine placed fountains depicting the Good Shepherd, and others forged with brass and finished with gold and silver depicting the famous story of Daniel in the lions' den. He built a new palace, and fixed in its sleeping quarters was a paneled ceiling made of gold, and in the center an enormous bejeweled cross. This cross, said Eusebius, "he seemed to have intended to be as it were the safeguard of the empire itself."[23] Proving his adeptness at translating pagan symbols into Christian contexts, Constantine ordered built a massive column, about 125 feet high, crowned with a golden statue of Apollo, whose face was remade with Constantine's. New walls were marked out by Constantine himself in a ceremony that imitated Romulus's mythical establishment of the walls of Rome. And of course he extirpated many pagan temples:

Being filled, too, with Divine wisdom, he determined to purge the city which was to be distinguished by his own name from idolatry of every kind, that henceforth no statues might be worshiped there in the temples of those falsely reputed to be gods, nor any altars defiled by the pollution of blood: that there might be no sacrifices consumed by fire, no demon festivals, nor any of the other ceremonies usually observed by the superstitious.[24]

In the place of pagan temples, which had been constructed by pagan emperors, Constantine found it fitting to embark on a sustained program of church building across the empire. At one point he commissioned fifty Bibles to be printed to be used in the multitude of newly built churches in the East; the *Codex Sinaiticus* highlighted in chapter 5 is often thought to be one of them. This new abundance of church buildings symbolized to a watching world the Christian victory over the pagan gods.

THE RISE OF THE BASILICA

By the early fourth century, the church was in need of new meeting places. The persecutions of Diocletian had destroyed many old churches just at the time the growth of Christianity had pushed centers of worship out of house churches. In response to the new need, Constantine's construction program popularized a new form of church style that not only accommodated throngs of believers but also reflected his imperial acceptance of Christianity. In Greek and Roman terms, a basilica (from the Greek *basileus*: "pertaining to the king") was initially any public or private structure that was "royal in scale": it could be used as a courtroom, market, or public meeting place.[25] In Christian terms, the basilica served the same purpose. Constantine dotted the urban centers of the Roman world with Christian basilicas: grandiose churches that communicated the emperor's power. The common element to almost all basilicas was the design. Worshippers entered the basilica through the narthex, a wide but shallow room. The narthex led to the nave, the large, long central room with high ceilings. The nave usually had two or even four aisles leading toward the front of the basilica. At the front of the basilica was the apse, a usually semicircular opening with a platform (tribunal), on which the altar stood. In the Constantinian

The interior of Constantine's Basilica in Trier, Germany.

era, the basilica represented the triumph of Christianity over paganism: new shrines to the old gods were hardly being built, and these new basilicas architecturally outdid the old pagan shrines in their scale.

Basilicas were designed to be imposingly tall and full of light, guiding the entrant's eyes toward the heavens and the God who reigned in them. Constantine's double-naved basilica in Trier, Germany, which is still standing today, is the textbook example of the early basilica. But the city that benefited most from the rise of the basilica, aside from Constantinople, was Rome. The church of Saint John Lateran in Rome, begun in 313, stood 312 feet long, 180 feet wide, and 98 feet high, and could house up to three thousand worshippers.[26] Splendidly adorned with marble columns, brilliant mosaics, and gold and silver, Saint John Lateran not only functioned as a place of worship but also served as a court of law, run by bishops whom Constantine had empowered with new legal and judicial authority. Even more impressive was Saint Peter's basilica on the Vatican Hill, now colloquially known as "Old Saint Peter's" to distinguish it from the "New Saint Peter's" basilica that was built on the site in the sixteenth century. Old Saint Peter's was larger than any other Constantinian church and featured a transept, a hall that intersected the nave, making the entire basilica into the shape of a cross. Because Saint Peter's was built on the site of where Peter is believed to have been buried, it quickly gained a reputation as a destination for religious pilgrims.

The other major shrine for pilgrims dating from Constantine's era was the Church of the Holy Sepulchre in Jerusalem. The church was a token of joy and gratitude for the ecclesiastical and doctrinal unity that was achieved (or, is said to have been achieved) at the Council of Nicaea in AD 325, an episode of major theological significance that will be discussed in chapter 7. Constantine declared that the Church of the Holy Sepulchre should "surpass all the churches of the world in the beauty of its walls, columns, and marbles,"[27] and ordered it built on Mount Calvary, the site of Jesus' crucifixion and burial. The only problem was finding the site, which in his day had evidently been forgotten. Legendary stories from the period's historians describe how Constantine's mother, Helena, took to the Holy Land in hopes of discovering it, along with her own plans of finding the remains of Christ's cross.

When Helena arrived in Jerusalem, she ascertained that the site of Jesus' tomb had been filled up with dirt, and a shrine to the pagan goddess Aphrodite had been erected on top of it. When Constantine heard how the site had been profaned, he ordered that the structure not only be torn down but that the materials it was built with "should be removed and thrown as far from the site as possible." Likewise, he also had "the soil which had been polluted by the foul impurities of demon worship transported to a far distant place."[28] Once the shrine was demolished and cleared away and the site excavated, Helena and her entourage found the tomb, inside of which were three crosses, as well as another piece of wood, on which was inscribed in Greek, Latin, and Hebrew "Jesus of Nazareth, King of the Jews." Macarius, the bishop of Jerusalem, had his own (historically dubious) method of determining which of the crosses had belonged to Jesus:

> There was a certain lady of rank in Jerusalem who was afflicted with a most grievous and incurable disease; Macarius, bishop of Jerusalem, accompanied by the mother of the emperor and her attendants, repaired to her bedside. After engaging in prayer, Macarius signified by signs to the spectators that the Divine cross would be the one which, on

being brought in contact with the invalid, should remove the disease. He approached her in turn with each of the crosses; but when two of the crosses were laid on her, it seemed but folly and mockery to her for she was at the gates of death. When, however, the third cross was in like manner brought to her, she suddenly opened her eyes, regained her strength, and immediately sprang from her bed, well.[29]

With the site discovered, the church could be built. Its length was 384 feet and its walls 36 feet high.[30] In addition to a centralized place for worship, the Church of the Holy Sepulchre featured a special *martyrion*, a resting place for a martyr, often marked with a small church or other monument. According to the church historian Sozomen, Constantine charged those responsible "to see that the work was executed in the most magnificent and costly manner possible."[31] Eusebius wrote that after the interior of the church was completed, Constantine "further enriched it with numberless offerings of inexpressible beauty and various materials—gold, silver, and precious stones, the skillful and elaborate arrangement of which, in regard to their magnitude, number, and variety, we have not leisure at present to describe particularly."[32] The old Church of the Holy Sepulchre was destroyed in 1009 by Muslim crusaders (and later rebuilt), but in Constantine's time it stood as an unmistakable landmark to the Christian faith.

THE DONATIST CONTROVERSY

With a formal entrenchment of Christian values in public life now under way, Constantine's interaction with church theology became inevitable. Constantine's involvement with the Donatist controversy of the fourth century showed how comfortable he was intervening in ecclesiastical matters. The Christians of North Africa, as in the rest of the East, had endured acute suffering during Diocletian's persecutions. Now, in the Constantinian era, many who had denied that they were Christians while under punishment or had performed a sacrifice to the emperor sought to be restored to the church. This included many bishops and presbyters, who often explained their decisions to worship false gods or turn over Christian books to the authorities as a means of protecting their congregations. As was the case during the Novationist controversy (see chapter 4), however, the church became divided on the question of how those Christians—the lapsed—should be treated. Often the confessors—those who had not relented in the face of punishment, torture, or death—insisted that the lapsed should not be received back into the church, and that doing so would diminish the purity of the church. Those clergy who had handed Scripture over to the authorities were given the pejorative name of *traditores*—Latin for "hander-overs," or, more colloquially, "betrayers." Some insisted that they should have to be rebaptized into the church. Hotly disputed was the appointment of the new bishop of Carthage named Caecilian. The Donatists, led by a young presbyter named Donatus, argued that some of the bishops whom Caecilian had consecrated were *traditores*, and that Caecilian's appointment was invalid. The implications of this were major: First, they said, Caecilian had been declared a bishop by illegitimate authorities. Second, since a bishop often administered the sacraments of baptism and communion, the church had to be sure that a valid authority was dispensing them. The Donatists argued that the legitimacy of the sacraments hinged on the spiritual condition of the administrator and that a reprobate like Caecilian was not authorized to give them. In response, the Caecilians (the bishop's supporters) insisted that a bishop was only God's agent of the sacramental office, and his spiritual condition did not determine the efficacy of the sacrament to the recipient. In later times, Augustine would become the chief proponent of this theology in a stance commonly called *ex opere operato*.

Economic and political factors also influenced the Donatist controversy. Now that the emperor had embraced Christianity, many members of the upper classes thronged to become (or portray themselves as) Christians to gain favor with the emperor and his administration. This rankled the spirits of many Christians who had suffered through the persecutions only to find their church polluted by newcomers who didn't share their intensity of belief. The areas mostly populated by Caecilians were closest to Carthage, the seat of Roman power and commerce in North Africa, while the Donatists were farther out in the countryside. Hence, many Donatists saw the Caecilians propped up by adherents of questionable sincerity. The Donatists were more austere in their morals and saw the church becoming corrupted by the same people who ran the fallen, worldly institutions of the empire.

In the middle of this was Constantine, whose goal was to use the church as a vehicle to help reunite the empire, and so believed ecclesiastical disunity to be a hindrance to the good of the state. In 313, he had gotten wind of the Donatist situation, and he wrote a letter to the bishop of Rome, asking for advice. He worried that the Christians in North Africa were "following the baser course, and dividing, as it were, into two parties," in "those provinces which Divine Providence has freely entrusted to my devotedness, and in which there is a great population." He continued, "I have such reverence for the legitimate Catholic Church that I do not wish you to leave schism or division in any place."[33]

A council of bishops met in 313 to debate the issues, and when that proved unsatisfactory to resolving the argument, Constantine himself called another in 314—the first time an emperor ever called a church council. Bishops across the empire traveled to the town of Arles, in France. The Donatist position was voted down by a vast majority, but this far from settled the matter in their eyes. The Donatists went to Milan and appealed directly to Constantine himself. Constantine heard them out, but reaffirmed the decision of the bishops at Arles: Caecilian was the legitimate bishop of Carthage. But the turmoil didn't end there. In 317, riots broke out at Carthage over the matter. Groups of citizens and Roman soldiers began attacking a Donatist church and killed two bishops. Children and women were slain in the church, but the tough Donatists "flew undaunted to the house of prayer with a desire to suffer."[34]

Another problem was a group of radical Donatists called Circumcellions. The Circumcellions originally started as a social justice movement, renouncing ownership of property and agitating for the manumission of slaves. The Circumcellions were named by their contemporaries from Latin—*circum cellas euntes*, or "those who go around the storehouses," since they had a reputation for robbing peasants. Their cause was more one of banditry, and soon turned much more violent. As a group whose members shared an ascetic set of morals and were desirous of martyrdom, they would instigate fights with random travelers, shouting, "Laudate Deum" ("Praise God!") while beating them with clubs they called Israelites. The goal of this was to provoke retaliation leading to martyrdom. Likewise, some disrupted legal proceedings in the middle of the courtroom, an action that could be treated by the judge with a death sentence. Later in history, they blinded Catholic bishops by throwing powdered lime and vinegar into their faces. The Donatist bishops were not happy about the presence of the Circumcellions in their midst, but they often played a useful enforcer role in a time in which combat between Donatists and Catholics was real.[35]

All this was too much for Constantine, who saw the Donatists as causing more trouble to the stability of the empire than the defense of their cause was worth. Although he had initially given the church freedom to settle the dispute without his direct intervention, he now decided to suppress the Donatists by force. A letter at the time from the emperor made his sentiments plain: "it is as clear as the sun of noon-day, that they are of such a character as to be seen to be shut off even from the care of Heaven, since so great a madness still holds them captive, and with unbelievable arrogance they persuade themselves of things which cannot lawfully be either spoken or heard . . . Oh mad daring of their rage!" Over the next two years, Constantine confiscated Donatist property, ordered their churches closed, and put to death a few Donatist bishops. But in time Constantine had a change of heart and rescinded his orders. His rationale for forgiveness strikes us as profoundly Christian: "it is the mark of a fool to snatch at that vengeance which we ought to leave to God."[36]

For all his imperial power, Constantine realized that only God could heal the church in North Africa: "Until the Heavenly medicine shows itself, our designs must be moderated so far as to act with patience . . . all this we must endure with the strength that comes from tranquility."[37] The trajectory of Constantine's involvement with the Donatists is a curious one. At the outset, he removed himself from the dispute, but then became a persecutor of Christians before consigning the whole question to God. His involvement had negligible impact: the Donatist schisms endured for centuries afterward, and while it was barely relevant after the early fifth century, it wasn't until the Islamic conquest of North Africa in the seventh and eighth centuries that it vanished entirely. But Constantine had established an important precedent—that the emperor had it in his power to arbitrate in church affairs.

WAS CONSTANTINE REALLY A CHRISTIAN?

We have seen from Constantine evidence that seems to indicate genuine concern for the cultural advancement of Christianity: a restoration of civil liberties on the church, a concern for the purity of the church and its doctrines, and a campaign of church building. But these are not necessarily indicators of a personal faith in Christ. The central question of the Constantinian era is if the man (a) was genuinely converted to Christ, (b) was a pretender who callously used Christianity as a political tool, or (c) fell somewhere in between. Each major theological vein of the Christian tradition—Catholic, Protestant, and Orthodox, as well as each tradition's various sects—applies a different standard for ascertaining the state of the soul before God. As one scholar has noted, "the question as to whether he was a 'genuine' Christian or not depends on somewhat subjective definitions."[38] It is not the task here to judge whether Constantine, by the theological rubric of each denomination, was redeemed. But we can observe the totality of the man's life and actions to get an idea of what motivated him, and whether that motivation was more directed at building the kingdom of God, the kingdom of Rome, or the kingdom of Self.

Certainly there can be no question that Constantine was a great blessing to the church. Scarcely in history have we observed such a complete and rapid transformation of a state's values as the one that occurred in the age of Diocletian to Constantine. In one generation, the church went from suffering its greatest interference to enjoying its greatest patronage. The Edict of Milan restored the freedoms Christians tacitly enjoyed before the Great Persecution, and in subsequent years Constantine extended them. He embarked on a massive campaign of church building that gave the growing masses of Christians a place to worship, and afforded clergy and laypeople alike a number of civil protections previously unknown. But significant questions remain.

For one thing, Constantine killed his own son and his wife. In 326, well after his supposed conversion, Constantine ordered his son Crispus, from a previous wife, killed by poisoning. He may have perceived him as a threat to his rule. Since Constantine himself was born in 285, his son could not have been more than probably nineteen or twenty years old. The next month, his wife, Fausta, was put to death by being left in an overheated bath. For centuries afterward, historians speculated that Crispus and Fausta were entwined in some sort of immorality—perhaps with each other—but this remains questionable. Constantine's motivations for this wickedness remain very unclear. Perhaps he wanted to send a message to other relatives that he would protect what was his.

Another historian who wrote a few generations after Eusebius, Zosimus, was also less than kind to him. Zosimus retroactively criticized Constantine for breaking an oath to spare the life of his rival Licinius, and also reaffirmed another trait that does little to affirm the seriousness of his belief—selectively resorting to paganism and divination. Wrote Zosimus, "He indeed used the ancient worship of his country; though not so much out of honour or veneration as of necessity. Therefore he believed the soothsayers, who were expert in their art, as men who predicted the truth concerning all the great actions which he ever performed."[39] On the other hand, we might more likely view this sometimes-embrace of paganism as a sort of ceremonial action, in the same way a Protestant or Catholic United States president might attend a service at a synagogue to affirm the contributions of Jews to American life, and the idea that America is a place for people of any faith. President George W. Bush, for instance, heard the Torah read to him in a synagogue in Washington, DC, and was also the first president to host a Hanukkah party in the White House residence, even making the food kosher. Constantine was an adroit politician, and probably felt pressure to ensure the stability of the empire by accommodating different faith traditions, whether Christian or pagan. (Unfortunately, his policy on Jews precipitated a great deal of Christian persecution of Jews during the Middle Ages.) But a great number of Christians of Constantine's time (and today) were not comfortable with Constantine's sometimes outward displays of paganism.

Lastly, it is worth noting that Constantine was not baptized until he was on his deathbed. Yet Sozomen, sometimes a critic, still provided a laudatory summary of his reign: "He was a powerful protector of the Christian religion, and was the first of the emperors who began to be zealous for the Church, and to bestow upon her high benefactions. He was more successful than any other sovereign in all his undertakings; for he formed no design, I am convinced, without God."[40] It is probably best to conclude that Constantine was a Christian, but a deeply flawed one, and one who viewed his faith as a tool for executing the great office of Roman emperor. His mission on earth seemed at times much more political than spiritual, but it does not mean that he was not under the grace of God to fulfill it. He, and all the rest of the Christian world, would need this grace to resolve the great theological dispute of ancient Christianity that erupted in AD 325.

SEVEN

TARES AMONG WHEAT

Arianism, the Council of Nicaea, Athanasius

Sometime in AD 323, the emperor Constantine, now at the zenith of his power after a series of conquests, received a letter that detailed "a most serious disturbance which had invaded the peace of the Church."[1] This disappointing news was a most untimely occurrence. After the empire suffered a decade of merciless persecutions under Diocletian and the tetrarchs, Constantine now reigned as the first Christian Roman emperor, not only legalizing Christianity, but giving it a favored status in public life. The transformation of the faith from an outlawed one to one that enjoyed a privileged legal place had been fast. Theodoret, the bishop of Cyrus who lived a few decades after the period, described the age's transition from the previous rulers to Constantine: "The surge which those destroyers, like hurricanes, had roused was hushed to sleep; the whirlwinds were checked, and the Church henceforward began to enjoy a settled calm." He further described Constantine's reign by stating simply that, "for us, all was joy and gladness."[2] Eusebius recounted "a bright and most profound peace."[3] Despite the recent Donatist controversy, churches were full, pagan temples were closed, and sacrifices to idols were banned. But then, wrote Theodoret, "the devil, full of all envy and wickedness, the destroyer of mankind, unable to bear the sight of the Church sailing on with favourable winds, stirred up plans of evil counsel, eager to sink the vessel steered by the Creator and Lord of the Universe."[4] Eusebius's account is similar, saying that the consequence of this "contagion" was that "the sacred matters of inspired teaching were exposed to the most shameful ridicule."[5] What disturbance had Constantine read of, and what had provoked Theodoret and Eusebius to describe it in such language?

In the early part of the fourth century, there was "an obstinate conflict on the highest questions" in the city of Alexandria.[6] That it came from Alexandria is not surprising, since the city was already, as we have seen, a multiethnic and highly cerebral metropolis from which came some of the questionable doctrines of Origen and Clement. A priest in the city, an "expert logician" named Arius, was fixated on "absurd discourses," teaching with "audacity" things about the nature of Jesus Christ that "no one before him had ever suggested."[7] Contrary to orthodox doctrine, Arius held that Jesus Christ was not co-eternal with the Father, that there was a point in time in which he had not existed. To him, Jesus was created at a certain point at time, and although he was still the firstborn of all creation, he was not of the same substance as the Father. In the simplest terms, Arius held that "there was once a time when He was not."[8] This of course undercut the centuries of trinitarian doctrine, embedded in the New Testament, that scholars such as Justin Martyr and Tertullian had drawn out. "Hence," said Eusebius, "it was that a mighty fire was kindled as it were from a little spark."[9]

The bishop of Alexandria, Alexander, got wind of Arius's teachings and vacillated on the question of what to do about him. Besides the theological nature of the disagreement, there was perhaps an element of personal rivalry between the two men. Arius may have been incensed that Alexander, "a noble defender of the doctrines of the gospel," was chosen to be the bishop of Alexandria instead of him.[10] At first Alexander tried to reason with Arius, but when he saw that he was "enslaved by the lust of power," eventually he called a local council of church leaders, who reaffirmed the apostolic orthodoxy: Christ was co-eternal and consubstantial with the Father. But Arius would not relent, and had actually persuaded many different clergymen to agree with him.[11] As a consequence, Alexander had him stripped of his presbytery, and wasted little time in excommunicating him and his followers from the church. Alexander knew this would be controversial, and wrote the bishop of Constantinople (also, confusingly, named Alexander) describing in elaborate detail their bad theology and recommending how Constantinople should consider their claims: "Let none of you receive them, nor attend to what they say or write. They are deceivers, and propagate lies, and they never adhere to the truth."[12] This letter circulated to the other churches of the East and had the effect of inflaming the conflict further. Arius had obtained a powerful and influential ally in Eusebius of Nicomedia (not to be confused with the bishop-historian Eusebius of Caesarea), who then "vomited forth his own impiety"[13] and perpetuated the Arian heresy (so named after Arius) to other bishops. In time, Arianism spread down to the laypeople of the East, provoking a new round of church disunity. In some ways, the conflict at this time was as tragic as the persecutions, for Christians profess the unity of one worldwide body of Christ. The church was scarred:

> And so when the blasphemous doctrine had been disseminated in the churches of Egypt and of the East, disputes and contentions arose in every city, and in every village, concerning theological dogmas. The common people looked on, and became judges of what was said on either side, and some applauded one party, and some the other. These were, indeed, scenes fit for the tragic stage, over which tears might have been shed. For it was not, as in bygone days, when the church was attacked by strangers and by enemies, but now natives of the same country, who dwelt under one roof, and sat down at one table, fought against each other not with spears, but with their tongues. And what was still more sad, they who thus took up arms against one another were members of one another, and belonged to one body.[14]

Eventually Constantine learned of the disturbance, which he heard "with much sorrow of heart."[15] But he was as vigilant to keep public order as he was heartbroken at the disunity of the church, and sent a messenger, Hosius of Cordoba, "one whom he well knew to be approved for the sobriety and genuineness of his faith,"[16] to personally deliver a letter Constantine had written requesting peace between the factions of the Alexandrian church. Constantine's message was tough. He declared that he "[found] the cause to be of a truly insignificant character, and quite unworthy of such fierce contention."[17] He blamed both Arius and Alexander for the disturbance, saying that whatever disagreements they had should be kept private, and that they had now unleashed "an intolerable spirit of mad folly" on the churches.[18] The two should come to an agreement. To show how much the dispute displeased him, Constantine also canceled a planned tour of the eastern provinces. Yet his letter changed virtually nothing, and the conflict continued unabated.

CONSTANTINE CALLS THE COUNCIL OF NICAEA

When Constantine saw that his exhortations for unity had come to nothing, he decided to call a council of bishops to resolve the matter. The scale of this council, appropriate to the level of acrimony, far outdid the smaller regional synods and councils that had been called in the past. Constantine invited every bishop in the empire, about eighteen hundred total, to Nicaea, a small town on the northern coast of Turkey, forty-three miles from Constantinople. Although Nicaea was partly chosen for its relatively central location in the empire, the journey was still a very long, expensive, and dangerous one for bishops coming from faraway places like Spain, Gaul, and North Africa. Constantine sweetened the deal by providing an imperial stock of mules and horses for the bishops to use for the journey. Each bishop was also allowed to bring along two presbyters and three slaves.

About three hundred bishops took up Constantine's invitation.[19] They came from every part of the empire except Britain. It was quite an assemblage of piety, talent, and personalities. In addition to the bishops from the apostolic sees of Jerusalem, Antioch, and Alexandria, "many other excellent and good men from different nations were congregated together, of whom some were celebrated for their learning, their eloquence, and their knowledge of the sacred books, and others discipline; some for the virtuous tenor of their life, and others for the combination of all these qualifications."[20] Jacob of Nisibis, "the Moses of Mesopotamia," showed up looking ragged. Before becoming bishop, Jacob had lived a hermetic existence in the wilderness, living in forests and caves, eating roots and leaves. Although he was now a bishop, he had experienced no inclination to change his customs. John the Persian, who despite his name may have been the head of the church in Calcutta, India, probably traveled the farthest. An appropriate counterpart for John might have been Theophilus, the Gothic bishop from the extreme northern areas of the empire, whose shock of blond hair probably awed his fellow churchmen. Sylvester, the bishop of Rome, was too old to make the trip, but he did send two presbyters who were authorized to conduct business on his behalf. Many of the bishops still bore the scars of the persecutions of the previous decades. One bishop was missing an eye; another, Paphnutius ("dedicated to his God" in Greek), had his knee mutilated as well, leaving him with a limp. Paul of Neo-Caesaria "had been deprived of the use of both hands by the application of a red-hot iron, by which the nerves which give motion to the muscles had been contracted and rendered dead." "In short," wrote Theodoret, "the Council looked like an assembled army of martyrs."[21] Adding to the number of the assembled were a plethora of presbyters and deacons who had made the trip with their bishops, as well as "men present who were skilled in dialectics, and ready to assist in the discussions."[22] At the head of the proceedings was Hosius, the bishop of Cordoba, in Spain, the one whom Constantine had originally sent to Egypt to reconcile the two parties. The "magician from Spain" was a spiritual confidant of the emperor, fairly young, highly intelligent, and beyond reproach as a Christian.[23]

Before the council opened, informal gatherings of bishops met to examine and discuss the issues at hand. Their aides, laypeople, philosophers, and other hangers-on participated in these open-air disputes. Many of the bishops were probably illiterate and were incapable of matching the intellectual sophistication of their Arian opponents, most of whom could demonstrate an appreciable polish in Bible knowledge, rhetoric, and philosophy. But what many of the catholics (anti-Arians) lacked in erudition, they made up for in passion and a knowledge of sound doctrine. In the midst of one dispute, a layman who had been maimed during the persecutions stepped forward and declared in the middle of an argument, "Christ and the Apostles left us, not a system of logic, nor vain deceit, but a naked truth, to be guarded by faith and good works."[24] Many bishops took this pre-conference as an opportunity to straighten out personal disputes, and they individually petitioned Constantine on an appointed day that he had reserved to decide all such matters. Though not a bishop, emerging from the initial tumult was a most passionate defender of orthodoxy: a twenty-five-year-old archdeacon who had accompanied Alexander of Alexandria to the Council. Derisively called "the Black Dwarf" by his opponents because of his small stature and tanned complexion, Athanasius of Alexandria is now remembered as the most vociferous opponent of Arianism in church history. Sozomen remembered his role there as "seem[ing] to have the largest share in the counsel concerning these subjects."[25]

Athanasius could not have appeared more different from his opponent, Arius, who was also summoned to the council. Arius was sixty, a long and thin creature, with a tangled mess of hair and the shabby clothes of an ascetic. He was marked by a tremulous physical constitution and a kind of wild, nervous look in his eyes. Yet he could summon deft arguments, and for this reason, had gained a devoted following. In league with Arius was the bishop Eusebius of Nicomedia, who was called "the Great" by his followers, and several other bishops from the East, mostly from Egypt and Asia Minor. The Arians' most prominent opponents were up to the task of countering what they saw as a noxious heresy. One of these was Spyridion of Cyprus, who before and after his ordination as a bishop worked as a simple shepherd. Once when he caught some thieves trying to steal some of his sheep early in the morning, he gave them a ram and told them to go on their way, since he didn't want them to have stayed up all night for nothing. He once rebuked a preacher who, in quoting from one of the Gospels, used the loftier word for "couch" instead of the word for "bed." Spyridion piped up: "Are you better than He who said 'bed' that you are ashamed to use His words?"[26] Another attendee was the bishop Nicolas of Myra. Nicolas had a reputation for generosity, such as putting coins in shoes that were left out for him. His life and works became the basis for our modern conception of Santa Claus. Unlike the image of Santa as a red and rosy-faced man, a forensic survey of Nicholas's bones in 2004 revealed that the real Saint Nicholas was around five and a half feet tall, had suffered a broken nose, and probably had a slight frame. The composition of Nicholas's bones also suggested that he may have spent a good deal of time in dank prisons, perhaps while suffering in the persecutions of the early fourth century.[27]

On the day the council opened, the bishops, some young, some old, filed into a large hall that Constantine had prepared for the event, "in which a sufficient number of benches and seats were placed."[28] The hall, which still stands today, was later consecrated as a church, and the frescoes painted in later times of Jesus, Mary, and John the Baptist can still be found today. In 2012, as part of a nationwide campaign to Islamify the country, the deputy prime minister of Turkey had it turned into a mosque, just as it was beginning to attract attention from Western tourists.

The bishops fell silent as Constantine himself capped the procession with his own entrance. He wore a purple robe adorned with a brilliant array of precious stones. Conscious of his status among so many men of God, he kept his eyes down and blushed. Still, said Eusebius, "he surpassed all present in height of stature and beauty of form, as well as in majestic dignity of mien, and invincible strength and vigor."[29] When

121

he reached the end of the hall, a golden stool, sitting low to the ground, was brought for him. At the invitation of the bishops, he took his seat. Eustathius of Antioch, known for his learning, eloquence, and dignity, rose and placed on Constantine's head a garland of flowers, and with the aid of a translator, "delivered a concise speech, in a strain of thanksgiving to Almighty God, on his behalf."[30] Eustathius sat back down, and silence again filled the hall. Constantine, also aided by an interpreter, addressed the bishops in Latin, saying in part:

> And now I rejoice in beholding your assembly; but I feel that my desires will be most completely fulfilled when I can see you all united in one judgment, and that common spirit of peace and concord prevailing amongst you all, which it becomes you, as consecrated to the service of God, to commend to others. Delay not, then, dear friends: delay not, ye ministers of God, and faithful servants of him who is our common Lord and Saviour: begin from this moment to discard the causes of that disunion which has existed among you, and remove the perplexities of controversy by embracing the principles of peace. For by such conduct you will at the same time be acting in a manner most pleasing to the supreme God, and you will confer an exceeding favor on me who am your fellow-servant.[31]

Constantine had called for concord. The vast majority of the bishops were ready to seek it. This was easy, since they were already in theological agreement with one another. But some of the bishops, entirely from cities in the East, supported Arius. The council, which had begun with so much pomp and ceremony, quickly dissolved into strife. The argument exploded into the open, with little regard for the emperor's presence. Said Eusebius, "numberless assertions were put forth by each party, and a violent controversy arose at the very commencement."[32] Constantine "gave patient attention to the speeches of both parties; he applauded those who spoke well," and "rebuked those who displayed a tendency to altercation."[33] But Constantine remained neutral throughout and played

only the role of referee. He had called the council, but took no official position on the issue and
allowed the bishops to come to their own agreement on doctrine.

The irony of the council was that the two
theological stars from either side—Arius and
Athanasius—were not even bishops. Several
times they directly squared off, and it is a
great disappointment that no record of their
discourse survives. At one point, most of the
bishops recoiled in disgust at the revelation that

Eastern Orthodox icon
depicting the First Council
of Nicaea.

Arius had written a series of poems that helped popularize his teachings
among ordinary people unversed in the theological minutiae of his arguments. These poems were written in a meter usually reserved for erotic
love poetry, and Arius is said to have danced around fanatically while
reciting his lines, one of which was "God was not always Father." When
someone in the proceedings recited the lines, the bishops moaned and
shut their eyes and ears to avoid hearing them. It was at this point in the
legend of Saint Nicholas that he allegedly struck Arius in the face, on
account of the erroneous doctrine and lusty style of these poems.

After a month of contention, the Arian bishops drew up a document
detailing their theological positions and presented it to the assembly. It
was read out loud, declared "spurious and false," and torn up immediately.[34] The reaction was great enough to persuade all but two bishops,
Theonas, bishop of Marmarica (on the Libyan-Egyptian border), and
Secundus, bishop of Ptolemais in Egypt, to recant their support for the
Arian creed. Still, the question lingered: how sincere was the Arian
party's repudiation of what they had believed just hours or days before?
The council was at an impasse, and the figure of Constantine looming
over the assembly added pressure to the situation.

Then Eusebius of Caeserea, the bishop and great chronicler of the
church, had an idea. Why not write down a theological statement that
everyone could sign in good conscience? This of course was in deference

to Constantine's preference for obtaining ecclesiastical unity over theological truth, but one that might break the gridlock. Both parties labored
to produce a statement that would be at once true, comprehensive, and
vague enough not to offend. But this approach was rife with its own
problems. The most significant was a misunderstanding of theological
terms. The bishops had come from all over the empire, and predominantly the eastern part, where Greek and Latin were in many places
secondary languages. Hence, there was great disagreement in precisely
what certain words meant to certain bishops.

In writing the Nicene Creed, the word *homoousios* (Greek: "of the
same substance") produced a violent disagreement on both sides. The
word already had a long history in theological scholarship, and both parties understood it with different shades of meaning. Others favored the
term *homoiousios* (note the extra *i*), which meant "of a similar substance."
When Eusebius produced the first draft of his statement, the Arians tore
it in half, disqualifying the word *homoousios* as unscriptural and heretical.
Athanasius countered by saying that by their standards, Arius's theology
was equally unbiblical. One scholar has put the stakes of the debate in
stark terms: "the rejection of it [the creed] seemed to involve polythe-
ism, and a return to the ancient paganism."[35] Finally, with the *homoousios*
still in the statement, Eusebius presented it to Constantine, who in all
probability had very little understanding of the complexity of the issues
being debated. What he did comprehend was that the orthodox branch
of Christianity, led by Hosius and Athanasius, could never accept any
statement that was less than perfectly explicit on declaring that Jesus
and the Father were in every way of equal substance and divinity. In the
end, the creed was good enough for him. The Nicene Creed was modified over time, but it is still recited in many churches today in its original
iteration:

> We believe in one God, the Father Almighty, maker of all things
> visible and invisible; and in one Lord Jesus Christ, the Son of God,
> Light of Light, very God of very God, begotten [*gennethenta*], not

made, being of one substance [*homoousion* in Greek, *consubstantialem* in Latin] with the Father; by whom all things were made; Who for us men and for our salvation came down and was incarnate and was made man; He suffered and the third day he rose again, and ascended into heaven; from thence he shall come again to judge the quick and the dead. And in the Holy Ghost.

In time, the following section was added:

And whosoever shall say that there was a time when the Son of God was not, or that before he was begotten he was not, or that he was made of things that were not, or that he is of a different substance or essence [from the Father] or that he is a creature, or subject to change or conversion all that so say, the Catholic and Apostolic Church anathematizes them.[36]

The date was June 19, AD 325, when Hosius of Cordoba stood up to declare the creed complete. His was the first signature at the top of the document, attesting to the truth of the creed. Below him were the signatures of the two presbyters sent by the bishop of Rome. The placement of the bishop of Rome's name indicates, as we have seen before, the growing importance of Rome's opinion in church matters. Because Hosius's Greek was choppy, the first oral recitation of the creed was undertaken by a certain Hermogenes, a priest or deacon from Cappadocia serving as the secretary of the council. The Arian reaction was predictably unenthusiastic. Eusebius of Nicomedia, one of the leaders of the Arian opposition, begrudgingly signed on to it, but when Arius, Theonas, and Secundus refused to sign the document, they were excommunicated. This punishment was compounded by Constantine's swift and unambiguous affirmation of the creed. While he had earlier respected the theological position of both sides, he now denounced Arianism in the strongest way possible. Theonas and Secundus lost their bishoprics and were exiled to Illyria (modern-day former Yugoslavia), as was Arius.

Lastly, Constantine wrote letters to the major cities of the empire, stipulating punishment for anyone who harbored Arian writings:

> In addition, if any writing composed by Arius should be found, it should be handed over to the flames, so that not only will the wickedness of his teaching be obliterated, but nothing will be left even to remind anyone of him. And I hereby make a public order, that if someone should be discovered to have hidden a writing composed by Arius, and not to have immediately brought it forward and destroyed it by fire, his penalty shall be death. As soon as he is discovered in this offense, he shall be submitted for capital punishment.[37]

Eventually Arius's sentence of exile was lightened, and he was merely banned from returning to Alexandria. The controversy he had produced, as we will see, would live on for several generations. But the council had refuted his heresy. This was all the more impressive considering that the bishops at the Council of Nicaea had the enormously difficult task of clarifying the nature of God using only human paradigms of thought and language. Said the commentator A. W. Tozer in the twentieth century, "The authors of the Athanasian (Nicene) Creed spelled out with great care the relation of the three Persons to each other, filling in the gaps in human thought as far as they were able while staying within the bounds of the inspired Word."[38] Over the years, many writers, including Dan Brown (author of *The Da Vinci Code*), Richard Rubenstein, and Bart Ehrman, have incorrectly pointed to the Council of Nicaea as the moment when the church conferred on Jesus the status of God. In reality, the council merely reiterated what had already been expressed in passages such as John 1, Colossians 1, and Hebrews 1, as well as by commentators such as Justin Martyr. Through the ages, fringe sects of the church would from time to time embrace Arianism, as they had embraced Gnosticism. But in the Nicene Creed, the church had achieved substantial unity on the question of the divinity of Jesus. In time, the creed became, according to one fourth-century Christian philosopher, "the rampart and wall of orthodoxy."[39] But Arianism was quite prevalent in the decades to follow, and would not disappear as a mainstream theology until the Muslim conquests of the seventh century.

OTHER MATTERS RESOLVED BY THE COUNCIL OF NICAEA

The Council's most important agenda was the resolution of the Arian dispute. But the bishops took it upon themselves to examine several other questions of lesser significance.[40] Resolved was the old Paschal controversy, in which churches, mostly along lines of East and West, disagreed on the date of the celebration of Easter. Churches could differ on when Easter could be celebrated, but the Christian calendar—not the Jewish one—had to be the basis for their calculations of the date for celebration. The bishops also established twenty new church canons, many of which formed the basis for subsequent canonical laws. Most of them clarified gray areas of ecclesiastical authority—the bishops of Rome, Alexandria, and Antioch were recognized to have special jurisdiction over the customs of the churches in their regions. Some of the canons instituted practical regulations for the churches: kneeling in prayer on Sunday, for instance, was forbidden; the standing posture was the only one acceptable, and this rule is still observed in Eastern Orthodox churches. The most unusual of all canons was the first, which regulated self-castration. Apparently the same impulse that had motivated Origen to self-castration had found its way into the hearts of several other clergy members. The bishops agreed:

> If any one in sickness has been subjected by physicians to a surgical operation, or if he has been castrated by barbarians, let him remain among the clergy; but, if any one in sound health has castrated himself, it behooves that such a one, if [already] enrolled among the clergy, should cease.[41]

That wasn't the only matter of personal propriety that the bishops confronted. In the third canon, clerics were forbidden to allow a younger woman who was not a relative to live with them. Additionally, the council debated a provision that would have insisted on the celibacy of clergy—even for those who were married before they had become clerics. For Paphnutius, the maimed bishop from Greece, this could not stand. Although he himself was celibate, he insisted that a married cleric abstaining from sexual relations with his wife would surely lead to temptation for both parties. The measure was never adopted.

At last, after over a month of confabulation, the council adjourned its business. The culmination of the council came at a very timely moment. Constantine was celebrating his twentieth year as emperor, and every ten years of rule was marked by a celebration. On July 25, the empire celebrated with games and festivities, but Constantine held a feast for the bishops who had labored for truth. Ringed by armed guards, the emperor presided over a sumptuous banquet. As the evening progressed, he addressed all the assembled bishops individually, heaping praises and gifts on them. Constantine was especially fond of old Paphnutius, the half-blind and lame bishop, and had often begged to hear his tales of suffering persecution. This time Constantine threw his arms around him, kissing and stroking his eyeless socket, and eventually pressing his own eyeball into the hollow and his own purple robe onto Paphnutius's crippled leg.[42] Another bishop, Acesius, was the target of some ribbing. Constantine asked him if the creed and the Paschal controversy had been settled to his liking. Acesius had not, in fact, been enthusiastic about either outcome, but replied with deference that he was. Constantine pressed the question and inquired why, if Acesius did agree with the council, he was no longer taking communion with his brethren. This was too much for Acesius, who said he could not forgive those Christians who had denied the faith under threat of torture: "None, who, after baptism, have sinned the sin, which the Divine Scriptures call the sin unto death, have a right to partake in the Divine Mysteries. They ought to be moved to perpetual repentance. The priests have no power to forgive them; only God, who alone has the right to pardon sins." Constantine was nonplussed at this display of blustering moralism. "Ho ho!" he scoffed. "Acesius, plant a ladder, and climb up into heaven yourself."[43]

At the end of the celebration, Constantine, undoubtedly contented by the council's profession of unity, dismissed the bishops with an exhortation to harmony "in which he recommended them to be diligent in the maintenance of peace, to avoid contentious disputations, amongst themselves and not to be jealous."[44] They adjourned and dispersed to their respective sees, each one enjoying his own level of satisfaction or disappointment.

ATHANASIUS CONTRA MUNDUM

As we have seen, Constantine enforced the Council of Nicaea's conclusions by instituting a merciless campaign of destroying Arian literature and ordering death on anyone who concealed it. But Arianism actually lived on well past the Council of Nicaea in different churches. Arius himself eventually returned from exile and was in time allowed to preach again, after making a profession of faith that the bishop Alexander and others thought suspicious. Arius died in 336, still enjoying the adulation that had made him such a controversial figure. If the sources are to be believed, his death in 336 was a most gruesome sight:

> It was then Saturday, and Arius was expecting to assemble with the church on the day following: but divine retribution overtook his daring criminalities. For going out of the imperial palace, attended by a crowd of Eusebian partisans like guards, he paraded proudly through the midst of the city, attracting the notice of all the people. As he approached the place called Constantine's Forum, where the column of porphyry is erected, a terror arising from the remorse of conscience seized Arius, and with the terror a violent relaxation of the bowels: he therefore enquired whether there was a convenient place near, and being

directed to the back of Constantine's Forum, he hastened thither. Soon after a faintness came over him, and together with the evacuations his bowels protruded, followed by a copious hemorrhage, and the descent of the smaller intestines: moreover portions of his spleen and liver were brought off in the effusion of blood, so that he almost immediately died. The scene of this catastrophe still is shown at Constantinople, as I have said, behind the shambles in the colonnade: and by persons going by pointing the finger at the place, there is a perpetual remembrance preserved of this extraordinary kind of death.[45]

The fight over orthodoxy, or the idea of Arius being readmitted into the church, may have been too much for Alexander, for he died a mere five months after the council ended in 325. On his deathbed, the story goes, he tapped his young associate Athanasius to be his successor. Athanasius was not yet thirty, the traditional minimum age for a bishop. But he had proved himself such an ardent and skillful apologist at the Council of Nicaea that the choice was obvious. He was described by one historian of the times as "eloquent and intelligent, and capable of opposing plots, and of such a man the times had the greatest need."[46] He had also already shown himself to be a mortal enemy of the Arians, and his ascension to the episcopate of Alexandria, still the main locus of Arianism in the empire, alarmed them. They hatched a devious plan to get rid of the young deacon. A letter was written to Constantine, alleging that Athanasius was levying a tax upon Egypt and giving the gold to a man who threatened to usurp imperial power. Athanasius was summoned before the emperor, where he passionately defended himself against the charges. Constantine luckily relented and wrote a letter back to the Alexandrians, assuring them, "I have conversed with him as with one whom I know to be a man of God."[47]

But the Arian faction did not stop there, and they "devised so bold a fiction against him, that it surpassed every invention of the ancient writers of the tragic or comic stage."[48] Eusebius of Nicomedia, the wily Arian leader from the Council of Nicaea, and an Arian bishop named

Theognis wrote Constantine again, accusing Athanasius of unspeakable crimes and begging the emperor to convene a synod of bishops at Tyre on the eastern end of the Mediterranean. Constantine became exasperated with their protests and eventu-

The Ruins of the Church of Jacob of Nisibis, in modern-day Nusaybin, Turkey.

ally relented. When the synod opened, Athanasius was first accused of breaking a sacred chalice. Then a woman "of lewd life" was brought in,[49] and she claimed that Athanasius had personally robbed her of the perpetual virginity she professed to uphold. Then a hand from a corpse that had been kept in embalming fluid was presented, with the prosecutors declaring it belonged to a man named Arsenius, whom Athanasius had murdered. What the accusers didn't know was that Athanasius's allies had tracked down Arsenius ahead of time and hid him. Athanasius asked that Arsenius be brought forward and pointed out that both his hands were intact. But instead of confessing their treachery, his opponents insisted that Athanasius was a sorcerer, and that "he had by his magical incantations bewitched the eyes of men."[50] They lunged at him, thirsty for blood, but a group of imperial guards hustled him outside of the hall and onto a waiting ship.

When Constantine got wind of what happened, he commanded those perfidious bishops to give an account for their actions. Instead of showing remorse, they said that Athanasius had threatened to stop the exportation of corn from Egypt, an order that would have surely meant hunger for the whole empire. Constantine, amazingly, believed them and exiled Athanasius to Germany from 335 to 337. It wouldn't be Athanasius's last time in exile. During his forty-five years as bishop of Alexandria, Athanasius was exiled five different times under four different emperors, spending a total of seventeen years away. Much of the time was spent in the deserts of Egypt, being smuggled back and forth between different monasteries. During his last period of exile, in 365, he spent a great deal of time hiding in his father's tomb. Such was the life of one who stood so firmly for the truth, and his writings on the nature of the Trinity are still some of the finest in Christian history.

THE DEATH OF CONSTANTINE

In 337, Constantine fell ill in the town of Nicomedia, of which his friend Eusebius (the Arian) was bishop. Knowing the frailty of human life, he was baptized on his deathbed by Eusebius, a great irony considering how hard Constantine fought for the Catholic faith. His body was placed inside a golden coffin and borne to Constantinople by a train of provincial governors, army officials, and infantrymen, who all grieved the man who was "as an affectionate father to them all."[51] Constantine's death inaugurated anew the decades of turbulence that had been stayed under his reign. His empire would fall to his three sons: Constantine II, Constantius II, and Constans, none of whom displayed the magnanimity of their father. For about the next quarter century, political conflicts became enmeshed with ecclesiastical ones, and the empire again fell into factiousness and turmoil. Virtually all of Athanasius's terms in exile were a testament to his implacable opposition to Arian doctrine, a position that sometimes put him at odds with the emperors and their allies and earned him the nickname *Athanasius Contra Mundum* (Athanasius against the World).

Athanasius's legacy of holy combat is almost universally praised among the three great branches of Christianity. In the Catholic Church, he is one of the four Eastern Doctors of the Church. In Protestant Christianity, he is revered for his defense of the Trinity and his early definitive list of the books to be included in the New Testament. In the Eastern Orthodox Church, he is called "the Father of Orthodoxy," largely for his tireless work of keeping the province of Egypt from sliding into heresy. His writings, such as his *On the Incarnation of the Word of*

God, Apology Against the Arians, Orations Against the Arians, and *Against Heresies* were seminal works in their own time for their defense of trinitarian principles. But Athanasius's biography of one of his friends, Saint Anthony of the Desert, would help trigger a mini-revolution in Christian thought and living.

EIGHT

SAVING WASTELANDS

*Monasticism, Anthony, the Copts, Ephrem
the Syrian, Martin of Tours, John Cassian*

During Constantine's time as emperor, many Christians believed
that the church was losing its identity. In their view, Constantine's
legitimization of the church turned it into an outlet for ambitious men:
promotion through an ecclesiastical hierarchy was a substitute for
advancement through the decaying Roman civil service system. Bishops
competing for power and influence undermined the Christian idea of
brotherhood and unity. Newcomers filled the churches in hopes of gaining imperial favor. The schisms over readmitting the lapsed into the
church disheartened many. Previously, in the age of persecution, only
the genuinely committed wished to partake of Christ's kingdom. Now a
period of peace produced lukewarm disciples. Many desired to escape a
church that they viewed as enfeebled and polluted.

The response of a few Christians was to disengage from the church
and seek isolation from the world as a means of purifying their souls and
drawing closer to God. Around the middle of the third century, a few
Christians began living in isolation in the deserts of Egypt. We know
them today as the first monks. The root word for *monk* comes from the
Greek *monachos*: "solitary." Largely inspired by the biblical examples of
Elijah and John the Baptist's experiences in the wilderness, as well as

Jesus' forty days of temptation in the desert, the first monks lived lives of extreme abstinence from almost all earthly enjoyments, and lived with only the most minimal provisions of food, water, shelter, and human contact. The first monks were also influenced by Origen's austere personal habits, such as subsisting on the most meager fare, going shoeless, and performing self-castration as an act of Christian fleeing temptation.[1] And although the church had formally rejected Gnostic thought, which held that the human soul is inherently good and the physical body is inherently bad, pieces of it nonetheless had seeped into the church. Thus the monastic putting off of worldliness was intended to free the mind to concentrate on the things of God.

The first recorded ascetic monk was a man named Paul the Hermit, who retreated into the desolation of Egypt probably around 250. The details of Paul's life, some apocryphal, are recorded by Saint Jerome, who lived some one hundred years after him. Paul was born in the Egyptian town of Thebes to wealthy parents. Around the age of sixteen, during the reign of the persecutors Decius and Valerian, his parents died, leaving him a plentiful inheritance. But his brother-in-law, hoping to capture the fortune, reported Paul as a Christian to the authorities. Paul fled into the mountains of the desert to escape and discovered an ancient cave complex that had formerly been used as a mint hundreds of years before. Paul took up the cave as a residence and used palm leaves for his food and clothing. He regarded the cave as a gift from God and grew to appreciate it. He never left, and Jerome reported that he died at the age of 113, a lifetime of prayerful contemplation behind him.[2]

ANTHONY OF THE DESERT

If Paul was the vanguard of the monastic life, the example of Saint Anthony (ca. 251–356) touched off the great wave of monastic activity that consumed the imagination of many Christians during the third and fourth centuries. Anthony was also an Egyptian from a wealthy

Christian family. When he was around the age of eighteen or twenty, his parents died, leaving Anthony with a vast fortune. About six months later, as was his custom, Anthony went to church and heard a sermon on Matthew 19:21: "If you want to be perfect, go, sell your possessions and give to the poor, and you will have treasure in heaven. Then come, follow me." If we are to believe the tale, handed down to us by Athanasius, Anthony was blindsided by these words and ran out of the church, intent on doing just that. He promptly sold off three hundred acres, as well as all his other possessions, and donated the profits to the poor, reserving only a little money to care for his orphaned sister. He began to spend time with a handful of hermits who lived the contemplative life on the outskirts of town and adopted their spiritual practices:

> He observed the graciousness of one; the unceasing prayer of another; he took knowledge of another's freedom from anger and another's loving-kindness; he gave heed to one as he watched, to another as he studied; one he admired for his endurance, another for his fasting and sleeping on the ground; the meekness of one and the long-suffering of another he watched with care, while he took note of the piety towards Christ and the mutual love which animated all.[3]

Eventually Anthony took to the desert himself, living a rigorously ascetic lifestyle, sleeping on the hard ground, eating salted bread and water, and routinely staying up all night. Out of modest self-regard, he hated to be seen eating by anyone. He rarely bathed. Books were foreign to him and most of the other early monks—they were a worldly good unfit for the disciplinary lifestyle, and the possession of them could lead to the sin of pride. For Anthony, his physical punishment was an imitation of what the apostle Paul had stated in 2 Corinthians: "when I am weak, then I am strong" (12:10). But the stillness and isolation of the sands of Egypt were not without temptations. A popular theme in the writings and the biographies of the Desert Fathers is the endless battle with demons—a battle won only through steadfastness and prayer:

[The devil] attacked the young man, disturbing him by night and harassing him by day, so that even the onlookers saw the struggle which
was going on between them. The one would suggest foul thoughts and
the other counter them with prayers: the one fire him with lust, the
other, as one who seemed to blush, fortify his body with faith, prayers,
and fasting. And the devil, unhappy wight, one night even took upon
him the shape of a woman and imitated all her acts simply to beguile
Antony. But he, his mind filled with Christ and the nobility inspired
by Him, and considering the spirituality of the soul, quenched the coal
of the other's deceit.[4]

For twenty years, Anthony lived in solitude, barely seen by anyone.
At the end of the two decades, he emerged and attracted a great deal of
attention. People began flocking to the wilderness to get a glimpse of the
man, and many "enrolled themselves for the citizenship in the heavens."[5]
Anthony became the abbot (from the Coptic *abba*, "father") of a monastery and instructed many others in the way of the solitary Christian life.
Twice he visited Alexandria—once to offer himself as a martyr during
the persecutions, and another time to refute the Arians' claims that he
had adopted their theology. But the city life was entirely unfit for him,
said Sozomen:

When compelled to visit a city, he never failed to return to the deserts
as soon as he had accomplished the work he had undertaken; for, he
said, that as fishes are nourished in the water, so the desert is the world
prepared for monks; and as fishes die when thrown upon dry land, so
monastics lose their gravity when they go into cities.[6]

Despite his reclusiveness, Anthony became one of the most famous
men of his age. Constantine and his sons wrote to him, but Anthony
wasn't very interested in the content of their letters, whatever it was. He
replied back, urging them "not to think much of the present, but rather
to remember the judgment that is coming, and to know that Christ alone

was the true and Eternal King."⁷ The definitive account of Anthony's life was set down by Athanasius after the saint's death. *The Life of Saint Anthony* proved to be a wildly popular, if exaggerated instrument for spreading Anthony's fame across the Christian world, and the tales of Anthony fighting demons, performing miracles, and exercising body discipline enticed many to the sands of Egypt. Eventually Egypt became so overrun with monks that Athanasius wrote that "the desert was made a city."⁸

Michelangelo, *The Torment of St. Anthony*, 1487–1488.

PACHOMIUS AND CENOBITE MONASTICISM

Paul and Anthony practiced a form of monasticism later called *anchorite monasticism*, from the Greek *anchoretes*: "one who withdraws or retreats." But in time, another form of monasticism arose, *cenobitic monasticism*, which was distinguished by groups of monks living together in community but still removed from the world. Although there were groups of early monastic holy men in Egypt and elsewhere, the de facto founder of cenobitic monasticism was Pachomius, an Egyptian born near the end of the third century. Pachomius was originally a pagan who was impressed into army service against his will. A group of Christians recognized his despondency and consoled him. After he was released unexpectedly from military service, he gained instruction in the faith and was converted. In time, he became an anchorite monk.

One day, while contemplating God in a cave, Pachomius received a vision of an angel instructing him to gather young monks together so he could teach them in the way of monasticism. Pachomius obeyed and founded his monastery. Shortly after its founding, he had more than one hundred monks living in community together.

THE MONASTIC LIFESTYLE

The ritual for joining a monastery was not easy. Those who wanted to join the monastic community had to endure several days and nights outside the gatekeeper's quarters, begging to be let in. This was intended to be a confirmation of both the supplicant's desire to be a monk and his ability to obey his superiors, a characteristic Pachomius demanded. If admitted into the monastery, the candidate lived with the gatekeepers, perhaps for months, until he was considered ready to join the community. The new monk in Pachomius's monastery could expect a difficult existence:

> [T]hose who ate heartily were to be subjected to arduous labor, and the ascetic were to have more easy tasks assigned them; he was commanded to have many cells erected, in each of which three monks were to dwell, who were to take their meals at a common refectory in silence, and to sit around the table with a veil thrown over the face, so that they might not be able to see each other or anything but the table and what was set before them; they were not to admit strangers to eat with them, with the exception of travelers, to whom they were to show hospitality; those who desired to live with them, were first to undergo a probation of three years, during which time the most laborious tasks were to be done, and, by this method they could share in their community.[9]

Pachomius organized his community according to a monastic "rule," which later became known as the Rule of Saint Pachomius. (Subsequent monastic leaders, such as Saint Basil and Benedict, invented rules of their own.) Pachomius's Rule was a meticulous set of commands that governed every aspect of monastic life. Take, for instance, the rules applicable to the bakers of the monastery:

> When they pour the water in the flour and when they dough the pasta, nobody will talk to their neighbor. In the morning, when they take the bread to the ovens and hearths, they will be as silent and will chant psalms or passages from Scripture until they have finished their job. If they need anything, they will not talk, but they will make a sign to the ones that are able to take that which they need.[10]

And what happened to a monk who laughed during prayers?

> If during the chanting, the prayers, or the readings, someone talks or laughs, he will untie his girdle instantly and will go before the altar with his head bowed and downfallen arms. After the father of the monastery had reprehended him there, he will repeat this same penitence in the refectory, when all of the brothers had gathered.[11]

The monks who followed the Rule of Pachomius were far from idle. Work was an essential component of monastic life, both for the purpose of serving the other brothers and for keeping the mind occupied. As the monks worked, they might recite hymns, prayers, or portions of Scripture. Even the abbot and his deputies, called superiors, would often take on the most humbling occupations, so as to demonstrate their equality with the other brothers. The Pachomian communities

The ruins of the Monastery of St. Simeon, Aswan, Egypt.

also did not adhere to as strict a standard of discipline as the reclusive anchorites did: they often had fruit, vegetables, and fish (but still no meat). But books and outside visitors were still very rare. As is the case today, the monks usually sold their goods in marketplaces as a way of generating income for themselves and any travelers who needed a place to stay on a journey. Even more important than work was prayer. The monks prayed together at least twice a day and spent long hours away from corporate prayers doing the same. On Sundays, they emerged from their monasteries to attend a church service with other monks from the area.

MACARIUS AND MOSES THE BLACK

Like their anchorite counterparts, many of the cenobitic monks gained renown. One was a monk named Macarius, "the Lamp of the Desert," who bore the nickname because his face was said to have glowed in the dark with holiness. Macarius was an Egyptian whose life spanned nearly the entirety of the fourth century (ca. 300–391). When he first was called to the ascetic life, it was said that a woman accused Macarius of raping her. He endured the accusation in silence, but when she started going into labor months later, she could not give birth until she confessed her sin to Macarius. Macarius was a disciple of Saint Anthony who at the age of thirty became a monk, and at forty presided over a monastery for the remainder of his life. Still inhabited today is the Monastery of Saint Macarius, just one of a few dozen monasteries in the Wadi El-Natrun Valley of Egypt, about sixty miles northwest of Cairo.

Another famous monk of the age, and a follower of Macarius, was Saint Moses the Black, also known as "Abba Moses the Robber," "the Abyssinian," "the Ethiopian," and "the Strong." Before adopting the monastic life, Moses was an enormously built escaped slave who became a highway robber, terrorizing the Nile Valley with his gang. One day they attacked a monastery but were met by the abbot, who displayed a warm and peaceful countenance to them. Moses was convicted of his sins, repented, and begged to remain at the monastery. Now a monk, Moses set to work draining his body of its natural strength, eating only a little bread each day and praying fifty times daily, often while standing. Although Moses struggled with a violent temper, even after becoming a monk, he still found ways to extend grace to others. In 405, with his monastery under assault by barbarians, Moses refused to flee. When some other monks asked why he insisted on staying, he replied, "I have been expecting this day to come for many years past, so that might be fulfilled the command of our Redeemer, Who said, 'Those who take up the sword shall perish by the sword.'"[12] Moses and seven others were slain, and today he is remembered as the patron saint of nonviolence. There is a priory bearing his name in Mississippi, whose brothers work for racial harmony in a once racially acrimonious area of the country.

EVAGRIUS PONTICUS

Apart from leaders like Athanasius and Pachomius, most of the other monks of the great monastic period were illiterate. It wasn't until later in time that the monasteries of medieval Europe became great centers of learning. A great exception was the late-fourth- and early-fifth-century monastic leader Evagrius of Pontus (also known as Evagrius Ponticus): "a wise man, powerful in thought and in word, and skillful in discerning the arguments which led to virtue and to vice."[13] Evagrius was from a Christian family and had studied with the famous Gregory Nazianzus (a theologian presented in the next chapter) at Constantinople. Evagrius was a handsome young man, and this excited the jealousy of the husband of a female acquaintance. The husband plotted Evagrius's death, but Evagrius had a dream that foretold the event. Shaken, he fled the city, and resolved that he should devote himself to the monastic life. He first made his way to Jerusalem and later to Egypt, where he lived among the ascetics. "From the time that I took to the desert," he boasted, "I have not touched lettuce nor any other green vegetable, nor any fruit, nor grapes, nor meat, nor a bath."[14] Like Anthony, Evagrius was often tormented by demons, and in particular, lust. To mortify them, he once stood naked in a well all night, and his flesh became frozen. On another occasion, he stayed outdoors for forty days, and his physical mannerisms, it is said, became more animalistic during this time.

Evagrius's behavior was unusual, but he was a very learned man and wrote copiously on all kinds of theological topics. Evagrius was the first to set down the idea of what would later be called the seven deadly sins. The seven deadly sins had their roots in biblical lists, such as the Ten Commandments and a catalogue of sins in Proverbs 6, but Evagrius developed a list of eight evil thoughts in one of his works: gluttony, prostitution/fornication, avarice, hubris, sadness, wrath, boasting, and sloth. In the sixth century, Pope Gregory I modified Evagrius's list to become the seven deadly sins we know today: lust (*luxuria*), gluttony (*gula*), greed (*avaritia*), sloth (*acedia* or *socordia*), wrath (*ira*), envy (*invidia*), and pride (*superbia*). This list was later used by the Italian poet Dante in his epic poem the *Divine Comedy*. Of particular interest is *acedia*, which connotes a sense of being unable to work or pray because of an overwhelming listlessness or torpor. The monkish lifestyle—one of quietude, concentration, and routinized work—was particularly susceptible to bouts of *acedia*. If a monk felt a sense of boredom and spiritual dejection, it might stir up other sins. According to Evagrius, the "noonday demon" of *acedia* "causes the worst trouble of all":

> He presses his attack upon the monk about the fourth hour and besieges the soul until the eighth hour. First of all he makes it seem that the sun barely moves, if at all, and that the day is fifty hours long. Then he constrains the monk to look constantly out the windows, to walk outside the cell, to gaze carefully at the sun to determine how far it stands from the ninth hour, to look now this way and now that to see if perhaps [one of the brethren appears from his cell]. Then too he instills in the heart of the monk a hatred for the place, a hatred for his

very life itself, a hatred for manual labor . . . Should there be someone at this period who happens to offend him in some way or other, this too the demon uses to contribute further to his hatred.[15]

Perhaps the seriousness with which Evagrius addressed *acedia* stemmed from his own battle against lust. In the inability to work and contemplate the divine, laziness, boredom, and despair set in. This might partially explain our modern pornography epidemic: young men disengaged from work and spiritual contemplation succumb to great boredom, and in turn, lust. Evagrius was equally stern about the eight other sins and saw them as motivated by demonic attack. His *Praktikos* (Practices) exposits a series of tactics for identifying and fighting off demons:

When we are obliged to spend time in towns or villages, we should particularly hold to our self-control at such times in consorting with worldly people, in case our mind coarsens and loses its habitual vigilance because of its actual situation and so becomes a fugitive, tossed around by the demons . . . When the demons are helpless in their conflict with monks, they retire for a while and watch to see which area of virtue they are neglecting in the mean time, and then suddenly rush in and devastate the poor soul.[16]

Many parts of Evagrius's work, especially his advice for fighting sin, are useful. But like many others of his age, Evagrius's theology was heavily influenced by the works of Origen, which was itself influenced by Plato's philosophy. As a result, much of his thought seems to be close to Gnosticism, which the very first early church fathers, such as Irenaeus and Justin Martyr, would not recognize as orthodox. In 553, Evagrius's and Origen's work were both declared heretical at the Second Council of Constantinople. Still, Evagrius left behind a fascinating literary tradition that is too often neglected, and his ideas for how to conduct monastic life became part of the basis for the European ideas of monasticism.

DESERT WOMEN

Women also felt called to the monastic lifestyle, and there soon appeared a network of convents in Egypt. Pachomius's sister, Mary, founded a convent shortly after Pachomius founded his monastery. Melania the Younger (ca. 383–ca. 439) was the daughter of a wealthy Roman senatorial family who, despite taking a husband, still retained an ascetic lifestyle. She sold all her belongings—against the objections of the Roman Senate—and went to Jerusalem, where she and her husband built a monastery and corresponding nunnery. Despite owning nothing of her own, she was frequently entrusted with other people's money, since she distributed it so wisely. Like Melania, Saint Paula was also a very wealthy woman, who was carried around Rome by a team of eunuchs. After her husband died, she became attracted to the monastic lifestyle and established a convent. She also became a lifelong friend of Saint Jerome and assisted him with his translation of the Bible into Latin from the original Hebrew and Greek.

Saint Pelagia the Harlot was originally a courtesan in Antioch with beauty so great that "all the ages of mankind could never come to the end of it." When the bishops of Antioch and the surrounding regions gathered together one day, they got a glimpse of Pelagia, who dressed so promiscuously that "there was not one who did not hide his face in his veil . . . averting their eyes as if from a very great sin." One of the bishops who caught sight of Pelagia was named Nonnus. Nonnus broke down into a bout of hysterics, remonstrating that the woman had put more time into her appearance than he had into his own love of Christ, and he felt unworthy. The next day Nonnus gave a sermon in which he spoke "very earnestly about the future judgement and the good gifts in store in eternity." This was an especially powerful sermon that moved his hearers so much that "the floor of the church was awash with the tears of the hearers."[17]

As Nonnus was preaching, Pelagia happened to be passing outside of the church, and was "so struck that she despaired of herself and her tears flowed in such a flood that she could not control them." She went home and told her servants to find out where Nonnus was staying. When they reported his location, she wrote him a letter detailing her repentant heart. To confirm that her conversion was authentic, Nonnus, afraid of sexual temptation, wrote, "If you really do desire God, have strength and faith and come to me among the other bishops, for I cannot let you see me alone." Receiving his response, she ran to his church and begged him, "My lord, I am an ocean of sin, a deep pit of iniquity and I ask to be baptised."[18]

Pelagia was baptized, but eight days later disappeared. A few years went by with no trace of her. When James, a deacon who served with Nonnus, intended to take a trip to Jerusalem, Nonnus asked him to inquire about a monk named Pelagius living in solitude nearby. James reached Pelagius's cell and called out to him. Hearing no answer, he looked through the window, only to see him lying dead. When a group of monks came to anoint the body with oil in preparation for burial, they stripped off the clothes and saw that Pelagius had not been a man at all, but Pelagia! The former harlot had fled into the desert to become a monk in disguise. The monks cried out, "Glory to Thee, Lord Christ, who hast many treasures hidden on the earth, and not men only, but women also."[19]

Ephrem and Simeon

Although Egypt was the primary (but not only) locus of monastic activity, in time the lifestyle became popular in other areas of the East, especially Caesarea (Palestine) and Syria. The Eastern monastics could boast their own set of notable men, none more so than Ephrem the Syrian, a monastic born at the beginning of the fourth century. Despite never being formally trained in languages and literature, Ephrem ("the Harp of the Holy Spirit") was described in his own time as the "greatest ornament of the Catholic Church," who "surpassed the most approved writers of Greece" on the back of his exquisite hymns and poetry, which was reported to have totaled "three hundred thousand verses"![20] No less admirable was his ascetic lifestyle. Once, when Ephrem had just broken a fast lasting several days, an attendant bringing him food dropped the dish containing his meal. The attendant was angry and upset with himself. But Ephrem, undaunted, told him, "Take courage; we will go to the food, as the food does not come to us."[21] He then sat down and took his food from the floor.

An eleventh-century mosaic of Ephrem the Syrian.

Ephrem was also known for his concern for the poor. In 373, a famine decimated the town of Edessa. Ephrem quit his monastic cell and went into town to rebuke the rich people there for their stinginess, as many of the town's poor around them were dying from hunger and disease. Ephrem convicted the rich of their greediness and took up an offering to pay for the town's convalescence. The amount collected was enough to supply three hundred hospital beds. Ephrem attended to the sick daily, and when the worst of the plague had passed, he returned to his monastery. But it was too late. Ephrem died within a few days, a victim of his own compassion.

His legacy lies mostly in his literary output. He was a prodigious writer of many different genres—hymns, sermons, and theological speculations. Most of Ephrem's poetry is distinguished by reverence for Christ: "I will run in my affections to Him who heals freely / He who healed my sorrows, the first and the second, He who cured the third, He will heal the fourth. / Heal me, Thou Son the First Born!"[22] But in some hymns, his imagination runs wild. For instance, his Nisibene Hymn 52 is a dispute between Satan and Death over who is more powerful, which seems like an early version of the demonic dialogue of C. S. Lewis's *Screwtape Letters*:

> DEATH: To thee, O Evil One, none comes save he that wills: to
> me he that wills and he that wills not, even to me they come.
> SATAN: Thine, O Death, is but the force of tyranny: mine are
> snares and nets of subtlety.

DEATH: Hear, O Evil One, that he who so is subtle breaks off
   thy yoke: but none is there that is able to escape my yoke.

SATAN: Thou, Death, on him that is sick proves thy might: but
   I over them that are whole, am exceedingly powerful.

DEATH: The Evil One prevails not over all those that revile
   him: but for me he that has cursed me and he that curses
   me, come into my hands.

SATAN: Thou, Death, from God, hast gotten thy might: I
   alone by none am I helped, when I lead men to sin.

DEATH: Thou, O Evil One, are like a weakling: while like a
   king I exercise my dominion.

SATAN: Thou art a fool, O Death, not to know how great am
   I: who suffice to capture free will, the sovereign power.

DEATH: Thou, O Evil One, like a thief, lo! thou goest round:
   I like a lion break in pieces and fear not.

SATAN: To thee, O Death, none does service or worship: to me
   kings do service of sacrifice as to God.

DEATH: On Death there are many that call, as on a kind
   Power: on thee, O Evil One, none has called or calls.[23]

Another famed Syrian monk was an eccentric named Simeon the
Stylite, whose life spanned between the fourth and fifth centuries. Simeon
entered the monastic life very early, before the age of sixteen, and he used
to subject himself to corporal tests such as standing up straight until he
collapsed, and refusing to take food and drink during the entirety of
Lent. This kind of extreme behavior got him labeled by the other monks
as unsuited for communal monastic life. Simeon moved to the desert,
where he spent his time in a tight space less than twenty yards in diameter. Finding himself beset by people inquiring to know about his life and
practices, Simeon grew frustrated at the throngs of people who left him
distracted from prayer and contemplation. To escape them, he erected
a column nine feet high, and gained the nickname Simeon the Stylite
(*style* is Greek for "pillar"). In time, the pillar got higher and higher, and

by the time of Simeon's death it had gotten to be more than fifty feet high! Although no shelter of any kind was on top of the column, Simeon did have a platform on top of about one square meter and entertained visitors from time to time, who reached the top by climbing a ladder. For food, local shepherd boys would bring him bread and goats' milk. He passed his time praying; one observer recounted that Simeon bent over at the waist 1,244 times during one prayer session before he lost count, and each time Simeon's forehead almost touched his knees. Simeon, like Anthony, became enormously famous in his day. According to one of his biographers, Simeon's asceticism had an evangelistic purpose: "How many harlots came there and from afar saw him, the Holy One, and renounced and left their places the cities in which they had lived, and surrendered themselves to the Christ!"[24] All in all, Simeon spent about forty years on his column, all of them a testament to the sufficiency and provision of God. When Simeon finally expired in 459, his follow-ers "embraced the pillar and gave voice like jackals."[25] They went up to retrieve the body and discovered Simeon hunched over in his customary contortion of prayer. The ruins of the monastery of Saint Simeon, founded in his honor after his death, still stand on a desolate hill about forty miles from the nearest city in

All that remains of St. Simeon's Column, Syria.

northern Syria. In the center of the church, portions of Simeon's column can still be seen; generations of pilgrims to the site chipped away at the pillar, leaving today only a boulder on top of the base.

THE SYRIAC AND COPTIC LANGUAGES

Much of the monastic literature from the ancient Near East was written down in Syriac (the vernacular language of ancient Syria) and Coptic (the vernacular language of ancient Egypt). Both are still used as written and liturgical languages today in various rites of the Syriac Orthodox Church and Coptic Orthodox Church. Ephrem the Syrian's poetry is the most famous work from the ancient church written in Syriac, which was supplanted by Arabic as the region's main speaking language in the seventh century. Coptic managed to have a greater legacy of survival. Coptic had its roots in ancient Egyptian, but the first Christian writings were predominantly Greek. As Christianity spread to areas where Greek was less commonly spoken and read, writers such as Athanasius, Pachomius, and Anthony began to use Coptic to pass on Christian Scriptures and their own thoughts. The greatest Coptic writer was one Shenoute the Archimandrite, an abbot of a monastery who had gained an intimate knowledge of the Greek classics of Aristotle, Plato, and the Greek playwrights and myth makers. Another of the most popular Coptic texts is a collection of aphorisms, stylistically similar to Aesop's Fables, from the Egyptian abbots, collectively known as the *Sayings of the Desert Fathers*. The *Sayings* are intended to report the wisdom of the various abbots:

> Abba Theophilus, the archbishop, came to Scetis one day. The brethren who were assembled said to Abba Pambo, "Say something to the Archbishop, so that he may be edified." The old man said to them, "If he is not edified by my silence, he will not be edified by my speech."[26]

> One day Abba Arsenius consulted an old Egyptian monk about his own thoughts. Someone noticed this and said to him, "Abba Arsenius, how is it that you with such a good Latin and Greek education, ask this peasant about your thoughts?" He replied, "I have indeed been taught Latin and Greek, but I do not know even the alphabet of this peasant."[27]

151

One of the monks was told of the death of his father. He said to the one who brought the news, "Stop blaspheming! My father is immortal."[28]

The unusual lives and habits of the Desert Fathers were only amplified by these semimythical reports. With the help of these and other pieces of hagiography (the biographical depiction of Christian saints), these monks assumed a legendary status in future generations. Throughout the late antique and medieval periods, Christian hagiography was usually based on the real-life deeds and personality traits of each saint, but also used substantial fiction as a technique for capturing the essence of a saint's life and character. The ancient and medieval biography of a saint is frequently referred to as his or her *vita*, the Latin word for "life." Athanasius's *Life of Anthony* encapsulated well the essence of a *vita*, and as a result, it helped to touch off a frenzy of interest in the monastic life. But the western portion of the empire would soon discover a saint that inspired its own monastic fever: Martin of Tours.

The Life of Martin of Tours

The idiosyncratic devotion of the Desert Fathers captured the attention of Christians all over the known world, and monasticism eventually spread to western Europe. Athanasius, the great ally of the monks, visited Rome in 340, and several believers there took up the practice shortly after. But if the West could boast any inspiring example of personal piety, as Egypt could Saint Anthony, it was Martin of Tours. Martin was born in 316 along the northern frontier of the empire, and his father was a cavalry officer in the Roman army; by law, Martin was forced to join the cavalry at age fifteen. Martin had previously become a Christian against his parents' wishes and was uncomfortable with the idea of military service. He served two years, but later renounced his duty, saying, "I am the soldier of Christ: it is not lawful for me to fight."[29] The most famous episode of Martin's life is the apocryphal account of him cutting his soldier's cloak in two and giving half of it to a beggar in the middle of winter, as the words of Jesus resounded in his mind: "Inasmuch as ye have done these things to one of the least of these, ye have done them unto me."[30]

After being discharged from military service, Martin traveled back home to convert his family. Along the way, his *vita* says, he encountered numerous difficulties. At one juncture, he was beset by robbers, and as their axe was coming down upon his throat, one of the bandits snatched the assailant's arm in mid-stroke. The robber was curious who Martin was, and Martin shared the good news with the robber, leading to his conversion. Martin was then mercifully released. But his trials weren't over yet. Outside of Milan, the devil appeared to Martin in the form of a man, saying, "Wherever you go, or whatever you attempt, the devil will resist you." Martin replied, "The Lord is my helper; I will not fear what man can do unto me."[31] The devil vanished. Other episodes of Martin's life include him restoring to life a man who had hanged himself, interrupting a pagan burial ritual, and healing a leper with a holy kiss. Many of these are dubious, but some are no doubt rooted in truth; it is not hard to imagine Martin ministering to the sick, preaching the gospel to pagans, and struggling in his flesh against the devil. Whatever Martin did, his biographer, Sulpitius Severus, regarded him worthy of the highest praise: "I freely confess that if . . . Homer himself were to ascend from the shades below, he could not do justice to this subject in words; to such an extent did all excellences surpass in Martin the possibility of being embodied in language."[32]

Martin eventually founded a monastery in Gaul, and in 371 was made the bishop of the city of Tours. His consecration was an unwilling one; Martin reportedly hid among a flock of geese in a barn because of his unwillingness to be made a bishop. This unwillingness was characteristic of Martin's ascetic and humble way of life. He too, said Sulpitius, took very little food and spent virtually no time unengaged in prayer, even when he was doing something else. In time, Martin became one of the most revered saints in Europe, and many men and women of the fourth and fifth centuries were so attracted to his pious example that they themselves entered the monastic lifestyle, although the outlandish solitary asceticism of Egypt was less common in the West.

JOHN CASSIAN

A nother great disseminator of Egyptian monasticism in the fourth and early fifth centuries was John Cassian. Cassian was born in modern-day Romania or Bulgaria (or perhaps Gaul) and was called to a life of monasticism in Palestine and Egypt. After he was dismissed from his monastery because of a theological controversy, he spent time in Constantinople, studying under the greatest preacher of the age, John Chrysostom (a figure we will discuss later on). Eventually he settled in the south of France, where he founded two monasteries, one for men and one for women. Cassian was a learned man who, like Evagrius Ponticus, set down in writing the wisdom he had culled from his time in Egypt. The *Institutes* and *Conferences* were written in Latin, the reading language of the Western empire, and helped spread the ideas of monastic theology, organization, and disciplines to the West. In the *Institutes*, Cassian, like Pachomius, detailed the rules that governed behavior in the monastery, including what might happen, for example, if a brother broke an earthenware jar:

> If then any one by accident breaks an earthenware jar . . . he can only expiate his carelessness by public penance; and when all the brethren are assembled for service he must lie on the ground and ask for absolution until the service of the prayers is finished; and will obtain it when by the Abbot's command he is bidden to rise from the ground. The same satisfaction must be given by one who when summoned to some work or to the usual service comes rather late, or who when singing a Psalm hesitates ever so little.[33]

Cassian, almost certainly drawing from Evagrius, wrote his own exposition on the seven deadly sins, considering how each sin, like gluttony, drew the sinner away from God. Cassian even claimed that it was gluttony that led to God's destruction of Sodom in the book of Genesis:

> The belly, when filled with all kinds of food, gives birth to seeds of wantonness, nor can the mind, when choked with the weight of food, keep the guidance and government of the thoughts. For not only is drunkenness with wine wont to intoxicate the mind, but excess of all kinds of food makes it weak and uncertain, and robs it of all its power of pure and clear contemplation. The cause of the overthrow and wantonness of Sodom was not drunkenness through wine, but fullness of bread . . . And because through fullness of bread they were inflamed with uncontrollable lust of the flesh, they were burnt up by the judgment of God with fire and brimstone from heaven.[34]

Cassian's other great work, the *Conferences*, recorded a series of conversations that Cassian had with many of the great monks of the desert. The object of the work is to detail how the monk can exercise a moral life and have intimacy with God. One of the monks suggested, "And therefore if you would prepare in your heart a holy tabernacle of spiritual knowledge, purge yourselves from the stain of all sins, and rid yourselves of the cares of this world."[35] For Cassian, a lifetime of self-deprivation (*purgatio*—purging) and inner contemplation (*illuminatio*—illumination) would eventually produce a kind of (*unitio*—unity) with God. The extensive theology of Athanasius, Evagrius, and Cassian reveals a group of men and women fanatically fixated on the mortification of sin and purification of the flesh, whether it was ultimately accomplished in this world or the next.

NINE

FATHERS KNOW BEST

The Continued Fight Against Arianism
in the East, Julian the Apostate, Basil,
Gregory Nazianzus, Gregory Nyssa

After the death of Constantine, the Roman Empire, already teetering from the strain of civil and foreign wars, again splintered
apart. Now controlling the *orbis Romanus* were Constantine's three sons,
all of whom showed plenty of the ill temperament but none of the magnanimity that their father did. The confusingly named Constantine II,
Constantius II, and Constans, after killing off their other relatives who
threatened their claims on power, forged a tripartite treaty in 337. Each
son received a portion of the empire to call his own. But differing religious sympathies, as well as a hunger for more spoils of empire, quickly
tore their already unstable pact apart.

Constantine II had received Gaul (France), Hispania (Spain),
and Britannica (Britain) as his allotment. But this was insufficient for
him. As the firstborn son, he peevishly complained that his lot was less
than he deserved under the terms of primogeniture, the Roman custom that stipulated that a firstborn son should receive a greater share of
an inheritance than his brothers. Constans, who had been given territory in North Africa, begrudgingly gave over more of his land to allay

Constantine II. But the brothers soon began squabbling over which territories belonged to whom. By 340, Constans had had enough, and fatally ambushed his brother Constantine II while he was on the march with his own army. Constantius, controlling the eastern portion of the empire, was hardly sad to see Constantine II go, for Constantius was an Arian, while Constantine II had been a committed trinitarian. By 350, Constans himself and his successor were deposed and killed in a coup. Constantius was now in charge, and his actions set the stage for the great theme of the latter half of the fourth century: orthodoxy's fight against a militant form of Arianism.

ARIANISM FIGHTS BACK

From 337 to 361, Constantius exercised a great deal of power over church affairs, to the suffering of many Christians. To gain a sense of his estimation of his own authority, we can look at a declaration that he once made in which he insisted, "My will is also a canon of the church."[1] The emperor's imposition on church affairs made clear that the pronouncements of the Council of Nicaea a generation earlier were only as binding as the emperor wished. Constantius too came under the sway of the old trickster, the bishop Eusebius of Nicomedia, who soon became bishop of Constantinople.

After his appointment, ninety-seven bishops from the East traveled to Antioch under the guise of consecrating a new church, but in actuality, they "intended nothing else than the abolition of the decrees of the Nicæan Council."[2] They installed a new bishop at Antioch and slandered Athanasius to Constantius's face, saying he had seized the bishopric of Alexandria unlawfully and had also condemned several people to death without due process. A manhunt for Athanasius ensued, and soldiers surrounded the Alexandrian church in which he was hiding out. Athanasius asked the congregation to sing a psalm as the soldiers assembled outside, and the soldiers, out of a sense of propriety, waited until the psalm was concluded before entering the church to search for him. In the meantime, under the cover of night, Athansius had slipped out and fled to Rome, which, like the great majority of the West, was firmly attached to the doctrine that had been reaffirmed at the Council of Nicaea.

In the decades that followed, Constantius embraced Arianism more heartily and permitted several Arian bishops to conduct campaigns of terror against Nicene bishops and congregants. We have to admire many of the Eastern bishops who held fast to the Nicene Creed and lost their episcopates as a result. One of them was Gregory of Alexandria, a faithful bishop who was displaced by George the Cappadocian, an Arian whom nearly everyone despised. George, said Sozomen, was "hated by the rulers because he scorned them . . . and the multitude detested him on account of his tyranny."[3] George had a notorious deputy named Sebastian, who carried out his heartless whims against anyone, even young girls, orphans, and widows. George's entire reign as bishop of Alexandria was a nightmare:

> When Easter-week was passed, the virgins were cast into prison, the bishops were led in chains by the military, and the dwellings even of orphans and widows were forcibly entered and their provisions pillaged. Christians were assassinated by night; houses were sealed; and the relatives of the clergy were endangered on their account . . . Having kindled a fire, he set the virgins near it, in order to compel them to say that they were of the Arian faith: but seeing they stood their ground and despised the fire, he then stripped them, and so beat them on the face, that for a long time afterwards they could scarcely be recognized. Seizing also about forty men, he flogged them in an extraordinary manner: for he so lacerated their backs with rods fresh cut from the palm-tree, which still had their thorns on, that some were obliged to resort repeatedly to surgical aid in order to have the thorns extracted from their flesh, and others, unable to bear the agony, died under its infliction.[4]

George was also famously cruel to the pagans of the town, and this eventually proved to be his undoing. In 361, the pagans of Alexandria believed that the time was right for vengeance to be taken on behalf of the gods. "Away with George!" was the cry, and he was seized and thrown into prison. Four weeks later, on December 24, George was dragged out of prison and kicked to death by a mob. His body was placed upon a camel and paraded around the city, and subsequently burned. His ashes were then cast into the Mediterranean Sea.

Macedonius, a heretic, seized the leadership of the church at Constantinople from Paul, a faithful adherent to the Nicene doctrine. "The exploits of Macedonius," said Socrates Scholasticus, "on behalf of Christianity, consist[ed] of murders, battles, incarcerations, and civil wars."[5] Macedonius instituted a campaign against the Nicenes, confiscating property, stripping them of citizenship, and inflicting torture. One of his tactics was to brand some of them on the head with an iron. Other men of faith who refused to take communion with him were seized and had their mouths forced open with a piece of wood. The bread and wine of the Lord's Supper were then rammed down their throats. Women who refused to take communion with the Macedonians (who denied the power of the Holy Spirit) had it even worse. Their breasts were placed in a wooden casing and burned with irons or eggs that had been heated in a fire. Sometimes they were sawed off. Macedonius and his followers also forced women and children to be baptized. If they refused, they were whipped.[6]

Even the emperor Constantius became uneasy at Macedonius's behavior. In 358, Macedonius decided to remove the remains of Constantine from the church in which it had been buried. He claimed the church was structurally unsound and about to crumble; the Catholics cried that he was desecrating a holy site. Constantine's body was moved to another church, which was quickly surrounded by two mobs of differing convictions. The factions "attacked one another with great fury, and great loss of life was occasioned, so that the churchyard was covered with gore, and the well also which was in it overflowed with blood, which ran into the adjacent portico, and thence even into the very street."[7] Constantius was angered not because of the slaughter but because Macedonius hadn't bothered to tell him that he intended to move Constantine's body. In time, Macedonius was stripped of his bishopric, both for his violence and for his admission to the diaconate a man accused of fornication.

THE COUNCIL OF SARDICA

As the Arian offensive intensified in the 340s, many of the Eastern bishops who fled from their sees, like Athanasius, found refuge at Rome. Their great defender there was the bishop Julius I. When Julius learned of what was happening in the East, he wrote a sternly worded letter to the Eastern bishops, reproaching them for their conduct. The Eastern bishops responded that the Roman bishop was in the wrong for receiving Athanasius and others into communion with the Roman church, and that insulting their episcopal decisions was "unjust and discordant with ecclesiastical right."[8] Peace between the Arian East and trinitarian West, they said, was only possible if the West recognized their authority to depose some bishops and install new ones.

Julius decided to call a synod to resolve the issue. The place was Sardica, today called Sofia, the capital of Bulgaria. Three hundred Western bishops and only seventy-six Eastern bishops attended, an indication of where the sympathies of most of the attendees laid. The bishops wanted further unity on the Arian question, an indication that the Council of Nicaea, for all its rejection of Arianism, was ultimately powerless to enforce its pronouncements. The bishops also wanted clarification on the status of Athanasius, a man of the people who was alternately subject to hero or outlaw status, depending on who was in power and where he happened to be in the empire. The Eastern bishops were implacable on this question—Athanasius, they said, had caused too much disruption in Egypt by fighting tooth and nail for orthodoxy. The result of the Council was the excommunication of a handful of Eastern bishops, and "because they separated the Son from the substance of the Father,"[9] they were declared alien to the Nicene church. The council's Western orientation was confirmed by a letter from Julius emphasizing that Rome was the arbiter of the significant questions in the universal church. Even if Athanasius was to blame for undermining episcopal authority, he conceded, "Can you be ignorant that this is the custom, that we should be written to first, so that from here what is just may be defined?"[10]

After Sardica, relations between the two sides of the fading empire drifted toward a nadir. According to the historian Sozomen, East and West "ceased to maintain the intercourse which usually exists among people of the same faith, and refrained from holding communion with each other."[11] Constantius himself even felt that things were getting out of hand; he called yet another two councils in the 350s to resolve the Arian question, at Sirmium (in Italy) and Seleucia (Iraq). Both were unsuccessful, and Sirmium was actually a major victory for Arianism, so much so that Saint Jerome later wrote that at the conclusion of it, "the whole world groaned, and was astonished to find itself Arian."[12] This sentiment is no doubt an exaggeration, but it is true that several of the councils of the 350s produced a succession of Arian creeds that denied the *homoousios* of the Father and Son. It wasn't until the Council of Constantinople in 381 that the tide of Arianism, so strong among church leaders in the East, was definitively reversed.

JULIAN THE APOSTATE

The Arian church lost its most powerful patron when Constantius died in 361. The emperor who came after him, Julian, was openly antagonistic to Christianity. Julian was the last emperor to adhere to the religion of the ancient Romans, and, like Diocletian, he believed that a revival of the old pagan customs would restore the might and prosperity of the empire. Because Julian had been brought up as a Christian (under the watchful eye of Eusebius of Nicomedia) but had renounced the faith at age twenty, history has bestowed on him the name Julian the Apostate. Upon taking power, his first campaigns of reestablishing paganism were fairly mild. Temples were reopened, priests were restored, and Julian himself participated in the ancient Roman custom of examining the entrails of animal sacrifices in order to divine the future. One day when Julian was sacrificing in the Temple of Fortune in Constantinople, the bishop of the town, Maris, came to him and rebuked him as an atheist and an apostate. Julian scoffed at the aged and nearly blind bishop, "The Galilean, your God, will not cure you." Maris replied, "I thank God for my blindness, since it prevents me from beholding one who has fallen away from our religion."[13]

A noseless bust of Julian the Apostate, Archaeological Museum, Athens.

Julian's persecution of Christians took a very different character than the bloodletting of centuries past. Julian sought to rip the church apart by exploiting its internal tensions: bishops were recalled from exile; taxes were levied on Christians to rebuild pagan temples they had destroyed; civil liberties and meeting places were taken away. Christians who would not sacrifice to the emperor were deprived of the rights of citizenship and could not hold civil office, and Julian also issued an edict that Christian children were prohibited from attending the public schools, where they would study the works of the ancient Greeks. "If they want to learn literature," Julian said, "they have Luke and Mark: Let them go back to their churches and expound on them."[14] Julian (rightly) believed that studying the Greek masters honed one's rhetorical skills, and he did not want to equip Christian children to be able contenders against the forces of paganism. This irritated the writer Apollinaris of Laodicea, who in response composed an epic poem based on the Old Testament to stand in the place of the *Iliad* and the *Odyssey*, as well as tragedies that echoed Euripides and comedies that hinted at

Menander. Said Sozomen, "Were it not for the extreme partiality with which the productions of antiquity are regarded, I doubt not but that the writings of Apollinaris would be held in as much estimation as those of the ancients."[15] It is very unfortunate that most of these intriguing creations do not survive.

But the persecution of Julian's reign was not confined to putting pressure on Christians to retreat from their civic and intellectual high ground. In the absence of a strong Catholic emperor to protect them, pagans and Arians brought humiliation and death to Christians in the fourth century. At Gaza, enterprising pagans had young Christian women stripped naked and paraded around as a public spectacle. Lastly, their heads were shaved, and they were split open at the torso. Into their bodies was stuffed slop for swine, and their bodies were then torn apart by hungry pigs, unable to distinguish between human remains and their usual food. At Arethusa, the bishop of that town, Mark, fled from the threat of persecution, but returned when he heard that many of his people were being tortured. Mark stepped forward and offered himself to the mobs to absorb the entirety of any torture they wished to inflict. The people obliged him:

> The entire people . . . rushed upon him, dragged him through the streets, pressing and plucking and beating whatever member each one happened upon. People of each sex and of all ages joined with alacrity and fury in this atrocious proceeding. His ears were severed by fine ropes; the boys who frequented the schools made game of him by tossing him aloft and rolling him over and over, sending him forward, catching him up, and unsparingly piercing him with their styles. When his whole body was covered with wounds, and he nevertheless was still breathing, they anointed him with honey and a certain mixture, and placing him in a fish-basket made of woven rushes, raised him up on an eminence. It is said that while he was in this position, and the wasps and bees lit upon him and consumed his flesh, he told the inhabitants of Arethusa that he was raised up above them, and

could look down upon them below him, and that this reminded him of the difference that would exist between them in the life to come.[16]

Thankfully, Julian's reign was fairly short. In 363, he died in modern-day Iraq on a campaign against the Persians. One historian reported that before Julian embarked for battle, he said that after the war was over he would increase the severity of his dealings with Christians, and that the Son of the Carpenter would not be able to help them escape it. The Christian mystic Didymus was said to have had a vision of Julian's death before the battle, and responded that the Son of the Carpenter was then preparing for Julian a wooden coffin in view of his death.[17] Didymus's version came to pass. Amid an ambush, a Persian cavalryman pierced his side with a spear, which penetrated into the lower part of his liver. A botched surgical procedure to fix the wound sealed his fate. Julian died that night, and an apocryphal tale suggests that his last words were an acknowledgment of the rising tide of Christianity in his day: "O Galilean, you have won."[18]

VALENS

Under Julian, Christians were forced to keep a lower profile, and this meant that many of the theological quarrels of the previous decades went dormant. But strife soon emerged again now that the church enjoyed another period of toleration. Sozomen, the church historian, wrote axiomatically, "It is thus that men, when attacked by foreign enemies, remain in accord among themselves; but, when external troubles are removed, then internal dissensions creep in."[19] The cause for ease was the ascension of Jovian, Julian's successor, who at Athanasius's urging reversed many of Julian's decrees, but unfortunately died within a year.

Following Julian as co-emperors were Valentinian and his brother Valens. Valentinian, according to Christian sources, was "a good man and capable of holding the reins of the empire," who "maintained the faith of the council of Nicæa."[20] But early in his reign, Valentinian decided that he, unlike his predecessors, preferred to remain aloof from church matters. When a petition for another doctrinal council was brought to him, his response was, "I am but one of the laity, and have therefore no right to interfere in these transactions; let the priests, to whom such matters appertain, assemble where they please."[21] This stance was a weak one, especially since Valens, his brother and co-emperor, was a committed and active Arian. Gregory Nazianzus said that Valens was "an Emperor, most fond of gold and most hostile to Christ, infected with these two most serious diseases, insatiate avarice and blasphemy."[22] Consequently, the Arian persecution of the 340s and 350s experienced a revival under Valens in the 360s and 370s. Nicene Christians were forced out of their churches and deprived of priests. Huge fines were levied against them, sending them into impoverishment. Again the old issue of Athanasius came up, and the Egyptian church, controlled by Arians, begged Valens to send him into exile. But Valens was not prepared to pursue the indefatigable Athanasius as others were, and Athanasius returned peaceably to Alexandria.

Some of the most shocking incidents, if the sources are to be believed, were commissioned by Valens himself. Valens ordered the prefect of Constantinople to round up a number of presbyters who would be sent away into exile. The men agreeably boarded a ship, which they believed was destined for some exilic destination. Once the ship sailed a good distance from Constantinople, the sailors on board set fire to it and climbed into a rowboat. The unguided ship and its human cargo burned up before it reached the shore: "So, fighting at the same time against both sea and flames, at last they were delivered to the deep, and won the martyrs crown."[23] On an imperial tour to Edessa, in Syria, Valens punched a local governor, Modestus, for allowing Nicene churches to assemble in a field outside the city walls. Modestus, although he was a heretic, then secretly warned the town that they should not appear for prayer the next day or Valens would punish them. He believed only a few would show up, but the next morning, the meeting place was more crowded than usual. One woman, with her child following her, pushed through an armed detachment to get there. Modestus ordered her arrested and questioned what she was doing:

> "Know you not," replied Modestus, "that the prefect is on his way there for the purpose of condemning to death all who are found on the spot?" "I have heard so," replied she, "and this is the very reason of my haste; for I am fearful of arriving too late, and thus losing the honor of martyrdom for God." The governor having asked her why she took her child with her, she replied, "In order that he may share in the common suffering, and participate in the same reward."[24]

At Antioch, the Orthodox Church had no rest from persecution, so much so that they took to the region's mountaintops to worship, and suffered rain, snow, cold, and heat to do so. But Valens couldn't even endure this, and he sent soldiers up the mountain to disrupt their worship. Alexandria, as in previous decades, remained the great hotbed of Arianism during the period of Valens's reign. Lucius of Alexandria served two terms as Arian bishop of the town between 363 and 380, and so thoroughly persecuted the Nicene sect that it filled the historian Theodoret with anguish to even write it down: "Ah! Woe is me. Many a virgin underwent brutal violation; many a maid beaten on the head, with clubs lay dumb, and even their bodies were not allowed to be given up for burial, and their grief-stricken parents cannot find their corpses to this day."[25] Lucius, who enjoyed Valens's protection, sent the orthodox bishop Peter into exile, and regarded the storms that beset the church "as a season of brilliant festivity."[26]

One of Lucius's goals was to disrupt and destroy the monastics in the desert. Christians around the Roman world looked to the monks as spiritual leaders because of their piety and insistence on orthodoxy; Arianism was unheard-of among them. Hence, the monastic refusal to accept any principles of the Arian doctrine limited its growth among the laity. One day Lucius thought it a good idea to round up many monks and ecclesiastics and ship them off to Heliopolis, "a place where none of the inhabitants, who are all given over to idols, can endure so much as to hear the name of Christ . . . where every man is given over to superstition, where flourish the devil's ways of pleasure, and where the situation of the city, surrounded on all sides by mountains that approach the sky, is fitted for the terrifying lairs of wild beasts."[27]

One of the passengers on that gloomy ship was a deacon sent by Damasus I, the bishop of Rome, carrying with him letters of condolences and encouragement. The deacon was whipped with stones and bits of lead before being bound and marched onto the ship, his destination the salt mines of the East. The city grieved as the ship departed from the shore: "up went a mingled cry of maids and matrons, old men and young, all sobbing and lamenting together, and the noise of the multitude overwhelmed the roar raised by the waves on the foaming sea."[28] But Lucius's exile of many monks did nothing to change the monastic refusal of Arian theology. "The monks," said one source, "were prepared to subject their necks to the sword rather than to swerve from the Nicene doctrines."[29] The monks, so revered as holy men, became guardians of doctrine, and the Arians could never convert them. This was not only true in Egypt, where Athanasius allied himself with the Desert Fathers, but also in a region of Asia Minor called Cappadocia, which emerged as a home to its own set of churchmen with ties to the monastic life.

THE CAPPADOCIAN FATHERS

In 373, Athanasius died, leaving something of a void in Nicene leadership in the East. For fifty years, he had devoted his life to guarding the truth revealed in the Scriptures, and now "received release from his labours and passed away to the life which knows no toil."[30] The notables who continued his work were three men from the rocky and remote region of Asia Minor called Cappadocia (in Turkish, Kapadokya). Cappadocia's unique desert terrain served as a natural locus for monastic activity: its very soft yet mountainous rock formations could be easily carved into domiciles. Hence, it served as a perfect place for monks to fashion elaborate cave churches and monasteries out of whole mountains.

The remains of ancient cave churches and monasteries can be seen there even today, alongside whole communities who dwell in cliffs and caves hewed from the rock.

Uchisar Castle, Cappadocia, Turkey.

The most famous of the Cappadocians was Basil of Caesarea, also known as Basil the Great (ca. 329–379). Basil came from a faithful and wealthy family, and at an early age showed a remarkable aptitude for learning. He was eventually sent away to study at Athens, even then still the home of the great rhetoricians, where one of his classmates was Julian the Apostate. After school, where he amassed "all the learning attainable by the nature of man,"[31] Basil used his education to teach law and rhetoric until he had a spiritual awakening at the age of twenty-eight:

> Much time had I spent in vanity, and had wasted nearly all my youth in the vain labour which I underwent in acquiring the wisdom made foolish by God. Then once upon a time, like a man roused from deep sleep, I turned my eyes to the marvelous light of the truth of the Gospel, and I perceived the uselessness of the wisdom of the princes of this world, that come to naught. I wept many tears over my miserable life and I prayed that guidance might be vouchsafed me to admit me to the doctrines of true religion.[32]

After his conversion, Basil went to live with the monks around Alexandria, but realized that the solitary life, while worthy of honor, was not for him. Basil and his brother, Gregory of Nyssa, instead founded a monastic community on their family's property. Basil's monasticism, codified in the Rule of Saint Basil, emphasized a communal existence and care for the poor, like the Rule of Pachomius, often through networks of hospitals, soup kitchens, and shelters for the impoverished. Other church leaders recognized Basil's gifts for ministry; in 365, he was made a presbyter, and in 370, he was called to be a bishop of the very influential episcopate of Caesarea. Basil continued to preach to and pastor the congregations around Caesarea, conducting his affairs with a personal touch that was unusual for a bishop. His contemporary and friend Gregory Nazianzus said Basil was distinguished for "blending his correction with consideration and his gentleness with firmness."[33] One of his letters, to a woman who had committed sexual sin, contains a lengthy reproof, but ends with a tender assurance of heavenly pardon: "If you give yourself to Him He will not hold back. He, in His love, will not disdain even to carry you on His own shoulders, rejoicing that He has found His sheep which was lost."[34] In another letter, he gave encouragement to a soldier, a profession that, at the time, many deemed incompatible with Christianity: "I have learned to know one who proves that even in a soldier's life it is possible to preserve the perfection of love to God, and that we must mark a Christian not by the style of his dress, but by the

Icon painting of Basil the Great, Church of the Theotokos Peribleptos in Ohrid, Macedonia.

disposition of his soul."[35] Basil's gifts for writing and servant-hearted ministry made him famous in his own time: "his extreme addiction to the philosophic life and astonishing powers of eloquence attracted great celebrity."[36]

As gentle and fair-minded as he was in pastoring his flock, Basil was an equally uncompromising advocate for orthodoxy, whose fearless fervor gained the attention of several emperors. Basil is often credited with writing a letter from a group of Nicene bishops that circulated up to the emperor Julian, its contents a declaration that the pagans were "far from having attained right opinions of God." Julian snidely dismissed the bishops' efforts, writing of them, "I have read, I have understood, and I have condemned." The bishops sent the following reply to their rejection: "You have read, but you have not understood; for, had you understood, you would not have condemned."[37]

After Julian, Basil, and Valens dueled as titans of their respective sects. Valens once dispatched the local governor to persuade Basil to drop his theological quarrels or face exile. The prefect sweetened his proposition by saying that Basil's place in the emperor's good graces would confer on him and many others a great deal of privileges. But Basil was unmoved: "This sort of talk . . . is fitted for little boys, for they and their like easily swallow such inducements. But they who are nurtured by divine words will not suffer so much as a syllable of the divine creeds to be let go, and for their sake are ready, should need require, to embrace every kind of death."[38] Another time, when the prefect actually did threaten Basil with death, Basil responded, "Inflictions of this nature have never excited in my mind one pang of sorrow. I possess nothing but a cloak and a few books. I dwell on the earth as a traveler. The body through its weakness would have the better of all sensation and torture after the first blow."[39] Another famous story goes that Valens was about to exile Basil permanently, until his child fell ill and died. Valens attributed the death to God's vengeance against him for planning to expel Basil, and he decided against expulsion.[40]

Although he faced many threats of exile, Basil was never removed from his episcopate. In his writings, Basil wrote a lengthy treatise on the unity of the Father, Son, and Holy Spirit, and more than three hundred of his letters survive, giving us a detailed insight into the man and his time. For his contributions to monasticism, his care for the poor, and his contention for right theology, Basil is regarded as a saint in both the Western and Eastern churches, and holds a special title as one of four Doctors of the Eastern Church.

GREGORY OF NAZIANZUS

B asil's crucial co-laborer for years was Gregory of Nazianzus (Gregory Nazianzus), originally a schoolmate of Basil's who eventually became the bishop of Constantinople and was perhaps the greatest orator of the early church age. In Basil and Gregory's intimate friendship, we find one of history's great partnerships, albeit one that later unraveled, similar to the careers of John Adams and Thomas Jefferson. Gregory was aptly suited to be Basil's lifelong friend; he too possessed a sharp intellect and skill for oratory. Socrates Scholasticus wrote:

> If any one should compare Basil and Gregory with one another, and consider the life, morals, and virtues of each, he would find it difficult to decide to which of them he ought to assign the pre-eminence: so equally did they both appear to excel, whether you regard the rectitude of their conduct, or their deep acquaintance with Greek literature and the sacred Scriptures.[41]

After Gregory finished school at about the age of thirty, he briefly went into the monastic life with Basil, where they jointly worked on editing a volume of Origen's works. He contemplated becoming a lifelong monastic, as his friend Basil had decided to do, but this decision did not seem to accord with his education and his enthusiasm for studying and expositing the Scriptures, as well as his gift for oratory. Moreover, he was needed at home, where his aged father, the bishop of the small town of Nazianzus, was beset by a disunited church and accusations of heresy. At Basil's urging, Gregory returned home and was made a presbyter in 361. At some point in the 360s, Basil and Gregory joined forces in a series of debates against the Arians that the emperor Valens presided over himself. Which side had the upper hand was never in doubt; Socrates said that "whenever they [the Arians] attempted to enter into controversy with Gregory and Basil, they appeared in comparison with them ignorant and illiterate."[42]

Gregory became known as one of the greatest orators and theologians of the ancient church, and one of his most famous sermons is a lengthy exposition on the duties and concerns of a pastor. In one section, Gregory made it clear that anyone who leads others cannot himself be engrossed in sin:

> With these thoughts I am occupied night and day: they waste my marrow, and feed upon my flesh, and will not allow me to be confident or to look up. They depress my soul, and abase my mind, and fetter my tongue, and make me consider . . . how I myself am to escape the wrath to come, and to scrape off from myself somewhat of the rust of vice. A man must himself be cleansed, before cleansing others: himself become wise, that he may make others wise; become light, and then give light: draw near to God, and so bring others near; be hallowed, then hallow them; be possessed of hands to lead others by the hand, of wisdom to give advice.[43]

In 371, a rift suddenly opened between Basil and Gregory. After Basil was made a bishop, he now gained authority over Gregory, who, although a great orator, was still merely a presbyter. Basil appointed Gregory the bishop of a small town called Sasima, an outpost in the war against Arianism. This rankled Gregory, but he went anyway. He found the place unsuited to a man so learned as himself, and quit the town and returned to his hometown of Nazianzus. This caused a great rift between Basil and Gregory that was never fully healed; in fact, there are no recorded letters between the two men after Gregory's return to Sasima. Still, in 379, Gregory delivered Basil's funeral oration, a masterpiece of classical oratory, even if at times it fawns over its subject:

> One of his [Basil's] devices was of the greatest service. After a period of such recollection as was possible, and private spiritual conference, in which, after considering all human arguments, and penetrating into all the deep things of the Scriptures, he drew up a sketch of pious

doctrine, and by wrestling with and attacking their opposition he beat off the daring assaults of the heretics: overthrowing in hand to hand struggles by word of mouth those who came to close quarters, and striking those at a distance by arrows winged with ink.[44]

After the rupture with Basil, Gregory stayed in the desert, living quietly and contemplating the Scriptures. In time, Gregory was called to be the bishop of the Nicene community at Constantinople, a vastly different town from Sasima. It was then that he delivered most of his great orations; his chief subject was the defense of the unity of the Trinity. But age and his opponents wore him down, and in 381, a fight with the Arians loomed over whether his appointment as a bishop had broken canon law or not. This was too much for the aged Gregory, and in 383, he retreated to Nazianzus, where he served as bishop again before retiring to write some more. Gregory's fame as a theologian and orator gained him, like Basil, the title of one of the four Doctors of the Eastern Church.

GREGORY OF NYSSA

The third of the Cappadocian Fathers, and the younger brother of Basil the Great, was Gregory of Nyssa. Unlike Basil and Gregory Nazianzus, both of whom embraced monasticism and never married, Gregory of Nyssa was married with children, although he later did take up the contemplative life after his wife's death. The details of Gregory's life are fairly colorless, just as he would have wanted. Whereas his older brother Basil was brash and intense, Nyssa sought quietude and anonymity. Yet he still took up the fight against Arianism, and he became the leader of the Nicene opposition after Basil's death. Basil had also made Gregory the bishop of Nyssa, but this appointment was not without its difficulties, and in 376, the governor of his province seized him and accused him of embezzling church monies and rigging his own episcopal election. Gregory at first consented to be led away, but soon had a change of heart and fled from his captors. Now a fugitive, Gregory was forced to move from town to town until Valens's death in 378. When Basil died in 379, Gregory became the foremost defender of Nicene doctrine in works such as *Against Eunomius* and *On the Holy Spirit*. He would also figure prominently in the Council of Constantinople in 381, as we will see in the next chapter.

THE DEATH OF VALENS

After twelve years of imperial power, Valens's rule abruptly came to an end in AD 378 at the battle of Adrianople, one of the great military disasters of all time. Valens was jealous of his nephew's recent victory over barbarians in Gaul and wanted an equal honor for himself. He marched east from Antioch to Adrianople (now Edirne in Turkey, not far from the Bulgarian border) to meet a Gothic army, which vastly outnumbered his own. As he passed by Constantinople, a monk from the city named Isaac prophetically shouted at him:

> Where are you going, O emperor? To fight against God, instead of having Him as your ally? 'Tis God himself who has roused the barbarians against you, because you have stirred many tongues to blasphemy against Him and hast driven His worshippers from their sacred abodes. Cease then your campaigning and stop the war. Give back to the flocks their excellent shepherds and you shall win victory without trouble, but if you fight without so doing you shall learn by experience how hard it is to kick against the pricks. You shall never come back and shall destroy your army.[45]

Valens responded:

> I shall come back; and I will kill you, and so exact punishment for your lying prophecy.[46]

As Isaac predicted, Valens's offensive turned out to be a deadly act of hubris. On an excruciatingly hot day, his men stayed in the field for hours, unsuccessfully fighting off the Goths. In the end, Valens either died on the battlefield or was burned alive inside a farmhouse in which he was hiding (the historical accounts differ). In some ways, Isaac's harangue encapsulated all the frustration of the past thirty years. A succession of emperors who were either unorthodox or unchristian harassed the Nicene church to the point of spilt blood. As a new emperor, Theodosius, took the throne, it remained to be seen how much honor he would give to the church's petitions for security and peace. It would take Gregory of Nyssa and a hard-nosed bishop from Milan to find out.

TEN

Doctors' Orders

Theodosius, the Council of Constantinople,
Ambrose, Jerome, Damasus, the Vulgate

Valens's death in 378 signified that the Roman Empire was certainly in its hour of twilight. The defeat at Adrianople was a debacle, and from this point onward barbarian invasions overwhelmed the great realm: groups from Northern and Eastern Europe like the Avars, Goths, Huns, Persians, and Vandals began to nibble and chomp away at the frontiers of the empire. By 406, the great scholar Jerome wrote with sorrow:

Who could believe that Rome, built upon the conquest of the whole world, would fall to the ground? That the mother herself would become the tomb of her peoples? That all the regions of the East, of Africa and Egypt, once ruled by the queenly city, would be filled with troops of slaves and handmaidens? That to-day holy Bethlehem should shelter men and women of noble birth, who once abounded in wealth and are now beggars?[1]

But although the storms of invasion were making landfall ever closer to Rome, for most of the fourth century, the Western church had experienced a great deal of peace. This was a situation very different from the

East, mostly because Arianism was generally an Eastern phenomenon. "The west," wrote Theodoret, "had escaped the taint." Even though they had been at odds with one another, the lineage of Constantine in the West had "kept the true religion undefiled."[2] The West experienced a succession of Nicene emperors, such as Constantine II, Constans, and Valentinian II, and then Gratian, who became co-emperor from 367 to 383. Gratian reacted to his uncle Valens's cruel policy toward the Nicene church by recalling many exiled bishops home and declaring that heretical sects, such as the Eunomians, the Photinians, and the Manichaeans, should be excluded from the churches.

A portrait of the emperor Theodosius, from a German book, 1836.

Gratian, however, was far more preoccupied with the barbarian onslaught than being a mediator in church disputes, and "perceiving that the state was in need of a brave and prudent man," put a general named Theodosius in charge of the Eastern empire.[3] Theodosius, like Gratian, was primarily concerned with beating back the barbarian invasions, a task at which he was generally unsuccessful. But his influence over the church was enormous, and as one who embraced Nicene doctrine, he was eager to drive away the Arian darkness that had overtaken much of the Eastern church.

The Edict of Thessalonica

Beginning in 380, the emperor Theodosius, with the blessing of his co-emperors, Gratian and Valentinian II, took a number of major steps that put Nicene Christianity back on the offensive. The most major of these was his Edict of Thessalonica, as the decree came to be known, which commanded all subjects of the Roman Empire to profess the Nicene faith of the bishops of Rome and Alexandria:

We desire all people, whom the divine influence of our clemency rules, to turn to the religion which from Peter to the present day declares to have been delivered to the Romans by blessed Peter the Apostle, the religion which it is clear that the Pontiff Damasus and Peter, the bishop of Alexandria, a man of apostolic holiness, follow; this faith is that we should believe that there is one Godhead, Father, Son and Holy Spirit, in an equal Majesty and a holy Trinity. We order those who follow this doctrine to receive the title of Catholic Christians, but others we judge to be mad and raving and worthy of incurring the disgrace of heretical teaching, nor are their assemblies to receive the name of churches. They are to be punished not only by divine retribution but also by our own measures, which we have decided in accordance with divine inspiration.[4]

A reading of the edict reveals several major developments. First, it stipulated that only those who followed the theology of the bishop of Rome could rightly be called Catholic Christians. Hence, we have the most definitive evidence for the emergence of the term *Catholic* as referring to that kind of Christianity practiced by the bishop of Rome and his followers. Secondly, it reaffirmed the bishop of Rome as the guardian of the apostolic doctrine. It is here most definitively that we see the bishop of Rome becoming the pope. The issuance of the edict is a critical historical moment from which emerges much of the theology regarding the primacy of the Roman bishop above all others.

The Edict of Thessalonica was quickly published at Constantinople. But the Arians still controlled the churches there, and would not go down without a fight. They recruited an Arian bishop named Eunomius to approach Theodosius to try and win him to the Arian side, as they had done with Constantius and Valens. "These machinations," wrote Sozomen, "excited great anxiety and fear among the members of the Catholic Church." But the empress Flacilla, "the most faithful guard of the Nicene doctrines," was alert to the Arian schemes, and prevented Eunomius from going near her husband. Instead, a number of Nicene bishops from around the city came to pay respects to the emperor. Accompanying the delegation was an aged priest, "simple and unworldly, yet well instructed in Divine subjects." All of the bishops greeted Theodosius and his son, the prince, with careful reverence. When the old priest greeted the prince with an embrace, calling him his child, Theodosius flew into a rage, saying that the priest had acted dishonorably, with too much casualness, and ought to be ejected from his presence by force. As the priest was being dragged off, he turned and shouted at Theodosius, "Reflect, O emperor, on the wrath of the Heavenly Father against those who do not honor His Son as Himself, and who have the audacity to assert that the Son is inferior to the Father."[5]

Theodosius was struck by the priest's cunning example; he intended to show that God would similarly dismiss Theodosius at the last judgment if he abandoned the Nicene precepts. Theodosius apologized and confessed that the priest had spoken the truth, and from that point on was "less disposed to hold intercourse with heretics."[6] Later that same year, Theodosius expelled the Arian bishop Demophilus and installed Gregory of Nazianzus, the great defender of orthodoxy, as bishop at Constantinople. At first, Gregory had to fight off a coup from a rival archbishop named Maximus, who had once been a friend. But after being reaffirmed in his election by Theodosius and Pope Damasus I in the West, Gregory called together the Council of Constantinople in 381, an event that he hoped would help put an end to the violence of the past generation.

THE COUNCIL OF CONSTANTINOPLE

At Constantinople, Gregory gathered about 150 of the Eastern bishops together and begged them to put an end to the madness that had consumed the church over the past forty years: "I shall be released from many cares and once more lead the quiet life I hold so dear; while you, after your long and painful warfare, will obtain the longed for peace."[7] To attain that peace, Gregory knew that he had to sacrifice his own position as bishop. Gregory was deeply unpopular with many of the Arians, and he knew his episcopacy would be an impediment to the first great attempt at reconciliation in a generation. In the capstone oration of his career, he begged to be released from his duties as a bishop and quit the chaotic city, the politics of which he was ill suited to engage in: "But behold, I pray you, the condition of this body, so drained by time, by disease, by toil. What need have you of a timid and unmanly old man, who is, so to speak, dying day by day, not only in body, but even in powers of mind, who finds it difficult to enter into these details before you?"[8]

Theodosius and the bishops relented and granted the old man his wish. In his place, Theodosius elected a surprise choice, an obscure bishop originally from Tarsus named Nectarius. However unlikely Nectarius's appointment was, he proved to execute faithfully the design that Theodosius and Gregory had intended for the council: "Nectarius and the other priests assembled together, and decreed that the faith established by the council of Nicæa should remain dominant, and that all heresies should be condemned."[9] The bishops also decreed that "the bishop of Constantinople should have the next prerogative of honor after the bishop of Rome, because that city was New Rome."[10] Although Damasus and the other bishops in the West initially rejected the election of Nectarius, eventually they relented. As had been the case at Nicaea, the orthodox bishops of the empire once again presented a united front in the battle against Arianism and issued the Creed of Constantinople, a statement very similar to the Nicene Creed.

Theodosius presides over the Council of Constantinople, wall painting at the church of Stavropoleos, Bucharest, Romania.

THEODOSIUS CAMPAIGNS AGAINST ARIANISM

Theodosius's campaign to stamp out Arianism did not end with a mere written statement. Like Constantine, Constantius, and Valens before him, he went to great lengths to enforce his ideas of right religion. One of his ideas was to order all the dissenting sects to produce their own creeds, which Theodosius and his team of theologians would review. Copies of those creeds that denied the complete union of the Trinity were burned. Theodosius went even further, enacting laws that forbade heretics from holding church services, offering public instruction in their teaching, and consecrating bishops. Some aligned with the heterodox sects lost civic rights, or were thrown out of their cities. But many of Theodosius's orders were never enforced with punishment. As the historian Sozomen said rather coldly, "they were not always carried into execution, for the emperor had no desire to persecute his subjects; he only desired to enforce uniformity of view about God through the medium of intimidation."[11]

But Theodosius did doubtlessly undertake harsh punitive measures against heretical groups like the Arians, Eunomians, and Macedonians, as well as pagans. His chief tactic was the closing and eventual demolishing of pagan temples. In 391, Theodosius allowed the bishop Theophilus of Alexandria to "expose the pagan mysteries to contempt."[12] Theophilus, with the aid of imperial troops, demolished temples around the city, melting golden pagan idols down into pots and other utensils for use in the Alexandrian church. In the razing of a famous temple of the god Serapis, the Christians discovered ancient hieroglyphics in the shape of crosses. The Serapians and Christians rushed to claim the signs for their own, and many pagans converted as a result of seeing these crosses inscribed at their own place of worship. The Serapian priests also claimed that anyone who approached the statue of Serapis would cause a great earthquake. Theophilus considered these tales as "drivelling of tipsy old women," and ordered a man standing by with an axe to give it a healthy blow:

> No sooner had the man struck, than all the folk cried out, for they were afraid of the threatened catastrophe. Serapis however, who had received the blow, felt no pain, inasmuch as he was made of wood, and uttered never a word, since he was a lifeless block. His head was cut off, and forthwith out ran multitudes of mice, for the Egyptian god was a dwelling place for mice. Serapis was broken into small pieces of which some were committed to the flames, but his head was carried through all the town in sight of his worshippers, who mocked the weakness of him to whom they had bowed the knee.[13]

As time went on, Theodosius became progressively fiercer in stamping out paganism and heresies. He prohibited public sacrifices and augury, making confiscation of property the punishment for such offenses. Many famous temples around the empire, including the Altar of Victory and the Temple of the Vestal Virgins at Rome, and the oracle of Delphi in Greece, were closed or torn down. There is good reason to believe that Theodosius was also responsible in 393 for putting an end to the Olympic Games, an event that would not be revived again until 1896. Although he was a Christian, Theodosius's use of violence in enforcing his will sometimes went too far, as we will see in his often tempestuous relationship with Ambrose, the great bishop of Milan.

AMBROSE

The greatest churchman of the fourth century in the West was Ambrose of Milan. Ambrose came from a Christian family and originally practiced law. Ambrose gained a reputation for being fairminded and highly competent, and he rose to become the governor of the province of Liguria and Aemelia, the seat of which was Milan, in northern Italy. Shortly after arriving there, in 374, the local bishop, Auxentius, an Arian, died. The question of succession was one of such importance that the citizenry began to riot; both orthodox and Arian insisted on one of their own taking the episcopate.[14] Ambrose rushed to the scene and tried to calm the mob through his gift of oratory. As he was speaking, the voice of a small child cried out, "Ambrose, bishop!" Members of the crowd, seeing that Ambrose was a better alternative than the choice of the opposing side, also started chanting, "Ambrose, bishop, Ambrose, bishop!"[15]

At first Ambrose protested and tried to flee the city. But he eventually relented and was made bishop within eight days. Ambrose, still not yet baptized, embarked on a strenuous course of studying the Scriptures, and his powerful mind proved more than capable for the task. A later theologian (the great Saint Augustine) who once saw Ambrose reading marveled that he could read silently to himself (in ancient times, the custom, even for private reading, was to verbalize the words on the page as one read).[16] Ambrose, like Gregory Nazianzus, produced a hefty corpus of writings filled with references to classical authors. His work on pastoral ministry, *On the Duties of the Clergy*, directly imitates Cicero's *On Duties*. But even Ambrose recognized that the Christian's life was to be very different from the ancient philosopher's. In the *Republic*, Socrates suggested (but ultimately rejected) that harming one who has harmed you could be an exercise in justice. Not so, said Ambrose:

A late antique mosaic of Ambrose in the church of St. Ambrogio in Milan.

> But that very thing is excluded with us which philosophers think to be the office of justice. For they say that the first expression of justice is, to hurt no one, except when driven to it by wrongs received. This is put aside by the authority of the Gospel. For the Scripture wills that

the Spirit of the Son of Man should be in us, Who came to give grace, not to bring harm.[17]

Like Basil the Great, Ambrose was also fervently devoted to material provision for the poor. When refugees from a barbarian attack streamed into Milan, Ambrose felt compelled to care for them. Lacking funds, he procured some by melting down some of his church's golden ornaments. For this he came under criticism, especially from the Arians. But he replied, "It is better to preserve for the Lord souls rather than gold. He who sent the apostles without gold also gathered the churches without gold. The church has gold, not to store it, but to give it up, to use it for those who are in need . . . It is better to keep the living vessels, than the golden ones."[18]Ambrose was also one of the first to venerate Mary the mother of Jesus as an example of female virtue, and in particular, chastity:

> What is greater than the Mother of God? What more glorious than she whom Glory Itself chose? What more chaste than she who bore a body without contact with another body? For why should I speak of her other virtues? She was a virgin not only in body but also in mind, who stained the sincerity of its disposition by no guile, who was humble in heart, grave in speech, prudent in mind, sparing of words, studious in reading, resting her hope not on uncertain riches, but on the prayer of the poor, intent on work, modest in discourse; wont to seek not man but God as the judge of her thoughts, to injure no one, to have goodwill towards all, to rise up before her elders, not to envy her equals, to avoid boastfulness, to follow reason, to love virtue.[19]

Although certainly not the first churchman to compose hymns, Ambrose has also commonly been referred to as "the father of Western hymnody" for introducing into Latin (the language of the West) an array of musical techniques. As one of a shrinking number of men in the West who could read Greek, Ambrose imported many Greek musical ideas, such as the antiphonal chant, in which parts of a chorus alternate in singing different parts of a hymn. Ever a bishop attuned to the people, Ambrose was the first to use the tool of rhyme, and he incorporated rhythms from Roman soldiers' marches into Latin hymns so that people could easily learn about trinitarian theology in a time of great theological confusion. Note the second stanza of his hymn *Veni Redemptor Gentium* (a title itself that features three consecutive rhyming short *e* sounds):[20]

> *Begotten of no human will*
> *but of the Spirit, Thou art still*
> *the Word of God in flesh arrayed,*
> *the promised fruit to man displayed.*[21]

Although Ambrose's hymns are unpolished, by the standards of the Middle Ages, the musical innovations, popular styles, and rich theology he injected into them helped lay the foundation for centuries of Western hymnody.

AMBROSE AND THE ARIANS

Judging from the content of his hymns, Ambrose too looked with concern on the spread of Arianism, and resolved to stamp it out. He had an ally in the emperor Gratian. In 381 (the same year, coincidentally, as the Council of Constantinople), two Arian bishops, believing that they had a superior number of sympathetic bishops, asked Gratian to hold a council on the trinitarian question. Although the West was generally unaffected by the scourge of Arianism, the district around Milan was an exception. Gratian obliged the bishops, and the council was held at the Italian town of Aquileia. Thirty-two bishops participated in the Council of Aquileia, and Ambrose presided over the whole council. Preserved in Ambrose's correspondence is a transcript of the council, including his inquest of Palladius, an Arian bishop:

Palladius said; "I speak to you according to the Scriptures: I call the Lord the very Son of God."

Ambrose, Bishop, said; "Do you call the Son of God very Lord?"

Palladius said; "When I call Him very Son, what more is wanted?"

Ambrose, Bishop, said; "I do not ask only that you should call Him very Son, but that you should call the Son of God very Lord."[22]

Ambrose and the other bishops proved able enough inquisitors that two bishops who supported Arianism were excommunicated. But that wouldn't be the end of Ambrose's fights with heresy. Around 385, Ambrose made a very powerful enemy in the empress Justina, the mother of the emperor Valentinian, who had recently adopted Arianism. Justina demanded two churches for the Arian population to worship in, a request that Ambrose of course refused. In defiance, Justina offered honors and offices to anyone who would kidnap Ambrose from his church and force him into exile. One man, a certain Euthymius, took up her offer and rented a house next door to the church. Euthymius concealed a wagon in the backyard, in order to expedite the deed if he ever got the chance to snatch Ambrose up. But he was found out and was sent into exile (whether by Ambrose or the emperor is not clear). Even in the midst of this, Ambrose was gracious and gave Euthymius enough money to live on. But even this did not allay Justina's anger, and she managed to persuade Valentinian, her son, that Ambrose had insulted her. Valentinian angrily sent a detachment of soldiers to arrest Ambrose in his own church, but Ambrose "treated them all like the ghosts and hobgoblins with which some men try to frighten babies."[23] When they tried to lead Ambrose away by force, his congregation surrounded the soldiers and said they would have to kill them if they wanted to take Ambrose. Ambrose too said he would rather die than be taken alive:

If you demand my person, I am ready to submit: carry me to prison or to death, I will not resist; but I will never betray the church of Christ. I will not call upon the people to succour me; I will die at the foot of the altar rather than desert it. The tumult of the people I will not encourage: but God alone can appease it.[24]

Only then did the soldiers relent, and instead of hauling off Ambrose, they barricaded everyone inside. They didn't seem to mind too much; they passed the time singing hymns (probably composed by Ambrose himself) and holding prayer vigils. Ambrose had played a very dangerous and significant gambit, but eventually the emperor backed down. In contrast to the church's subordinate position during the reign of Constantine, Constantius, and Valens, Ambrose's resistance to Valentinian was a confident assertion of the church's role in the world. Said Ambrose, "The emperor indeed is within the church, not above the church."[25] Ambrose would demonstrate this philosophy in his relationship with Theodosius.

AMBROSE AND THEODOSIUS

Theodosius's rule carried over from the 380s into the 390s. He claimed to be a Christian, but he was also very much an emperor, and he exercised his prerogative of imperial power accordingly. In 390, the local population of a town in Greece revolted against a detachment of Gothic mercenaries stationed there. In the violence, the commander of the Gothic force was killed. When Theodosius heard the news, he was furious, and he "allowed his rage to be the minister of his vengeance."[26] As retribution, Theodosius ordered that the town be punished and dispatched military units to carry out the sentence. Civilians were imprisoned, and many were indiscriminately killed without trial. The number slain totaled about seven thousand: "like ears of grain in harvest-tide."[27]

Theodosius spent the next few years putting down civil wars and usurpations. In 392, having finally placated all rebellion and unified the empire (for the last time, it turns out), Theodosius went to Milan to pray. Ambrose ran out to meet him as he approached the church. But he did not deliver the welcome that Theodosius wanted. Ambrose stood at the doors of the church and would not let Theodosius enter. He grabbed his purple robe, and in the presence of his congregation said, "Stand back! A man defiled by sin, and with hands imbrued in blood unjustly shed, is not worthy, without repentance, to enter within these sacred precincts, or partake of the holy mysteries."[28] Ambrose condemned Theodosius as an unrepentant sinner for his ordering of the massacre in Greece, and prevented him from taking the Lord's Supper with God's people. What this amounted to was excommunication: "How in such hands will you receive the all holy Body of the Lord?" he told Theodosius. "How will you who in your rage unrighteously poured forth so much blood lift to your lips the precious Blood? Begone."[29] Theodosius, somewhat surprisingly, accepted Ambrose's condemnation and retired to his palace, "sighing and weeping." For eight months, Theodosius languished at Constantinople, and as Christmas came, was still "shedding a storm of tears."[30] Ambrose defended himself in a letter to the emperor, saying that his duty as a minister of God necessitated such a hard stance:

> What, then, could I do? Should I not hear? But I could not close my ears with the wax of the old fables. Should I utter what I heard? But I was bound to be on my guard in my words against that which I feared in your commands, namely, lest some deed of blood should be committed. Should I keep silence? But then my conscience would be bound, my utterance taken away, which would be the most wretched condition of all.[31]

As time dragged on, Theodosius's chief adviser, Rufinus, suggested that he could go to Ambrose to petition him for readmission to the church on Theodosius's behalf. "He will not yield," said the emperor. "I know the justice of the sentence passed by Ambrose, nor will he ever be moved by respect for my imperial power to transgress the law of God." Rufinus's pleas did not persuade Ambrose either. Finally, Theodosius realized he must go to Milan himself and face Ambrose's wrath if he wanted to be restored to the church. "I will go," he said, "and accept the disgrace I deserve."[32]

Theodosius made the trip to Milan and approached Ambrose in his cathedral. Predictably, Ambrose was not exactly pleased to see him. "Your coming," said Ambrose, "is the coming of a tyrant. You are raging against God; you are trampling on his laws."

"No," said Theodosius, "I do not attack laws laid down, I do not seek wrongfully to cross the sacred threshold; but I ask you to loose my bond, to take into account the mercy of our common Lord, and not to shut against me a door which our master has opened for all them that repent."

The bishop replied, "What repentance have you shown since your tremendous crime? You have inflicted wounds right hard to heal; what salve have you applied?"

Ambrose stops Theodosius, painting in the church of St. Ambrogio in Milan.

"Yours is the duty alike of pointing out and of mixing the salve," said Theodosius. "It is for me to receive what is given me."[33]

Ambrose ordered that any outstanding death sentences decreed by Theodosius be stayed for thirty days, and then examined them to see if they were issued according to his passion or his reason. Ambrose also told him that he was no longer to sit with the priests during mass (his longstanding custom), but with the rest of the congregation. Ambrose must have also observed Theodosius's obvious grief over his sin, an indication of genuine repentance. Theodosius agreed to Ambrose's terms, and entered the church to pray and perform penance. He lay prostrate on the ground, weeping and striking his own head and plucking out his hair. Soon after, he went to the altar of the church and placed an offering on it. His restoration was complete, and he returned to Constantinople. Later he reflected: "It is not easy to find a man capable of teaching me the truth. Ambrosius alone deserves the title of bishop."[34]

The relationship between Ambrose and Theodosius remained one of mutual respect. Ambrose genuinely honored the emperor and had a personal affection for him, while Theodosius submitted to Ambrose's pastoring. Ambrose delivered a moving funeral oration for Theodosius in 395, and on Easter day 397, expired himself, a long career of tough and faithful ministry behind him. Today Ambrose is recognized as one of the four Doctors of the Western church, along with one of his contemporaries, Jerome.

JEROME

Jerome was born in modern-day Slovenia. As a young man, he was shipped off to Rome to begin his training as a scholar, a vocation in which he diligently engaged for the entirety of his life. But, although professing himself a Christian, Jerome also gave himself to days and nights of drinking and debauchery. To appease his conscience, he would visit the Catacombs, the underground network of crypts in which ancient Roman Christians were buried. In time, Jerome put off his sinful impulses for good and headed out for the desert to become a monk. But he was unwilling to leave behind his carefully cultivated collection of Greek and Roman authors, and did not appropriately esteem the value of the Bible, calling the style of the prophets "rude and repellent." As a consequence, he wrote, "The old serpent was thus making me his plaything."[35] On the way to Jerusalem, he fell ill with a fever, and in a bout of sleep (or delirium), he received a vision of Christ, who rebuked him for loving classical literature: "Thou liest, you are a follower of Cicero and not of Christ!" Jerome also experienced a psychosomatic experience of being scourged and cried out, "Have mercy upon me, O Lord: have mercy upon me."[36] Jerome resolved to make studying the Bible his priority. When he finally reached his destination and took up the monastic lifestyle, he felt tormented day and night in his inability to forget the sexual passions in which he had indulged as a young man:

> How often, when I was living in the desert, in the vast solitude which gives to hermits a savage dwelling-place, parched by a burning sun, how often did I fancy myself among the pleasures of Rome! I used to sit alone because I was filled with bitterness. Sackcloth disfigured my unshapely limbs and my skin from long neglect had become as black as an Ethiopian's. Tears and groans were every day my portion; and if drowsiness chanced to overcome my struggles against it, my bare bones, which hardly held together, clashed against the ground. Of my food and drink I say nothing: for, even in sickness, the solitaries have nothing but cold water, and to eat one's food cooked is looked upon as self-indulgence. Now, although in my fear of hell I had consigned myself to this prison, where I had no companions but scorpions and wild beasts, I often found myself amid bevies of girls. My face was pale and my frame chilled with fasting; yet my mind was burning with desire, and the fires of lust kept bubbling up before me when my flesh was as good as dead. Helpless, I cast myself at the feet of Jesus, I watered them with my tears, I wiped them with my hair: and then I subdued my rebellious body with weeks of abstinence.[37]

Jerome eventually managed to get control of himself, and set to intense study of Scripture that would not stop until he was in the grave. In the process, he became the most prolific scholar of the Bible since Origen (though his contemporary Augustine was the superior theologian). In the desert, Jerome learned Hebrew from a converted Jew in order to better understand the Old Testament, and began copying theological commentaries and writing some of his own works: a life of Paul the Hermit and a translation of Eusebius of Caesarea's massive work on church history. Jerome later examined Origen's works, and while he found some good points of biblical exegesis, found that some of his interpretations were much too unorthodox to be correct:

He has erred concerning the resurrection of the body, he has erred concerning the condition of souls, he has erred by supposing it possible that the devil may repent, and—an error more important than these—he has declared in his commentary upon Isaiah that the Seraphim mentioned by the prophet are the divine Son and the Holy Ghost.[38]

JEROME AND DAMASUS I

In 379, Jerome went to Constantinople to study Scripture with Gregory Nazianzus and then, in 382, came back to Rome, where he formed a relationship with Pope Damasus I, recently affirmed in Theodosius's edict as the true guardian of the faith. Damasus had been the bishop of Rome since 366, a position he had acceded to under a great deal of controversy. When Liberius died, Damasus stood for election to the office, but so did Ursinus, a rival claimant to the Holy See who may have been an Arian. The clash between supporters of the two factions was bloody: more than one hundred people died over the course of three days.[39] Ursinus and his followers were exiled by the emperor to northern Italy, and for at least ten years afterward, Damasus consistently resisted enemy efforts to remove him.

Feeling empowered by Theodosius's decrees, Damasus, who may be rightly called a pope, acted swiftly to solidify control over the church. He was the first to habitually refer to Rome as the "Apostolic See."[40] Latin, still the common language of the West, was made the liturgical language of the Western church. He commissioned a restoration of the Christian crypts throughout Rome known as the catacombs. Damasus was also active in keeping the Arian menace at bay. In 369, he excommunicated the Arian bishop Auxentius of Milan,[41] and he wrote to the Eastern bishops at Constantinople in 381, "If any one speaks of Christ as having had less of manhood or of Godhead, he is full of devils' spirits, and proclaims himself a child of hell."[42]

THE VULGATE BIBLE

D amasus also chose Jerome as his personal secretary, and the two men developed a long-standing friendship. Jerome's correspondence shows the growth of the belief in the West that the bishop of Rome really was the vicar of Christ on earth: "My words are spoken to the successor of the fisherman [Peter], to the disciple of the cross. As I follow no leader save Christ, so I communicate with none but your blessedness, that is with the chair of Peter. For this, I know, is the rock on which the church is built!"[43]

Damasus no doubt noticed Jerome's scholarly gifts and assigned him one of the most monumental tasks in church history: a comprehensive translation of the Hebrew Old Testament and the Greek New Testament into a new Latin translation of the entire Bible. The Bible had been, of course, translated into Latin (the Old Latin version) over time, but this had been a piecemeal effort down the centuries, using various manuscripts, some of them riddled with copyists' errors. The Latin in these Old Latin translations was also very colloquial and did not adhere to classical standards of style. Additionally, the Latin Old Testament had been translated from the Greek translation of the Hebrew Old Testament (in scholarly terms, the Septuagint). The better route was to translate directly from the Hebrew into Latin, and Jerome, because of his comprehensive understanding of Scripture and Hebrew, was the man for the task. By the Middle Ages, Jerome's new edition had become so widespread that it became known as the *versio vulgata*, or "Vulgate," from the Latin word meaning "common, popular."

Jerome was keenly aware of the difficulty of his undertaking. For one thing, he knew his translations couldn't please everyone. He wrote to Damasus expressing his concerns: "Is there indeed any learned or unlearned man, who when he picks up the volume in his hand, and takes a single taste of it, and sees what he will have read to differ, might not instantly raise his voice, calling me a forger, proclaiming me now to be a sacrilegious man, that I might dare to add, to change, or to correct anything in the old books?"[44]

Jerome first tackled a new translation of the four Gospels, which he managed to complete before Damasus's death in 384. The pope's death meant Jerome had lost the greatest patron of his work. In the absence of his friend and benefactor, Jerome's enemies, many of them secularists who managed to obtain clerical positions, confronted him over the nature of his relationships with a number of women at Rome. The most

important of these was his friendship with Paula, a wealthy widow who financed a great deal of his scholarship and later built a monastery for men and women in Palestine. Jerome became to her a lifelong platonic companion and spiritual guide. Jerome also managed to become a friend to Paula's daughter, a young girl, just twenty, named Blaesilla, who upon her conversion adopted an ascetic lifestyle so severe that she died within just three months of becoming a Christian. Jerome wrote a letter to Paula, comforting her, but

St. Jerome in his study.

the same missive also included some admonitions that Paula was improperly steeped in grief ("I am the more surprised, therefore, that you should act in a manner which in others would justly call for reprehension").[45] Such an attitude, combined with allegations of (unproven) sexual dalliances with Paula, stirred up many of his fellow Romans against him, and in 384, they called for him to leave the city. Jerome obliged them. After a tour of the monasteries of the East, Jerome eventually settled at Bethlehem in 386, where he would spend the rest of his life.

Having relocated, with Paula, to the East, Jerome next moved to translating or substantially revising from old sources the remainder of the New Testament, most of which he finished by 390, followed by a period of fifteen years devoted to producing a new version of the Old Testament, all thirty-nine books of which he translated directly from the Hebrew. He faced resistance from many scholars for his decision to translate from the Hebrew rather than the Septuagint. In their view, the Septuagint was itself directly inspired, and a new translation was unnecessary. Many Christians at the time also wanted to distance the church from its Jewish roots, something a translation from the Hebrew would not do. Lastly, argued Augustine, translating from the Hebrew rather than Greek would offend the Greek-speaking Eastern church, which had a much higher degree of reverence for the Septuagint than the West did. For proof, Augustine told Jerome about a bishop in Libya who used Jerome's new translation of the book of Jonah in his church and experienced a congregational riot because the lesson was so unfamiliar.[46]

Also complicating Jerome's efforts were questions, still of great concern to modern Bible translators, of how literal or idiomatic his translation should be. Jerome, drawing on Cicero, believed that the general best course of action was to translate literally (especially in the case of the Bible), while retaining the essence of the text's style. He addressed the paradox in the preface to his translation of Eusebius's *Church History*: "A literal translation sounds absurd; if, on the other hand, I am obliged to change either the order or the words themselves, I shall appear to have forsaken the duty of a translator."[47] Jerome had to invent new words in Latin to express theological terms that older editions of the Latin Bible had inadequately addressed or had no terms for: for instance, *coheres* (coheirs), *concorporalis* (belonging to the same body), and *conelectus* (chosen).[48] Consequently, the Vulgate as a whole displays a style that alternates between idiomatic and literal renderings of Greek and Hebrew passages.

Lastly, Jerome was confronted by the question of which books to include in the canon of Scripture. The Jewish rabbis of Palestine did not regard books in the Septuagint, such as Wisdom, Ecclesiasticus (Sirach), Tobit, Judith, Baruch, and 1 and 2 Maccabees, as truly inspired

Scripture, and Jerome, a conservative scholar, did not translate them. At the Catholic Church's Council of Trent in the 1500s, the church affirmed the inclusion of these books in their canon, probably in response to the Protestant Reformers' acceptance of Jerome's limited canon. In looking back to the Vulgate, the Council of Trent affirmed that Jerome's work was still the preferred:

> But if any one receive not, as sacred and canonical, the said books entire with all their parts, as they have been used to be read in the Catholic Church, and as they are contained in the old Latin vulgate edition; and knowingly and deliberately contemn the traditions afore-said; let him be anathema.[49]

In any case, the Vulgate Bible and subsequent revisions to it became the standard version of the Bible before the emergence of new vernacular translations in the 1500s, and it very often served as the source material for those translations. Jerome would later be distinguished as a Doctor of the Church for his huge influence on the Bible and biblical scholarship. For this reason, he is the patron saint of librarians, translators, and encyclopedists.

For the final fifteen or so years of his life, Jerome wrote voluminous commentaries on Scripture and kept up an active personal correspondence. But he was also a guardian of doctrine, and he positioned himself in opposition to a new teaching that was largely seen as heretical: Pelagianism.

Pelagius was a British-born theologian who came to Rome sometime in the late fourth century. As Pelagius looked around the church, he saw rampant immorality, and he decided that an overreliance on God's grace was to blame for this kind of wantonness. Pelagius developed a theology that denied the existence of man's inborn sinful nature. He believed that man was able to perform good works apart from God's grace; willpower was enough to avoid being tainted by sin. Jerome recoiled at this teaching, since he, and every other orthodox teacher, believed that sin was an unquestionable aspect of human existence. In the preface to his commentary on Jeremiah, Jerome denigrated Pelagius as a Scot whose brain was addled because he was "stuffed with Scottish porridge."[50] The battle against the Pelagians raged just as Jerome died in 420. But it would be continued by the greatest theologian of the ancient church, Augustine.

ELEVEN

TWO GIANTS

John Chrysostom and Saint Augustine

Above the main entrance to the Basilica of the Shrine of the Immaculate Conception at the Catholic University of America in Washington, DC, stand engraved portraits of two churchmen, one Eastern, one Western. It should not be surprising that John Chrysostom and Augustine of Hippo were chosen to have two of the most visible places on one of the most prominent church buildings in the country. At the dawn of the fifth century, both men were pillars of orthodoxy and prolific writers, the best the church could boast at that time. Both were bishops, but their influence pervaded areas far beyond their dioceses. And each man served in his own ways as a spiritual bridge from the crumbling ancient world into the emerging medieval one.

The beginning of the fifth century was very different from the beginning of the fourth. Instead of the church weathering Diocletian's state-sponsored persecutions, it was now the dominant social organization of the age; the emperors Honorius and Arcadius, following their father, Theodosius, also claimed to be Christians. The contentions over Christ's divine nature that consumed Constantine and his successors had (for a time) mostly dried up after Theodosius's campaign against

199

Arianism. Many Arians, wrote the historian Sozomen, "in reflecting upon the diversity of sentiments which prevailed among those of their own persuasion, judged that the truth of God could not be present with them, and went over to those who held the same faith as the emperors."[1] But, as in every age, the church was not without problems. In the West, the church had to adapt to a new role amid the disintegrating Roman Empire. And in the East, the leaders had to contend with churches full of tepid, selfish, wrongly ambitious believers. Nobody took up the task with more enthusiasm than John Chrysostom.

JOHN CHRYSOSTOM

The greatest heir to the tradition of orthodox leadership established by Basil and Gregory was the greatest preacher of the age and the bishop of Constantinople, John Chrysostom. The name Chrysostom means "golden-mouthed," quite an honorific. But John was not uniformly praised in his own lifetime. In fact, he made many enemies by speaking truth to the wealthy and powerful.

John was born in Antioch, Syria, in 347, and was baptized as a Christian around 367. Like Basil and Gregory, he was naturally eloquent. He studied with a famous pagan orator of the day named Libanius. When Libanius was on his deathbed, he was asked who should head his academy after him. "It would have been John," he replied, "had not the Christians taken him from us."[2]

John began his career as a presbyter around Antioch, and he quickly distinguished himself as a brilliant orator; in his congregations he "excited to the love of virtue,"[3] and they found "sweet refreshment from the bitterness of life" at his tender pastoral hand.[4] One time the population of Antioch went on a destructive spree and defaced in that city a number of statues of the emperor Theodosius. The emperor was not pleased. John, in response, preached nearly two dozen sermons to his congregation, urging them to see the error of their ways.[5] This impressed Theodosius and attracted the notice of the emperor's court. Moreover, John did not have a reputation as one who gained popularity merely because he spoke with "rhetorical art and strength," but "expounded the sacred books with truth and sincerity" as well. John "strenuously convicted sinners even in the churches, and antagonized with boldness all acts of injustice, as if they had been perpetrated against himself."[6] His simple, practical style won him a great deal of admiration among the common people, and provided a stark contrast to the Alexandrian style of preaching, which often too much contorted the Scriptures to find "hidden" meanings. One of the main themes in John's homilies was injustice committed against the poor. Many wealthy Christians of the day were hoarding their money for themselves and failing to contribute to the needs of their brothers and sisters in Christ. For John, this was reprehensible:

> Would you do honor to Christ's body? Neglect Him not when naked; do not while here you honor Him with silken garments, neglect Him perishing without of cold and nakedness. For He that said, This is my body, and by His word confirmed the fact, This same said, You saw me and hungered, and fed me not? For what is the profit, when His table indeed is full of golden cups, but He perishes with hunger?[7]

Such preaching did not win him a great deal of favor with the moneyed classes of Antioch, and they were probably not unhappy to see him depart in 398 for Constantinople, the greatest city of the age, of which John had recently, surprisingly, been made bishop.

John's Episcopate

When the bishop Nectarius, the unlikely successor to Gregory Nazianzus, died in 397, a mad dash for the episcopate of Constantinople ensued: "Immediately a crowd of people who were not called for rushed forward to secure the supreme position—men who were not men, presbyters by office, yet unworthy of the priesthood; some battering at the doors of officials, others offering bribes, others again going on their knees to the populace."[8] This kind of scramble repulsed much of the clergy, who asked the emperor Arcadius to appoint someone who was experienced and worthy of respect. Eutropius, the emperor's chief adviser, was familiar with John from some business that had once taken him east, and convinced Arcadius that John was the man for

Eleventh-century mosaic of John Chrysostom, Hosios Loukas Monastery, Boeotia, Greece.

the job. John was ordered by imperial letter to meet with the emperor and was secretly smuggled out of Antioch by the emperor's personal detachment at night, a request that was motivated out of concerns for peace. The citizens of Antioch, one historian believed, "would probably have excited a sedition, and have inflicted injury on others, or subjected themselves to acts of violence, rather than have suffered John to be taken from them."[9] The same day John arrived at Constantinople, he was ordained the bishop of the city, a position he had not sought.

John's tenure as bishop, predictably, started off on a reformer's note. He inveighed against clergy who took up women despite their vows of chastity, calling them worse than brothel keepers. Next, "he put his hand to the sword of correction against the rich, lancing the abscesses of their souls, and teaching them humility and courtesy towards others."[10] John did an audit of the church's expenditure books and found that huge sums of money were being spent on bishops' comforts. He put a stop to this largesse and used the money to build a hospital, complete with two priests, some cooks, a few doctors, and several volunteers to help the operation. Laypeople were encouraged to attend evening prayer sessions at the churches, a practice that "annoyed the less strenuous clergy, who made a practice of sleeping all night."[11] And John kept preaching his strongly worded sermons. As a result of all this, "the tone of the whole city was changed to piety, men delighting their souls with soberness and psalmody."[12] The city seemed to be experiencing a revival.

But John was making enemies as well. Even before his election, Theophilus, the bishop of Alexandria (the same bishop who had conducted a destructive campaign against pagan temples during the reign of Theodosius), wanted to put up his own candidate for the position. He was defeated in his effort, but still longed to bring down John. He had his chance a few years later when a controversy broke out in Alexandria over the writings of Origen. Theophilus, in accordance with the general opinion of the day, refuted Origen's scholarship. However, a group of Egyptian monks, known as the "Tall Brothers," continued to teach that certain aspects of Origen's theology were true. Although they had a disagreement, Theophilus treated them in a most disgraceful way. He ordered them expelled from their monasteries without giving any reasons. The Tall Brothers went to Alexandria to get an explanation:

> Theophilus stared at them, like a dragon, with bloodshot eyes, glaring like a bull; in his uncontrollable temper, he was livid one moment, pale the next, the next again smiling sarcastically. He took the tippet[13] upon the shoulders of the aged Ammonius, and twisted it round his neck with his own hands, punching him in the face, making his nose bleed with his clenched fists, and shouting, "Anathematize Origen, you heretic!"[14]

Despite such foul treatment, the monks went back to their cells in the desert with their opinion unchanged. Theophilus next petitioned the civil governor, saying that the monks needed to be expelled from Egypt for supporting excommunicated bishops. The governor acquiesced and gave Theophilus license to drive them out of the province. Theophilus rounded up a gang of young ruffians, primed them with booze, and set them loose on the Tall Brothers' monastery. The Tall Brothers managed to escape through a well to safety, but Theophilus still decided to burn up the monastery, destroying one of the boys, some copies of the Scriptures, and the monks' communion elements in the process. The Tall Brothers, along with three hundred other monks, priests, and deacons, first fled to Palestine and then Constantinople, which they believed would be a safe place for them to argue their grievances before John and the emperor.

Although John wasn't sure if the Tall Brothers were telling the truth about how much they had suffered, he still received them warmly and "afforded them every aid and encouragement in his power."[15] John's hospitable reception of the monks made Theophilus angry, and he set in motion a series of measures to get John removed from power. He wrote letters to all the bishops of the East, stirring up an anti-Origen frenzy. He also appealed to the empress Eudoxia,

John Chrysostom confronts the empress Aelia Eudoxia, oil painting by Jean-Paul Laurens, 1880s.

who also had become an enemy of John because of his denunciation of the aristocracy's greediness and excessive luxury. John had also referred to Eudoxia during a sermon as a Jezebel, a reference to a famous Old Testament harlot.

At the same time, Theophilus was called to Constantinople to answer for the accusations against him. He arrived with twenty-nine of his allied bishops, said one source, "like a beetle loaded with the dung of the best that Egypt, or India itself, produces, emitting sweet scent to cover his stinking jealousy."[16] He stayed three weeks, and in violation of episcopal tradition, never once had a conversation with John, but instead "spent night and day in his efforts to expel Bishop John not only from the Church, but even from life itself."[17] He recruited two bishops who had been excommunicated for murder and fornication to levy false accusations of impropriety (and treason, for the Jezebel comment) against John. At Eudoxia's approval, a synod was called against John. His response was a plea to his supporters for prayer and loyalty: "Pray for me, brethren, and, if ye love Christ, let none desert the Church of which he is in charge on my account."[18]

The Synod of the Oak—so named for a suburb of Constantinople distinguished by an ancient oak tree—commenced in 403. The court was stacked with Theophilus's bishops from Egypt and Syria. John refused to participate in a show trial in which his sworn enemies were his judges, but thinking resistance would ignite a public riot, submitted himself to their judgment anyway. The punishment was exile, but an earthquake rocked Constantinople the day after John was sent to a remote region on the Black Sea. For the empress Eudoxia, this was a frightening omen that she had acted wrongly, and John was recalled by royal decree a few days later.

Two months later, a cabal of corrupt bishops again decided to try to rid themselves of their nemesis. They appealed once more to Theophilus, now back in Alexandria, to help them devise a scheme for John's removal. They petitioned the emperor Arcadius over John's highly technical violations of church law. Arcadius eventually lost interest in resisting their overtures and allowed the case to go forward. Yet the more likely motive for John's ultimate dismissal was again an incident involving the empress Eudoxia. A large statue of her, cast in silver, had been erected in front of the main cathedral in Constantinople. John criticized the artifice as excessive, a waste of money. From the pulpit, he compared Eudoxia to Herodias, the granddaughter of King Herod who whimsically asked for John the Baptist's head on a platter: "Herodias is again enraged; again she dances; again she seeks to have the head of John in a basin."[19] Eudoxia was infuriated. She called another council, whose bishops pronounced the same result as the first council: exile. John's supporters were defiant in defeat. Expelled from the churches, they held services in the public baths, and they formed an unofficial bodyguard to prevent the bishop from being taken away. But John sneaked away from them to face his captors, who treated him "more severely than murderers, sorcerers, and adulterers."[20] Before he left, John managed to say his good-byes to his bishops, tenderly kissing some of them and urging them on: "Stay here for the present, and let me go and have a little rest."[21] This time his exile was permanent: a desolate spot on the Black Sea near the Caucasus Mountains. Reprisal against John's followers was swift. Many were beaten and thrown into prison, and the women were despoiled of all their most precious belongings. Sozomen reported that earlobes were ripped off in the grab to forcibly take their earrings.[22]

Exile did not stop John's ministry. He wrote letters frequently to his supporters in Constantinople and abroad, a practice that eventually got him exiled even farther from civilization, all the way to modern-day Georgia. Not even the pleas of Pope Innocent I could persuade Arcadius to call John home. On the way farther inland, in 407, John died. His last words were reported to have been "Glory to God for all things," a testament to his unyielding love of Christ.[23] His influence would spread over the Byzantine church for generations, not just as a moral example and a picture of the height of eloquence in giving sermons, but for his work on the Eastern Orthodox catechism as well.

Over the next few centuries, the eastern portion of the empire would live on as the Byzantine Empire—a polity that had a distinct identity from the Roman Empire, and one that will be addressed in a later chapter. But the West was in relative chaos, politically speaking; some even imagined the barbarian invasions as a harbinger of the end times. But the decades immediately preceding the death of the empire also managed to produce the greatest theologian of the ancient world—one who viewed the immediate chaos in an eternal context, and reassured the church that this too would pass.

AUGUSTINE

Augustine was born in Hippo, a town in modern-day Algeria near the Tunisian border. His family was not particularly wealthy, but from boyhood Augustine received financial support from a local dignitary so that he could receive a classical education. "Even as a boy," he wrote in his magnificent autobiography, the *Confessions*, "I had heard of eternal life promised to us through the humility of the Lord our God."[24] There's no doubt that the message of the cross came to him through his mother, Monica, who throughout Augustine's young life begged God to redeem her son. Augustine later remembered the woman "who for many years had wept over me, that I might live in your [God's] eyes."[25]

As Augustine entered his sixteenth year, he began to make mischief. One of the most famous episodes from his boyhood was his theft of pears from a tree, an act done, as Augustine told us, "simply that I might steal."[26] He also around the same time developed an almost insatiable obsession with sex: "the thorns of lust grew rank over my head, and there was no hand to pluck them out."[27]

At eighteen, the young man went to Carthage to continue his studies, something for which he had an incredible talent. His scholarship was not entirely motivated by intellectual curiosity, however: "I craved, through an excess of vanity, to be thought elegant and urbane."[28] Augustine jumped to the head of his class, and at this time, prompted by a reading of Cicero's *Hortensius*, began to fall in love with philosophy and rhetoric. Yet even as he experienced a great deal of academic success, his heart was still restless. He recognized in himself a need to discover truth, and he decided to study the Scriptures to explore that need. Like Jerome, however, Augustine's first serious encounter with the Bible left him unimpressed: "They [the Scriptures] appeared to me to be unworthy to be compared with the dignity of Tully [Cicero]; for my inflated pride shunned their style, nor could the sharpness of my wit pierce their inner meaning."[29]

Around this time, Augustine attached himself to a semiheretical sect of Christians called the Manicheans, who, like the old Gnostic heresies, emphasized the goodness of things spiritual and the evil of the physical world and developed many bizarre, unscriptural theories to explain their beliefs. Augustine's spiritual hunger remained unsatisfied: "How inwardly even then did the marrow of my soul pant after You."[30]

His mother, Monica, continued to pray for him, and asked a local bishop to sit down with Augustine and set him straight. The bishop, noting Augustine's involvement with Manichaeism and his propensity for "vexatious questions," refused. "Leave him alone for a time," he told Monica, "only pray God for him; he will of himself, by reading, discover what that error is, and how great its impiety." Monica was disheartened at the response and begged with tears that the bishop would change his mind. He wouldn't, but felt confident that the day of salvation was coming: "Go your way, and God bless you," he told Monica, "for it is not possible that the son of these tears should perish."[31]

In his twenties, Augustine and his friends "went on seduced and seducing, deceived and deceiving."[32] Augustine still involved himself with Manichaeism, but didn't know God. He subscribed seriously to astrology. He lived with a concubine for a decade, having a child out of wedlock named Adeodatus. Grief struck: a dear friend, one whom Augustine had known from boyhood and who was also a teacher of rhetoric, died of a fever. Being at home only reminded him of the sorrow from this loss; his father's house became a "wondrous unhappiness."[33] He soon after renounced Manichaeism, finding it lacking philosophical substance. The only thing Augustine loved at the time was his career as a professor of rhetoric. His rise became meteoric, and by the end of his twenties he decided to move to Rome, motivated, he claimed, by a desire to teach better-behaved pupils; "Many outrages they perpetrate with astounding phlegm," he complained about his Carthaginian students.[34] Monica was beside herself with the thought of her son moving so far away from her and her Christian influence. But despite her prayers that Augustine not depart, Augustine later reflected on God's providence in the matter:

> But You, mysteriously counselling and hearing the real purpose of her
> desire, granted not what she then asked, in order to make me what
> she was ever asking. The wind blew and filled our sails, and withdrew
> the shore from our sight; and she, wild with grief, was there on the

morrow, and filled Your ears with complaints and groans, which You disregarded; while, by the means of my longings, You were hastening me on to the cessation of all longing.[35]

At Rome, Augustine found himself with access to the best students, but he regarded them as fraudsters, as they would flee the school as the term of study ended, not wanting to pay their tuition bills. Augustine then went to Milan, partly out of a desire to meet the great Ambrose, who even the unbelieving Augustine regarded as "among the best of men."[36] Ambrose received Augustine "like a father," and Augustine went to hear him whenever Ambrose preached. But Augustine the rhetorician only went to hear *how* Ambrose spoke, not *what* he said. Still, Augustine retrospectively admitted, the experience drew him nearer to God "gradually and unconsciously."[37] Augustine's process of conversion, as ever, was spurred on by Monica's arrival in Milan. She swore to him that before she departed this life, she would see him a Catholic believer. Augustine still was not a Christian, but began the catechesis (the course of study necessary for baptism). He reflected that he, now thirty-two, had been striving for true wisdom since age nineteen, yet had not found it. And still he felt enslaved to his lustful desires, restraining him from coming to faith. Augustine's prayer in those days was a paradoxical one: "give me chastity and continency, but not yet."[38]

By 386 (about age thirty-two), the internal pressure overwhelmed him. One day, amid conversation with a friend, Augustine suddenly fled from his house into a little garden behind it, "being most impatient with myself that I entered not into Your will and covenant, O my God, which all my bones cried out unto me to enter."[39] He tore at his hair, clenched his knee, and beat his body involuntarily. A shower of tears burst forth as Augustine lay prostrate under a fig tree. Separation from God overwhelmed him, and he was at a loss about what to do. Suddenly, he heard a child's voice saying in a singsong tone from the house next door, *"Tolle lege, tolle lege"*—"Take up and read." Augustine interpreted this as a command to open the Bible, and he ran back into the house. He grabbed the Bible he had been reading with a friend and flipped it open to a random page. His eyes fell upon Romans 13:13–14: "Let us behave decently, as in the daytime, not in carousing and drunkenness, not in sexual immorality and debauchery, not in dissension and jealousy. Rather, clothe yourselves with the Lord Jesus Christ, and do not think about how to gratify the desires of the flesh." Augustine recalled his response: "Instantly, as the sentence ended—by a light, as it were, of security infused into my heart—all the gloom of doubt vanished away."[40] Augustine had finally become a Christian.

POST-CONVERSION

After his conversion, Augustine resigned his professorship (partly out of a problem with his lungs) and decided to move back to Africa. On the way there, tragedy stuck: Augustine's mother, traveling with him, died of a fever. So departed the woman of unmatched influence on his life, and the young man was heartbroken: "As, then, I was left destitute of so great comfort in her, my soul was stricken, and that life torn apart."[41] But she had seen his conversion and was at peace. Augustine sold all his possessions and devoted himself to fasting, prayer, and study of the Word. In time, his hometown of Hippo needed a new presbyter. In 391, Augustine reluctantly accepted the post, weeping at his ordination at the spiritual weight of the office as his bishop laid hands on him. By 395, he himself had become bishop, a position he held until his death in 430. In the days before his

Fra Angelico, *The Conversion of St. Augustine*, ca. 1430–1435. Note on the left a peacock, an early Christian symbol of immortality.

death, he asked that the shortest penitential psalms be put on the wall opposite the bed so that he might read them. He left no will, his biographer said, because he owned no property.[42] All that was his he had donated years before for the foundation of a monastery.

In every respect, Augustine seems to have executed the office with utmost faithfulness, showing restraint in his personal habits and fidelity in his communal ones. One of the things Augustine despised was gossip, and at his table was an inscription:

> *Who injures the name of an absent friend*
> *May not at this table as guest attend.*[43]

There was at least one occasion when Augustine's guests ignored this rule, wrote his biographer Possidius, and Augustine "became exasperated and so sternly rebuked them as to declare that either those verses would have to be removed from the table or he would leave in the midst of the meal and retire to his chamber."[44]

In financial oversight of his see, Augustine personally examined the account books at the end of the year, and "for new buildings he never had any desire."[45] Lastly, although Augustine managed to churn out hundreds of written works over the course of his life, he never ceased ministering to his

A sixth-century fresco of Augustine, Archbasilica of St. John Lateran, Rome.

congregations: "[W]henever it happened that he was requested by the sick to come in person and pray to the Lord for them and lay his hand upon them, he went without delay."[46] Undoubtedly, there were many bishops like Augustine, whose manner of life commended the gospel. But it is Augustine's contributions to theology and philosophy that make him so revered and studied even today.

AUGUSTINE'S THEOLOGY

Augustine was for the most part not a systematic writer, and ideas critical to his theology are scattered across multiple works. Undoubtedly the most compelling Augustinian product is his *Confessions*, the story of his journey to faith and the first Western autobiography (which has been quoted generously in this chapter). But his true magnum opus is *City of God*, a massive exposition of Christianity's place in the world amid competing religions, ideologies, and historical events. Augustine conceived of all creation being divided into two "cities." The first is the City of Man, or the natural world and every idea (including pagan philosophy) in it. The City of Man is a temporary phenomenon that will pass away and face judgment at the end of time. The City of God, on the other hand, is distinguished by all things hopeful for Christ, and will prove triumphant over the City of Man at the last judgment. For one scholar, "The city of humanity contrasts with the city of God: the struggles of secular human beings for sex, power, and possessions are juxtaposed with the condition of Christians who have surrendered their own desires and now regard themselves as journeying on a lifelong pilgrimage to the City of God."[47]

The emphasis on the two cities was intended to give encouragement to Christians who fearfully looked on the barbarian destruction of the empire as evidence that they were living in the biblical end times, a period distinguished by tribulation for God's people. Particularly terrifying for the Christian population of the Roman Empire was the sack of Rome by the Visigoths in AD 410. Augustine wrote that the second coming of Christ, not the sack of Rome, would mark the end of history:

> It is in vain, therefore, that we try to reckon and put a limit to the number of years that remain for this world, since we hear from the mouth of Truth that it is not for us to know this. And yet some have asserted that 400, 500, or as much as 1,000 years may be completed between the Lord's ascension and his final coming. But to show how

each of them supports his opinion would take too long, and is unnecessary, for they make use of human conjectures, and quote no decisive
evidence from the authority of canonical scripture.[48]

The other great object of *City of God* was to refute pagans who
claimed that the destruction that befell the Roman Empire was the fault
of the Christians—that the Roman gods had turned their back on the
empire as a consequence of their abandonment. Not so, said the bishop
of Hippo. If this was the case, he claimed, "why was Troy or Ilium, the
cradle of the Roman people . . . conquered, taken and destroyed by the
Greeks, though it esteemed and worshipped the same gods as they?"[49]

Augustine also developed a highly refined explication of sin and
God's redemptive grace. For him, all human beings, as well as all creation, were tainted with sin because of the Fall. Because the Fall was
a consequence of human free will, Augustine wrestled with questions
about the relationship of human free will versus God's omnipotent control of the universe. Ultimately, he accepted that "we are by no means
compelled, either, retaining the prescience of God, to take away the freedom of the will, or, retaining the freedom of the will, to deny that He is
prescient of future things, which is impious. But we embrace both. We
faithfully and sincerely confess both."[50] Although human sin originates
in human free will, Augustine reasoned, human salvation originates in
the unasked-for, irresistible grace of God. Augustine's emphasis on God
as the true agent of salvation put him in conflict with the Pelagians, a
group that since the third century denied the doctrine of original sin and
believed that Christians, by their own effort, could attain a perfect moral
state. Augustine considered this impossible; the enduring presence of sin
in the human condition could never allow it. The practical outworking
of the Pelagian position was that Christians, finding themselves unable
to attain perfection, would rapidly become discouraged, even to the
point of abandoning the faith. Augustine spent copious volumes refuting the Pelagians,[51] who suffered significant setbacks at the Council of
Carthage in 419.

Even to old age, Augustine spent huge amounts of time attacking the Pelagians, as well as the Manicheans, Arians, and Donatists, in works such as *On the Trinity*, *On Christian Doctrine*, and *On Grace and Free Will*. In refuting the Donatists, Augustine continued to contest a movement that the church had now encountered for over a century. The Donatists were a breakaway sect of Christians, primarily located in Africa, who, like the old Novationists, insisted that sacraments (the Lord's Supper, baptism, ordination) dispensed by clergy who had betrayed the faith during times of persecution were of no value. Augustine responded that the moral state of the administrator had no bearing on the sanctity or efficacy of the sacraments.[52] This theology was later described as *ex opere operato* ("from the work worked"). Largely because of Augustine's efforts, this view won out, and the Donatists ceased to be popular by the midway point of the fifth century. Augustine wrote on dozens of other topics, including human sexuality, education, and just war theory. His bibliography is so extensive, in fact, that Isadore of Seville, a writer of the sixth century, scoffed that anyone who claimed to have read all of Augustine's works was a liar.[53]

THE LEGACY OF AUGUSTINIAN THOUGHT

Augustine is sometimes justly described as "the first medieval man." This title has been awarded on the back of his worldview, which proceeded from his maxim *Credo ut intellegam*, "I believe that I may understand." For Augustine, secular philosophies are useless unless seen in the light of God and his lordship over all creation; only those who have faith can rightly interpret them. To that end, Augustine drew heavily on the Greek philosopher Plato, using classical arguments of reason and the soul to demonstrate the existence of God and the unity of body and soul. It is largely thanks to Augustine that classical philosophy retained a place in medieval thought. Secondly, Augustine's high view of God's dominion over creation influenced subsequent generations of medieval thinkers, who themselves saw the world ordered according to God's purpose. Augustine's belief in God-appointed hierarchies was used later to argue for the divine right of kingship and the authority of the church over the people. In time, both institutions abused this doctrine, having an understanding of it that allowed for expansive authority over subject people, but without any accountability to God.

Augustine has been an important source for Catholic and Protestant thinkers through the generations. For Catholics, Augustine's thought lives on in the Catholic approach to ecclesiology and the sacraments. The great medieval theologian Thomas Aquinas also drew heavily on Augustine to formulate his views, and Augustine is one of the four original Doctors of the Church. But Augustine was also popular with the Protestant Reformers, who claimed him as one whose views on sin, grace, and justification before God mirrored their own. The Protestant Reformer Martin Luther, originally an Augustinian monk, quoted Augustine nearly one hundred times in his *Commentary on the Epistle to the Romans*.[54] Undoubtedly, the bishop of Hippo was the indispensable man of the fifth-century church, and his influence is little diminished since.

TWELVE

FROM ANCIENT
TO MEDIEVAL

Germanic Invasions and the Fall of Rome,
Theodosius II, Council of Ephesus, Leo I and
Attila the Hun, Council of Chalcedon

During the years when Augustine was laboring to produce what would become the most influential corpus of Christian writings from the ancient world (ca. 400–430), the Western empire continued to shrivel. The sons of Theodosius—the emperors Arcadius and his Western counterpart, Honorius—were feckless men who did nothing to buttress the empire against the barbarian onslaughts. For the most part, the barbarians had come originally from beyond the northeastern frontiers of the Roman Empire, places we know today as Russia and the Ukraine. From the fourth century onward, it was as if these steppe regions of Central Asia acted as one big people spigot; the period saw numerous groups spill into the empire. Crossing the loosely (if at all) guarded borders of northern Europe, the Visigoths primarily took up residence in Spain, the Franks and Burgundians in France, the Huns and Ostrogoths in Italy, and the Vandals in North Africa. All around the empire, men looked fearfully on a changing world. An anonymous chronicle from 452 remembers the year 408: "The fury of various peoples began to tear Gaul to pieces . . . at this time, as the host of enemies grew stronger, the powers of the Romans were weakened to their very foundation."[1] The year 410 saw the event most emblematic of the Roman decline. Alaric, king of the Visigoth tribe, led the first foreign sack of Rome in eight hundred years. The effect on the city was cataclysmic. The greatest structures and pieces of art of the ancient world were burned. Anything that could not be destroyed was stolen; "nothing whatever of public or private wealth" remained.[2] The principal senators of the city were put to death. A local monk begged Alaric to stop his rampage, but the barbarian chief claimed that he could not help it. "I am not going on in this course of my own will; but there is a something that irresistibly impels me daily, saying, 'Proceed to Rome, and desolate that city,'" he said.[3] Around the same time, the Roman way of life had largely degenerated into a lackadaisical torpor: "The magnificence of Rome is defaced by the inconsiderate levity of a few, who never recollect where they are born, but fall away into error and licentiousness as if a perfect immunity were granted to vice."[4] Hydatius, a Spaniard writing in the 450s to 460s, believed he was seeing the foretold end of the world:

> As the barbarians ran wild through Spain and the deadly pestilence continued on its savage course, the wealth and goods stored in the cities were plundered by the tyrannical tax-collector and consumed by the soldiers. A famine ran riot, so dire that driven by hunger human beings devoured human flesh; mothers too feasted upon the bodies of their own children whom they had killed and cooked with their own hands; wild beasts, habituated to feeding on the bodies of those slain by the sword, famine, or pestilence, killed all the braver individuals and feasting on their flesh everywhere became brutally set upon the destruction of the human race. And thus with the four plagues of sword, famine, pestilence, and wild beasts raging everywhere throughout the world, the annunciations foretold by the Lord through his prophets came to fulfillment.[5]

In 455, the Vandals destroyed a great part of North Africa (hence the origin of the English word *vandalism* stemming from the reputation of this particular tribe). In 476, the last Roman emperor in the West (if he could even be rightly referred to as such), a fifteen-year-old boy named Romulus Augustulus, was deposed. The year 486 saw the establishment of the Franks (from which the modern name of France comes) as the dominant power in Gaul. Yet the forcible transformation of Europe from a Roman-dominated continent into an ethnically pluralistic one did not mean that the institution of the church disappeared. Even as the political and social milieu of Europe was transformed by the barbarian invasions, the church contended for and preserved a high level of theological and ecclesiastical continuity. As had been the case in the fourth century, the Eastern church in the fifth century featured yet more Christological controversies—ones that often reflected the competition for power and authority among different cities. From the ashes of the West would rise a new civilization in which the church became the conduit for classical and Christian ideas of the past.

THEODOSIUS II AND THE THEODOSIAN CODE

The last Roman emperor of significance was Theodosius II, the grandson of Ambrose's friend Theodosius I. Theodosius II became the Eastern emperor at age seven, but his life apparently displayed few princely mannerisms, as he was described as "neither stultified nor effeminated by the circumstances of his birth and education."[6] Young Theodosius II was aided in his office by an ample number of advisers, one of whom was his older sister Pulcheria, a Christian. Under her tutelage, Theodosius II gained a hearty interest in the Christian faith. On Wednesdays and Fridays he fasted, and his palace was "little different from a monastery."[7] He and his sister rose early in the morning to sing hymns and recite Bible verses, and he often passed the time in discourse with bishops over spiritual matters. It was this attachment to faith that led Theodosius II to fight the Persians, who were persecuting Christians in the East, "inflicting on them a variety of Persian punishments and tortures."[8] When Theodosius II defeated the Persians in battle, many Persian prisoners of war were held captive in the East, and there is a wonderful anecdote stemming from this bondage.

The frontier city of the Eastern Roman Empire was the city of Amida (Diyarbakir, Turkey), where enormous walls (which still stand today) stood as a bulwark against Persian invasions. The bishop of that city was Acacius, who noticed that the Romans were starving many of their Persian captives to death. Moved by the Persians' suffering, Acacius directed all his clergy to relinquish the golden cups in their churches. He then had them melted down and sold off. His rationale was simple: "Our God, my brethren, needs neither dishes nor cups; for he neither eats nor drinks, nor is in want of anything. Since then, by the liberality of its faithful members the church possesses many vessels both of gold and silver, it behooves us to sell them, that by the money thus raised we may be able to redeem the prisoners and also supply them with food."[9]

The bishop had ransomed the very people who were persecuting his fellow Christians. It was a kind of mercy that could only be motivated by the love of Christ. After feeding the Persian captives, Acacius sent them back to Persia. The Persian king was shocked at this kind of clemency, and requested from Theodosius II a personal audience with Acacius, a wish that the emperor granted. The Persian king was so moved that he ended the persecution of Christians in his empire.

Theodosius II was a man concerned with order, and this was reflected in the publication of one of the most important works of jurisprudence in Western history: the *Codex Theodosianus* (Theodosian Code). In 429, Theodosius II ordered that a compilation of all of the laws published since the time of Constantine (a span of about 125 years) be put together. This was a very ambitious work that took eight years and twenty-two scholars to complete. Although Theodosius died before the codex was completed, his successor, Valentinian III, continued the work, and the new code went into effect across the empire on January 1, 439. The Theodosian Code bequeathed to us even today some of the more important principles of Roman law, like the right of appeal in judicial decisions, or the imposition of penalties for breaking a contract. Some of the Theodosian laws were downright bizarre: in Constantinople, for instance, there were to be no more than 950 practicing undertakers at one time.[10]

The code set a number of critical precedents still found in Western law. But undoubtedly the signature aspect of the code was its affirmation of Christianity as the official religion of Roman society. This gave the church a level of stature that in many ways enabled it to perform good work. But in preserving a very privileged place for the church, Theodosius sanctioned some rather heavy-handed laws that had accumulated over the centuries. The right of making a will was stripped from those who had converted to paganism from Christianity. No theaters or horse-racing tracks were to be open on Sunday[11]—that day was for the worship of God. Meetings of Manichaeans (a heretical sect) were to be broken up immediately,[12] and their property seized by the civil government. Astrologers were to be exiled and their books burned.[13] However much Constantine and his Christian successors desired to spread Christianity, elements of the Theodosian Code revealed that they seemed to have had little grasp of religious tolerance themselves.

THE COUNCIL OF EPHESUS

Theodosius II also took it upon himself to wade into a significant theological controversy. When the patriarch of Constantinople died in 428, Theodosius, on account of disputes among the clergy, resolved not to appoint anyone from the city's clergy to fill his post. Instead, he looked outside the city and found a choice in Nestorius, a bishop from Antioch known for his "excellent voice and fluency of speech."[14] It became clear almost instantly that Theodosius had picked the wrong man. In his opening sermon, Nestorius begged the emperor,

"Assist me in destroying heretics, and I will assist you in vanquishing the Persians."[15] Such language was disconcerting and betrayed an unstable mind. Nestorius seems to have been a charlatan, and one ancient historian regarded him as "being a man of natural fluency as a speaker, he was considered well educated, but in reality he was disgracefully illiterate."[16] As it turned out, Nestorius had a "violent and vainglorious temperament" that quickly displayed itself in the persecution of heretics.[17] After only five days, for instance, he burned down the Arians' church in the city, a completely unjustifiable action for a professing Christian to take. When another local bishop, believing he was acting in accordance with what Nestorius wanted, started harassing his local Macedonian sect, the Macedonians retaliated by assassinating him. In response, Nestorius stripped the Macedonians of all their churches in his district.[18] He seemed to be agitating for more conflict.

Nestorius also held to a peculiar doctrine that would eventually lead to his demise. He had brought with him from Antioch a certain priest named Anastasius, whom he respected greatly and trusted with the management of many affairs. One day when Anastasius was preaching, he declared, "Let no one call Mary *Theotocos*: for Mary was but a woman; and it is impossible that God should be born of a woman."[19] This shocked his audience, for his words, like so many other heretical pronouncements, effectively amounted to a denial of the idea that Jesus was God. For Anastasius, Mary was not the *Theotocos*, the mother of God. Confusion set in. Nestorius supported Anastasius, a decision that did not sit well with the people. Meanwhile, Nestorius, believing himself completely in the right, convinced Theodosius II to call a council at Ephesus in 431 to resolve the issue. About 250 bishops, delayed at times by flooding and by a plague, found their way to the town. As had happened at Nicaea, the bishops informally gathered together before the council to hash out various issues, a process that would actually, in the words of one scholar, "exasperate rather than heal their differences."[20]

The leader of the anti-Nestorian faction was Patriarch Cyril of Alexandria, at that time a city in which pagan, Christian, and Jewish groups grappled for authority and influence. Cyril was the highly educated nephew of Theophilus of Alexandria, the patriarch who had caused so much trouble for John Chrysostom. Though Cyril's theology was on the whole quite orthodox, he also displayed a good bit of the temper that made Theophilus so hated, as we will see in another historical episode. Before the council, Cyril declared Nestorius's teaching about Christ anathema, calling it a "putrid sore" in a letter to Pope Celestine I.[21]

The opening of the council was heavily controversial. A large deputation of bishops loyal to Nestorius had not arrived. The council agreed to give them two weeks to appear. When the time passed and they were still unaccounted for, Cyril called the opening of the first session, and soon after declared Nestorius anathema. As evidence for the rectitude of his convictions, Cyril invoked Pope Celestine I's declaration of Nestorius as anathema. Owing to an advantage in numbers, Cyril's party voted to excommunicate Nestorius: "We have come, with many tears, to this sorrowful sentence against him, namely, that our Lord Jesus Christ, whom he has blasphemed, decrees by the holy Synod that Nestorius be excluded from the episcopal dignity, and from all priestly communion."[22]

Then the group of missing bishops, headed by a bishop named John of Antioch, showed up. Hearing that Nestorius had already been excommunicated under questionable circumstances, they formed their own council and condemned Cyril! Over the course of several weeks, all the bishops spun a web of accusations, motions, proclamations, condemnations, canons, and other procedural measures against one another. Eventually the bishops reaffirmed the divine and human nature of Christ, that Mary was the mother of God, and that it was "unlawful for any man to bring forward, or to write, or to compose a different Faith as a rival to that established by the holy Fathers assembled with the Holy Ghost in Nicæa."[23]

But Theodosius II was torn between the decision of the council and his personal loyalties to Nestorius. He decided to ratify the decisions of both the Cyrilians and the Nestorians. Cyril was imprisoned, and Nestorius voluntarily went into exile at a monastery, where he spent the rest of his life. Cyril eventually escaped from prison, fled to Egypt, and convinced a mob of citizens, led by a character named Dalmatius the Hermit, to plead his case before Theodosius II. Eventually Cyril became a confidant of the imperial household.

The effect of the council of Ephesus was substantial. Nestorius was condemned, but divisions between some churches in the East and the churches in the West (who had opposed Nestorius) deepened, as did the rift between the churches in Alexandria and Constantinople, and between those in Alexandria and Antioch. What was clear is that very often in these ancient council decisions, personal and political rivalries overlaid questions that were purely theological in nature. Over time, the nascent churches of Persia adopted Nestorius's doctrine as authoritative, a decision that put them at odds with Western Christianity and some branches of Eastern Christianity for centuries. It wasn't until 1994 that the Catholic Church and the Assyrian Church of the East came to a reconciliation on the issue, issuing a statement that, among other things, declared that "the divinity and humanity are united in the person of the same and unique Son of God and Lord Jesus Christ, who is the object of a single adoration."[24]

CYRIL AND ORESTES

Well before his involvement in the Council of Ephesus, Cyril was at the center of three very ugly episodes in the year 415 that called into question just how much respect was due him. All stemmed from his quarrels with the Roman governor of Egypt, a man named Orestes, who pushed back against Cyril's ecclesiastical intrusions into his civic power. Already the city of Alexandria, with its array of diverse religious groups, seemed to maintain an environment of hostility. The historian Socrates Scholasticus noted that the Alexandrians were "more delighted with tumult than any other people: and if at any time it should find a pretext, breaks forth into the most intolerable excesses; for it never ceases from its turbulence without bloodshed."[25]

The first episode began with the Jews, who frequented dancing exhibitions on Sundays, a practice forbidden by the increasingly Christianized Roman law. At one such spectacle, the Alexandrian Jews noticed one of Cyril's most loyal followers, Hierax, in the crowd, reading the prohibition out loud and applauding it. This made them suspect that Hierax had been planted there by Cyril to stir up some kind of commotion. Evidently Orestes believed something similar, for he seized Hierax and had him tortured in public as a show of his power. In response, Cyril confronted the Jewish leadership and threatened them with "the utmost severities" unless they desisted from their machinations. This made many of the Jews even madder, and they vowed revenge. One night they ran into the street, screaming that one of the city's churches was on fire. Christians ran out of their homes to put out the fire, and were waylaid and killed by the Jews, who wore special rings made of bark to identify themselves to each other. When Cyril discovered what had happened, he led a mob to the city's synagogues and plundered them, expelling nearly the whole of the Jewish population from Alexandria. Cyril tried to plead his case to Orestes, and even offered him a Bible in friendship, but this would not be enough to mollify Orestes's anger.[26]

Some time later, either at Cyril's urging or by their own will, five hundred armed monks loyal to Cyril came down from the mountains of Egypt to confront Orestes, calling him a "pagan idolator" as he rode along in his chariot. Orestes protested that he was a Christian, but it did not seem to convince the monks. One of them, Ammonius, threw a stone at Orestes, opening a gash in his forehead. Blood streamed down his face. Orestes's personal guard abandoned him, but the citizens of Alexandria came to his rescue. Ammonius was captured and then tortured to death. When Cyril recovered the body, he gave Ammonius a lengthy and orotund funeral speech, hailing him as a martyr. But most other Christians saw through Cyril's ploy. They "did not accept Cyril's prejudiced estimate of him; for they well knew that he had suffered the punishment due to his rashness, and that he had not lost his life under the torture because he would not deny Christ."[27] Cyril himself apparently must have been convicted about the true terms of Ammonius's punishment, for he too eventually "suffered the recollection of the circumstance to be gradually obliterated by silence."[28] The whole episode did nothing to diffuse the tension between Cyril and Orestes.

The third act in this tragic drama is one that drove Orestes from the town permanently. There was a prominent woman philosopher in Alexandria named Hypatia, who "made such attainments in literature and science as to far surpass all the philosophers of her own time." Owing to her "self-possession and ease of manner," Hypatia would even frequently debate men in the public assemblies. This was an unorthodox thing for a woman to do, but the men of the city had no issue with it, for they, "on account of her extraordinary dignity and virtue," admired her. But Hypatia had a friendship with Orestes, and the Christians began to speculate that it was she who had poisoned his mind against Cyril. A madman named Peter led a band of thugs, who kidnapped her from her carriage and brought her into one of the churches. They stripped her naked, and murdered her by scraping the skin off her with pieces of tiles and seashells. They then tore her body limb from limb and burned her remains. "This affair," wrote the historian Socrates, "brought not the least opprobrium, not only upon Cyril, but also upon the whole Alexandrian church . . . Surely nothing can be farther from the spirit of Christianity than the allowance of massacres, fights, and transactions of that sort."[29] It is impossible to know whether the murder of Hypatia was directed by Cyril or not. But it is emblematic of the kind of violence that characterized Cyril's time as patriarch of Alexandria. After this, Orestes quit the town, discouraged and intimidated by the enmity there.

Pope Leo I Turns Back Attila

On the other side of the Mediterranean, far removed from the contentions of Constantinople, the Italian peninsula was dealing with problems of its own. The Huns, a tribe of barbarians originally from Eurasia, were rampaging across Europe. In 440, they crossed the Danube River in Hungary, reaching Constantinople by 445, where the city's impenetrable walls slowed them down. Undaunted, they turned to Gaul, which was conquered in 451. By 452, they entered Italy. Some terrified residents fled to a ring of islands inside a lagoon on the nation's northern coast. In time, their temporary refuge became a permanent settlement: the city of Venice. At the head of the Hunnic invasions was one of the most fearsome characters in world history: Attila. Attila had been co-ruler over the Huns since 434, and had recently come into sole possession of power after slaying his own brother. According to Jordanes, a Gothic historian from relatively the same period:

> He was a man born into the world to shake the nations, the scourge of all lands, who in some way terrified all mankind by the dreadful rumors noised abroad concerning him. He was haughty in his walk, rolling his eyes here and there, so that the power of his proud spirit appeared in the movement of his body. He was indeed a lover of war, yet restrained in action, mighty in counsel, gracious to suppliants and lenient to those who were once received into his protection. He was short of stature, with a broad chest and a large head: his eyes were small, his beard thin and sprinkled with grey: and he had a flat nose and a swarthy complexion showing the evidences of his origin.[30]

Attila was even more fearsome in deed than in appearance. One source claims that the Huns were responsible for so many murders and bloodlettings "that the dead could not be numbered. Ay, for they took captive the churches and monasteries and slew the monks and maidens in great numbers."[31] Another source describes him as "utterly cruel in inflicting torture, greedy in plundering, insolent in abuse."[32] In time, his nickname became "the Scourge of God" for the devastation he inflicted upon Gallic cities like Paris, Orleans, and Troyes. Along the way, he impressed other barbarian tribes into joining his army or feeling death. As he made his excursions into Italy, the need to feed his troops became greater, and Attila set his sights on Rome as a source of food for his starving men.

But Pope Leo I, who received word of Attila's advance, was not about to let the city suffer the same fate as hundreds of others across Europe. Leo had become pope in 440, largely due to his success as a deacon in mediating a dispute between two civil officials in Gaul. His personality was apparently winsome enough to extract commitments of peace from barbarians as well. In 452, Leo, along with two Roman civil officials, met with Attila outside Mantua in northern Italy. The scene, according to an anonymous source, went something like this:

> The old man of harmless simplicity, venerable in his gray hair and his majestic garb, ready of his own will to give himself entirely for the defense of his flock, went forth to meet the tyrant who was destroying all things. He met Attila, it is said, in the neighborhood of the river Mincio, and he spoke to the grim monarch, saying "The senate and the people of Rome, once conquerors of the world, now indeed vanquished, come before thee as suppliants. We pray for mercy and deliverance. O Attila, thou king of kings, thou couldst have no greater glory than to see suppliant at thy feet this people before whom once all peoples and kings lay suppliant. Thou hast subdued, O Attila, the whole circle of the lands which it was granted to the Romans, victors over all peoples, to conquer. Now we pray that thou, who hast conquered others, should conquer thyself. The people have felt thy scourge; now as suppliants they would feel thy mercy."[33]

Attila was obviously moved by some force of Leo's speech, because he did decide to refrain from marching on Rome. But there were undoubtedly other considerations. For one thing, Attila knew that the last chieftain to sack Rome, Alaric the Visigoth, in 410, had died shortly afterward. This ominous coincidence may have discouraged him from making an assault on the Eternal City. Secondly, the Italian crop that year was meager, and Attila may have thought that an incursion down the spine of Italy would stretch his army too far from their supply sources. Lastly, a Roman army from the Danube had recently won a major victory over Attila at Chalons, in France. The battle was a bloody one; both sides incurred tens of thousands of casualties. A historian acknowledged straightaway what a famous contest it was:

> Hand to hand they clashed in battle, and the fight grew fierce, confused, monstrous, unrelenting—a fight whose like no ancient time has ever recorded. There were such deeds done that a brave man who missed this marvelous spectacle could not hope to see anything so wonderful all his life long. For if we may believe our elders a brook flowing between low banks through the plain was greatly increased by blood from the wounds of the slain. Those whose wounds drove them to slake their parching thirst drank water mingled with gore. In their wretched plight they were forced to drink what they thought was the blood they had poured out from their own wounds.[34]

Attila's timidity outside Rome perhaps was evidence that he did not want to risk another such defeat. Thus it was probably a combination of all four factors that dissuaded him from marching any farther. But Leo's legendary stance was not soon forgotten by future church historians, and the account was adapted in new ways as the years went on; one even claims that Attila was frightened into retreat by a vision of Saints Peter and Paul at the spot he met Leo. Leo also performed a similar feat of peacemaking again in 455, when he dissuaded Genseric, king of the Vandals, who was already rampaging across Africa, from annihilating the city of Carthage and slaughtering its inhabitants. A few months later, Attila's fear of death became a reality, and he perished as the victim of either a nosebleed suffered during a drunken stupor or internal hemorrhaging caused by alcohol poisoning.

The Papacy of Leo I

The famous episode with Attila occurred near the end of Leo's life, but the rest of his papacy was very important for a number of other reasons. In 1910, the editors *of The Catholic Encyclopedia* wrote that "Leo's pontificate, next to that of Saint Gregory I, is the most significant and important in Christian antiquity."[35] Leo was born around AD 400 and spent twenty-one years as pope, beginning in 440. As can be seen from his negotiation with the Huns, Leo had a keen sense for providing for the local needs of the Roman city; to this end, he also led a campaign of church reconstruction that rebuilt, among other places, the famous Saint Peter's Outside-the-Walls. His sincerity of heart as a shepherd of souls was also unquestionable. As destruction engulfed the empire, and the bonds of ecclesiastical communication became strained by marching armies, destroyed roads, or dead friends, Leo worked to preserve church unity, and also kept a vigilant eye on bishops who were drifting toward heresy or immorality. As one of his letters suggests, he wasn't afraid to succinctly telling disobedient bishops that practices like ordaining twice-married men and practicing usury would lead to excommunication: "This admonition of ours, therefore, proclaims that if any of our brethren endeavour to contravene these rules and dare to do what is forbidden by them, he may know that he is liable to deposition from his office, and that he will not be a sharer in our communion who refuses to be a sharer of our discipline."[36]

Leo also encouraged all the churches in Rome, and later the bishops in Italy, to inform the civil authorities which citizens were part of the heretical Manichean sect: "We call you to a share in our anxiety, that with the diligence of shepherds you may take more careful heed to your flocks entrusted to you that no craft of the devil's be permitted."[37] Leo's tactics were oppressive, but by mid-century, he had even persuaded the emperor Valentinian III to issue imperial decrees against the Manicheans, which resulted in the expulsion of nearly all Manicheans from Italy.

Leo's eagerness to enforce doctrine stemmed from his belief that he had a divine mandate to do so. A great deal of his papacy was spent advocating for papal supremacy: the right of the bishop of Rome to exercise authority over the churches. Though past churchmen such as Irenaeus and Damasus had also defended this idea, as did the emperor Theodosius I, Leo's efforts were even more influential, to the point of being in some ways foundational for the medieval church. Leo believed that Peter and Paul had been sent to Rome so that the knowledge of God could radiate from what was at that time the center of the civilized world: "Here it was that the tenets of philosophy must be crushed, here that the follies of earthly wisdom must be dispelled, here that the cult of demons must be refuted, here that the blasphemy of all idolatries must be rooted out," he wrote.[38]

Leo's eagerness to assert papal authority led him into conflict with the churches of the East, who increasingly rejected the authority of one bishop located far from Alexandria and Constantinople, both of which claimed a degree of ecclesiastical autonomy. It was on this account that Dioscorus of Alexandria, at that time the patriarch of the city, became Leo's rival. Dioscorus, like the Alexandrian patriarchs before him, did not believe that his churches should submit to Leo's authority. The Alexandrian church had its own tradition and traced its founding back to Mark the Evangelist (the author of the book of Mark and probably a companion of Peter's). That church thus believed it had equal claim to its own unique theology, a claim with which Leo disagreed: "For since the most blessed Peter received the headship of the Apostles from the Lord, and the church of Rome still abides by His institutions, it is wicked to believe that His holy disciple Mark, who was the first to govern the church of Alexandria, formed his decrees on a different line of tradition."[39] The disagreement between the two men would be a basis for one of the most controversial church councils in history.

THE SECOND COUNCIL OF EPHESUS AND THE COUNCIL OF CHALCEDON

Around 444, Eutyches, a monk living near Constantinople, began teaching that Christ's nature was only divine, not human. This teaching earned him the label of being a "Monophysite" (in Greek, *mono* meaning "one," *physis* meaning "nature"), and an excommunication from Flavian, the bishop of Constantinople. This caused no shortage of controversy, and a second council was called at Ephesus to examine more closely Eutyches's teaching. He pleaded that his inquisitors misunderstood him—that he fully subscribed to the Nicene Creed, and that his only error had been an infelicity of speech. In reality, the dispute was not as fierce as earlier disputes about whether Jesus was God at all; this debate centered on precisely *how* the transcendent God could take the form of a mortal man. The two rival schools of thought were the Alexandrian (Jesus' divinity came at the expense of his humanity) and Antiochian (both divinity and humanity were united in one, mysterious way).

Pope Leo did not buy Eutyches's Alexandrian views, and sent a letter now known as the "Tome" to Flavian, concurring with his decision to excommunicate Eutyches for his positions. The Tome cited Scripture extensively to prove that Christ had two natures united in one form, and declared Eutyches "very unwary and exceedingly ignorant," and his theology "the height of stupidity and blasphemy."[40] With the two most powerful bishops in the Christian world in agreement, it seemed an easy decision for the council to make. Yet the assembled bishops, under the presidency of the aforementioned Dioscorus of Alexandria, labeled Flavian a heretic when he presented the letter and killed him. The council then reaffirmed Eutyches's teaching as orthodox, probably as a way to assert their independence from Leo. One of Leo's deputies to the council managed to escape with his life and flee back to Rome. Leo was furious when he heard the news, and he denounced the proceedings as a "Robber Council" (*latrocinium*) for its unsatisfactory resolution of the questions at hand.

Leo appealed to the emperor Theodosius II for another council, but he refused. Apparently he had been paid a large sum of gold by the Alexandrian church. But in 451, Theodosius II died in a horseback-riding incident, and by October of the same year, Leo convinced Theodosius's sister Pulcheria to call another at Chalcedon, at that time an independent city on the Asian side of the Bosphorus strait, but today just one neighborhood in the megalopolis known as Istanbul. About eighteen representatives of the emperor presided over the proceedings, which included about five hundred bishops. After several weeks of haggling, this time Leo got his way. The Tome was read again, and the council reaffirmed the two natures of Christ—fully God and fully man. Eutyches and Dioscurus were condemned and sent into exile. The council passed thirty resolutions to conclude the proceedings, most of them regulating who could be ordained to the clergy. But one of them, number twenty-eight, was highly controversial: "The bishop of New Rome [i.e., Constantinople] shall enjoy the same honour as the bishop of Old Rome, on account of the removal of the empire. For this reason the [metropoli-tans] of Pontus, of Asia, and of Thrace, as well as the Barbarian bishops shall be ordained by the bishop of Constantinople."[41]

The intent of this canon was to establish Constantinople as superior over Antioch and especially Alexandria, from which many heresies and controversies had emanated over the past two centuries. But for Leo, only one bishopric—Rome's—could have primacy over all others. He protested vigorously, but to no avail. Though professing unity, Rome and Constantinople now absolutely viewed themselves as operating autonomously from the other because of diverging theological views and ecclesiastical practices. In later centuries, this rift would widen to the point of schism.

THIRTEEN

CHRISTIANITY IN THE EARLY BARBARIAN KINGDOMS: THE BARBARIANS BECOME ARIANS

Isidore; Theodoric, Boethius, and Cassiodorus; France and Gregory of Tours; Gregory the Great and the Germans; Britain and Ireland

In the previous chapter we examined a great clash of civilizations as barbarian tribes came in violent contact with the Romans. By the end of the fifth century, the Roman Empire as a political entity was gone, but the cultural legacy of the Romans lived on in the language, law, commerce, and manners of Europe. The new kingdoms that arose in place of the empire had absorbed many of these influences. The chief relic of the Roman world that would shape the barbarians the most was the Christian worldview. One churchman, Orosius, even claimed that he didn't mind that the Roman Empire fell, since that meant that the pagan barbarians were coming into contact with the Christian world: "If only to this end have the barbarians been sent within Roman borders . . . that the church of Christ might be filled with Huns and Suevi, with Vandals and Burgundians, with diverse and innumerable peoples of believers, then let God's mercy be praised . . . even if this has taken place through our own destruction."[1]

As Orosius wished, the barbarian tribes that settled in Europe in the fifth and sixth centuries did find themselves, by various means, at various times, attracted into the church. In this chapter we will examine how Christianity grew in those new barbarian kingdoms. Europe had unquestionably entered the Dark Ages (ca. 500–1000), a time period originally so described because so few written historical sources survive to adequately describe it. But the Light of the World that had come into earthly existence five hundred years earlier was still illuminating some of the most dismal places on the planet.

THE GOTHS CONVERT

Although the Romans had fought the barbarians (initially, a term that merely meant peoples who were non-Greeks, and later, also non-Romans) for generations, it wasn't until the third century that the Goths, a tribe from east of modern-day Romania, migrated into Roman lands. Trace amounts of Christianity coming from Roman Christians in captivity permeated the Gothic tribes in the first few decades of contact with the Romans, but it wasn't until the reign of the emperor Valens, an Arian, that any form of Christianity started to permeate the barbarian tribes en masse. As much as the barbarians fought the Romans, they also fought one another. On one occasion, a faction of Goths, embroiled in a civil war, beseeched Valens for help in vanquishing the other side. Valens agreed and sent troops to help them. When the Roman-backed side proved victorious, many of the Goths, at the behest of their leader, Fritigernes, "converted" to Arianism as a sign of respect for Valens. A half-Gothic, half-Greek Arian named Ulfilas ("little-wolf") was installed as the Gothic bishop and invented a written alphabet of the

Gothic language in order to copy down the Scriptures. Of course, the transformation from pagan to Arian Christian was a highly questionable one, since the Goths knew next to nothing about who their new God really was.

But even Arian Goths from time to time suffered persecution from their own people because of their decision to forsake the pagan traditions of their ancestors. One of the most famous persecutors of Gothic Christians was a leader named Athanaric. In one episode, Athanaric placed a statue of a Gothic god in a chariot and drove it around from tent to tent, forcing people to worship it. Those who would not worship the statue were burned alive in their tents, including some women who were "nourishing their new-born infants at the breast."[2]

In time, as the Goths spread out over Europe, their Arian theology spread to other barbarian tribes like the Vandals, Burgundians, Visigoths, and Ostrogoths. The differences between the Arianism of the barbarians and the Nicene beliefs of the Roman world sometimes contributed to cultural friction between the two ethnicities. The most extreme case of this is the Vandal conquest of North Africa. The Vandals initially came from Eastern Germany and Southern Poland, and by the 430s had found their way to North Africa, where they encountered the Catholic communities of the Romans. Under their king, Genseric, they set up a kingdom across modern-day Algeria, Tunisia, and Libya. The establishment of their new homeland came with a merciless persecution of the church there. Victor of Vita, a historian of the Vandal persecution in North Africa, remembered that "the storm of their rage has been like the wind of a tempest . . . why the hangings, why the fires, why the claws and the crosses? Why has the serpent-like progeny of the Arians devised for use against the innocent such tortures?"[3] In proportion to the brutality of the Vandals was the mercy of Deogratias, the Nicene bishop of Carthage. When in 455 the Vandals imported men, women, and children from Rome to sell them off as slaves, Deogratias, out of a desire to keep marriages and families from being torn apart by the slave trade, sold off all the gold and silver vessels from his church in order to ransom them. He then used his churches as refugee camps:

> And since there were no places big enough to accommodate so large a multitude, he assigned two famous churches, the Basilica Fausti and the Basilica Novarum, furnishing them with beds and bedding . . . And since so many were in distress owing to their inexperience of a voyage by sea and to the cruelty of captivity, there was no small number of sick people among them. Like a devoted nurse, that saintly bishop went the round of them constantly with doctors and food; so that the condition of each was looked into and every man's need supplied in his presence. Not even at night did he take a rest from this work of mercy.[4]

The Vandal persecutions did not stop until the region was reconquered by the Byzantine Empire nearly one hundred years later. By that time the region had experienced such a great deal of fragmentation that the Muslims who conquered North Africa in the 600s discovered a church mired in a severe state of disunity.

THE VISIGOTHS

One place that experienced a much greater degree of comity between Roman and barbarian was the Iberian peninsula: modern-day Portugal, Spain, and parts of southern France. After several decades of itinerant conquests, including a sack of Rome in 410, the Visigoths settled down in Iberia to enjoy the rich farming soil. At times, the Romans enlisted the Visigoths to fight alongside them against other barbarian tribes, and in 418, the Visigoths were rewarded with gifts of land to settle in. These land grants along the border with Gaul became the basis for their later expansion into modern-day Spain and Portugal.

The Visigoths, as an offshoot of the Gothic tribes of earlier times, were also halfhearted Arians, but relations with the native Romans, predominantly Catholics, were mostly peaceful, despite the religious differences. The Visigoths did experience, however, a great deal of clan warfare among themselves. As the historian Justo González noted, only fifteen of thirty-four Visigoth kings died of natural causes.[5] Such violence forced the Visigoths to realize that they needed to participate more fully in the institutions of culture that produced political stability. Above all, this meant the necessity of joining the Catholic (Nicene) church.

In 589, the king of the Visigoths, Reccared I, formally embraced Catholic Christianity at the Third Council of Toledo. Toledo, in Spain, was the capital of the Visigothic kingdom, and Catholic bishops from around the country traveled there to participate in the event. The leader of the proceedings was Leander of Seville, a bishop who had been instrumental in Reccared's conversion. The council began with three days of prayer and fasting, and on the opening day of ceremonies, Reccared read a lengthy confession of faith based on the creeds of Nicaea, Constantinople, and Chalcedon that had been written by Leander for him. Twenty-three anathemas against the Arian doctrine were pronounced, as well as twenty-three canons that governed ecclesiastical affairs in the Visigothic kingdom. Because Reccared's "conversion" had the great goal of political unity in mind, many Jews who were living in Visigothic Spain with relative freedom felt immediate pressure to convert to Christianity or be exiled. Included in the twenty-three canons was one that forbade Jews to have Christian wives, concubines, or slaves. Such prescriptions only intensified at the Fourth Council of Toledo in 633. Christians were barred from converting to Judaism, and any Jew who was found married to a Christian wife either had to convert or was forbidden from staying with his wife and children. By 687, a document drafted during the reign of King Erwig (who reigned from 680 to 687) stipulated that Jews must either convert to Christianity or face expulsion from the kingdom:

Therefore, if any Jew, of those, naturally, who are as yet not baptized or who have postponed their own or their children's baptism, should prevent his slaves from being baptized in the presence of the priest, or should withhold himself and his family from baptism, or if any one of them should exceed the duration of one year after the promulgation of this law without being baptized, the transgressor of these [conditions], whoever he may be, shall have his head shaved, receive a hundred lashes, and pay the required penalty of exile. His property shall pass over into the power of the king; it shall remain perpetually in the possession of him to whom the king wishes to bestow it, inasmuch as the stubborn life of the Jew shows him to be incorrigible.[6]

This kind of Christian persecution of the Jews would, unfortunately, only become more common in later centuries.

ISIDORE OF SEVILLE

The greatest churchman and intellectual of the Visigothic kingdom in Spain was Isidore of Seville. Isidore was the brother to Leander, the bishop of Seville and agent of Reccared's conversion. From an early age, Isidore attached himself to the pursuit of knowledge according to the ancient educational rubric of the *trivium* (grammar, logic, rhetoric) and the *quadrivium* (arithmetic, geometry, music, and astronomy). When Leander died, Isidore became the bishop of Seville, and continued his brother's work of unifying the Visigothic kingdom through Christianity and cultural refinement. At the Fourth Council of Toledo (which also

A tenth-century manuscript illustration of the Visigoth Council of Toledo.

leveled additional opprobrious laws against Jews), Isidore ordered the bishops of Spain to establish seminaries in their cathedral cities—places where bishops had their headquarters, *cathedra* being a Latin word for "seat." The study of Greek and Hebrew, the original languages of the Bible, was encouraged, as was medicine and law. By 654, near the end of Isidore's life, a Visigothic law code known as the *Liber iudiciorum* (Book of Judgments) emerged with a set of limitations on royal power. One provision, for instance, insisted that "the monarchy and the people of the kingdom are to be subject to the same reverence for the laws."[7] Beginning with Isidore's tenure, the Visigoth kingdom showed a level of political sophistication that came to an end with the Islamic conquest of Spain in 711.

Isidore's signature achievement, however, was his massive written compendium of human knowledge, an encyclopedia called the *Etymologies*. The *Etymologies* is a highly organized attempt to preserve a vast quantity of knowledge that might be lost because of the barbarian disruption of the Roman world. A great majority of the citations in it come from classical authors, and much of the material preserved within would have otherwise been lost if not for its inclusion in the great tome. The *Etymologies'* comprehensive nature, containing information on subjects as diverse as farming, grammar, law, medicine, art, animals, theology, warfare, and more, allowed the *Etymologies* to serve as the classic reference work of Western civilization for nearly one thousand years. For instance, we see the inclusion of the medical idea of the four humors in the chapter on medicine: "All diseases come from the four humors, that is, blood, bile, black bile, and phlegm."[8] Modern science now knows this to be nonsense, but the point remains that Isidore's *Etymologies* was titanically reflective of the classical world and influential in shaping the medieval one. In the years after his death, a subsequent council of Toledo remembered Isidore as "the extraordinary doctor, the latest ornament of the Catholic Church, the most learned man of the latter ages, always to be named with reverence."[9] Like other medieval figures whom we will examine, Isidore realized that the church could be a useful conduit for transmitting indispensable knowledge that was in danger of being lost.

ITALY: THEODORIC, BOETHIUS, AND CASSIODORUS

Control of the Italian peninsula changed hands multiple times among different barbarian tribes during the second half of the fifth century. Eventually the kingdom of the Ostrogoths, who had initially come from the Black Sea area in the third and fourth centuries, won out over the others. The Ostrogoths were a short-lived but powerful group who reached their apex under the king Theodoric. Theodoric was born in 454, and the first years of his life were spent as a hostage at Constantinople (again, an arrangement in which members of one royal family were given as collateral to another as a guaranty of peace). There he gained exposure to all the refinements of cosmopolitan city life, including reading and writing. This early contact with classical learning would later influence his monarchy. By 475, Theodoric became the king of the Ostrogoths, and in 493 became the sole ruler of all Italy after strangling a rival barbarian chieftain whom he had just toasted at a banquet.

No doubt influenced by his cultured upbringing, Theodoric established his kingdom at Ravenna in northern Italy, and ran Italy with an eye focused on administrative detail and respect for his new, Roman subjects. In particular, he took steps to re-beautify Rome itself. In one letter, he wrote to the prefect of the city, "Let nothing lie useless which may rebound to the beauty of the City. Let your illustrious Magnificence therefore cause the blocks of marble which are everywhere lying about in ruins to be wrought up into the walls by the hands of the workmen whom I send herewith."[10] In another letter, Theodoric rebuked the Senate of Rome for paying less in taxes than they owed:

We hear with sorrow, by the report of the Provincial judges, that you the Fathers of the State, who ought to set an example to your sons (the ordinary citizens), have been so remiss in the payment of taxes that on this first collection nothing, or next to nothing, has been brought in from any Senatorial house. Thus a crushing weight has fallen on the lower orders, who have had to make good your deficiencies and have been distraught by the violence of the tax gatherers.[11]

Theodoric, though an Arian, was aided in his administration by two Catholic, culturally Roman advisers. The first was named Boethius, a man sometimes called "the last of the Romans." Boethius came from a distinguished family, and despite being orphaned, attained a reputation for learning at a young age. Around 510, he began to gain high-level posts in Theodoric's administration, and in 522 became the *magister officiorum* (master of the offices), the highest rank in the civil service. But Theodoric's confidence in him was not to last long. Boethius was suspected by Theodoric of trying to restore the Ostrogothic kingdom's relationships with the Byzantine Empire. Compounding that division lay the fact that Theodoric was an Arian, while Boethius, the suspected spy, adhered to a more Nicene version of Christianity. In 523, Theodoric sentenced him to death for treason.

But Boethius's time as a prisoner produced one of the most important works of Western philosophy of the Middle Ages—a book that some scholars have deemed as secondary in importance during the medieval period to only the Bible. The *Consolation of Philosophy*, as Boethius titled his magnum opus, depicts a forlorn Boethius in conversation with a woman (an allegorical character that represents the discipline of philosophy), discussing the eternal questions: how God can permit evil, the changing nature of life, the inconsistency of human beings, and the unpredictable consequences for doing good. One of the images that Boethius used to capture his thinking was a wheel (probably the source of our modern idea of a Wheel of Fortune). The wheel may lift someone up to great heights, but we shouldn't be surprised when it inexplicably casts him back down. Yet at the end of all things, said Boethius, is a greater good that must be pursued; everything is subordinate to it. In some ways, the *Consolation of Philosophy* reads like the Psalms: a great man wrestling with the will of God, alternately praising and questioning, but ultimately realizing his authority and goodness over the world. At one point, he ponders why creation rebels against God's good established order before resigning himself to the fact that it may not be for him to know:

> *Why does a strange discordance break*
> *The ordered scheme's fair harmony?*
> *Hath God decreed twixt truth and truth*
> *There may such lasting warfare be,*
> *That truths, each severally plain,*
> *We strive to reconcile in vain?*[12]

In 524, Boethius was put to death on an estate 450 miles from Rome. But the ideas expressed in the *Consolation* profoundly influenced the medieval worldview. Though written by a Christian, the *Consolation* is not a specifically Christian book. It does not mention Christ, or suggest that Christ is the hope of all men. But it does capture the essence of classical philosophy, hence the title, suggesting that the character receives relief from the anxieties of impending death through inward contemplation. Extensive copying of the work through the Middle Ages meant that a classical worldview, especially one defined by Plato's philosophy, was preserved in a Christian context. Boethius pointed to internal joys (by this he meant Christ) as the source of true happiness; satisfaction cannot be found in materialism. This kind of introspection, generally unseen in ancient pagan literature, reaffirmed the Christian ethos, even if it did not point to Christ explicitly. It also helped establish the individual's search to know himself as a major line of inquiry in Western thought and literature.

CASSIODORUS

Succeeding Boethius as *magister officiorum* was a learned lawyer named Cassiodorus. As indicated in his surviving letters, Cassiodorus oversaw all sorts of matters for Theodoric and his successors, including topics as diverse as the manufacture of purple dye,[13] the allotment of retirement funds for a former chariot driver,[14] and restitution to a merchant for losing a grain shipment in a shipwreck.[15] But Cassiodorus was especially eager to continue one of Theodoric's personal missions of preserving the Greek and Latin literature that the king had no doubt enjoyed as a boy. In times past, many Christians destroyed or, at a minimum, refused to read Greek and Roman literature, believing it a sinful output of paganism. Cassiodorus realized such work was profitable to the reader, and that Christian schools should be set up to teach the material:

> When I realized there was such a zealous and eager pursuit of secular learning, that the majority of mankind hope thereby to obtain worldly wisdom, I was deeply grieved that Holy Scripture lacked public teachers, since secular authors certainly have a powerful and widespread tradition. Together with blessed Agapetus, pope of Rome, I made efforts to collect money for expenses to enable Christian schools in the city of Rome to employ learned teachers from whom the faithful might gain eternal salvation for their souls and the adornment of fine, pure eloquence for their speech.[16]

For Cassiodorus, as for Clement of Alexandria, Augustine, and many other Christians of antiquity, secular literature had value as a reference point for understanding the world. Many of the ideas in classical thought also pointed toward theological truths. Where Plato speculated on the idea of the Good, for instance, the classical Christians saw mankind longing to understand the true form of the eternal Good: God. "Any mention of the ancients in the midst of praising the Lord is not considered tasteless boasting," Cassiodorus wrote in his *Institutes of Divine and Human Learning.* "Furthermore, you indicate your satisfaction with a serious teacher if you question him often; even if you return many times to these books, you will not be checked by any severity."[17]

After his retirement from the Ostrogothic court, Cassiodorus founded a monastery at Vivarium, in southern Italy. As the level of literacy and the dispersion of the written word across the former Roman Empire declined, Cassiodorus sensed a need to preserve the great texts of the pagan and Christian past. He persuaded the monks to undertake the work of copying and editing manuscripts, a job usually reserved for the infirm:

> The books should be corrected to prevent scribal errors from being fixed in untrained minds, because what is fixed and rooted in the depths of memory is hard to remove. Happy indeed is the mind that has stored such a mysterious treasure in the depths of memory, with God's help; but much happier the mind that knows the ways of understanding from its own energetic investigation.[18]

This reproduction of ancient writings would become one of the signature achievements of the later Middle Ages. Though unknown to most, we owe a great deal of thanks to Cassiodorus for his desire to preserve these manuscripts. Cassiodorus firmly believed that "[e]ducation lifts an obscure man on to a level with nobles, but also adorns him who is of noble birth."[19] To that end, Cassiodorus insisted that the classical educational model of the *trivium* (grammar, rhetoric, and dialectic) and the *quadrivium* (arithmetic, astronomy, music, and geometry) were entirely suitable for the Christian as well as the pagan. It was this formula on which he structured his course of studies at Vivarium, and one that still is used in schools today.

Cassiodorus lived to be ninety-five, dying around 585 as a symbol of the new civilization in western Europe. He had been born when his father could still remember the Roman Empire of the West. By the time of his death, the political and military structure of Rome had long ago vanished. He had spent the prime years of his life laboring for a barbarian king who appreciated the classical tradition of his conquered subjects. Under Cassiodorus, the church, as happened under Isidore and others, became the repository for the very philosophical and literary works that the Bible had supplanted in cultural importance. Amid medieval Europe's rising patchwork of non-Roman cultures and kingdoms, the monks in Italy and elsewhere vouchsafed the ancient classical and Christian ideas.

THE FRANKS

As the Visigoths were rising to prominence in Spain, the area to the north of it, Gaul, was quickly coming under the control of a barbarian tribe called the Franks. The Franks initially came from the North Sea, migrating down from modern-day Holland and Belgium until reaching Gaul in the third and fourth centuries. By AD 500, they had unified the whole region under their command and established their capital at Paris. The central figure of the Frankish kingdom, who emerged at the end of the fifth century, was a fifteen-year-old boy named Clovis (466–511), who eventually blossomed into a king with a wild penchant for violence, often putting to death his own family members.

One instance reflects well Clovis's notorious temper. In 486, the Franks, not yet Christianized, conquered and

Clovis, King of the Franks, drawing, 1885.

looted the town of Soissons. His men carried away from one of the churches a vase of enormous size and beauty. The bishop of the town sent a messenger to petition Clovis that he might return the vase, even if he kept all other spoils. Clovis agreed, and went out to examine the lot of captured plunder. Clovis asked for the vase to be given to him, and all of his soldiers acquiesced. All, that is, but one man, "impetuous, envious, and vain," who raised his battle-axe and brought it down upon the vase, crushing it. Clovis responded calmly, but nurtured the injury deep in his heart. He sent the vase, now broken into pieces, back to the bishop. A year later, Clovis ordered his entire army to come out, arrayed in battle formation, for an inspection. As they stood in tight ranks, Clovis approached the vase-breaker and said to him, "No one bears his arms so clumsily as thou; for neither thy spear, nor thy sword, nor thy ax is ready for use." He then grabbed the soldier's ax and threw it on the ground. As the soldier bent down to pick it up, Clovis raised his own ax with two hands and smashed it down on the offender's head. "Thus," he said, "didst thou to the vase at Soissons."[20]

Clovis allied himself with the Gallo-Roman bishops in Gaul (who probably reciprocated out of fear of defying such a brute), but it wasn't until around 500 that Clovis became the first Frankish king to convert to Catholicism. Unlike the Arian Visigoths and Ostrogoths, the Franks worshipped a set of pagan deities. But Clovis's wife, Clotilde, was a Catholic, and Gregory of Tours, the key historian of post-Roman Gaul, painted her as instrumental in his conversion. When Clovis and Clotilde's first child was born, Clotilde begged to have him baptized as a Christian. Clovis refused, not believing that the God of the Bible was a real god: "By the will of our gods all things are created and produced. Evidently your god can do nothing, and it is not even proved that he belongs to the race of gods." But Clotilde persisted, extravagantly decorating the church for the event in hopes that Clovis would be moved by the splendid ornamentation. The child was baptized, but soon after he suddenly died while still wearing his baptismal robe. Clovis berated Clotilde: "If the child had been consecrated in the name of my gods he would be alive still. But now, because he is baptized in the name of your god, he cannot live." Soon after this, Clotilde bore him another son, who too fell ill. Clovis lectured her again, "Because he, like his brother, was baptized in the name of Christ he must soon die." But Clotilde prayed, and soon the baby was restored to health.[21]

It wasn't until Clovis one day found himself cornered in battle against a rival barbarian tribe that he felt his need of Christ. Seeing his army was "near to utter destruction," Clovis cried out:

> Jesus Christ, whom Clotilde declares to be the son of the living God, who it is said gives aid to the oppressed and victory to those who put their hope in you, I beseech the glory of thy aid. If you shall grant me victory over these enemies and I test that power which people consecrated to thy name say they have proved concerning you, I will believe in you and be baptized in thy name. For I have called upon my gods, but, as I have proved, they are far removed from my aid. So I believe that they have no power, for they do not succor those who serve them. Now I call upon thee, and I long to believe in thee, all the more that I may escape my enemies.[22]

Immediately, the legend goes, his enemies began to flee, and Clovis eventually won the day. Clovis reported back to the queen what had happened, and she sent for Remigius, the bishop of Rheims, who gave Clovis theological instruction. The only thing standing in the way of a full conversion, according to Clovis, was "that the people who follow me are not content to leave their gods. I will go and speak to them according to thy word."[23] Clovis managed to convince his people to follow this new, immortal God, and was baptized, along with three thousand members of his army.[24]

Clovis died in 511, and the kingdom he had fought to unify was soon subdivided among his heirs. Several centuries of warfare between increasingly small principalities followed, and France experienced no true level of unity until the emergence of the great king Charlemagne in the 700s. Still, the formal introduction of Catholic Christianity into the kingdom of the Franks meant that the country had now come into the orbit of the Catholic Church.

COLUMBANUS'S MISSION TO THE FRANKS

C lovis's conversion did not persuade all the Franks to give up their own pagan gods, and the likely outcome of it in many places was that Christ was worshipped alongside the other deities. The conversion of Clovis and others did little for the culture of sixth-century France; as Gregory of Tours made clear, it was a bleak and violent cauldron of death. As a consequence, France soon became the target of the church's missionary activity. By 573, for instance, the bishops of the city of Tours, in France, had planted at least twenty-four churches in the villages in the surrounding areas.

One of the most fervent missionaries of the age was a monk named Columbanus, who was born in Ireland in 543. As a boy he had a keen mind for studying the Scriptures, but in his youth, said his biographer, the devil was wont to arouse against him the "lust of lascivious maidens, especially of those whose fine figure and superficial beauty are wont to enkindle mad desires in the minds of wretched men."[25] Fearing that he would submit too much to temptation and thus forfeit a career in the church, Columbanus decided to leave his hometown and go study with the monks at Leinster. His mother was distraught, but Columbanus paid her no heed. Though she lay stretched out on the ground in front of the door, weeping, Columbanus leaped over his mother and assured her that though he would never see her again, he would be content to go wherever the way of salvation led him.[26]

Columbanus's way apparently led first to a monastery, where he stayed for several years, acquiring further knowledge of the Bible. But he soon "longed to go into strange lands,"[27] for missionary activity, and subsequently took a team of twelve others into France, where he spent twenty-six years until his death in 611. On one occasion, Columbanus was passing through Paris, where, the story says, he performed an exorcism:

When he arrived there, he met at the gate a man having an unclean spirit, who was raving and rending his garments, while babbling. The latter addressed the man of God complainingly: "What are you doing in this place, O man of God?" From afar he had been crying out for a long time with his growling voice as he saw Columbanus, the man of God, approaching. When the latter saw him, he said: "Depart, evil one, depart! Do not dare to possess any longer the body washed by Christ. Yield to the power of God, and invoked by the name of Christ." But when the devil resisted for a long time with savage and cruel strength, the man of God placed his hand on the man's ear and struck the man's tongue and by the power of God commanded the devil to depart. Then rending the man with cruel violence so that bonds could scarcely restrain him, the devil, issuing forth amid great purging and vomiting made such a stench that those who stood by believed that they could endure the fumes of sulphur more easily.[28]

Columbanus's missionary urge was not uncommon in the age of the new barbarian kingdoms. It was also shared by one of the greatest popes of all time, Gregory the Great.

GREGORY THE GREAT

Undoubtedly one of the most important church figures of the early Middle Ages was Pope Gregory the Great, a man who did so much for the faith that even John Calvin, one of the great fathers of Protestantism and an unsmiling opponent of the Catholic Church, referred to him as "the last good pope."[29] Only two popes have ever been given the honorific "the Great," and Gregory was one of them.[30] Gregory came from an aristocratic Roman family, and when his father died, Gregory used some of his inheritance to found six monasteries in Sicily, and the rest he gave to the poor. As a young man, Gregory himself became a monk, and he cultivated a set of spiritual disciplines that he adhered to throughout his life. As Gregory's reputation for piety and competence grew, Gregory was appointed to serve as papal ambassador to Constantinople. Gregory had always felt more comfortable with his monastic origins and wasn't excited to serve in this capacity. Yet the practices he acquired from his fellow monks in years past "proved an anchor-cable that held him fast to the peaceful shore of prayer while he was tossed on the restless waves of worldly affairs."[31]

Gregory was even more perturbed at his election to the papal office, an event that happened in 590: "Under the pretense of being made a bishop, I am brought back into the world; for I am now more in bondage than ever I was as a layman. I have lost the deep joy of my quiet, and while I seem outwardly to have risen, inwardly I am falling down."[32] Still, he exerted the greatest degree of energy in fulfilling his commission. His *Pastoral Rule*, written shortly after his ascension to the Papal See, became a hugely influential exposition of his philosophy of pastoral ministry, and its principles were adopted by clergymen all over western Europe. In his letters, hundreds of which survive, he referred to himself as *servus servorum Dei*, "the servant of the servants of God," a title that later became common for popes down the ages to use. His actions matched his words; once during a war-induced famine, Gregory himself cooked meals for the poor with his own hands and then sent them out as gifts, so that the recipients might be spared the shame of begging for their food.

Gregory Evangelizes Europe

As a boy in Rome, Gregory had once witnessed a slave trader showing off his latest haul from Britain, and he inquired as to who the blond-haired boys before him were. Gregory sighed, "How sad that such handsome folk are still in the grasp of the Author of darkness, and that faces of such beauty conceal minds ignorant of God's grace! What is the name of this race?" "They are Angles," said a bystander. Gregory was moved to pity for them, and retorted with a play on the word *Angles*: "That is appropriate, for they have angelic faces, and it is right that they should become fellow-heirs with the angels in heaven."[33] The story, perhaps true, reflects Gregory's lifelong desire to bring the name of Christ to the far-off places of the world. Gregory's greatest legacy was the true evangelization of the Germanic tribes that inhabited Europe. As we have seen in the conversion narratives of the Goths, Visigoths, and Franks, the meaningfulness of the early barbarian "conversions" was questionable. Kings sometimes adopted the name of Christianity out of political expedience, and often forced their armies or their people to convert at the point of a sword, absent the kind of heart change that is inherent in true conversion. Even if people were converted, these rural folk, especially in France and Germany, had very few priests or churches, and the practice of the early Germanic tribes was usually to assimilate the Christian God into their belief system. Gregory recognized this, and insisted that it should not be.

Gregory worked with Reccared to implement Christianity in Spain, and in an event that recalled Clovis's conversion, Gregory developed a relationship with the Christian queen of the Lombards ("long-beards") as they slashed and burned through northern Italy. Gregory was able to get her to convince her husband, King Agilulf, to show mercy to the Italian peninsula. Eventually, "the king . . . moved by her wholesome supplications, not only embraced the Catholic faith, but also bestowed much wealth upon the Church of Christ, and restored to the honor of their accustomed dignity certain bishops who were in a straitened and abject condition."[34]

Gregory also commissioned full-scale missions to the Germanic areas in northern France and beyond the Rhine River in Germany. Gregory knew that the cultural traditions of these peoples were not going to be quickly given up, and he instructed that the priests he dispatched to those areas to plant churches and make disciples should have patience, "For it is undoubtedly impossible to cut away everything at once from hard hearts, since one who strives to ascend to the highest place must needs rise by steps or paces, and not by leaps."[35] A letter to one of his bishops demonstrates Gregory's philosophy. In ages past, many Christians had destroyed the pagan temples in which the natives worshipped. But Gregory emphasized a gentler, more gradual approach:

> I have decided that the peoples' temples to their false gods should not be destroyed, not on any account. The idols within them should be destroyed, but the temples themselves you should simply purify with holy water; moreover, you should set up Christian altars in them and place sacred relics in them. If the temples are solidly built, they should be purified from demon worship and re-dedicated to the service of the true God. This way, I hope the people, seeing that we have not destroyed their holy sites, may abandon their erring ways: by continuing to congregate regularly in their accustomed site, therefore they might come to know and adore the true God.[36]

Gregory was immediately canonized after his death in 604, and is, along with Ambrose, Jerome, and Augustine, one of the four Doctors of the Latin church. A famous English monk of the period, the Venerable Bede, described him in the most laudatory terms: "Much might be said of his imperishable genius, which was unimpaired even by the most severe physical afflictions; for while other popes devoted themselves to building churches and enriching them with costly ornaments, Gregory's sole concern was to save souls."[37] Gregory's passion for the lost was seen nowhere more clearly than in the missions to the Britons.

THE CHURCH COMES TO BRITAIN

Until the first century BC, the area that we today call the United Kingdom (England, Scotland, Ireland, and Wales) was virtually untouched by the Romans. The indigenous inhabitants there were the Celtic peoples, who, subdivided into various tribes, inhabited much of Europe by the first century AD. The priestly and ruling classes of the Celtic peoples in Britain were called the Druids, best known for their construction of Stonehenge in stages between 3000 and 1520 BC. Modern languages derived from the original Celtic tongues, such as Gaelic, Welsh, Irish, and Cornish, are still spoken a bit in the United Kingdom today. Although the existence of a group of islands off the coast of mainland Europe was known to the Greeks in the fourth century BC, it wasn't until 55 BC that the Romans, under Julius Caesar, tried to conquer the island, a task that was fully completed by his successors in AD 43. To mark off the farthest reaches of Roman inland expansion, the emperor Hadrian constructed in 122 a stone wall that stretched for seventy-three miles. Substantial segments of the wall, known as Hadrian's Wall, still remain today.

Christianity first came to Britain probably during the reign of the emperor Tiberius (d. AD 37). Gildas the Wise, the earliest source for the history of the church in Britain, said that the fledgling faith was first received slowly by the island's inhabitants, but that the number of converts grew nonetheless. Yet the persecution of Diocletian, which happened around AD 300, did much to damage the progress of the church. Gildas said, "The churches throughout the whole world were overthrown, all the copies of the Holy Scriptures which could be found burned in the streets, and the chosen pastors of God's flock butchered, together with their innocent sheep, in order that not a vestige, if possible, might remain in some provinces of Christ's religion."[38]

It is around this time that we encounter the first and greatest martyr story of the early English church, that of Saint Alban. Alban was a pagan who one day took into his home a clergyman who was fleeing from his persecutors. After a few days of watching the cleric's example of prayer and watchfulness, he became a Christian "in all sincerity of heart."[39] Eventually the local authorities found out that the clergyman was hiding in Alban's house, and they went there to drag him off to court. When they arrived at the home, Alban, dressed in a cleric's cloak, presented himself as the man they were looking for.

Alban was brought before a local judge, who told him, "Because you have chosen to conceal a rebellious and sacrilegious person, rather than to deliver him up to the soldiers . . . you shall undergo all the punishment that was due to him, if you seek to abandon the worship of our religion."

Alban said he would not worship the pagan gods.

The judge replied, "Of what family or race are you?"

"What does it concern you," answered Alban, "of what stock I am? If you desire to hear the truth of my religion be it known to you, that I am now a Christian, and bound by Christian duties."

"I ask your name," said the judge. "Tell me it immediately."

"I am called Alban by my parents," said Alban, "and I worship and adore the true and living God, who created all things."

Then the judge, furious, said, "If you will enjoy the happiness of eternal life, do not delay to offer sacrifice to the great gods."

Alban fired back, "These sacrifices, which by you are offered to devils, neither can avail the subjects, nor answer the wishes or desires of those that offer up their supplications to them. On the contrary, whosoever shall offer sacrifice to these images shall receive the everlasting pains of hell for his reward."[40]

The infuriated judge had Alban whipped for this comment, but Alban "being most cruelly tortured, bore the same patiently, or rather joyfully, for our Lord's sake."

Seeing that this punishment would not persuade Alban to recant, the judge ordered him beheaded: "Here, therefore, the head of [the] most courageous martyr was struck off, and here he received the crown of life, which God has promised to those who love Him."[41]

A cathedral now stands today in the town where Alban is said to have been martyred, also called Saint Alban's.

As was the case in other places across the empire, the number of martyrs dying for their faith gave comfort and strength to many Christians, and after the persecution of Diocletian passed around 313, Gildas observed that churches were rebuilt, sacraments were celebrated, and that "all Christ's young disciples, after so long and wintry a night, begin to behold the genial light of heaven."[42] But later in the century, as was also the case in other places, the Arian heresy also fractured the new ecclesiastical unity that had come to Britain in the wake of persecution. Said Gildas, "For this holy union remained between Christ their head and the members of his church, until the Arian treason, fatal as a serpent, and vomiting its poison from beyond the sea, caused deadly dissension between brothers inhabiting the same house."[43]

THE ISLE OF THE DEAD

The Roman army withdrew from Britain in 410, viewing it as a cumbersome territorial luxury at that point. Although the culture of the great island was by then heavily Romanized, the power vacuum that opened up in place of a central administration was filled by numerous warlords competing for power across the country, as well as Scottish and Pictish armies coming from the north, "like worms which in the heat of mid-day come forth from their holes."[44] In 446, some Roman Britons despaired of their situation and wrote to a Roman general a letter that later became known as "The Groans of the Britons." "The barbarians drive us to the sea; the sea throws us back on the barbarians: thus two modes of death await us, we are either slain or drowned."[45] Later in the century, Britain began to suffer incursions from Germanic tribes from southern Denmark (the Angles) and northern Germany (the Saxons). This period of British history is now known as the Anglo-Saxon period, and our world *England* is today a variation of the Old English words *Angle-land*. This is the period that gives rise to the medieval legends of King Arthur, and in reality there is a shred of historical evidence to suggest that there was a Briton named Arthur who at one point organized some resistance to the Anglo-Saxon invaders around AD 500.

King Arthur or not, post-Roman Britain was an unmistakably dismal place. Writers around the Mediterranean referred to it as "the Isle of the Dead." Wrote one modern scholar, "Having virtually no trade with continental Europe, no known state organization, no Christian Church, and a reputation as a superstitious violent wasteland, Anglo-Saxon England was widely regarded by the rest of western Europe as the end of the world—the last, poorest, and most backward frontier of civilization."[46] To say that there was no Christian church is figuratively true; although there were scattered pockets of believers, the church of Rome had virtually no presence there. As the Roman government left Britain, so the church shriveled too.

GREGORY SENDS AUGUSTINE TO THE BRITONS

The gruesome conditions in England did not escape the notice of Pope Gregory, who undoubtedly had recalled his boyhood memory of the Angle slaves. It was Gregory the Great, said the Venerable Bede, who "transformed our still idolatrous nation into a church of Christ."[47] In 596, Gregory commissioned a missionary expedition to the Britons, an endeavor led by a monk named Augustine.[48] Things got off to a tough start. After Augustine and his forty fellow monks had traveled some ways to their destination, they were "seized with a sudden fear, and began to think of returning home, rather than proceed to a barbarous, fierce, and unbelieving nation, to whose very language they were strangers."[49] Augustine wrote a letter to Gregory, asking that they might not be forced to go any farther. But Gregory wrote back, exhorting them, "Let not, therefore, the toil of the journey, nor the tongues of evil speaking men, alter you; but with all possible earnestness and zeal perform that which, by God's direction, you have undertaken; being assured, that much labour is followed by an eternal reward."[50] Augustine was strengthened by the reply, and eventually made it to Britain, where he found a receptive audience in the form of King Ethelbert of Kent, one of the seven kingdoms into which the island was partitioned.

Using Frankish interpreters, Augustine "assured to all that took advantage of it everlasting joys in heaven and a kingdom that would never end with the living and true God."[51] Ethelbert was intrigued. He already had a Christian wife whom he had taken from the Franks, but the new message was still so mysterious and foreign to him that he ordered Augustine and his men to shelter where they were until he could figure out what to do with them. Several days later, Ethelbert invited Augustine and his cohort into his royal chamber (he was wary of being cursed by black magic if they entered his home). The visitors entered with a silver cross painted on a banner, singing liturgical hymns. They preached to Ethelbert, who was not quite ready to renounce the pagan customs of his people. He was, however, willing to allow them to take up residency in Kent: "But because you are come from far into my kingdom, and, as I conceive, are desirous to impart to us those things which you believe to be true, and most beneficial, we will not molest you, but give you favourable entertainment, and take care to supply you with your necessary sustenance; nor do we forbid you to preach and gain as many as you can to your religion."[52]

Augustine was allowed to take up residence in Canterbury, the seat of Ethelbert's power, in southeast England. To win converts, the Augustinians adapted their dress and behavior to the local customs,

> applying themselves to frequent prayer, watching and fasting; preaching the word of life to as many as they could; despising all worldly things, as not belonging to them; receiving only their necessary food from those they taught; living themselves in all respects conformably to what they prescribed to others, and being always disposed to suffer any adversity, and even to die for that truth which they preached.[53]

The small church already established in Kent, Saint Martin's (remember, the queen herself was already a Christian), flourished, and it is still today the oldest standing church in the entire English-speaking world. Augustine was appointed archbishop of all England. Today, the head of the Anglican Church in England is still the archbishop of Canterbury. To further establish the church, Gregory sent to Augustine "sacred vessels and vestments for the altars, also ornaments for the churches, and vestments for the priests and clerks, as likewise relics of the holy apostles and martyrs; besides many books."[54] Sometime later, probably around the year 600 or 601, Ethelbert converted, becoming the first English king to convert to Christianity. Ethelbert's conversion spurred other kings to convert as well, and set in motion the gradual Christianization of Anglo-Saxon Britain, a process that was almost entirely completed by the time William the Conqueror inaugurated a new period of English history in 1066.

THE VENERABLE BEDE

The great historian of early England, whom we have already referred to, was a monk known as the Venerable Bede (ca. 673–735). Bede's work *The Ecclesiastical History of the English Peoples* chronicled the events of the English church from the time of Augustine to the time of Bede's own death. A very significant aspect of the *Ecclesiastical History* is its usage of the anno Domini ("in the year of our Lord") system of dating historical events. The AD system, which later became the basis for the Julian and Gregorian calendars, was initially invented by a monk named Dionysius Exiguus (in English, "Dennis the Dwarf") around 525. Previously, the Romans reckoned time according to the years of consuls and emperors, and later, from the reign of Diocletian. But Dionysius couldn't bear the thought of ordering time by using a great persecutor of Christians as a reference point. Consequently, his new AD system accounted for time by counting upward from the year of Jesus' birth. It wasn't until Bede used this system in his chronicle (the most important historical work from Anglo-Saxon England) that it became widespread. In addition to his history (which is often cited here), Bede was also a very learned man who, like Cassiodorus and Isidore, was instrumental in preserving copies of Greek and Latin texts in their original languages.

EARLY CELTIC CHRISTIANITY

The regions of modern-day Scotland, Wales, and Ireland had never come under the Roman yoke, but they did experience some contact with Christianity. The first missionary from Rome who went to Ireland was Palladius, in 431, but the most famous missionary to the Irish people was Saint Patrick, "the apostle to the Irish," who conducted his work during the second half of the fifth century. The name *Patrick* is derived from the Latin word *patricus*, a reference to the upper class of ancient Roman society from which Patrick came. Patrick and his family lived in Britain, and when Patrick was sixteen, they were captured and sold into slavery by a band of Irish raiders. In time, his experience among the Irish, who still practiced the Druidic religion and spoke a Celtic language, helped him later assimilate to their culture. While he worked as a shepherd for a local chieftain, Patrick became gripped day by day by a desire to pray, one that knew no physical constraints:

> I used to pray many times a day. More and more did the love of God, and my fear of him and faith increase, and my spirit was moved so that in a day [I said] from one up to a hundred prayers, and in the night a like number; besides I used to stay out in the forests and on the mountain and I would wake up before daylight to pray in the snow, in icy coldness, in rain, and I used to feel neither ill nor any slothfulness, because, as I now see, the Spirit was burning in me at that time.[55]

One night while sleeping, Patrick heard a voice telling him, "Soon you will depart for your home country . . . Behold, your ship is ready."[56]

Patrick got up and fled to an unknown ship that he believed was waiting for him two hundred miles away! Patrick reached the port, and initially the sailors, not knowing Patrick's purposes, rejected him from coming with them. But after Patrick committed himself to prayer, they changed their minds and invited him aboard. After three days of sailing and an arduous overland journey in which he almost starved to death, Patrick finally reached his homeland of Britain and his parents. In time, Patrick entered the priesthood and served in a variety of roles

A bust of St. Patrick at Dublin Castle, Ireland.

across England. But one day Patrick had another dream and heard the voice of the Irish people crying out to him, "We beg you, holy youth, that you shall come and shall walk again among us."[57] In 433, Patrick and some companions landed again in Ireland, where they faced continual hardship for their gospel message. For one thing, the Druidic classes rejected the new faith. Patrick also never accepted any payment for his ministry, and so could not participate in the cultural institution of gift-giving that solidified friendships. Several times he was beaten or robbed, and no fewer than twelve times was he imprisoned, once for sixty days. Still, Patrick managed to baptize "thousands of people"[58] and establish churches all over Eyrie.

The seeds that Patrick sowed in Ireland bloomed in the early sixth century. Ireland became a hotbed of monasticism (more on this in another chapter), and the greatest abbey or monastery of early Ireland was called Clonard. Clonard was a place of extraordinary learning (this meant study and copying of Latin and often Greek texts), and it produced the "Twelve Apostles of Ireland," a group of holy men who built up the Irish church. The most famous of the Twelve was named Columba, a monk responsible for bringing Christianity to the Scots in the latter 500s. Columba was born in Ireland, and in 520 went to study at Clonard, which at its height contained no fewer than three thousands monks! Sometime afterward, Columba was sent out to study with another monk, but a plague referred to by the Irish as "yellow disorder" ravaged that community, and they broke up. Columba spent the next few decades as an itinerant founder of monasteries, and in 563, he was invited to Scotland, where he became a tireless evangelist to the Scots.

One of his great missions was that to the Northern Picts, a group of people who inhabited modern-day Inverness, the farthest reaches of the rugged Scottish wilderness. When he first visited King Brude, the ruler of these people, Columba's admittance to Brude's palace was denied, and the gate to the castle was locked. But Columba (so the legend goes) made the sign of the cross, and the bars and locks to the entrance flew open! The startled king listened to the man who could perform such a miracle and was converted. The next several decades of Columba's life were marked by his itinerant ministry to the peasants who inhabited the woods and glades of Scotland. Although we have scant evidence for the true account of his ministry, there is recorded in his hagiography a set of fantastical stories, highly entertaining, even if not true. On one occasion, it is said, Columba approached a spring whose water caused anyone who drank it to contract leprosy. The local population, at Druidic urging, worshipped this fountain as a god because of its (they thought) demonic power. As Columba neared the fountain, the Druids rejoiced at his impending illness. Yet Columba invoked the name of Christ, washed his hands and feet, and drank from the fountain. On that day, the nature of the fountain was changed, so that it instead poured forth water capable of healing instead of sickening. Countless stories like these reflect the kind of benevolent works that Columba did all around the Scottish countryside as a testimony to the Christian faith. Columba also founded Iona, a monastery off the Scottish coast, which became his base of operations. As probably the most learned man in the Scottish realm, Columba was a man of many energies: planting churches and monasteries, intervening in royal disputes between kingdoms, and finding the time to copy down, it is said, three hundred books. Nobody did more to Christianize Scotland than Columba.[59]

Whether it was Pope Gregory, the Irish monks, Germanic queens, or ordinary people, many Christians of the early Middle Ages were deeply preoccupied with bringing the gospel to the new barbarian kingdoms. By the end of the sixth century, their efforts had been very successful. As we will see, one of the great stories of the Middle Ages was how the church reflected the fusion of Germanic, Christian, and classical cultures. But there was also a burst of church expansion taking place outside of the Roman sphere of influence. It is to these distant places that we will now turn our attention.

FOURTEEN

THE BYZANTINE EMPIRE

Justinian, Hagia Sophia, Maurice, Heraclius

B y the end of the fifth century, the area formerly known as the Western Roman Empire had been engulfed by new barbarian king-doms. But the eastern part of the empire, although frequently enduring attacks from groups like the Huns, the Avars, and the Persians, remained relatively unscathed from destruction. Ever since Constantine founded Constantinople in the early fourth century, the Eastern empire had enjoyed a greater degree of peace and security. This stability was largely due to the amount of wealth concentrated in the urban centers there, from which the emperors could more easily pay their own soldiers and offer tribute to their adversaries. Additionally, the emperor Theodosius II had constructed the massive walls of Constantinople during his reign in the 400s. Thus, the crown jewel metropolis of the Roman world became an oft-assailed stronghold that never fell. The remains of these hulking fortifications can still be seen even today ringing the old city of Istanbul.

After the collapse of the western portion of the empire in 476 (a canonical number that denotes the year the last Western emperor was deposed), the emperors Zeno, Anastasius, and Justin managed to hold things together quite well in the East, in spite of some political controversies.

The Byzantines understood themselves to be Romans (the term they used to describe themselves), and it wasn't until the ascendency of the emperor Justinian in 527 that the eastern portion of the Roman Empire could be characterized as a distinct civilization of its own.[1] Justinian, for instance, created new standards for government, law, and architecture. His reign was the greatest in the history of the Eastern empire, which lasted until 1453. But it was his view of the relationship between church and state that constituted a significant break from the traditions of other emperors. His conception of how the emperor should relate to the church became a uniquely Eastern Roman phenomenon that resonated down the ages. As the Byzantines confronted ecclesiastical and military challenges through the centuries, the concentration of authority in one man over both secular and religious matters proved simultaneously beneficial and destructive.

JUSTINIAN

Justinian was born in modern-day Serbia in about 482, the son of an illiterate peasant. Justinian's mother, however, was the sister of Justin, a member of the imperial guard who would eventually become emperor. Justin's rise to the imperial throne meant a privileged place for his nephew, and the young man learned Greek and Latin (he was the last Roman emperor to speak Latin as his first language) and gained a familiarity about the inner workings of empire. In fact, Justinian himself may have exerted de facto control over imperial affairs even before Justin's death. In 527, Justinian formally became the head of the empire. It appears that though his achievements were enormous, his character was at least somewhat unsavory. The *Secret History* at the time an unpublished history of Justinian's reign composed by a court secretary named Procopius, which we must read with some skepticism, is the main source for this opinion:

> [He] this man was both an evil-doer and easily led into evil, the sort of a person whom they call a moral pervert, never of his own accord speaking

the truth to those with whom he conversed, but having a deceitful and crafty intent behind every word and action, and at the same time exposing himself, an easy prey, to those who wished to deceive him. And a certain unusual mixture had developed in him, compounded of both folly and wickedness . . . Nature seemed to have removed all baseness from the rest of mankind and to have concentrated it in the soul of this man . . . if one should care to estimate all the misfortunes which have befallen the Romans from the earliest times and then to balance against them those of the present day, it seems to me that he would find a greater slaughter of human beings to have been perpetrated by this man than has come to pass in all the preceding time.[2]

Justinian's main preoccupation as emperor was reconquering territory that the empire had lost to barbarians. Justinian delegated authority to his top general, Belisarius, who launched campaigns against the Ostrogoths in Italy and the Vandals in North Africa. These campaigns were for a time successful; the Byzantines even recaptured Ravenna, the capital of the Ostrogothic kingdom in Italy, where the most beautiful mosaics from the Byzantine period can still be seen today. In North Africa, Justinian rebuilt towns, aqueducts, and forts.

But Justinian did not prove the most able commander in chief. He always, claimed Procopius, went to war at the wrong time, and when he was at war, quickly had his attention diverted from the matter at hand, preferring to spend his time ruminating on philosophical concerns, like the nature of God, rather than making battle plans. The consequence of Justinian's incompetency and poor timing were protracted campaigns that took a great toll on both sides: "the whole earth was constantly drenched with human blood shed by both the Romans and

Sixth-century mosaic of Justinian in the church of San Vitale in Ravenna, Italy.

267

practically all the barbarians."[3] But Justinian's warring, for all the blood and treasure spilled, was actually quite successful. By the time of his death, Justinian's kingdom could rightly be called an empire. Almost all of Italy and North Africa were recovered, in addition to gains in places such as the Balkans and Armenia. These territories would remain in Byzantine hands for over a century.

THE FIRST GREAT PLAGUE

B ut Justinian's time held its fair share of calamities, none of which was more destructive than the First Great Plague, a form of bubonic plague that devastated the Byzantine Empire, and Constantinople in particular. At the time, plague was thought to have come from the fleas of rats riding on Egyptian grain ships, but more likely those fleas came from China. Procopius, ever the exaggerator, wrote that a consequence of the plague was that "the whole human race came near to being annihilated."[4] Another scholar, the wonderfully named Evagrius Scholasticus, also said that "no part of the human race remained unvisited by the disease."[5] There is some exaggeration in these words, but the extent of the destruction these men witnessed was severe—Procopius's own estimate was five thousand per day[6]—about 40 percent of the city's population in the final reckoning, over the course of four months. Victims suffered a long, slow fever that doctors at first thought ordinary. But suddenly the fever would be accompanied by large boils (boubons) on the abdomen, armpits, and inner thighs, a sign that it was probably too late to save the patient. Oftentimes victims died within a single day. Vomiting of blood often accompanied the mental delirium and open sores. One of the worst consequences was the lack of room to bury all the dead bodies:

> And when it came about that all the tombs which had existed previously were filled with the dead, then they dug up all the places about

the city one after the other, laid the dead there, each one as he could, and departed; but later on those who were making these trenches, no longer able to keep up with the number of the dying, mounted the towers of the fortifications . . . and tearing off the roofs threw the bodies there in complete disorder; and they piled them up just as each one happened to fall, and filled practically all the towers with corpses, and then covered them again with their roofs. As a result of this an evil stench pervaded the city and distressed the inhabitants still more, and especially whenever the wind blew fresh from that quarter.[7]

Justinian himself contracted the plague, though he managed to survive. The pestilence, which also visited western Europe and the Persians in the East as well, impeded his plans to keep a hold on parts of the Mediterranean. As Justinian's wars with the Persians intensified and his lavish public treasury dwindled, the plague limited his ability to muster the manpower or the money to fight simultaneous wars against the barbarians in the West and Persians in the East.

DOMESTIC AFFAIRS

Justinian's exertions abroad were matched by avarice at home. His wars drained the formerly well-stocked public treasury; the wars in Italy alone also cost over three hundred thousand pounds of gold. "Like an everflowing river . . . ," said Procopius, "each day he plundered and pillaged his subjects, yet the inflow all streamed straight on to the barbarians."[8] Such measures had a destructive effect on everyone else: Justinian squeezed every last penny out of landholders, merchants, and even the poor. When Justinian levied a tax on bread, bakers responded to the tax by cutting costs: bread was now baked with sawdust and crushed-up seashells mixed in. The consistent, often arbitrary levying of taxes on citizens of all social classes meant that the tempers of the citizenry in Constantinople were constantly on a slow boil.

The other great infamy of Justinian's reign was his marriage to Theodora. Theodora was the young daughter of the Hippodrome's[9] bear-keeper and allegedly the most promiscuous prostitute in all of Rome. Procopius's account of her is world-class slander: the least racy of his passages describe her as one who "gave her youth to anyone she met, in utter abandonment . . . on the field of pleasure she was never defeated."[10] Theodora was unquestionably one of the most beautiful women in Constantinople, however, and when

Sixth-century mosaic of the Empress Theodora in the church of San Vitale in Ravenna, Italy.

Justinian was forty, against the protestations of his family, he shocked the empire by taking the twenty-five-year-old girl as his wife! The king and queen, both originally of common backgrounds, proved a power couple well suited to one another. Theodora acted as Justinian's top adviser, and the two apparently staged public disagreements in order to manipulate different political factions into believing the two were actually divided. Theodora, like Justinian, seems to have been a prideful and snobbish personality, even making foreign deputations grovel at her feet when they arrived at the palace. But she still managed to use her power to affect social legislation that served women, such as prohibiting the trafficking of young girls as sex slaves, implementing the death penalty for rape, and outlawing the exposure of infants. Her most important achievement, however, was an act of encouragement to her husband in a moment of panic.

THE NIKA RIOT

The center of civic life at Constantinople was the Hippodrome, a large racetrack for horses with seating for thousands of spectators. In Justinian's day, rival fans of chariot drivers organized themselves into factions that resembled modern European soccer hooligan gangs. The most prominent of these two squads were the Blues and the Greens, and both sides often carried their passions over into political or theological disputes, which also had a tendency to become violent. Justinian's palace abutted the Hippodrome, and he would often go out on his private balcony overlooking the racetrack to observe the shows. At his appearance, the Blues and Greens would often take the opportunity to shout advice or abuse at him, though Justinian himself personally supported the Blues.

On the afternoon of January 13, 532, tensions between Blues and Greens were already at a fever pitch because of a violent episode a few days before. Justinian had refused to commute the sentences for two men involved in a Blue-Green fight, and was also facing the ire of the crowd because of his perpetually high taxes. On this day, the Blues and the Greens unified against him and stormed the palace, shouting, "Nika!" ("Conquer!"). For five days, fires and rioting engulfed the neighborhoods around the palace. The Blues and Greens stormed the city's prison, emptying it of political prisoners. Whole portions of the city were set on fire, and civil servants were killed indiscriminately. Justinian considered fleeing, and readied a fleet to take him across the Bosphorus, but it was Theodora who talked him out of it. "For one who has been an emperor it is unendurable to be a fugitive. May I never be separated from this purple, and may I not live that day on which those who meet me shall not address me as mistress.

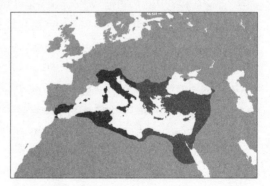

The Byzantine Empire at its height in the sixth century. The purple represents areas reconquered from the barbarian empires.

If, now, it is your wish to save yourself, O Emperor, there is no difficulty . . . as for myself, I approve a certain ancient saying that royalty is a good burial shroud."[11]

At these words, Justinian gathered himself and resolved to stay. He concocted a plan with his advisers in which they bribed the leadership of the Blues to call off their men. At the moment when the Blues and Greens were poised to crown a new emperor in the Hippodrome, the Blues stormed out, leaving only the stunned Greens as Justinian's feeble challengers. Justinian sent his army out to quell the rebellion, and they slaughtered thousands of rebels in that single day. The Nika riot was the last serious domestic political opposition that Justinian would ever encounter, and indirectly produced one of the greatest masterworks of architecture the world has ever seen.

THE HAGIA SOPHIA

In the course of the Nika Riots, great portions of Constantinople were burned to the ground. One of the casualties of the chaos was a church originally built in 415 during the reign of Theodosius II that the rioters left "a charred mass of ruins," according to Procopius.[12] Justinian decided to rebuild a church on the site, one that would be more splendid than any church that had come before it. The new church, like the old, would be called the Hagia Sophia (Greek: "Holy Wisdom"). His decision to erect a new church had many motives. He probably felt a religious duty to rebuild a shrine that had been destroyed. But a new church would also project an image of Byzantine power, and would be a token of beneficence to the many mobs that seethed at his heavy-handed policies.

Work on the great edifice began in 532. The principal architects were a physicist named Isidore of Miletus and a mathematician named Anthemius of Tralles. Ten thousand workers contributed to the project. Blocks of marble were quarried (or stripped from pagan temples) and hauled in from all over the empire. Justinian, "disregarding all questions of expense, eagerly pressed on to begin the work of construction, and began to gather all the artisans from the whole world."[13] In the end, such a huge and talented labor force managed to produce one of the great architectural wonders of all time in only five years. Procopius gasped that the structure "exults of indescribable beauty . . . the beholder is utterly unable to select which particular detail he should admire more than all the others."[14] Justinian, in a reference to the Israelite king Solomon's temple in Jerusalem, is said to have exclaimed at the sight, "Solomon, I have outdone thee!"

The signature stylings of the church certainly are worthy of admiration. The church's many arched windows allowed for an abundance of sunlight to gleam off of the rich marble inside, illuminating the interior. The central dome of the church, ringed by arches at the base that let in sunlight, seemed to float above the rest of the building (this can be confirmed even today). The ceiling was overlaid entirely with gold, and dozens of columns and precious stones adorned the inside. Procopius noted that although the building "towers above the whole earth," it was still distinguished for its "harmony of proportions, having neither excess nor deficiency."[15] This proportionality reflected the classical Greeks' view of physical beauty, an aesthetic that was transmitted down the centuries. In time, the residents of the city came to call it simply the Great Church. Its position was most prominent: near Justinian's palace, on one of the highest hills of the old city, and easily viewable from ships entering the harbor at Constantinople. Most impressive was the spiritual effect that entering the church had on the worshipper. Said Procopius:

The interior of the Hagia Sofia today.

> [W]henever anyone enters this church to pray, he understands at once
> that it is not by any human power or skill, but by the influence of God,
> that this work has been so finely turned. And so his mind is lifted up

toward God and exalted, feeling that He cannot be far away, but must especially love to dwell in this place which He has chosen.[16]

The Hagia Sophia stands as the finest achievement of Byzantine architecture, and its many features were later copied by the Western and especially Islamic architects. Many architectural elements of mosques that are commonly described as "Islamic" in style in reality trace their architectural heritage to the Hagia Sophia. In 1453, the Turkish conquest of Constantinople meant that the church was converted into a mosque. Many Christian frescoes and mosaics were covered over by Islamic designs, and minarets were added to the outside. In 1935, Ataturk, the secular ruler of Turkey, declared that the Hagia Sophia would become a tourist exhibition. Over the past few decades, a remarkable restoration effort has uncovered many of the great artistic details of Christian mosaics and frescoes that were formerly considered lost or destroyed, and both Christian and Islamic details can be seen today.

The exterior of the Hagia Sofia today.

THE *CORPUS IURIS CIVILIS*

Despite the heavy-handedness with which Justinian ran his kingdom, he did manage to institute a number of reforms that strengthened the empire. None were more important than the publication of the *Corpus Iuris Civilis* (Body of Civil Law), the last great work of law from the ancient world. The *Corpus* was much more comprehensive than anything that had come before it, and sought to put order to thousands of various laws governing the empire since ancient Roman times. In 528, Justinian ordered a ten-man commission, headed by an adviser of his named Tribonianus, to account for, revise, and reorganize the laws of the empire. The commission counted two thousand extant books of law, some of them contradictory, but also discovered that most lawyers referred to no more than six. This cumbersome system could not last. In the preface to the *Corpus*, Tribonianus wrote, "We have found the entire arrangement of the law which has come down to us from the foundation of the City of Rome and the times of Romulus, to be so confused that it is extended to an infinite length and is not within the grasp of human capacity."[17]

After months of work, the commission produced a massive set of books in 529 that helped shaped Western law for centuries. Instead of the law being a collection of individual pronouncements, it became a systematized set of rules guiding multiple areas of public life, including later systems of canon law. More pieces were issued over time, and the code included a law textbook called the *Digest*, one of the very first legal textbooks in the world. The code also reaffirmed what had been officially established in 391 by Theodosius: that Christianity was the official state religion of the Roman Empire. But the code went a step further in claiming that the emperor, a civic authority, also had full jurisdiction over church matters. Though in both East and West the church and the civil authorities had often blessed one another's endeavors, and at times the emperor had embarked on ad hoc interventions in church matters, Justinian broke new ground by legally codifying his permanent, perpetual authority over church and state.

JUSTINIAN'S RELIGIOUS POLICY

Justinian, for all his faults, apparently took God seriously. He often spent long nights in prayer and fasting, and loved to hold theological discussions. But he was also an emperor whose goal was to consolidate and preserve political power. Justinian's religious policy became what in modern times became known as *caesaropapism*: the concentration of a high degree of secular and religious authority in one man. As had increasingly been the case from the time of Constantine, the emperor's power meant he could willfully blur distinctions between his authority as an emperor and his authority over the church. But Justinian's reorganization of the entire Roman law code included a more formal expansion of this authority than ever before. This made the Byzantines strikingly different from the West: the pope, though a powerful man, could not boast the kind of secular authority Justinian and his successors did. Moreover, the West was fragmented into many different principalities at this point; there was no great political leader in which power could be concentrated.

The great object of Justinian's concentration of power was unity and peace within the empire, a goal sometimes obtained through brutal means. In the *Corpus*, apostasy (converting from Christianity to paganism) was made punishable by death. Civil authorities had a say in nominating bishops, and the *Corpus* even listed a number of rules that had to be obeyed during a church service, including the volume of the bishop's voice: "We order all bishops and priests to repeat the divine service and the prayer, when baptism is performed, not in an undertone, but in a loud voice which can be heard by the faithful people, in such a way that the minds of the listeners may be induced to manifest greater devotion, and a higher appreciation of the praises and blessings of God."[18] Justinian's decision to assert control by fiat over the church allowed him to consolidate his power and place allies in influential places. But it occasionally produced a major headache for him.

THE THREE CHAPTERS CONTROVERSY

In chapter 13, we saw that the Council of Chalcedon in 451 condemned the Monophysite doctrine as anathema. Monophysites believed that

Christ only had one distinct nature (a mysterious combination of human and divine) while the Chalcedonian opposition to this doctrine believed in two distinct but fully complementary natures. Although formally condemned, the Monophysite doctrine lived on in many churches of Egypt and Syria. Over time, these churches' refusal to accept the decision of Chalcedon put them at odds with Justinian. Justinian's quest for political and ecclesiastical unity thus pitted him in the middle of multiple competing interests: the Monophysite churches, the Chalcedonian churches, the pope, and his wife, Theodora.

In 543 or 544, Justinian declared anathema the writings of three Monophysite theologians. Justinian believed these contrary to the theological creed that the Council of Chalcedon had produced more than one hundred years earlier, which affirmed the dual nature of Christ as both man and God. Justinian's purpose was to bring the Monophysites back into the church. But not everyone agreed with Justinian's theological assertions. The Monophysites, though a minority movement, had influence in high places. Justinian's own wife, Theodora, was said to have been a Monophysite, and through her influence had installed a Monophysite patriarch over Constantinople. Quarrels broke out all over the empire, and even the pope was unsure which side to support. A bishop in North Africa named Facundus of Hermione wrote to Justinian in the 540s, and cited as a warning to Justinian an Old Testament passage that detailed what happened to a king who overstepped his boundaries:

> One should remember the fate of Oziah who ruled over many nations, rose to fame, and felt such pride in his heart that he placed incense on the altar, which was the exclusive privilege of the priests and the sons of Aaron. For this sin his impudent face, which had lost all sense of reverence, was stricken with leprosy. Our very humble Prince [i.e., Justinian] knows that Oziah did not go unpunished for daring to usurp the function of a priest.[19]

Finally, in 553, Justinian, without papal approval, called a council to decide on the Monophysite question. One hundred sixty bishops from around the empire came together and ultimately decided to condemn the Monophysite doctrine. Western denial of the Monophysites was often simply the result of the fact that the Latin-speaking West could not properly understand the Monophysite writings, which were composed almost entirely in Greek. The pope, Vigilius, alternately supported or denied the Council's conclusions four different times before he died in 555. His successor, Pelagius I, declared his support for it, which led to a schism of many churches in northern Italy and North Africa. But the pope's decision to condemn the Monophysites did not fully put the controversy to rest. At the time of the Muslim conquests, the churches of the East were still bickering over the question.

PERSECUTION IN THE BYZANTINE EMPIRE

Justinian did not always resolve religious differences with edicts and councils. The proclamation in his *Corpus* of Christianity as the official religion of the empire also legitimized state-sponsored persecution of heretics. All pagan temples were to be immediately closed, and anyone who was caught performing an animal sacrifice was bidden to be "laid low with the avenging sword,"[20] a holdover law from the time of Constantius. The offender's property was to be confiscated.

One man whom Justinian used to impose orthodoxy was a Syrian churchman named John of Ephesus. Justinian sent John on a mission in 542 to convert pagans living in the hinterlands of the empire, on the border with the Persian Empire. At the end of his mission, John reported that he had converted seventy thousand pagans and built more than ninety monasteries. But he didn't produce his "conversions" through evangelism alone: a great deal of temple smashing took place. Likewise,

Justinian used John at Constantinople to eradicate a secret cadre of intellectuals accused of paganism. John's own *Ecclesiastical History* reported on the inquisition, which may have been driven by motives more political than theological:

> After they were discovered and tortured they rushed to denounce one another; some were beaten, others flogged or put in prison, some turned over to the church where they accepted Christian faith after admitting their false belief . . . A rich and powerful man named Phocas, who was a patrician, was arrested. Since he knew that the men already arrested had denounced him as a pagan, and since he knew that a severe judgment had been rendered against him because of the fervor of the emperor, he swallowed a deadly poison during the night and died. When the emperor heard of this, he rightly ordered that Phocas be buried like a donkey and that there be no funeral for him and no prayers offered for him. So Phocas' family collected him during the night on a cart and carried him to an open grave where they threw him like a dead animal.[21]

For all of Justinian's intolerance of pagans, heretics, and apostates, it is highly ironic that toward the end of his life, Justinian "became entangled among thorns and briers,"[22] and expressed a growing interest in the very Monophysite theology he had long combated. His interest in preserving relations with the Western church, which steadfastly condemned the Monophysites, probably prevented him from adopting the Monophysite doctrine in its full measure. Justinian died in 565, after a reign of thirty-eight years and eight months. As both priest and king, he had at times exercised tyrannical control over his political and ecclesiastical world. But he also reconquered a great deal of once-Roman territory, imposed orthodoxy on his subjects, and laid the foundation for Western law. Despite a character often stained by ruthlessness and profligacy with money, Justinian is perhaps the most important figure of the early Middle Ages.

AFTER JUSTINIAN

After the death of Justinian, the empire passed into the hands of his nephew Justin, who, according to a biographer, was "dissolute, utterly abandoned to luxury and inordinate pleasures . . . possessed alike by the vices of audacity and cowardice."[23] Justin's reign did not last long, nor did the imperial tenures of those who came after him. The most notable Byzantine emperors from the time of Justinian until the Muslim conquests of the Middle East and Mediterranean in the seventh century were two men named Maurice and Heraclius. Maurice was an accomplished general who reigned as emperor from 582 to 602. The entire tenure of his reign was marked by a kingdom teetering on the brink of financial ruin (something he inherited from his predecessors) and constant wars with barbarians and Persians. Maurice was a competent general and carved out a good deal of space from the barbarian tribes along the Danube and the Persians in the East. But his financial difficulties proved to be a good deal of his undoing. In 588, military wages were slashed. In 599, Maurice was unable to pay the ransom of twelve thousand Byzantine soldiers who had been captured by a barbarian tribe called the Avars, and all of them were slaughtered. In 602, Maurice decided that his army would spend the winter beyond the Danube River in central Europe, a location much more frigid than the Mediterranean. A centurion named Phocas decided this was the last straw of abuse and marched on Constantinople with a band of mutineers. Maurice fled, but the soldiers caught up to him and murdered him and his six sons. His wife and daughters were forced into a monastery.

HERACLIUS

From 610 to 641, the leader of Byzantium was a general named Heraclius. Heraclius's rise to power began with his own insurrection against the usurper Phocas, who had committed many abuses of power in his short tenure. When Heraclius met the captured Phocas face-to-face, he asked him, "Is this how you ruled, wretch?" Phocas replied, "And you will rule better?" Heraclius became so engaged that he had Phocas instantly beheaded. He later ordered Phocas's genitalia severed from his body because he had raped an aristocrat's wife.

Like his predecessors, Heraclius mostly occupied himself by fighting with the Sassanian (Persian) Empire. The Persians had been quite successful in the first decade of Heraclius's reign, capturing the major cities of Alexandria, Antioch, and Jerusalem. The devastation of Jerusalem was particularly acute. After twenty-one days of besieging the town, the Persians managed to smash through the walls with a battering ram. They poured in through the cracks and began indiscriminately slaughtering the citizens who hid in their homes, cisterns, and the walls themselves. What was believed to be the True Cross was carried off. One monk who was an eyewitness to the Persian destruction of Jerusalem believed the event to be a punishment for the empire's sins, and reported a detailed numbering of more than sixty-six thousand killed. The penalty inflicted on the church was particularly great:

> They [the Persians] listened not to appeals of supplicants, nor pitied youthful beauty, nor had compassion on old men's age, nor blushed before the humility of the clergy. On the contrary they destroyed persons of every age, massacred them like animals, cut them in pieces, mowed sundry of them down like cabbages, so that all alike had severally to drain the cup full of bitterness. Lamentation and terror might be seen in Jerusalem. Holy churches were burned with fire, others were demolished, majestic altars fell prone, sacred crosses were trampled underfoot, life-giving icons were spat upon by the unclean. Then their wrath fell upon priests and deacons: they slew them in their churches like dumb animals.[24]

The Persian destruction continued to the gates of Constantinople in 618 and 619. With the town besieged, Heraclius was forced to offer a tribute to the Persian king in exchange for peace. The price was steep: an annual offering of a thousand talents of gold, a thousand talents of silver, a thousand silk robes, a thousand horses, and a thousand virgins. But over the next few years, Heraclius was able to rebuild the army and put the empire on solid financial footing. In 622, he launched a counteroffensive, and in 627 sacked the Persian king's palace in northern Iraq following the Battle of Nineveh. The True Cross was recovered and restored to Jerusalem, an event that, though devoid of theological significance, elicited joy nonetheless:

> Now when the holy Cross of the Lord had fallen to the venerable, pious, and blessed king Heraclius, he enthusiastically and joyfully assembled his troops. Then, taking all the royal attendants and revering the blessed, miraculous, and divine discovery they took the Cross back to the holy city of Jerusalem. They also took there all the vessels of the church which had been saved from the enemy, in the city of Byzantium. And there was no small amount of joy on the day they entered Jerusalem, with the sound of sobbing and moaning, an outpouring of tears from their excited and moved hearts, and there was a tightening feeling in the king, the princes, all the troops, and the inhabitants of the city. No one was capable of singing the sacred songs due to the tremendous and deep emotion felt by the king and the entire multitude. Heraclius took the Cross and re-established it in its place; he put each of the vessels of the churches back in its place; and he gave wealth and incense to all the churches and inhabitants of the city.[25]

The restoration of the True Cross signified an end to the Persian threat that had menaced the Romans for four hundred years.

HERACLIUS AND THE CHURCH

Heraclius's wars had required a great deal of money. He raised taxes as high as he could, short of causing a revolt. But his greatest source of wealth was the church. The church had at times exhibited generosity toward the public interest and volunteered to melt down its precious metals to fund war efforts. But Heraclius's relationship with the patriarch of Constantinople, Sergius, was especially close. Sergius conceived of the wars against the Persians and European barbarians as having a religious character. Hence, he was all too happy to contribute church wealth to the cause. This practice of having the church contribute finances to military expeditions became an important historical development of the Middle Ages.

Like Justinian, Heraclius also had a sense of religious obligation that overlapped with his desires for political unity. Heraclius too was forced to deal with the conflict between the Monophysites and Chalcedonians that had been going on for nearly two centuries. These religious differences only added to a lack of unity in the war against the Persians; Monophysites were less willing to aid the Byzantine cause. As a solution to the problem, Sergius and Heraclius proposed a compromise doctrine called Monothelitism (Jesus had two natures but "one will"). In 638, at Heraclius's direction, Sergius drafted a statement called the *Ecthesis* and nailed it up in the narthex of the Hagia Sophia. The *Ecthesis* stated that Monothelitism was the official state form of Christianity, and must be adopted by everyone. The proposal was highly unsatisfying to both Monophysites and Chalcedonians, and mild persecution against both groups broke out in the East.

Though the Monophysite-Chalcedonian debate may seem too abstract to modern readers to produce the level of madness that it once did, the rivalry stirred up intense feeling in many Christians. One such man was Maximus the Confessor. Maximus was from a noble Christian family and rose to become one of the emperor Heraclius's top advisers. But he was disturbed by Heraclius's decision to adopt the Monothelite heresy and, convicted that he could no longer serve Heraclius in good conscience, abandoned the emperor's court for a monastery. When the *Ecthesis* was posted in 638, Maximus went around visiting various bishops, clergymen, and secular officials, urging them to hold steadfast to their orthodoxy. In 649, Maximus, along with 186 other bishops and clergy, condemned the Monothelite heresy, against the will of the emperor Constans II. At Constans's orders, Maximus and Pope Martin (also a Chalcedonian) were arrested in 653 and charged with treason for denying the Monothelite doctrine. Maximus was imprisoned, exiled, and then recalled in 662 to face charges of treason again. At his trial, a Byzantine official, perhaps the emperor himself, asked, "Do you think that the emperor will make a supplication to Rome?" "Yes," said Maximus, "if he will humble himself as God has humbled Himself."[26] Maximus would not relent, the charges of treason stuck, and Maximus paid for his theological views by having his hand and tongue cut off so that he would write and speak no longer. Fortunately, the Monothelite heresy never really caught on. Pope Honorius and his successor, John IV, were also bitterly opposed to the declaration. In time, orthodoxy made a resurgence, and Monothelitism was soundly condemned at the Third Council of Constantinople in 680 and 681. It was the Waterloo for a doctrine that had divided the church for more than two hundred years.

Heraclius ruled for thirty-one years, not as long as Justinian, but long enough to make a significant impression on the course of Byzantine history. Another of his great legacies was to do away with Latin and make Greek the official language of the empire. The emperor, who for centuries possessed the title *Augustus* ("the Honorable"), now adopted the honorific used by the ancient Greeks: *Basileus* ("King"). If anyone had any doubts that Byzantium was merely an extension of the Roman Empire, here marks a profound statement that it was, on the contrary, a civilization of its own. But even as Heraclius had achieved in 629 the long-desired permanent victory over the Persians, he soon had to confront a new juggernaut rising from the desert of Arabia: the Muslims.

FIFTEEN

CRESCENT AND CROSS

Muhammad, the Qur'an, the Byzantines
Fight Muslims, the Islamic Invasions
of Spain, the Battle of Tours

Sometime in the 630s, the Byzantine emperor Heraclius had a dream. Someone was saying to him, "Verily there shall come against you a circumcised nation, and they shall vanquish you and take possession of the land." Heraclius interpreted the dream to mean that the Jews of the Eastern provinces, by custom a circumcised people, would orchestrate an insurrection against him. Heraclius attempted to resist the prophecy by ordering that the Jews and Samaritans in the East should be baptized. Some of his advisers reportedly advised that they be beheaded, advice Heraclius resisted. But soon after, a bedouin from the Arabian peninsula who had made his way to Constantinople was brought before Heraclius, describing "curious events happening in his country." The bedouin went on: "A man from our midst claims to be a prophet and some people have followed and believed him. Others did not and battles occurred between them in many places."[1]

"This is, by God, the dream that I saw!" exclaimed Heraclius.[2] The premonition of more warfare is probably not what Heraclius wanted to hear. At the time of his dream, he had finally concluded decades of

285

warfare against the Persians, and had recently triumphantly restored what was purported to be the True Cross to Jerusalem. He must have wondered what these curious events were that the bedouin described, and who this prophet was.

THE DAWN OF ISLAM

The prophet whom Heraclius had heard about was, of course, Muhammad, the founder of Islam. Many of the biographical details of Muhammad's life are unreliable, having been written down centuries after he lived, but we will give here the ones that are most commonly accepted. Muhammad was born around 570 in the Arabian city of Mecca. He became an orphan at an early age and was raised by his uncle Abu Talib. Muhammad was supposedly a merchant who would sometimes retreat to a remote cave near Mecca to pray to the Arabian gods. On one such occasion, in 610, Muhammad claimed to have received a revelation from the angel Gabriel, a fact that reveals Islam's early incorporation of Judeo-Christian elements. Muhammad was disturbed and went on a period of soul-searching to find out whether what he experienced was true. Three years later, Muhammad began to preach publicly the message he had received: he was a true messenger of God, and that the only true god was God (Allah). In addition to this Islamic statement of faith, called the *shahada*, Muhammad warned that Allah would execute punishment on all those who did not practice complete *Islam* ("submission") to him. One early Christian source was puzzled at Muhammad's view of the afterlife:

> He taught his subjects that he who kills an enemy or is killed by an enemy goes to Paradise; and he said that this paradise was one of carnal eating and drinking and intercourse with women, and had a river of wine, honey, and milk, and that the women were not like the ones down here, but different ones, and that the intercourse was long

lasting and the pleasure continuous; and other things of profligacy and stupidity.[3]

In time, Muhammad began preaching his message in Mecca, where he managed to attract about several hundred followers, but mostly faced persecution from the polytheistic inhabitants there. Muhammad and his men fled to the town of Medina, about two hundred miles away in Arabia, where he stirred up

Muhammad receiving his revelation from the angel Gabriel. Illustration on vellum, ca. 1307.

the more disaffected elements of the population there to rebel against rival Arab traders. Muhammad tried to even co-opt into his new religion many Jews living in Medina who might have believed that Muhammad was the promised Messiah who had been predicted in the Old Testament. They soon realized, however, as they saw him eating camel meat (forbidden by the Mosaic law), that he was not.

Despite the Jewish (and Christian) rejection of him, Muhammad preached and fought at Medina for nearly a decade to unite the inhabitants there under the banner of Islam. One of the more gruesome episodes from this period is Muhammad's massacre of the Jewish tribe of the Benu Quarizah: hundreds of men who surrendered to Muhammad were decapitated and buried, and the women and children were given to the Muslims as booty.

The Prophet, Ali, and the companions at the massacre of the prisoners of the Jewish tribe of Beni Qurayzah. Illustration of the nineteenth-century text by Muhammad Rafi Brazil, British Museum, London.

287

Yet in spite of these atrocities, the Islamic idea of *ummah*, brotherhood, appealed to many Arabs who were constrained by traditional tribal loyalties and infighting. Eight years later, Muhammad emerged from Medina victorious, and eventually went back to conquer Mecca. The Bedouin tribes of northern Arabia soon came under his dominion also, providing manpower for continual expansion. Eventually Muhammad took Mecca unopposed with an army of ten thousand men, and in 630 led an army of thirty-thousand men against the Persians to the north. By the time of Muhammad's death in 632, nearly the entire Arabian peninsula was unified in one Islamic kingdom. But the spread of the new religion would not stop there.

EARLY ISLAMIC THEOLOGY AND THE BIBLE

Before we trace the history of the early Islamic conquests after Muhammad, it is best to further explore the theology of early Islam. The most basic teachings of Islam are known as the Five Pillars of Islam. They are *shahadah*, the Muslim profession of faith; *salat*, prayer performed five times each day; *zakat*, giving to benefit the poor and the needy; *sawm*, fasting during the month of Ramadan; and the *hajj*, the major pilgrimage to Mecca that a Muslim should undertake during his life if he is able.

Undoubtedly Muhammad's career as a merchant brought him into contact with Christian areas, such as Syria and northern Iraq. It is most likely that he developed a great deal of his theology from these influences. Although Muhammad claimed that Islam was an extension of the true religion of Adam, Abraham, Moses, and Jesus, the social features of early Islamic religion showed very little of New Testament theology and ethics. Christianity, Judaism, and Islam all believe in one God; but where the New Testament made clear the divinity of Jesus, Islam denies it, believing him merely a prophet.[4] Muhammad also emphasized that, unlike the Christian Trinity, there is only one God, and that God is One.[5]

Muhammad's sexual ethics clearly differ from those found in the Old and New Testaments. Passages like 1 Corinthians 7 and Ephesians 5 insist that a Christian may have only one wife. Islamic historians of the period claim that Muhammad had at least fifteen wives (but only was married to eleven at one time), and at least four concubines, who served as his sexual slaves.[6] Also, according to Sura al-Nisa' 4:34, a man can beat (the literal Arabic verb is *daraba*, which means "strike, hit") his wives (plural), a stance directly in conflict with Christian admonitions to live with one's wife "in an understanding way" (1 Peter 3:7 NASB). His favorite wife was Aisha, who was only six when the marriage was contracted, and nine when it was consummated.[7] On the basis of this marriage, child-bride arrangements have persisted even today in parts of the Islamic world. Such clear contradictions of what the New Testament teaches suggest that Islam is absolutely not the continuation of biblical revelation that Muhammad suggested it was.

Muhammad's theology was obviously not a part of the Christian tradition, but there is sufficient evidence to believe that what Muhammad seems to have done was plagiarized a great deal of his revelations, which became the basis for the first written editions of the Qu'ran, which appeared about 150 years after his death. Let us compare the following examples of the Bible against the Qu'ran:

> Genesis 1:1: "In the beginning God created the heavens and the earth."
> Qu'ran 6:1: "[All] praise is [due] to Allah, who created the heavens and the earth."[8]

> Deuteronomy 32:39: "There is no god besides me. I put to death and I bring to life."
> Qu'ran 15:23: "And indeed, it is We who give life and cause death, and We are the Inheritor."

Psalm 44:21: "Would not God have discovered it, since he knows the secrets of the heart?"

Qu'ran 3:29: "Whether you conceal what is in your breasts or reveal it, Allah knows it."

Even later Islamic traditions of what Muhammad said or did (known as the *Hadith*) reveal a conspicuous similarity between his words and the God of the Bible's:

1 Corinthians 2:9: "'What no eye has seen, what no ear has heard, and what no human mind has conceived'—the things God has prepared for those who love him."

Compare this to a quotation of Muhammad's repeated by a later Islamic scholar:

The Prophet said, "Allah said, 'I have prepared for My righteous slaves (such excellent things) as no eye has ever seen, nor an ear has ever heard nor a human heart can ever think of.'"[9]

Christophe Luxenberg, a German scholar of Semitic languages who publishes under a pseudonym for fear of Muslim retribution, has postulated that the vast number of incomprehensible passages in the Qu'ran that Muslims claim only Allah can understand are actually a corruption of Syrian and Aramaic languages that flourished in Late Antiquity. Luxenberg claims that Christian missionaries who spoke or wrote Syro-Aramaic introduced Christianity to the Arabic tribes sometime in that period. Hence, the earliest writers of the Qu'ran composed it out of a hodgepodge of Christian literature written in Syriac or Aramaic and Arabic oral traditions. A failure to appreciate the Syro-Aramaic influences has produced some puzzling Islamic conclusions about the Qu'ran. For instance, the *huri* that are traditionally taken to mean the seventy-two virgins that Islamic warriors will receive in heaven should actually be translated, claims Luxenberg, as "white grapes."[10]

THE MUSLIMS FIGHT THE BYZANTINES

After subduing the Arabian Peninsula and instituting a state governed by the doctrines of early Islam, Muhammad died in 632. He left behind no immediate male heir, which led to a generation of bloody strife that saw only one of the first four Islamic caliphs (in whom is concentrated all of the state's religious and political power) die a natural death. It is from the rivalry of two claimants to the Caliphate, Ali and Uthman, that the division between Shia and Sunni Muslims emerged.[11] In spite of the conflict, which culminated in the murder of both men, the early caliphs continued in expanding their state across the Middle East. From 632 to 750, the Islamic Empire experienced its greatest degree of military success, storming over lands that had been in Greco-Roman hands for hundreds of years, some since the time of Alexander the Great. It is not clear exactly what motivated the Muslims to press forward with expansion. One of the major factors that has been suggested was the proximity of the new state to lucrative trade routes that would supply the first Islamic state with resources. But Fred Donner, one of the most respected scholars of early Islam, has urged modern historians not to discount the idea that Islam itself drove expansionism:

> [T]here is the possibility that the ideological message of Islam itself filled some or all of the ruling elite with the notion that they had an essentially religious duty to expand the political domain of the Islamic state as far as practically possible; that is, the elite may have organized the Islamic conquest movement because they saw it as their divinely ordained mission to do so.[12]

The idea that Islam's expansion was driven by its theology can be supported by what the Qu'ran commands Muslims to do:

When ye encounter the unbelievers, strike off their heads, until ye have made a great slaughter among them; and bind them in bonds . . . He [Allah] commandeth you to fight his battles that he may prove the one of you by the other. And as to those who fight (or those who are slain) in defense of God's true religion, God will not suffer their works to perish—he will lead them into paradise, of which he hath told then, O true believers, if ye assist God by fighting for his religion, he will assist you against your enemies . . . as for infidels, let them perish—catastrophe awaiteth the unbelievers.[13]

Many revisionist scholars would have readers believe that the first Muslim-Christian interactions were full of accommodation and harmony, but as the Islamic conquerors came into contact with Christians living in places such as Iraq, Syria, Palestine, and Egypt, they committed a great deal of violence against their opponents. The first churchmen who encountered Muslim invasions were repulsed by their opponents' brutality. Many monasteries and holy places were raided and destroyed. During the invasion of Alexandria, the Muslims burned down the church containing the body of Saint Mark. One Coptic homily from the seventh century describes them as "oppressors, who give themselves up to prostitution, massacre and lead into captivity the sons of men saying: 'We both fast and pray.'"[14]

Several Christian writers interpreted the Islamic invasions as a divine punishment for lax morals, just as God punished the ancient Israelites of the Old Testament for their idolatrous behavior. The Islamic invasions, to a bishop named Methodius of Patara, were a sign of the coming apocalypse: "The barbarians who conquered and governed tyrannically were not humans but sons of the desert, corrupted, bringing dissolution, personifying hate. They have no respect for old age, orphans, the poor, pregnant women, or priests, whose holy altars they defile."[15] John of Nikiu was a bishop in Egypt who chronicled the Islamic invasions of that part of the world around AD 700. When Muslims conquered the city of Fajum, he wrote, "these Ishmaelites[16] came and slew without mercy the commander of the troops and all his companions. And forthwith they compelled the city to open its gates, and they put to the sword all that surrendered, and they spared none, whether old men, babe, or woman."[17] John also mentioned that the Muslims levied heavy taxes on Christian inhabitants, which made some so poor that they were forced to sell their children into slavery.

Retaliation against clergy for instigating Christian-Islamist apologetic dialogues was common. When Metropolitan Peter of Damascus challenged Islamic theology during the Caliphate of Walid II (743–744), Walid ordered that Peter's tongue be cut out. He was then exiled to Arabia, where he died.[18] The bishop of Maiuma, also named Peter, invited Arab elites to criticize the "pseudo-Prophet" Muhammed and to believe in the Holy Trinity. Peter was beheaded for his invitation.[19] Still, as had happened with the Roman persecution of Christians during the first three hundred years of the faith, much violence against Christians was sporadic. The superior intellectual and philosophical culture of Christianized areas meant that Muslims often put Christians into service in governmental offices, or as teachers, scientists, and artists. Many times, the best way of dealing with Christians in conquered cities (for there were so many of them) was not to massacre them outright but to group them together in areas of the city where they could be closely monitored. One Nestorian patriarch wrote to a bishop that the Muslims "have not attacked the Christian religion, but rather they have commended our faith, honoured our priests . . . and conferred benefits on churches and monasteries."[20]

Heraclius was very unsuccessful in his wars against the Muslims. At the battle of Firaz (near Baghdad) in 633, Heraclius cobbled together a force of probably close to 150,000 Greeks, Persians, and Christian Arabs. Although they were outnumbered, the Muslims somehow turned back the Byzantine advance, producing a victory that made the Muslims unquestionable masters of Mesopotamia. But the most decisive battle between Byzantines and Muslims during the seventh century was the Battle of Yarmouk, in Syria, the outcome of which gave control of the province of Syria to the Caliphate. In 636, Heraclius decided to launch a massive counteroffensive against the Muslim armies that had recently conquered Iraq and parts of Syria. He mustered a force of at least close to one hundred thousand men[21]—Greeks, Christian Arabs, Georgians, Armenians, Slavs, and Franks among them—to take the field against a Muslim army of about twenty-five thousand. Undermining the Byzantine effort was the division between different Monophysite and Chalcedonian units. The battle was of "the fiercest and bloodiest kind." Seventy thousand Greeks were slain. Many Muslim women fought alongside the men; one of them reportedly screamed out in the heat of battle, "Cut the arms of these 'uncircumcised' with your swords!"[22] After six days of fighting, the Byzantines were smashed. Many of them perished by drowning in a steep ravine that ran alongside their escape route. An anguished Heraclius heard the news and blamed his misfortune on his marriage to his niece Martina (an incestuous arrangement). Later, he confided to one of

The Byzantines using their vaunted "Greek Fire" against the Arabs. Twelfth-century manuscript, Bibliteca Nacional de Madrid.

his commanders, "I knew they [the Muslims] were going to defeat you because they love death as much as you love life."[23]

Hotly disputed in the wars between Byzantines and Muslims was the city of Jerusalem. In Christianity, Jerusalem had special significance as the capital of ancient Israel, the city in which Jesus was crucified and resurrected and the site of the first Christian church depicted in the book of Acts. Islam claimed Jerusalem as the place to which Muhammad made his famous "Night Journey," in 620, during which he rode a mystical horse overnight from Mecca to Jerusalem, ascended into heaven, and was given a tour of heaven and hell by the angel Gabriel. Today, Jerusalem is regarded as the third-holiest site in Islam (after Mecca and Medina), and Israeli police enforce the law preventing Jews from even moving their lips in prayer on the old Temple Mount area. In November 636, the Muslims stormed Jerusalem and laid siege to it. The patriarch of Jerusalem, Sophronius, was in charge of deciding whether the city would surrender or not, and recorded his thoughts. He groaned at "the Saracens,[24] who, on account of our sins, have now risen up against us unexpectedly and ravage all with cruel and feral design, with impious and godly audacity."[25] Sophronius continued, "Those God-fighters boast of prevailing over all, assiduously and unrestrainably imitating their leader, who is the devil, and emulating his vanity, because of which he has been expelled from heaven."[26] Eventually Sophronius capitulated and agreed to hand over the city, but only on the condition that he sign the surrender agreement with the caliph himself, Omar. The Islamic commanders at that time were reluctant to call Omar all the way from Medina, and instead sent forth one Khalid ibn Walid, pretending to be the caliph. Khalid had been the commander of the Muslim forces at the triumphant battle of Yarmouk, but was perhaps not famous enough to be recognized. But Sophronius was not deceived, and refused to negotiate with Khalid.

THE PACT OF UMAR

Omar finally made the journey and signed an agreement with Sophronius known as the Pact of Umar. Under the pact, Christians and Jews were given the status of *dhimmi*—non-Muslim citizens of an Islamic state. Under *dhimma*, non-Muslims could live in a certain place and practice their religion provided that they paid a tax to Muslims— *jizya*—which relegated them to second-class-citizen status. The historical Islamic sources for the pact (the earliest of which date from nearly three centuries after it was written) often claim that Christians were given large degrees of freedom. But an examination of the pact shows multiple provisions that radically altered Christians' way of life:

> We shall not build, in our cities or in their neighborhood, new monasteries, Churches, convents, or monks' cells, nor shall we repair, by day or by night, such of them as fall in ruins or are situated in the quarters of the Muslims.
>
> We shall not manifest our religion publicly nor convert anyone to it. We shall not prevent any of our kin from entering Islam if they wish it.
>
> We shall show respect toward the Muslims, and we shall rise from our seats when they wish to sit.
>
> We shall not sell fermented [alcoholic] drinks.
>
> We shall not display our crosses or our books in the roads or markets of the Muslims. We shall use only clappers in our churches very softly. We shall not raise our voices when following our dead. We shall not show lights on any of the roads of the Muslims or in their markets. We shall not bury our dead near the Muslims.[27]

These rules governing non-Muslims became the foundational approach for Islamic rulers throughout the centuries. There were at times great degrees of freedom for Christians to worship as they liked, especially in Spain, but *dhimmi* were not always treated as hospitably as early Islamic sources would contend. Christians in Eastern areas, such as Syria and Persia, were also subject to strictures like wearing a girdle around the waist to distinguish them from Muslims, and later, wearing a yellow patch on the back and front of their clothing. Christians had distinctive haircuts, cut very short in the front. On horseback, they rode sidesaddle, not like Muslims, and could not take up the center of the road. Beginning with the caliphs Walid I (ruled 705–715) and Suleiman (ruled 715–717), Christians became subject to some particularly notorious measures. Suleiman employed his tax collector to enforce a de facto extortion policy against his Christian subjects. This tax collector, named

Usama, used hot iron bars to burn symbols into those Christians who had paid the tax. If a Christian was discovered without a brand mark, Usama would amputate the victim's arms and then behead him.[28] In 723, sixty Byzantine pilgrims to Jerusalem were crucified for their refusal to convert to Islam.[29]

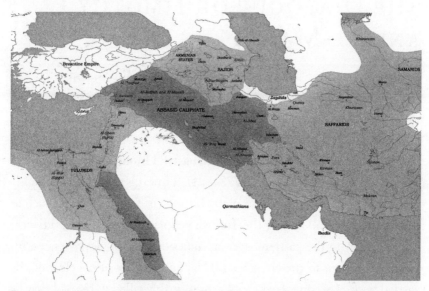

The extent of Islamic expansion, ca. 900. The light-green kingdoms indicate autonomous provinces allied with the Abbasid Caliphate.

After the last Umayyad caliph died out in 750, the new Abbasid dynasty (750–1258) continued the general theme of persecution that had started under the last Umayyad; the first caliph of the new dynasty called himself "the bloodshedder" (al-Saffah). One of his successors, the caliph al-Mahdi (ruled 775–785), commanded five thousand Christians in Aleppo, Syria, to convert or face death.[30] In the early eighth century, about seventy Christians set out from Iconium (Konya, Turkey) to make a pilgrimage to Jerusalem. When they reached the town, the Muslim occupiers ("the untamed and beastly, illogical in mind and maniacs in their desires") believed that they were spies. They insisted they were not, but nevertheless were forced to choose between becoming Muslims or being put to death. Seven chose conversion (as was a fairly common occurrence among persecuted Christians), but the other sixty-three chose martyrdom.[31]

THE DIALOGUE OF TIMOTHY I AND AL-MAHDI

Christians often lived uneasy lives under the caliphs, and often had to respond with sensitivity to direct threats. Sometimes they had to dance around difficult theological questions at the core differences of Islam and Christianity. Timothy I was the greatest patriarch of the Eastern church during the Abbasid dynasty. Throughout the course of his forty years as patriarch (ca. 778–821), Timothy maintained a highly missionary focus and ordained many bishops in faraway places, such as Iran and Tibet, and among the Turkish peoples of central Asia. His initial accession to the patriarchate was aided by a bit of cleverness on his part. As he went to the church on the appointed day of his election, he carried with him some heavy sacks, presumably filled with gold that he would distribute to his supporters. After he was elected, the sacks were opened, and the only thing found were piles of heavy rocks. Timothy used the moment to be didactic: "The priesthood is not to be sold for money," he said.[32] His reputation for faithfulness and diplomacy led him to obtain occasional interviews with the caliph himself. Once, he prayed openly before the caliph that the "pearl" of the gospel would be shared with Muslims, declaring that "God has placed the pearl of his face before all of us like the shining rays of the sun, and every one who wishes can enjoy the light of the sun."[33]

In 782, Timothy had an opportunity to participate in a very candid theological exchange with the third Abbasid caliph, al-Mahdi. The caliph, wanting to demonstrate a level of tolerance to (in his mind) the more intolerant Shia Muslims, hosted a religious debate with Timothy I. Scarcely had Timothy given his opening remarks when the caliph wanted to know, "O Catholicos, [how can] a man like you who possesses all this knowledge and utters such sublime words concerning God, [say that God] married a woman from whom He begat a Son?"[34] Timothy equivocated: "Who would say such a thing?" On the second day, the caliph asked Timothy, "What do you say about Muhammad?" The question was pregnant with tension. If Timothy denied Muhammad, he risked death. If he embraced him, he would be a traitor to his own beliefs. He again was delicate with his answer: "Muhammad is worthy of all praise, by all reasonable people, O my sovereign." Timothy was, however, a bit more forceful and articulate in his defense of the Trinity. Al-Mahdi insisted that God, "If He is three, He is not one." Timothy responded that God wasn't really like that; he was like a three-denarii gold coin, "one in its gold, that is to say in its nature, and three in its persons, that is to say, in the number of denarii."[35] The dialogue between Timothy and al-Mahdi showed that the various Islamic polities (in this case, the Abbasid Empire) did exhibit some degree of tolerance for Christians. But there was still a great degree of sporadic persecution that marked the early Islamic state. Under the same Mahdi who managed to have a fairly enlightened discourse with Timothy, Christian women were hung and whipped with the hide of a bull up to one thousand times in an effort to make them deny their faith.

As a result of being despoiled of their places of worship, as well as having experienced often intense pressure to convert to Islam, the church in the Middle East began to experience a great deal of decline. It had already been bruised by the divisions over the Monophysite-Chalcedonian controversy of the previous centuries (a disagreement that had never totally gone away). Persecution was not always as constant as we might imagine (Christians living under the Caliphate, for instance, probably experienced a greater degree of freedom than Christians living in Saudi Arabia or Iran today), but a general atmosphere of unease and intimidation probably hindered the spread of the faith through missionary activity.

Such a shrinkage of belief contrasts with the Christian experience in the Roman Empire during the first few centuries of the millennium, when persecution actually caused the church to grow. The difference might best be explained by the progressive drift of the Eastern church away from orthodox, biblical doctrines. By the 850s, the church of the East was experiencing a great deal of inner turmoil. The ecclesiastical histories of the time recount an abundance of sinfully ambitious rivalries, briberies, and greed within the churches. One patriarch tried to steal a monastery's jewel-adorned copy of the Bible. Another bribed a caliph into preventing a Jacobite sect of Christians from having a patriarch in Baghdad. Monks secretly took wives, and the liturgy of the churches was inconsistent all over the Caliphate. But despite the sin of the clergy and the yoke of the caliphs, the Eastern churches managed to endure all the way to the present.

THE MOORS INVADE SPAIN

The succession of Caliphates and smaller, breakaway Islamic king- doms that imposed themselves on what is now called the Middle East stretched at their height from parts of India and Afghanistan through the North African coast to Morocco. In 710, the Caliphate decided to expand even farther and landed a force of Berbers (North Africans) and Arabs on the shores of Gibraltar, on the northern end of the strait where Africa and western Europe almost touch. Within a year, most of Spain was conquered. By 732, the Muslims (Moors), hungry to acquire the wealth deposited throughout the churches of Spain, had conquered the Visigoth inhabitants of Hispania (Spain) and reached the Pyrenees mountains, which marked the border of France. One Muslim historian of the early invasion of Spain related an especially gruesome story of Muslim invaders intimidating the inhabitants of a remote island:

> When the Moslems settled in the island, they found no other inhabi- tants there, than vinedressers. They made them prisoners. After that

they took one of the vinedressers, slaughtered him, cut him in pieces, and boiled him, while the rest of his companions looked on. They had also boiled meat in other cauldrons. When the meat was cooked, they threw away the flesh of that man which they had boiled; no one knowing that it was thrown away: and they ate the meat which they had boiled, while the rest of the vinedressers were spectators. These did not doubt but that the Moslems ate the flesh of their companion; the rest being afterwards sent away informed the people of Andalus that the Moslems feed on human flesh.[36]

This story, however sickening, was an outlier. Many Christians in the Visigoth Empire hated Visigoth rule and actually fought on the side of the Muslims. By 781, the whole Iberian Peninsula was unified in one province of the Caliphate, known as al-Andalus, which would eventually become an independent emirate until 1031. It wasn't until the reign of Ferdinand and Isabella in 1492 that the last Muslim occupiers were expelled from Spain. Under the Moors, the *dhimmi* Christians and Jews of Spain usually enjoyed a fairly high degree of freedom. But as was the case in the Middle East, the degree of tolerance that Christians experienced under the Caliphate is often overstated. Under Islamic law, Christians were still regarded as second-class citizens who were stripped of political rights and were forced to pay the *jizya* tax. The Rabbi Maimonides, the greatest thinker of medieval Judaism, was forced to flee Cordoba in 1148 under the threat of violence. Medieval Spain was not a place of unrestrained butchery, but neither was it a perfectly harmonious blend of religious pluralism.

CHARLES MARTEL SAVES EUROPE

By 732, the Moorish invaders had crept up the Iberian Peninsula and over the Pyrenees mountains into the kingdom of the Franks. At the time, the Umayyad Caliphate, with its capital at the strategic city of Damascus, was the most powerful military force in Europe and the Middle East. Their desire for expansion seemed inexhaustible. The resistance they encountered was negligible; the various dukes of southern Gaul proved no match for the battle-hardened Muslim armies. The destruction experienced was so bad, wrote one historian, "that God alone knew the number of the slain and wounded."[37] Another source claimed the Islamic army "laid waste the country, and took captives without number. And that army went through all places like a desolating storm. Prosperity made those warriors insatiable . . . everything gave way to their scymetars,[38] which were the robbers of lives."[39] The Muslims had a sense of confidence about their conquests. One Arab chronicler recorded a conversation between an Islamic general, Musa, and the Caliph, all the way back in Damascus:

> "Now tell me about these Franks—what is their nature?"
>
> "They," replied Musa, "are a folk right numerous, and full of might: brave and impetuous in the attack, but cowardly and craven in event of defeat."
>
> "And how has passed the war [between] them and thyself? Favorably or the reverse?"
>
> "The reverse? No, by Allah and the prophet!" spoke Musa. "Never has a company from my army been beaten. And never have the Moslems hesitated to follow me when I have led them; though they were [outnumbered two to one]."[40]

Without any recourse to avoid destruction, the nobles of the area encompassing what is modern-day France appealed to King Charles of the Franks for protection. He agreed to help them. Charles was the most powerful sovereign in Europe at the time, and he had proved his prowess in battle many times. In 721, a Frankish force under one of Charles's lords had defeated the Ummayad advance at Toulouse, in southern France. But Charles knew that this victory was only a respite from a larger assault. But what he needed now, he realized, was an army that could stand up to the battle-tested Islamic forces, who numbered about twenty thousand. Anticipating further incursions into France, Charles spent nearly ten years training a set of conscripts, and he requisitioned land from the church to sell in order to raise money to train his troops. When the Battle of Tours commenced in October 732, the Muslims were surprised to encounter such a talented fighting force. Also to Charles's advantage was the weather. The battle took place the middle of autumn, a time when the Franks expected the annual cold spells in France. The Muslims, on the other hand, were unaccustomed to the cold. The battle commenced with a week of minor parries, but eventually Charles's stall tactics induced the Islamic commander, Abd al-Rahman, to charge at his lines with his cavalry. Charles's tight ranks held their formations, and weathered the assault: "In the shock of the battle the men of the North seemed like a sea that cannot be moved. Firmly they stood, one close to another, forming as it were a bulwark of ice; and with great blows of their

swords they hewed down the Arabs."[41] Another source wrote that Charles's army fought in the battle "as fiercely as the hungry wolf falls upon the stag."[42] As night fell, the fighting drew to a close. The next morning Charles sent out spies to scout the Islamic camp, which was strangely quiet. He feared an ambush, but upon a closer examination, all the tents were empty. The Muslims had retreated from Tours.

Charles de Steuben, *Bataille de Poitiers, En Octobre 732*, 1837. A depiction of the battle of Tours. Charles Martel is on the left, and Abd al-Rahman on the right.

    The campaigns of Charles and other Frankish leaders against the Muslims would continue until about 759, when the Islamic advance was beaten back into Spain. In successive centuries, Muslim raiders would from time to time launch successful incursions against mainland Europe. One of the most famous of these was a voyage up the Tiber in 846 that culminated in the sack of Rome and the plundering of thousands of pounds of gold and silver from Saint Peter's Basilica. The next year the pope constructed new walls twelve meters high around the perimeter of the Vatican. Large sections still remain, and it is curious to think that they were constructed for the purpose of defending the Holy See from Islamic raiders.

Charles's victory at Tours was so decisive that he earned the nickname *Martellus*: "the hammer." The Battle of Tours was quickly interpreted as evidence for a great civilizational triumph: the Europeans had halted the Muslim advance into Europe. But when he determined to take the field against Muslim troops, Charles had no grand visions of saving European civilization; he was merely intent on preserving his own kingdom. But it is not hyperbole to suggest that the Battle of Tours was the most important battle in European history prior to the Battle of Hastings in 1066. Like the European victory over the Ottoman Turks at Vienna in 1683, the Frankish victory over the Muslims in 732 drove back a force that threatened Western civilization: who knows how far the Muslim army might have penetrated into Europe, making *dhimmi* out of their vanquished opponents? Charles Martel probably did not understand the civilizational implications of his victory. But within a few generations of the Battle of Tours, one of Charles's heirs to the Frankish throne would take up a mission to consciously make his royal kingdom a vehicle for the defense of Christianity. That man's name was Charlemagne.

SIXTEEN

EUROPE IS BORN

Merovingian Dynasty, Boniface, Pepin, the Donation of Constantine, Charlemagne, the Holy Roman Empire, the Carolingian Renaissance

The Islamic empires that roared out of the sands of Arabia in the seventh century needed only a few generations to almost totally occupy the Middle East, North Africa, and parts of Asia. As a consequence of the Islamic invasions, the Byzantine Empire lost a great deal of territory, and Christian communities in places such as Egypt, Syria, and Persia felt the choice of subjecting themselves to Islamic law or facing death. It was Charles Martel's decisive defeat of the Moors at Tours in 732 that kept the Muslims from expanding north of their western-most foothold, Spain. Throughout the seventh century, western Europe, apart from Spain and southern Italy, remained mostly unscathed from the Crescent. To many historians, Charles Martel's greatest legacy is his role of the savior of Europe from the Muslims.

But Charles also worked consistently to ally himself with the ecclesiastical authorities of the day, and the relationship that he forged with the church in his Frankish kingdom, and with the pope, would help lead to the birth of Europe as a cultural idea. Charles was a member of the Merovingians, a dynastic family that had held significant power in the

Frankish kingdoms for several hundred years, since the time of King Clovis's grandfather. The Merovingian hold on authority was enforced mostly through senseless clan warfare, complicated gift-giving rituals, and suppression of rebellions. But Charles Martel also kept up a mutual arrangement with the church that helped both parties. The church helped him consolidate his authority, and he aided the church in evangelizing the unreached Germanic peoples of the Frankish Empire. Living along the Rhine river (in modern Germany) and northern coasts of what is today the Netherlands were the Saxons and the Frisians, peoples who, if they were Christianized at all, probably regarded the Christian God as just one among many deities, as many Germanic peoples did. Charles, out of sincere political and religious concerns, hoped to Christianize these people and bring them into the orbit of Frankish-Christian civilization. To do this, he looked to Rome. In 739, for instance, the pope wrote to Charles in the face of a Lombard attack, begging him to send troops. "For by doing this," the pope's letter said, "you will attain lasting fame on earth and eternal life in heaven."[1] At the same time, the missionary fire that had begun with Pope Gregory I in the late 500s and early 600s was still burning, especially in the British Isles. In 722, Charles Martel had received from the pope a letter commending an Englishman who now stood before him, "a man of sterling faith and character." This man's mission was "to preach the faith to the peoples of Germany who dwell on the eastern bank of the Rhine."[2] His birth name was Winfrid, but he would later become known as Saint Boniface.

SAINT BONIFACE

Winfrid was born in England around 675, and from an early age, wrote his biographer, "he conceived a desire to enter the service of God and began to think deeply on the advantages of the monastic life." Whenever holy men would come to his town to preach, he would have spiritually minded conversations with them, and "would ask them to advise him on the best means of overcoming the frailties of his nature." At a young age, he resolved to become a monk, and asked his father to give his blessing on the idea. His father reacted violently, and, desiring the boy to become his heir, tried to convince him that the fulfillment of worldly desires and the acquisition of wealth was the superior path, and "in order to turn the boy aside from pursuing his purpose he paraded before him all the inducements of pleasure and luxury." But Boniface's desire persisted, and eventually his father gave him his consent to enter the monastery.[3]

Boniface's training took him to two different monasteries, where he became "proficient not only in grammar and rhetoric and the writing of verses but also in the literal and spiritual exposition of the Bible." One of Boniface's early works was a textbook known as the *Ars Grammatica* (Grammatical Arts). His learning as an adult was profound, partly because "he did not refuse to learn from his pupils," and Boniface became perhaps the most respected, and certainly the most famous teacher of his time. In his study of the Scriptures he was most diligent and gave thanks to God in everything. "Lust was impotent in the presence of his chastity, and gluttony was unable to break down his abstemiousness," wrote his biographer. His character was above reproach, and he demonstrated no partiality, neither "flattering and fawning upon the rich nor oppressing and browbeating the freedmen and slaves."[4]

In 716, Winfrid felt called to pursue missionary work among the unreached Frisian peoples in modern-day Belgium. In that year, he and another missionary, Willibrord, roamed the country in hopes of preaching to the peoples there. But he picked a most unfortunate time to go. Radbod, king of the Frisians, and Charles Martel were at war, and the nascent Frankish church there was persecuted as a means of retaliating against Frankish invasion. Churches were burned, and priests were driven away. Few were receptive to Winfrid's message. He went home to England, secluding himself in the monastery for two years. But before he left, he had resolved "that if at any time he could see his way to approach the people he would minister to them the Word of God."[5]

After an extended period of reflection, Winfrid decided to go to Rome to obtain a papal commission (and a supply of resources and fellow workers) to evangelize the Frisians. Ignoring the pleas of his brother monks that he not go, he eventually obtained the blessing (and resources) of the pope to go back to Frisia and preach the gospel. When he arrived, he found that King Radbod, formerly a persecutor of Christians, was dead. The new freedom there "permitted him to scatter abroad the seed of Christian teaching to feed with wholesome doctrine those who had been famished by pagan superstition."[6] Over the next several decades, Boniface spent his life sharing the gospel with the Frisians and Saxons of the Frankish Empire. For this he earned the nickname "the apostle to the Germans." His missions were in general very successful in bringing pagan or semi-Christian peoples to a full acceptance of the Christian God.

The most legendary story of Boniface's work is known as the felling of the Donar Oak, or Oak of Jupiter. Germanic pagan tribes attached a great significance to trees, and one of the most revered was a colossal oak in a place called Gaesmere. To show that the tree was empty of any true spiritual power, Boniface resolved one day to cut it down. In front of a crowd of skeptical but curious onlookers, Boniface took a mighty thwack at the great oak, and aided by a fortuitous wind, felled it in only one blow. The effect of this, claims the story, was that the false power of the tree was broken, and many turned from pagan idols and worshipped the true God.[7]

By 723, Charles Martel had noticed and approved of Boniface's work, and decreed that Boniface should be brought under his political protection: "We have seen fit to issue and seal with our own hand an order that wheresoever he goes, no matter where it shall be, he shall with our love and protection remain unmolested and undisturbed," Charles (actually, some court scribe) wrote.[8] Partly through the beneficence of Charles and his successors, Boniface established formal dioceses in Bavaria, and later became the first archbishop over Germany (his archiepiscopal see of Mainz became the hub of German Christianity during the Middle Ages).

But despite an abundant amount of divine grace, Boniface also endured frequent hardships in his work. One problem he faced was disobedient and apostate clergy, men who "choke with weeds or pervert into a poisonous weed the Word of God."[9] These rebellious clergy taught falsehoods, such as abstinence from certain foods, and abused their authority to take land and money from poor peasants. Many lived lascivious lifestyles of heavy drinking and fornicating. Worst of all, these clergymen were especially numerous at the Frankish court, which Boniface depended upon for support. Boniface faced a dilemma on whether to correct these men or not: "I am afraid of contracting sin by associating with them . . . on the other hand, if, in avoiding them, I fail to approach the Frankish prince, I fear that my missionary work amongst the people will greatly suffer."[10]

Boniface ultimately took his concerns to Carloman, the Frankish king, who decreed, as Boniface suggested, that a council be held. The *Concilium Germanicum*, as the event came to be known, was held in April 743. Only Boniface's allies attended, which allowed him and his fellow bishops to pass (with Carloman's approval) a new set of rules governing the Frankish church:

1. Bishops and archbishops would now be in charge of the dioceses (plural) once headed by nobles.
2. Bishops were required to visit their parishes.
3. Clergy had to give an account of their parishes and conduct before a bishop once a year.
4. Clergy could no longer carry weapons or hunt (sport hunting was considered an activity too luxurious for bishops).
5. The Rule of Saint Benedict, which governed monastic life, became mandatory for all monasteries.

In his day, Boniface became one of the most well-known and revered men in Christendom. His zeal for converting the Germans and reforming the Frankish church was insatiable, even to the point of death. In 754, as Boniface was about to perform a confirmation service, a band of robbers, believing he and his companion clergy to be in possession of great wealth, ambushed the event. His comrades wanted to fight back, but Boniface's final words were Christian to the last: "Cease fighting. Lay down your arms, for we are told in Scripture not to render evil for good but to overcome evil by good."[11] The robbers slit his throat and stole his chest. When they broke it open, all they found were books on theology. Boniface is remembered in Germany and the Low Countries today as a major national historical figure, and his efforts served a great purpose in bringing the pagan tribes of northern Europe into the light.

PEPIN THE SHORT

Charles Martel died in 741, and his two sons, Carloman and Pepin, succeeded him. Carloman ruled in the southern regions of the Frankish kingdom, while Pepin, nicknamed "the Short" by posterity,[12] occupied the northern parts. Like Charles Martel, both men supported the work that Boniface had begun of bringing reform to the Frankish church and Christianizing the Germanic tribes. But the kingship of Pepin and Carloman was contested. Both men were Charles Martel's sons from his first wife, but were not thoroughly Merovingian enough in blood to command the respect and unity of all the Frankish tribes. As a result, Pepin and Carloman placed a noble named Childeric III, a man more completely Merovingian, on the throne as a puppet ruler. But when Carloman retired to the religious life of the monastery in 747, Pepin decided to take power for himself. Predictably, and problematically, however, Childeric had become so accustomed to holding power that he refused to abdicate.

A crisis of power loomed. But instead of starting an outright civil war, Pepin devised an ingenious method of usurping Childeric. Pepin had cultivated a close relationship with the church (which, in turn, looked to the Franks for help in defending the borders of Italy), and he felt comfortable writing to Pope Zacharias in 750, asking the question, "Is it wise to have kings who hold no power of control?"[13] Pepin held the real power in the Frankish kingdom, he stated, and it was only right that the pope honor the situation and give a blessing on his usurpation of Childeric. The pope answered, "It is better to have a king able to govern. By apostolic authority I bid that you be crowned King of the Franks."[14] In 751, Pepin was appointed king by an assembly of Frankish nobles and confirmed in his authority by Boniface I in a ceremonial anointing with oil. Childeric, meanwhile, had his head shaved and was imprisoned in a monastery.

In 753 and 754, Pope Stephen II endured the Alpine winter and made a journey to France. The purpose was to beg Pepin to repay the favor the pope had done for him in legitimizing his kingship. The Lombards were ravaging the northern portions of Italy and even threatened to sack Rome itself. Pepin promised he would send help, and accompanied the pope home to Italy with his army later in the year. As a show of gratitude for Pepin's commitment, Pope Stephen II himself proclaimed Pepin *patricus Romanorum* ("king of the Romans") in a ceremony at the Abbey of Saint Denis. But did the pope really have the authority to decide who was king or not?

As a statement that the pope did in fact have the right to determine who sat on the Frankish throne, Stephen II supported his choice of king by citing a forged document now known as the *Donation of Constantine*. The Donation was not proved a forgery until the Renaissance, but it was one of the most influential documents of the Middle Ages. It purported to be a decree written long ago by the Roman emperor Constantine, investing in the church a huge degree of authority, even making the imperial government subordinate to it: "We decree that his holy Roman church shall be honoured with veneration; and that, more than our empire and earthly throne, the most sacred seat of Saint Peter shall be gloriously exalted; we giving to it the imperial power, and dignity of glory, and vigour and honour."[15] Anyone with knowledge of church history would have suspected that *Donation* was inauthentic. After all, the pattern of church history in the centuries after Constantine thoroughly indicated that the emperor had absolute control over what went on in the churches, and that each pope had varying degrees of success in allying with or influencing the emperor. But the arrangement stood, and the *Donation* had enormous implications for medieval history. For one thing, it served as a kind of legal basis for many papal claims to political power for centuries to come. Secondly, it established the legitimacy of the Frankish kingdom over the lands it occupied now and in the future. Lastly, the cooperation of church and state in the Merovingian period—especially in the conversion of the Saxons, Germans, and Bavarians—proved that both parties could enjoy a relationship that proved mutually beneficial to each other. The church-state relationship, with alternating periods of cooperation and tension, would become the political framework in which the social and cultural aspects of the Middle Ages developed.

CHARLEMAGNE

Pepin's dethronement of Childeric and ascension to the unified throne of the Franks inaugurated the Carolingian dynasty, which would rule France until nearly the year 900. The rest of King Pepin's life would be spent in almost ceaseless campaigning against tribes such as the Lombards, Franks, Saxons, and Bavarians. Pepin was quite an accomplished ruler in his ability to forge alliances, consolidate Germanic tribes under the Frankish banner, and repel barbarian invasions. But his legacy would, perhaps unfairly, be overshadowed by his son Charlemagne, one of the most famous and successful figures of the Middle Ages.

Charlemagne was born sometime in the 740s and became the king of the Franks in 768. He was a giant of a man who towered over his contemporaries:

Charles was large and strong, and of lofty stature, though not dispro-
portionately tall (his height is well known to have been seven times the
length of his foot); the upper part of his head was round, his eyes very
large and animated, nose a little long, hair fair, and face laughing and
merry. Thus his appearance was always stately and dignified, whether
he was standing or sitting; although his neck was thick and somewhat
short, and his belly rather prominent; but the symmetry of the rest of
his body concealed these defects. His gait was firm, his whole carriage
manly, and his voice clear, but not so strong as his size led one to expect.[16]

Charlemagne's physical hulk did not suggest a man whose passions might lie in the life of the mind. But he loved to devote time to
studying and fancied himself something of a scholar. He loved learning,
and although he was a gifted speaker, his ability to write down his own
thoughts was limited:

Charles had the gift of ready and fluent speech, and could express
whatever he had to say with the utmost clearness. He was not satisfied
with command of his native language merely, but gave attention to the
study of foreign ones, and in particular was such a master of Latin that
he could speak it as well as his native tongue; but he could understand
Greek better than he could speak it. He was so eloquent, indeed, that
he might have passed for a teacher of eloquence. He most zealously
cultivated the liberal arts, held those who taught them in great esteem,
and conferred great honors upon them . . . The King spent much time
and labour . . . studying rhetoric, dialectics, and especially astronomy;
he learned to reckon, and used to investigate the motions of the heavenly bodies most curiously, with an intelligent scrutiny. He also tried
to write, and used to keep tablets and blanks in bed under his pillow,
that at leisure hours he might accustom his hand to form the letters;
however, as he did not begin his efforts in due season, but late in life,
they met with ill success.[17]

In his off hours, Charlemagne loved to eat and drink, and even take in some theology and music at dinnertime:

> His meals ordinarily consisted of four courses, not counting the roast, which his huntsmen used to bring in on the spit; he was more fond of this than of any other dish. While at table, he listened to reading or music. The subjects of the readings were the stories and deeds of olden time: he was fond, too, of St. Augustine's books, and especially of the one entitled "The City of God."
>
> He was so moderate in the use of wine and all sorts of drink that he rarely allowed himself more than three cups in the course of a meal. In summer after the midday meal, he would eat some fruit, drain a single cup, put off his clothes and shoes, just as he did for the night, and rest for two or three hours. He was in the habit of awaking and rising from bed four or five times during the night.[18]

But for all of Charlemagne's academic and leisure pursuits, he took the business of being king very seriously. Like Pepin, Charlemagne (a combination of the name *Charles* and the Latin title *magnus*, "great," thus Charles the Great) became a protector of the papacy, and spent a great deal of time campaigning against the Lombards in northern Italy. Charlemagne also launched an invasion in 778 against the Muslims, who still held some territory in the south of France. Although he was not exactly successful in his undertaking, the lands that he had sought to win back were freed from Muslim presence. As Charlemagne's army retreated, a Muslim ambush on his rear guard killed a Frankish nobleman named Count Roland. This episode later became enshrined in the legendary *Song of Roland*, one of the enduring works of medieval literature.

Charlemagne especially had to work to hold on to the gains that Pepin had made with groups such as the Bavarians and Saxons. Einhard, Charles's biographer, said that he spent thirty-three continuous years engaged in warfare with the Saxons, "a fierce people, given to the worship of devils, and hostile to our religion, and did not consider it dishonorable to transgress and violate all law, human and divine."[19] The wars against the Saxons must have exasperated him, and despite his professions of Christian belief and enlightened habits, Charlemagne's character sometimes displayed a trace of unconscionable brutality. In one battle, near the town of Verden, he lost a total of two envoys, four counts, and about twenty nobles. The loss made him furious. As retaliation, he ordered that all the Saxons in the vicinity be rounded up and brought to him. In a single day, he ordered forty-five hundred of them beheaded, and then attended Easter Mass. It took several more generations before the Saxons were subdued and Christianized. Charlemagne also took his campaigns into eastern regions of modern-day Austria, Hungary, and the Balkans. According to scholar Clifford Backman, on one trip, no fewer than sixty oxen were required to haul Charlemagne's booty of jewels, gold, spices, and fabrics back to France.[20]

What was Charlemagne trying to accomplish with such military expansionism? The desire to create a kind of Christian empire was already somewhat present in rulers like Constantine and Justinian, but Charlemagne was more intent on establishing a state founded on Christian ideals than any previous ruler in history. The idea of the grandeur of Rome lived on through the Middle Ages, and Charlemagne also saw it as his great duty to restore what had been formerly Roman territory. Hence, Charlemagne wanted to be the king of a Christianized world that overlapped the geography of the former Roman Empire. At the height of his reign, Charlemagne controlled most of modern France, Germany, Austria, Hungary, Italy, and parts of the Balkans. Charlemagne was an absolute monarch, but generally tried to rule with a spirit of justice and reason. His system of imperial administration was highly developed for its time, and as we will see, he generally inserted a Christian ethic into his court (massacres of Saxons notwithstanding).

CHARLEMAGNE CROWNED HOLY ROMAN EMPEROR

Charlemagne was regarded by himself and others as a serious Christian who "cherished with the greatest fervor and devotion the principles of the Christian religion, which had been instilled into him from infancy."[21] Like his father, Pepin, he aligned himself closely with the pope, and often served as the defender of Italy from Lombards and others. Charlemagne also recognized the special significance of the city of Rome:

> He sent great and countless gifts to the popes; and throughout his whole reign the wish that he had nearest at heart was to re-establish the ancient authority of the city of Rome under his care and by his influence, and to defend and protect the Church of St. Peter, and to beautify and enrich it out of his own store above all other churches.[22]

In 799, the new pope, Leo III, was a victim of an attack instigated by his rival claimants to the papacy. An angry mob had tried but failed to cut out his tongue and eyes. Leo begged Charlemagne, a self-conscious defender of the papacy, to hasten on to the Eternal City, and he arrived in November 800 to help resolve a dispute between Leo and his enemies. As a token of gratitude and a state-ment of political power, Leo invited Charlemagne to a coronation ser-vice on Christmas Day, 800, in which Charlemagne was crowned the Holy Roman emperor. His title sums up well his position in the world: not only did the pope view him as a legitimate successor to the Roman Emperors of old, but one

The coronation of Charlemagne, ca. 800.

who administered a "holy," or Christian, empire. Charlemagne claimed to be uncomfortable with the honor. His biographer, Einhard, claimed that Charlemagne never would have set foot in Saint Peter's Basilica that day if he could have foreseen what the pope was about to do. It is highly unlikely that Charlemagne didn't know what would happen that day. But it is a probability that Charlemagne feared the consequences of having the pope legitimize him as a ruler. Contrary to what the *Donation of Constantine* had stated, Charlemagne did not believe, nor desire, that the pope should exercise authority over him, and he most likely feared the perception that he was somehow subordinate to Rome.

CONFLICT WITH THE BYZANTINE CHURCH

Charlemagne's power and authority as the Holy Roman Emperor made the Byzantines unhappy. For one thing, the Byzantine monarchs saw themselves as the true heirs to the Roman throne, and the idea of another king calling himself *imperator Romanorum* ("king of the Romans") undermined Byzantine political preeminence. But Charlemagne's coronation was not just a blow to their pride. The Carolingian-papal alliance in the West threatened Byzantine influence over Western areas such as Italy, the Balkans, the Germanic areas, and even the papal lands. Over time, European kingdoms and tributary nations would look more frequently to the Holy Roman emperor (the office lived on after Charlemagne) than to the Byzantines in considering their courses of political action.

Adding insult to injury were the ways Charlemagne's own political decisions rankled the Greeks. Pope Leo's crowning of Charlemagne amounted to a signal that the wishes of Empress Irene of Byzantium were now, in Rome's eyes, of less importance than Charlemagne's. In 797, Irene had assumed the throne by blinding her emperor husband,

Constantine IV, and leaving him to die. She had remained unmarried, and now Charlemagne (who lost three wives to early death and kept multiple mistresses) saw an opportunity to unify the two great kingdoms that were, at least in name, Christian. He sent envoys to Constantinople, requesting that Irene marry him. Irene said she would consider it. The marriage would have been a masterstroke of reunification between the two increasingly alienated kingdoms (and churches), but it was never to be. Irene's advisers could not stomach the thought, and after kidnapping her, shaved her head and imprisoned her in a convent, where she died in 805.

Charlemagne was furious at this rejection and took retaliatory actions against the Byzantines. One step was entering into a temporary alliance with the Islamic caliph against them. Charlemagne already had come in contact with the Caliphate from his conquests of southern Italy; in 797, the caliph sent him as gifts an ornate clock and an Asian elephant. This alliance, however, was short-lived, and the two powers never jointly took the field against the Byzantines. Much more serious and more harmful to the relationship of the Eastern and Western churches was the Council of Aachen, a meeting of bishops at his capital called by Charlemagne in 809. Presiding over the council was Paulinus of Aquileia, a scholar and theologian closely attached to Charlemagne's court. The purpose of the council was to insert what became known as the *filioque* clause into the Nicene Creed. The *filioque* was a highly controversial doctrine disputed between East and West for centuries, centering on whether the Holy Spirit proceeded from the Father *and* the Son (in Latin, *filioque*). The *filioque* was originally used in the West to catechize Arians, but in 809, Charlemagne ordered its insertion into the Frankish church's Nicene Creed as a way of antagonizing the Byzantines, who, as was evident from their own Christological controversies, did not always agree on the nature of Christ. Charlemagne also asked Pope Leo to declare it a doctrine necessary for salvation. Leo would not agree to Charlemagne's request, and instead put up a silver-cast copy of the Nicene Creed without the *filioque* outside of Saint Peter's Basilica. The silver creed bore the inscription *Haec Leo posui amore et cautela orthodoxae fidei* ("I, Leo, put these here for love and protection of orthodox faith"). But the pope's decision to crown Charlemagne in 800 was in the eyes of the Byzantines much weightier than the erection of the silver Nicene Creed. In the end, Leo had cast his lot with the West, and never again would the Byzantines hold pride of place with the pope.

THE CAROLINGIAN RENAISSANCE

Charlemagne's glorious ambitions for the size and character of his kingdom seem almost laughable in light of what Carolingian Europe actually looked like. The vast majority of people were peasant farmers who rendered tribute to a lord. Commerce and trade barely existed, and most commercial transactions were bartered, not conducted with money, which was mostly nonexistent. The old system of Roman roads had long since crumbled apart, and lawlessness pervaded in areas outside of the few true towns that existed, which were mostly fortresses for nobles. Hunger and early death was ubiquitous.

Additionally, the Frankish kingdom was still rather spiritually undeveloped. By the time of Charlemagne's kingship, Christianity had been in France for almost seven hundred years. Most recently, Boniface had done a huge amount of missionary work in the northern parts of the Frankish kingdom, and another of Charlemagne's intimates, Paulinus of Aquileia, had become known as the "apostle to the Slovenes" for his work around modern-day Slovenia. Pepin and Charlemagne enjoyed cordial dealings with the pope, and the church's footprint in France had grown as a result of it. But the church in most areas of the Holy Roman Empire was still a disorganized and dissolute mess. Most clergy were ill trained, or even illiterate altogether. Many of them lived double lives as adulterers or men greedy for dishonest gain. Patches of paganism, often comingled with Christianity, still lived on, and liturgies across the churches could vary considerably. Even worse, many Christians' idea of worship was fanatical and nugatory devotion to local ascetics or holy men and women. Few were well taught in the doctrines of the faith.

Charlemagne set out to reform these deficiencies. Although modern historians' decision to call the period a "Renaissance" is an exaggeration of the cultural transformation that actually took place, the Carolingian years percolated with cultural activity not seen since at least late antiquity, and

Medieval serfs harvest grain. Illustration, ca. 1310.

which would not be seen again for another four hundred years afterward. At the head of the Carolingian Renaissance was Charlemagne himself. The king, as we have seen, was a man of letters, and viewed learning, and especially literacy, as not just a good for its own sake but as necessary to the continual Christianization of Europe: "I have in fact begun to fear that these monks' illiteracy could result in a serious misinterpretation of Holy Scripture," he wrote, "and we all know that, as dangerous as spoken words are, even more dangerous are misunder-

A golden bust of Charlemagne, Aachen Cathedral, Germany.

standings of God's Word."[23] Consequently, Charlemagne embarked on a program of cultural revival, commanding the members of his court, "Let every single episcopal see and every single monastery provide instruction in the singing of psalms, musical notation, [Gregorian] chant, the computation of the years and seasons, and grammar. Moreover, let all the appropriate texts be carefully corrected."[24] To fulfill these tasks, Charlemagne scouted out intellectual talent from all over Europe, and found one of the most important figures in Western history.

ALCUIN OF YORK

The greatest engine of the Carolingian Renaissance, besides Charlemagne himself, was an English monk named Alcuin (pronounced "AL-swin") of York. Charlemagne's biographer rightly called him "the greatest scholar of the day," and Alcuin was known to spend long hours with Charlemagne personally, teaching him "rhetoric, dialectics, and especially astronomy."[25] Alcuin had gotten his start as the head of a school in England, which quickly developed into one of the preeminent centers of learning in Europe. For this he gained the attention of the archbishop of York, who sent him to Rome in 781 to report the news of a new archiepiscopal election. On the way home, in Padua, Italy, Alcuin met Charlemagne, who offered him a position at the imperial court teaching his own children. In time, Alcuin gained regular access to Charlemagne as an adviser and was able to influence him on many issues, including his practice of putting pagans to death.

Alcuin had moral and theological influence at the Carolingian court, but he must be chiefly remembered as a scholar. His educational philosophy looked back to the Greek *trivium* (grammar, rhetoric, and dialectic) and *quadrivium* (arithmetic, geometry, astronomy, and music). From this sprang Alcuin's own intellectual interests: he wrote textbooks on myriad topics. One of his books, a mathematics textbook called *Propositiones ad Acuendos Iuvenes* (Problems to Sharpen the Young), still survives, and the problems, mostly algebraic, are quite challenging:

> (33) A head of household had 30 servants whom he ordered to be given 30 measures of corn as follows. The men should each receive three measures, the women should each receive two measures, and the children should receive a half measure each. How many men, women and children servants are there in the household?[26] (Answer in endnotes.)
>
> (43) A certain man had 300 pigs. He ordered all of them slaughtered in three days, but with an uneven number being killed each day.

He wished the same thing to be done with 30 pigs. What odd number of pigs out of 300 or 30 were to be killed on each of the three days?[27]

Another of Alcuin's great achievements was inventing the script of writing known as Carolingian minuscule. In Alcuin's day, the existing letter formations of the copyists were difficult to read, and ill suited for writing out mathematics problems. The Carolingian script added spaces between words, a trait unknown to Greek and Roman scripts. Thus, this new Carolingian style made copying everything much easier, and it is largely due to the invention of this new form that many ancient mathematical works of the ancient Greeks were able to survive. The superior readability of Carolingian minuscule was also critical to the successful communication of writers across Europe, who could only count on being understood by one another in Latin. And Carolingian minuscule also was the first Western alphabet to feature lowercase letters, a crucial help for distinguishing one word from another.

Alcuin also put on a massive effort to copy the great works of antiquity. More than seven thousand manuscripts from the eighth and ninth centuries, thanks to Carolingian *scriptoria* (portions of monasteries devoted to hand-copying manuscripts), still survive today, a highly impressive number, especially when we consider that the copying of manuscripts had almost ceased entirely in France before his time. Many of these manuscripts were new copies of Jerome's Vulgate Bible, which by

The Benedictine monk Maurus, supported by Alcuin, dedicates his work to the archbishop of Mainz. Ninth-century manuscript illustration, National Library of Austria.

this time was well established as the standard edition of the Latin Bible across Europe. Alcuin had undertaken the task of examining hundreds of manuscripts of the Vulgate for errors in copying that had crept in over time. By examining multiple manuscripts, he was able to identify and correct those errors that were obviously the fault of the copyists. This task too pointed to Charlemagne's and Alcuin's goal of transmitting classical and Christian knowledge for the education of men and the growth of the faith. A literate clergy, schooled in the Scriptures, was a necessary brick in building a new intellectual culture suffused with Christian thought. In a letter to Charlemagne, Alcuin wrote, "If only there were many who would follow the illustrious desire of your intent, perchance a new, nay, more excellent Athens might be founded in Frankland; for our Athens, being ennobled with the Mastership of Christ the Lord, would surpass all the wisdom of the study of the Academy."[28]

Alcuin, along with his three assistants, Witzo, Fridugis, and Sigulf, did not just teach boys, but grown men and women also. He personally instructed the royal court and made them work hard. But he also showed flashes of humor. Nicknames were given out in class: Charlemagne would often be called David, or sometimes Solomon, and his advisers, Angilbert and Adelhard, would become Homer and Antony. Once, when Alcuin was recounting the biographies of Augustine and Jerome, Charlemagne cried out loud, "Why can I not have twelve clerks such as these?" Alcuin wryly responded, "What? The Lord of heaven and earth had but two such, and wouldst thou have twelve?"[29]

In time, Alcuin's drive to educate the top officials of the Frankish kingdom bore a great deal of fruit. The Frankish church became more literate, and clergy began to be selected not just from noble families but common ones too. Charlemagne also issued strict orders for the reform and growth of church music. Music was not just a recreational pursuit, as we generally think of it today. To ancient and medieval thinkers, music was critical to the individual's moral and behavioral development. Plato wrote that music "imparted grace to the soul," and the medieval school-men considered it one of the seven essential liberal arts for young people. So also Charlemagne believed in the power of music as an intellectual and spiritual force. He ordered his singers to come with him to Rome for training from the papal singers, and even took back several papal singers with him to his capital, Aachen. He declared that all clergy must learn psalms, chants, and musical notation in conformity with the *cantus Romanus* (the form of chant sung at Rome), and personally supported the schools of music already established in a dozen towns across his empire.

Other church figures from all over Europe also spurred the Carolingian Renaissance on. Theodulf, the bishop of Orléans, who was of Visigothic descent, served as an important theological voice who helped reform the priesthood. Paul the Deacon wrote the first history of the Lombards, a barbarian tribe who from the sixth century became progressively accultur-ated to European manners. Peter of Pisa was one such Lombard who was highly educated, and in his old age served as Charlemagne's personal Latin teacher. An Anglo-Saxon named Angilbert served as Charlemagne's court poet, and he wrote an epic poem, now lost, that incorporated elements of Virgil and Ovid.

AFTER CHARLEMAGNE

After forty-seven years as king, Charlemagne died in 814. The event produced hysteria across his kingdom, as one monk recounted:

> From the lands where the sun rises to western shores, people are cry-ing and wailing . . . the Franks, the Romans, all Christians, are stung with mourning and great worry . . . the young and old, glorious nobles, all lament the loss of their Caesar . . . the world laments the death of Charles . . . O Christ, you who govern the heavenly host, grant a peaceful place to Charles in your kingdom. Alas for miserable me.[30]

As was the case with other great rulers in history, such as Alexander the Great or Constantine, his kingdom broke apart within a genera-tion of his death. His son, Louis the Pious, and Louis's son Charles the Bald were not nearly as competent or passionate as their predecessor had been. By the year 900, the Carolingian Empire had broken apart. Some intellectual culture from the Frankish kingdom, most notably the work of the Christian philosopher John Scotus Eriugena, survived. But the intellectual and spiritual culture of medieval Europe would hit its lowest points in the generations after Charlemagne.

The Carolingian era was a fairly brief glimmer of progress for the church. After centuries of illiteracy and corruption, Charlemagne managed to inject reform into the body of Christ. At the same time, the transmission of ancient Mediterranean knowledge through the labors of the monks allowed for the preservation of classical knowledge that might have been lost. Later medieval and Renaissance scholars owe mighty debts to these efforts. Without the dutiful efforts of Alcuin and others, European civilization may well have been bereft of some of the most important works of antiquity. Charlemagne had hoped to make a theocratic empire that was distinguished by Christianity at the cultural, intellectual, and social level. But his grasp of learning, rare for a medieval king, endowed the West with a much more lasting legacy. At Charlemagne's instigation, the fusion of the Christian, classical, and Germanic civilizations marked the dawn of a distinctly European identity. It is fitting to illustrate this point with a quotation from Alcuin of York, an Englishman who understood the perpetual value of the classics and of God. Near the end of his life, Alcuin reflected on how he had spent his career:

In the morning, at the height of my powers, I sowed the seed in Britain, now in the evening when my blood is growing cold I am still sowing in France, hoping both will grow, by the grace of God, giving some the honey of the holy scriptures, making others drunk on the old wine of ancient learning.[31]

SEVENTEEN

DECLINE AND REFORM

The Papacy of the Ninth and Tenth Centuries, Benedictine Monasticism and Cluny, Radbertus and Gottschalk, the Medieval Pilgrimage, Anglo-Saxon England

The Carolingian Renaissance (ca. 780–820) was a bright spot for western Europe during an otherwise dreary time. It is here that we can describe Europe as groaning through a truly Dark Age. One scholar has claimed that all the surviving writings (not counting duplicates) from roughly the last two centuries of the first millennium can be piled atop a single dining room table.[1] With the death of Charlemagne, the hope of a Christianized, politically unified Europe died as well. His successors were relatively inept men who lacked his vision and ability. The names of these unremarkable men sound more like New York mob bosses than medieval kings: Louis the Pious, Charles the Bald, Louis the Stammerer, Charles the Simple, Charles the Fat, Louis the Blind, and Louis the Child. There was even at one point a man named Bozo on the throne. The condition of Charlemagne's former kingdom, and the church, suffered under these men:

> Our cities are depopulated, our monasteries wrecked, and put to the torch, our countryside left uninhabited . . . Indeed, just as the first

humans lived without law or the fear of God and accordingly only to
their dumb instincts, so now does everyone to whatever seems good in
his eyes only, despising all human and divine laws and ignoring even
the commands of the Church. The strong oppress the weak, and the
world is wracked with violence against the poor and the plunder of
ecclesiastical lands . . . Men everywhere devour one another like the
fishes of the sea.[2]

Compounding the ecclesiastical corruption and unending violence
of the day was a general apocalyptic fervor that plagued Europe as the
continent lurched forward toward the year 1000. Many believed that
Christ would return in apocalyptic judgment at the beginning of the
millennium, a terrifying prospect. Others believed that the antichrist
predicted in the Bible would appear and inaugurate a period of uniquely
horrifying anti-Christian persecution. This millennial panic was mostly
the result of an interpretation of biblical prophecy that foretold the
return of Christ a literal one thousand years after his incarnation. Others
believed that the apocalyptic end of the world would come in 1033—one
thousand years after his death and resurrection. What is curious about
this expectation is that although medieval men knew that roughly one
thousand calendar years had passed since Jesus walked the earth, even
learned men in Europe at the time did not always know with confidence
in precisely what year they were living.[3]

The medievals were also quick to interpret natural phenomena, such
as comets, meteorites, plagues, famines, albino cattle, and floods, as prophetic signs of certain doom. One writer, the eleventh-century Raoul
Glaber, saw a famine so severe that "grown-up sons devoured their
mothers, and mothers, forgetting their maternal love, ate their babes."
Glaber was convinced that the last judgment was very near when he
learned that Mount Vesuvius, in Italy, "belched forth a multitude of vast
stones mingled with sulphurous flames, which fell even to a distance
of three miles around; and thus by the stench of his breath he began to
make all the surrounding province uninhabitable."[4] Glaber, like many

other medieval writers, also pointed to an unusual intensity of depravity that seemed to mark the age:

> But, alas for shame! the human race, forgetful of God's loving kindness and prone from its very beginning to evil, like the dog returning to his own vomit again or the sow that was washed to her wallowing in the mire, made the covenant of their own promise of none effect in many ways; and, as it is written, they waxed fat, and grew thick, and kicked. For even the princes of both orders, spiritual and secular, turned to covetousness and began to sin in theft and greed as grievously as before, or even worse. Then those of middle rank and the poorer people, following the example of the greater, declined into horrible Crime. For who ere now had heard of such incests, adulteries, and illicit alliances between close kindred, such mockery of concubines and such emulation of evil men?[5]

To Glaber, the other great indication of the end of the age was the moral degradation of the church. Trends of immorality that had begun in the seventh and eighth centuries had now spread throughout the Western church. And the people noticed. Beginning sometime in the tenth century, the feudal masses of Europe began organizing themselves into crude mobs to protest the corrupted relationship between church and state. These rallies became known as the "Peace of God" movement, which demanded that local lords extricate themselves from dealing too closely with the church. These rallies were partly the impetus for reforms at multiple levels. And no area was more badly in need of reform than the papacy.

THE PAPACY OF THE EARLY MEDIEVAL AGES (867–1049)

Ralph Waldo Emerson once wrote that "an institution is a lengthened shadow of a man."[6] By this he meant that founders or decision makers at the top of any organization shape its overall character. Near the year 1000, the repugnant character of the early medieval popes had produced moral rot throughout the church. Wrote Glaber:

> For whenever religion has failed among the pontiffs, and strictness of the Rule has decayed among the abbots, and therewith the vigor of monastic discipline has grown cold, and by their example the rest of the people are become prevaricators of God's commandments, what then can we think but that the whole human race, root and branch, is sliding willingly down again into the gulf of primeval chaos?[7]

The genesis of the papal degeneration had begun long before any one man became pope. For centuries, the pontiff was a powerful man who attracted many overtures of flattery and favor. Secondly, even after the end of the Roman Empire, the city of Rome and its surrounding areas retained a great deal of symbolic importance and practical power. Italy was for centuries the target of barbarian invasions, and as a politically fractious area, it never produced a strong, unifying leader of its own. Consequently, the papacy became the best bastion of stability, authority, and talent, and over time the pope assumed power over the secular affairs of Rome and the surrounding countryside. Later, the papacy became an office subject to ordinary political considerations, and eventually was used as a bargaining chip between powerful Roman families. Predictably, the office of Pope was sometimes inhabited by men who had little or no interest in shepherding the church, and popes were at times poisoned, imprisoned, and killed.

The first known case of papal simony (the buying or selling of ecclesiastical privileges) seems to have taken place with two different candidates for pope under the rule of the ill-tempered Ostrogothic king Theodoric II.[8] From that point, the use of deceitful or outright violent tactics to obtain the papacy became fairly standard. And as the relationship between the pope and the Holy Roman emperor became formalized with Pope Stephen II's appeal to Pepin the Short in 751, the pope's preoccupation with secular matters increased even more. Popes Nicholas I (reigned 858–867) and Adrian II (reigned 867–872) were relatively good men who sought peace between Carolingian rulers who warred over the scraps of Charlemagne's kingdom. But Adrian's successor, John VIII, evinced the beginning of the decay of the papacy. Some historians believe him the best of the ninth-century popes, while others regarded him as "cruel, passionate, worldly-minded, and inconstant."[9] He involved himself very heavily in the affairs of the Carolingians, and feuded with the patriarch of Constantinople on the question of who should have more influence over the Bulgarian church. In the end, John was murdered by being smashed in the head with a hammer, after the poison slipped to him proved to work too slowly.

Most disgusting was the "Cadaver Synod" of 897. Pope Stephen VII, who ultimately ruled only fifteen days as pope, desired to humiliate his deceased predecessor, Formosus, as a heretic. When Stephen took the papal throne, he ordered the body of Formosus exhumed. The corpse was then brought into the papal palace for a synod, and Stephen commanded the deceased Formosus to testify in his own defense. Because the disinterred body could produce no testimony but silence, a guilty verdict was pronounced against Formosus, and his rotting body was stripped naked. Stephen ordered the three fingers used for blessings cut off from the hand of the corpse, the whole of which was then thrown in the Tiber River. Stephen's actions so shocked the church that a synod promptly removed him from the papal throne, and he was soon after strangled to death in prison.

The first half of the tenth century is often called the *saeculum obscurum* (Dark Ages) of the papacy. The popes of this age were almost without exception despicably violent and sexually depraved. In the beginning of the tenth century, a count from the outskirts of Rome, named Theophylact I, used an armed insurrection to become the head of the city of Rome, and began to exert a despotic control over the papal succession process until his death in 924 (the modern practice of the papal conclave did not begin until 1059, as a response to the abuses of the time). Theophylact I instituted a papal legacy that would last for more than one hundred years, and produced some of the vilest popes in history. Theophylact's first de facto appointee was Pope Sergius III, who had deposed not one but two rival claimants to the papacy in 904, and sometime later in the year had both men strangled in prison. Sergius also became involved with Theophylact's daughter, Marozia, and from their union would come a child who would later become Pope John XI (reigned 931–935). The worst of the popes from Theophylact's line was Pope John XII (937–964). John was only eighteen when he became the Vicar of Christ. His sexual exploits were legendary, and one historian wrote that he "made the sacred palace into a whorehouse."[10] This intemperance, in addition to his meddling in political conflicts, was too much for the German emperor Otto I. In 963, at Otto's behest, the church called a synod at Rome with the purpose of deposing him. Fifty Italian and German bishops called John to defend himself on charges of adultery, simony, incest, murder, and sacrilege. He never showed up, and responded that he in fact would have everyone involved excommunicated if they removed him from the Holy See. At the synod, a number of clerics supplied the details of John's seemingly endless indiscretions, sexual and otherwise. One said that they had seen him ordain a deacon in a horse stable. Another swore he had made a ten-year-old boy a bishop. He had fornicated with two widows, a concubine, and his own niece. He had a subdeacon castrated and killed. He played dice and invoked Jupiter and Venus for good luck. And he never made the sign of the cross. It is fitting that John is said to have died while in the act of adultery, an act that Otto's court historian described as the devil calling home his most faithful servant.

Other popes in the Theophrylactian line were hardly any better. Benedict IX (reigned 1032–1048) was only twenty when he became pope but had already established a reputation for hedonistic living. His entry into the papal office only increased his appetite. One historian wrote, "It seemed as if a demon from hell, in the disguise of a priest, occupied the chair of Peter and profaned the sacred mysteries of religion by his insolent courses."[11] Benedict too had a rapacious sexual appetite, which, it was said, extended to both men and women. Other accusations included organizing bands of priests to dress up as robbers, regular applications of burns and tortures on his enemies, and bestiality. Benedict's low point was his decision to sell the papacy to his godfather, and his subsequent decision to use his own army to take it back. Benedict's actions ultimately led to his dismissal for the charge of simony. By this time it was clear that some kind of reform of the papal office was needed.

THE REFORM OF THE PAPACY

Henry III, the king of Germany, had observed with disdain what had become of the church in general and the papacy in particular. He also heard from his subjects, who were growing angry at the unstable and noxious condition of the church in general. He decided to clean house, and in 1046 used his power to gather a council that decided (at his behest) to depose three men who simultaneously claimed to be pope. He then installed his own pope, Clement II, who crowned Henry the Holy Roman emperor. Maddeningly, Clement died very quickly after his appointment, and in 1049, Henry, fed up with the revolving door that had become the Vatican, appointed his own cousin, Bruno of Toul, as pope.

Though Henry's choice was obviously a nepotistic one, Bruno, now Pope Leo IX, proved to be a capable reformer. Leo was by blood a German, and had grown up far removed from the backstabbing and intrigue that marked the Roman families who typically vied for the papacy. Still, Leo had some unease about his own appointment. Henry had appointed Leo, but Leo worried that the transaction appeared to be a form of simony. Therefore, as he set out for Rome, barefoot as a sign of humility, he insisted that he would not accept the office of pontiff unless he was elected to the office by the clergy and the people of Rome. This gesture won him a great deal of approval, and the people of Italy cheered him on as he made his way down the spine of the Italian peninsula toward Rome.

Accompanying him were two clerics who shared his vision for reform. One was Humbert of Lotharingia, a monk who had written a powerful treatise called *Against the Simoniacs*. The other was a monk named Hildebrand, who would become a great reformer in his own right in his later office as Pope Gregory VII. Leo's program of reform concentrated on combating two evils in the church: sexual immorality and simony, the selling of ecclesiastical offices. Leo saw simony as a practice that guaranteed that positions in the church could be passed down through wealthy families over time, a process that limited the ability of able and righteous men to advance in the church hierarchy. Additionally, clerics who married or carried on sexual relationships could produce heirs to which these offices could be transferred. By reaffirming the practice of clerical celibacy and enforcing hard measures against simony, especially in France and Germany, Leo rooted out a huge amount of corruption. Leo also wanted to win back from the people of Europe their confidence in the pope as spiritual leader. Thus, as Gregory the Great had done, he made grand tours around Europe to forge a personal connection. One modern historian described Leo's reception among the crowds of Europe:

> Leo IX was virtually the first pope to be seen in the flesh by any Christians beyond those any relative few who made the pilgrimage to Rome . . . His entry into any given city was preceded by days, if not weeks or months, of advance notice. The gathered crowds ultimately saw a spectacle beyond their imagining: a parade of chanting clergy, colorful banners, trumpets and drums, relics and holy objects carried in triumph, a cavalcade of armed and mailed knights, and then finally, in triumph, the robed and tiared [*sic*] Holy Father on a brilliant golden throne carried on the shoulders of a crowd of papal servants.[12]

Once in town, Leo held public hearings and gave people a chance to vent their grievances against the church. Clergy who had fallen into sin were given a chance to publicly repent and restate their allegiance to the church. One bishop in Reims invited Leo to town to complain to him that he had been denied his right as an archbishop to enjoy the revenues coming in from his parishioners. Leo said he could fix the problem, and removed the bishop from office on the spot. Such decisions reaffirmed the authority that had been invested in the papacy down the centuries.

Leo restored some measure of health back to the church and laid a foundation for greater church reforms in the twelfth and thirteenth centuries. It was also under Leo's papacy that the Latin church definitively split from the Byzantine Orthodox Church in 1054, an event covered later in this book. Leo's successors, including Gregory VII (Hildebrand), continued his reforms. Notable is the Lateran Council of 1059, which stipulated that only cardinals could participate in an election of the pope (albeit with consultation from other clerics and the people). Gregory VII also had an important role in convincing the William the Conqueror, king of England, to fight simony.

Undoubtedly, men such as Henry and Leo exerted a great influence on the direction of the church. But it would be a mistake to suggest that it was popes and kings who were at the source of the reformation of the church. Their decision to confront church abuses was partly the cumulative, calculated political response of local lords to the Christian masses of Europe who protested the injustices of the church. But there was another great force in the eleventh-century reform of the church: the monastic orders.

THE MONASTERY

As we have seen in previous chapters, the monastic life that arose from the sands of Egypt in the late third century took many different forms over time. Many of the monks of Egypt and Syria embraced a highly ascetic lifestyle of mental contemplation and physical mortification. The monks who embraced the Rule of Saint Pachomius, also mostly located in Egypt, Syria, and Palestine, preferred a more communal and somewhat less severe experience, one guided by an abbot (a head of a monastery). The legend of the soldier-turned-monk Martin of Tours drove many in continental Europe to the monasteries in the fourth century. But there was another order that had flourished since the sixth century, and by the eleventh century was the most popular and influential in Europe: the Benedictines.

Benedict of Nursia was born at Umbria, in northern Italy. Around the age of twenty, while living in Rome, he renounced the world and entered a life of contemplation and prayer. For three years, Benedict lived in a cave as a holy hermit. In time, he emerged to found twelve different monasteries in the area between Rome and Naples. The most famous of these is called Monte Cassino, which unfortunately was destroyed by Allied bombing during World War II but was later rebuilt. Benedict developed his own way of running his monasteries, which was written down near the end of his life as the Rule of Saint Benedict. The great motto of Benedictine monasticism was *ora et labora* ("pray and work"). Under the Benedictine model, monks lived together in community, in obedience to their superiors. Prayer was essential for living the monastic lifestyle, and work was a form of community-sustaining love and service from each monk to the others. Benedict viewed work and communal life as great bulwarks against the devil's snares, and this very attitude helped impart a sense of dignity into manual labor—a notion once unheard-of among Greco-Roman aristocrats of the ancient world. Benedict's Rule was also much more lax than many other monastic rules that had come before it, and it is to this relative ease that we can ascribe the popularity of his movement. Benedictine monks had plenty to eat and drink, and were not forced to be frugal in conversation. Regimens of prayer (usually eight individual one-hour periods over the course of twenty-four hours, even at three o'clock in the morning) and work were supplemented with periods of study.

As was also the case with Cassiodorus's monastery at Vivarium, the

Benedictine monasteries became the repositories for virtually all classical and Christian knowledge during the Middle Ages. Charlemagne himself, impressed with the Benedictine commitment to learning, insisted that the Benedictine Rule be copied and disseminated across his empire. By the year 900, virtually every monastery on mainland western Europe was Benedictine in character. The popularity of Benedictine monasticism from late antiquity through the Middle Ages has led many to regard him as the father of Western monasticism. Other popular orders such as Franciscans and Dominicans didn't emerge until later centuries, and Benedict's rule is in fact the one used most commonly by monks today.

But not even the monasteries were immune to the corruption happening in the church. Though monasteries were generally given high degrees of autonomy, they often became play objects for local rulers whose territories they inhabited. Occasionally, the abbot of a monastery would be installed as an act of hereditary or political patronage. The cloistered environment of the abbey allowed sexual corruption to seep in. Monasteries were relatively wealthy places, and some abbots cheated and murdered their way to the top. In 909, Duke William I of Aquitaine (in France), perturbed at all such developments, decided to grant a charter to a new monastery on the lands he formerly used for hunting. What was unique about William's land grant is that he removed himself, and anyone else, entirely from any authority over the new monastery, writing:

> I warn and admonish everyone, in God's name and that of all his saints,
> and by the terrible Day of Judgment, that no secular prince, no count,
> no bishop, nor even the pontiff of the aforesaid Holy See is to attack
> the property of these servants of God, nor alienate it, harm it, grant it
> in fief, or appoint any prelate over it against these monks' will.[13]

The new monastery was founded at a place called Cluny, and because of its independence from political considerations, its size quickly grew, as did its influence over other monasteries. Throughout the tenth century, numerous monasteries began to submit themselves

to the authority of the abbot of Cluny, and other new monasteries copied the Cluniac program. Monasteries all over Europe also felt free to demand autonomy from the local warlords, and these warlords discovered they could become popular with their subject populations by sup-

A nineteenth-century artist's rendering of the monastery at Cluny.

porting ecclesiastical reforms. The abbot of Cluny, free from political entanglements, was free to push a reform agenda, and he eventually became the most powerful man in Western Christianity. One of these men was Hugh of Cluny, who worked closely with Gregory VII to eradicate simony and abuses of power, and who personally performed the most menial tasks in the leper's hospital he founded. Cluny also placed a special emphasis on the monastic offices of prayer and worship. At one point they sang 138 psalms in a single day![14]

But even Cluny, in time, became corrupted by wealth. Rich benefactors who admired the Cluniac model left large gifts for the monastery upon their deaths, and eventually Cluny too grew spiritually weak and neglectful of physical labor. The high point of Cluny's influence was in the tenth and eleventh centuries, but its influence endured through the later Middle Ages, as it also possessed one of Europe's most well-stocked libraries. Judging from the health of the later medieval church, when a corrupt papacy and simoniac clergy abounded, the Cluniac reform movement came up short, and in time the monastery itself fell into decline and disrepair. In 1790, at the height of the French Revolution, angry mobs viewed Cluny as a symbol of the *acien régime*, which had just been deposed, and almost entirely destroyed it.

THEOLOGICAL DEVELOPMENTS OF THE EARLY MIDDLE AGES

If we were to read a newspaper devoted to the events of the ninth and tenth centuries, undoubtedly the headlines would focus on the desultory condition of the papacy in those periods. In the post-Carolingian period, the church seemed to be more concerned with rooting out sin and corruption than with articulating theology. But there were a handful of important theological controversies during the period that are worth noting. The first was instigated by a Frankish abbot and theologian named Paschasius Radbertus. As an infant, Radbertus had been left as an orphan on the steps of a church, and he was raised by nuns. Eventually he devoted himself to being a monk, and in 831 released a treatise on the Eucharist, entitled *De corpore et sanguine Christi* (Concerning Christ's Body and Blood). Even though the patristic writers wrote with disagreement about the institution of the Eucharist, Radbertus's treatise was the most detailed exploration of the sacrament of the Lord's Supper of the first millennium. Radbertus concluded that since God is truth and cannot lie, Jesus' declaration that the elements of bread and wine used in communion were his body and blood must be taken literally. For Radbertus, the consecration of the elements mystically transformed the bread and wine into the physical body and blood of Jesus Christ. When he presented his work to King Charles the Bald, the king recoiled at some passages of it and asked another theologian, Ratramnus of Corbie, to clarify Radbertus's thinking. Ratramnus answered that the elements used in the celebration of the Eucharist were only figurative representations of Jesus' sacrifice, and not a physical incarnation of Jesus' body and blood. The disagreement between the two men was not settled in their lifetime, and it wasn't until 1215, at the Fourth Lateran Council, that the idea of "a change in substance," or transubstantiation, became codified doctrine of the Catholic Church, which it remains today.

The second noteworthy theological dispute of the period revolved around the doctrine of predestination. Sometime around 840, a Saxon (German) monk named Gottschalk of Orbais began preaching on the doctrine of double predestination. Gottschalk was a devoted student of Saint Augustine's works, and read his work *On the Predestination of the Saints* with great enthusiasm. Gottschalk concluded that the church had departed from Augustine's teachings on predestination, and had persisted in error on the question. For Gottschalk, God not only pre-destined the elect before the foundation of the world, but also the reprobate. This view was of course controversial, and made him a num-ber of enemies. Gottschalk was forced to appear at multiple synods, and in 849, he was declared a heretic, ordered to burn his writings, stripped of his priesthood, and whipped (a punishment for disobedient monks under the Rule of Saint Benedict). He was then imprisoned in a Germany monastery for another twenty years and went mad before his death around 869. Although the controversies of the early Middle Ages were not nearly as meaningful to the church as the ones of the patristic and Constantinian eras, they still exhibited the fact that serious con-sideration of God and his ways had not died out among the few true intellectuals of western Europe.

THE MEDIEVAL PILGRIMAGE AND RELICS

The vast majority of people who lived in the early Middle Ages were rural peasants, and their involvement in the church was lim-ited to taking communion and absolution from itinerant priests. The dominant social arrangement of the period, feudalism, was emerg-ing in parts of Europe, and most people spent their time farming on the large estates of local lords in exchange for the nobles protecting them from enemies in warfare. People who lived in the urban centers of Europe (which by our standards today were very much towns, not cities) attended mass more frequently and had closer contact with their bishop. But sometimes people expressed their devotion in ways that went beyond attending the mass or offering confession to a priest. One of these expressions was the pilgrimage—a journey that the medievals believed could be undertaken as a means of obtaining divine favor or expressing penance for sins.

The first Christian pilgrimages can be traced back to very shortly after the time of Christ, when people visited Jerusalem to see many of the sites depicted in the Gospels. Later on, pilgrims from around the Mediterranean began to visit Rome, and the Christian catacombs (crypts) there, even still today, are filled with frescoes of Christians kneeling and praying at the different stations of their pilgrimage. By the fourth and fifth centuries, ecclesiastical authorities in Jerusalem laid down strict rules regarding pilgrims who had come to town. This was partly for their own safety, as bands of robbers were known to disguise themselves, infiltrate groups of pilgrims, and then rob them. Each pilgrimage was also an opportunity for non-pilgrims to express Christian charity; because of the danger and exhaustion that a lengthy pilgrimage entailed, every chapel and monastery along the way was considered open to pilgrims for food and lodging. The pilgrimage also took on a very egalitarian character; virtually any Christian could participate in the sanctifying arduousness of it all. The most famous medieval pilgrimage route was known as the Camino de Santiago, or the Way of Saint James. From early Christian times, a shrine was established to Saint James, the disciple of Jesus who was beheaded at Jerusalem in AD 44. Since the shrine's beginning sometime in late antiquity, a legend had grown that James's body had been sent to Spain by the disciples, then shipwrecked, and then, covered in scallop shells, washed up onshore near Compostela, a tiny town in the extreme northwestern corner of Spain. In the ninth century, hearing legends that the bones of Saint James had been discovered there, pilgrims from across Europe started to make the difficult trek over the Pyrenees mountains and across the northern coast of Spain to visit the shrine. The tradition of visiting Compostela even endures today, and as in medieval times, the symbol of the Santiago de Compostela pilgrimage is a scallop shell; the curved vertical lines of the shell are supposed to represent the many diverse ways that medieval pilgrims took to reach the site.

Another very important facet of a pilgrimage was the collection of relics associated with all kinds of saints and martyrs. Even the smallest bit of body, clothing, or personal artifact from a deceased, famous Christian could excite fanatical devotion. Very often within minutes of a martyr's death, his body would be despoiled, his blood saved with sponges, and the sand on which he fell collected. Relics began to be displayed in churches as a means of attracting pilgrims, and churches would display the bones of saints, or some other artifacts, outside their buildings. In 608, Pope Boniface IV, dedicating a new church in Rome, ordered that twenty-eight chariot loads of bones be transported from the catacombs to adorn the new church.[15]

Unfortunately, the display of relics, which grew tremendously in popularity during the seventh century, also enabled the veneration of saints and icons of saints, a practice that eventually helped fuel the Great Schism of 1054 between the Catholic and Orthodox churches. The collection of relics often devolved into ridiculous claims: multiple versions of the True Cross were claimed during the Middle Ages; other common objects passed off as holy included Noah's beard, the horns of Moses, the stone on which Jacob slept at Bethel, the branch from which Absalom hung, Jesus' foreskin, his navel cord, his coat, tears he shed at the grave of Lazarus, milk from Mary's breasts, the table on which the Last Supper was eaten, the stone of Christ's sepulcher, Paul's thorn in the flesh, and a tooth belonging to Saint Lawrence. Superstitions and shysterism surrounded the authenticity, trade, and display of medieval relics, but they still played an important role in cultivating the faith of medieval men and women.

342

ENGLAND

In chapter 13, we saw how Augustine of Canterbury and his co-laborers reestablished the Roman church in England. In time, Christianity spread around the island, and the English abbot the Venerable Bede chronicled the early history of the British church. In the period after Pope Gregory the Great dispatched Augustine to resuscitate the British church, two figures predominated: Theodore of Tarsus and Wilfrid of York.

The England that Theodore of Tarsus (602–690) inhabited was still a wild place, with little footprint from its onetime Roman colonists. Absent an urban structure for the church to grow into, many varieties of Christianity sprang up around the backwoods island. Theodore had initially come to Rome as a refugee from the Muslim armies overrunning Tarsus, the hometown of Saint Paul on the southern coast of Turkey. But Theodore was a man with Eastern theological instincts and training who perhaps did not quite fit in, and he was considered a threat at Catholic Rome. As a result, the pope effectively exiled Theodore, already an old man, by naming him the bishop of Great Britain in 668. Theodore was a highly learned man with training in biblical exegesis and biblical languages from the seminaries of Constantinople. His arrival in England as bishop brought a highly needed dose of learning to the island. He published commentaries on Scripture, introduced new forms of sacred music, and founded a school at Canterbury that proved highly successful, claimed Bede: "They attracted a large number of students, into whose minds they poured the waters of wholesome knowledge day by day. In addition to instructing them in the holy Scriptures, they also taught their pupils poetry, astronomy, and the calculation of the church calendar . . . Never had there been such happy times as these since the English settled Britain."[16]

Especially enthusiastic were the Irish scholars who came to Canterbury, who peppered Theodore with questions "like a pack of hounds baying at a wild boar run to earth."[17] Theodore also reformed some of the ways of ecclesiastical administration: one story goes that Theodore met an elderly Irish bishop who still preferred to travel the island on foot, a penitential tradition that had been around for generations. Theodore picked up the old bishop himself and set him upon a horse, insisting that if a bishop was to care for his flock properly, he ought to make use of the most efficient means of doing so.

The story of Theodore and the bishop hints at another great accomplishment of Theodore's time as the archbishop of England: bringing into uniformity the English (and Irish) ecclesiastical customs that stood outside of the practice accepted by the church at Rome. As was the case in other parts of Europe, the placement of the church in the British wilderness meant that the worship practices of the early British church varied greatly by region. The British church was one of the last to adopt the practices of Rome, and this was especially true in the region of Northumbria, a vast kingdom in the northernmost part of Britain and Scotland. At the Synod of Whitby around 664, ecclesiastics from both places met to reconcile their many differences.

The basic disagreement at the synod was one that had been confronted before in the early church: when to celebrate Easter. The Northumbrians, heavily influenced by Irish Christianity, argued for their right to celebrate Easter in their own way because their calculation was used by Saint Columba, a famous early Irish missionary who had followed the traditions of the apostle John. Refuting the Northumbrians at the Synod was Wilfrid of York. Wilfrid was a Northumbrian noble by birth, who at the age of fourteen was exiled from the kingdom by his stepmother. Wilfrid became a monk and spent extensive time in Gaul. Upon his return to England, he rose quickly to become the archbishop of York, the largest city in northern England, and helped found the school that would eventually educate many English churchmen, including Alcuin, Charlemagne's tutor. Presiding over the Synod as judge was King Oswu of Northumbria, who, as the supreme authority over the Synod, might have been expected to retain his own Northumbrian customs. In reality,

Oswu was more eager to hold on to power than he was to preserve the Northumbrian custom, and at Wilfrid's urging, he willfully placed his kingdom under the rubric of the church at Rome.

Wilfrid spent the rest of his long career bringing the churches of Northumbria into conformity with the rest of England, and he did this using some showman tactics. He adorned his home monastery with massive displays of wealth, and usually traveled around the countryside with up to 120 attendants![18] In spite of some of his lavish habits, he brought the Rule of Saint Benedict into the English and Irish monasteries, educated the churches in the musical styles of Rome, and oversaw the production of Bibles produced in Roman scripts. Though these stylistic changes may seem insignificant to us now, in a harsh world minimally touched by Mediterranean learning, such changes drew the British ever tighter into the Roman orbit. But just as the British church was experiencing new levels of learning and unity as it entered the eighth century, it encountered a new, foreign threat to its very existence: the Vikings.

EIGHTEEN

NORTHERN LIGHTS

Vikings and Alfred the Great, the Christianization of Scandinavia, Cyril and Methodius, the Christianization of Eastern Europe

Thanks to the efforts of church reformers such as Theodore of Tarsus and Wilfrid of York, the English church in the Anglo-Saxon period attained a new level of unity near the end of the eighth century. But the English church would face an entirely new external challenge beginning around the same time. In 793, a race of strange men made landfall on the tiny island monastery of Lindisfarne, off the coast of northeast England. They sacked and burned the monastery, looted it of all its treasures, and slaughtered its peaceful inhabitants. A later Anglo-Saxon chronicler recalled the year in the bleakest terms:

> This year came dreadful fore-warnings over the land of the Northumbrians, terrifying the people most woefully: these were immense sheets of light rushing through the air, and whirlwinds, and fiery dragons flying across the firmament. These tremendous tokens were soon followed by a great famine: and not long after, on the sixth day before the ides of January in the same year, the harrowing inroads

347

of heathen men made lamentable havoc in the church of God in Holy-island [Lindisfarne], by rapine and slaughter.[1]

The moment was not the first continental contact with the Norse peoples, but it functionally inaugurated the Viking age in Europe. The first explorers from Scandinavia to explore the Anglo-Saxon and Frankish areas were only traders; but later, attracted by the relative wealth of the Carolingian world, they organized themselves into small bands of warriors who looked for foreign targets to plunder. The Viking encroachment on European civilization did not resemble the mass invasions of the Goths or Huns, in which whole populations, supported by huge land armies, overran and inhabited conquered territories. To the contrary, the swift and unpredictable Viking raids were of a much smaller scale, but they could be even more terrifying.

The fearsome invaders appeared in their warships without much notice, and without much resistance raided isolated monasteries, churches, and castles (virtually the only reliable repositories of any significant wealth in the early medieval era). From around 750 to 1100, kingdoms from England to Constantinople suffered the wrath of the Norsemen. The Vikings had great advantages over the people they stalked. For one thing, they possessed a menacing countenance. To the average European, these "Northmen" were demonic-looking giants: blond, bearded men usually much larger in body size than the average European. These physical advantages allowed them to swing their mighty axes with terrifying force. The Vikings also traveled overseas in the Viking longship, a masterwork of nautical engineering, its narrow and light design allowing it to coast easily through otherwise unnavigable rivers and oceans around the continent. The longships enabled their excursion parties to reach faraway inland destinations, such as Seville, the capital of Islamic Spain, and Kiev in the Ukraine. The ferocity of the Vikings, a trait exacerbated by their wild appearance, is summed up in a prayer frequently found in the English liturgy of the period: "From the fury of the Northmen, O Lord, please save us!"[2]

The Norsemen's incursions began as mere plunder grabs. But eventually many of them decided to relocate permanently from Scandinavia to other places. There were multiple reasons for this migration. The first was that the craggy, cold terrain of Norway, Sweden, and Denmark did not lend itself to farming. The early

The emblem on the front of a Viking warship, Culture and History Museum, Oslo, Norway.

Norse were polygamists, and as their population numbers grew in the eighth century and space in the rocky tundra became more limited, they fanned out in search of more fertile, warmer climates. The Norwegians looked to the west, and, along with the Danes, who were less skilled in sailing, settled in England, France, and the Low Countries (modern-day Belgium, Luxembourg, and the Netherlands). To the East went the Swedes, who (as we will address later) established themselves as the first rulers over the first Russian state. The growth of the Viking menace across Europe was partly responsible for the rise of so many different, tiny medieval principalities run by men who were really more local chieftains than true kings. Fearful peasants promised material tribute and civic loyalty to these local lords in exchange for protection. Most lords or peasants could do little to fend off their incursions. But in England, one of these lords looked scornfully on the new invaders and resolved to do something about them.

ALFRED THE GREAT FIGHTS BACK

By the end of the 800s, the Vikings controlled all of England except for the territory of Wessex in the south of England, held by King Alfred (later given the honorific "the Great"). Alfred is the only early

Viking raids and expansion through the eleventh century.

medieval ruler who can approximate Charlemagne in his seriousness toward governing and his sharp intellect. He had a lifelong thirst for knowledge, beginning in boyhood, when "day and night did he listen attentively to the Saxon poems, which he often heard others repeating, and his attentive mind allowed him to remember them."[3] Alfred desperately wanted to learn how to read as a boy, but as his biographer said, "In those days there were no men really skilled in reading in the kingdom of the West Saxons."[4] By the time he became king of the West Saxons in 871, he still had not learned how to read, though he would later acquire the skill relatively late in life. Such was the miserable condition of England at the time that even a king could not learn to read even though he ached for the opportunity.

Still, Alfred had a reputation as an intelligent man, and this was proved by his prowess in battle. In 870, a year known as the "year of battles," Alfred and his brother, King Aethelred, won multiple skirmishes over what the Saxons called the Great Heathen Army, a large band of Scandinavian fighters led by the spectacularly named Ivar the Boneless.[5] In 871, Athelred died in battle, leaving the twenty-two-year-old Alfred as king, "trusting in the aid of God alone, ever to withstand such great fierceness of the heathen."[6] Over the next six years, Alfred waged dozens, perhaps hundreds, of fights against the Scandinavian invaders, fending off "countless attacks by day and by night."[7] By 877, his force was reduced to a small band of men hiding in the forests and marshes of Wessex. But he managed to mount an effective campaign of guerrilla warfare, proving himself capable of slaughtering a king and eight hundred of his men in one of his forays. Little by little, Alfred raided the Viking armies of the countryside, and finally smashed them at a brutal battle at what is today the tiny town of Edington. This defeat prompted the Scandinavians to sue for peace, and in 880, they and Alfred agreed on a power-sharing agreement. Alfred received the western and southern parts of the nation, while the Danes held the east. Alfred remained preoccupied with occasional skirmishes against the Danes throughout the rest of his life. But his triumph and reclamation of England was a permanent foothold for Christianity in the nation. As a condition of surrender, the Danish king in England converted to Christianity and was baptized by Alfred himself. Alfred and his men were (at least in name) Christians, and his triumph delighted Pope Marinus; he sent Alfred (what was certainly not) a piece of the True Cross, and exempted him from rendering any kind of tribute.

Alfred's accomplishments for the faith did not end on the battlefield. He ruled from 871 to 899, and conducted himself in a highly thoughtful manner, in light of the grubby, violent, and unlearned period in which he lived. Alfred was a courageous warrior, but also suffered for twenty-five years from ceaseless bouts of painful internal illness, now thought to perhaps be Crohn's disease.[8] Alfred tried to pray away the pain, of which he lived in constant dread. In the mornings, his biographer Asser wrote, he would rise secretly, and "sought the churches and relics of saints for the sake of prayer," and "prayed that the almighty God, of his mercy, would strengthen him and turn him wholly to Him, making his mind more ardent in love and service to him."[9] He sometimes sneaked off in the middle of the night to pray in church. Half of all tax revenue that

Alfred collected was given to the poor, the churches, monasteries, and the schools. He was described as a generally good-natured man who mingled easily with his subjects and inquired into their welfare, and one who would stop and pray with strangers.

Still, Alfred's own inadequacies of learning ate away at him, and he often "made complaint to the Lord . . . that Almighty God had not made him skilled in divine wisdom and in the liberal arts."[10] Like Charlemagne, Alfred did not let his early deficits in learning hinder his passion for letters. Sometime after he became king, Alfred sent for help from a neighboring kingdom and received Werferth, Bishop of Worchester, "well learned in the Holy Scriptures,"[11] who translated the dialogues of Pope Gregory the Great from Latin into Saxon, which was then distributed to the bishops of Alfred's kingdom. Alfred also kept a commonplace book that he carried with him everywhere in his cloak, and insisted to his companions that they write profitable quotations and prayers in this book. Wrote his biographer, "As the busy bee travels far and wide, searching through the marches, so without pause and unceasingly did he gather many little flowers of Holy Scripture of divers kinds, wherewith he filled the full cells of his mind."[12]

He also established schools that taught Saxon and Latin, corresponded with the Patriarch of Jerusalem, and perhaps also sent a mission to India. He helped restore the city of London and "made it habitable, after the burnings of cities and slaughter of people."[13] His network of strategically placed military forts, called *burghs*, helped slow invasions from the Danes. He even developed a primitive navy that achieved some success in beating back pirates and Vikings. Alfred also issued a law code that was heavily informed by the Judeo-Christian tradition, and he himself heard many disputes. Alfred styled himself as a sort of Solomon, the

A miniature illustration of Alfred on a manuscript.

ancient Jewish king who glutted himself on divine wisdom and then dispensed judgments in accordance with it. Alfred, said Asser, "would carefully look into nearly all the judgements which were passed [issued] in his absence anywhere in the realm, to see whether they were just or unjust."[14]

Alfred's quest for piety, learning, and good government in many ways mirrored the mission that Charlemagne had endeavored to carry out a century earlier. Unfortunately, little is known about Alfred's relationship with the church, though he too, like Charlemagne, Justinian, and Constantine, saw no distinction between his secular and clerical authority. The Viking invasions of the eighth and ninth centuries effected a momentous disruption of English ecclesiastical life and literacy, and posterity is grateful to possess the little bit of writings that do happen to survive from the period. Alfred died in 899, leaving an immediate political legacy that, unlike Charlemagne's, did not quickly evaporate. By the end of the tenth century, the Scandinavians who had settled in England had assimilated into the local populations, and in 975, Alfred's grandson Edgar achieved the reunification of England under Anglo-Saxon rule. But England would soon be reconquered; in 1015, the Danish king Canute sailed for England with a massive army of Scandinavians. Canute, despite not being Anglo-Saxon, proved a highly effective ruler until his death in 1035. Canute's relative, Harald II, would famously lose the kingship of England at the battle of Hastings in 1066 to William the Conqueror, an event that marked the end of the Anglo-Saxon period in English history.

ANGLO-SAXON CULTURE

It must have come as a massive shock to the Anglo-Saxon realm that the monastery at Lindisfarne was devastated by what seemed to the medievals a supernaturally evil act of destruction. Alcuin of York was aghast: "Behold, the church of Saint Cuthbert spattered with the blood

of the priests of God, despoiled of all
its ornaments; a place more venerable than all in Britain is given as a
prey to pagan peoples."[15] After all,
Lindisfarne was the unquestionable
treasure of the English church. It was
in its time certainly the wealthiest
and probably the most learned monastery in all of England and Ireland.
Lindisfarne was founded by monks
from the important Irish monastery

A view of Lindisfarne Castle.

of Iona, and down to the age of the first Viking raids remained especially
influenced by the Irish monastic and artistic traditions. Nowhere do we
see this more definitively than in the Lindisfarne Gospels, one of the
most splendid works of art from the medieval period. Sometime in the
early 700s, a group of monks created a copy of the four Gospels, bound
it in a leather and bejeweled covering, and decorated it with some of the
most mesmerizing illustrations the world has ever seen.

The illuminator of the Gospels was Eadfrith, bishop of Lindisfarne,
and his elaborate, swirling colors on nearly every page demonstrate a
depth of precision and effort that could only have been performed as an
act of spiritual worship to God. Such was the nature of monastic art,
in everything from manuscripts to jewelry to coffins, the highly intricate style of any artistic production bespoke God's passionate concern
for detail as revealed in the splendor of creation. In the tenth century,
a monk took it upon himself to interpose an Old English translation of
the Lindisfarne Gospels between their lines of Latin, a helpful if ruinous
gesture that nonetheless stands as the first translation of the Gospels
into English. The true pinnacle of the illuminated manuscript genre
is the Book of Kells, created around 800 in an Irish monastery. The
book sits today in the Trinity College (Dublin) library, and is considered the national artistic treasure of Ireland. The Book of Kells, like the
Lindisfarne Gospels, betrays almost a surrealist element to some of its art

choices (such as its depiction of a monk with flowers for hands), and the jagged compression of letters into colorful word blocks is reminiscent of the most carefully wrought modern-day graffiti. But a twelfth-century Welshman traveling to Ireland felt no differently about the quality of these manuscripts than we might today:

> If you look at them carelessly . . . you may judge them to be mere daubs . . . You would see nothing subtle where everything is subtle. But if you take the trouble to look very closely and to penetrate with your eyes to the secrets of the artistry, you will notice such intracacies, so delicate, so subtle . . . so involved and bound together, so fresh still in their coverings, that you will not hesitate to declare that all those things must have been the work not of men but of angels.[16]

Other than impressive copies of the Bible, the other great cultural product of Anglo-Saxon England is the epic poem *Beowulf*, composed in Old English sometime around the year 1000. That *Beowulf* only survives in a single manuscript that barely escaped a fire in the 1700s shows how close it was to being completely lost to the ages, and the fact that it was barely studied until the 1800s is a reflection of the early modern era's low interest in, or regard for, the Anglo-Saxon period. The plot of *Beowulf* revolves around a Scandinavian warrior, Beowulf, who is hired to exact revenge on a set of monsters who have terrorized the local king, Hrothgar. It is here that we see the most prized ethic of the early medieval man: heroism and talent in combat. Beowulf is revered throughout the poem not only for his loyalty, but also for his courage in the face of

First page of the book of Matthew in the Lindisfarne Gospels.

danger and his prowess at slaughtering enemies. But *Beowulf* also hints at the ways Christianity had permeated the Anglo-Saxon world.

It is God who allows Beowulf to spot a useful weapon, and God to whom Beowulf ascribes victory in battle. There is a reference to Noah's flood, and Beowulf's rival, Grendel, is described as "the opposer of God."[17] *Beowulf* exhibits little interest in the transcendence of Christianity and the transformation of the heart that characterizes the believer, preferring to emphasize a self-serving theology of how God helps the brave. But *Beowulf* does indicate how Christianity's moral code was starting to influence the warrior peoples near the Arctic Circle.

The Christianization of the Danes and Swedes

Even before the beginning of the Viking excursions across the North Sea, both Britons and continental Europeans had come in contact with the pagan Nordic people through trade. Undoubtedly the Norse came in contact with symbols of Christianity, such as coins depicting crosses. The Norse people worshipped a panoply of gods, including Thor and Odin, but not much detail is known about these pagan religions. Moreover, as was the case with the Germanic peoples in the sixth and seventh centuries, the converted Nordic peoples often commingled their worship of the Christian God with the worship of traditional deities. Wrote one chronicler in 968, "The Danes formerly became Christians, but nevertheless they continue to venerate idols according to heathen customs."[18] Although missionary activity started in the 700s, Scandinavia did not receive a permanent archdiocese until the 1100s. Thus we must take accounts of Christianization with a grain of salt, especially since many Scandinavian tribes were converted at the point of another tribe's sword.

Denmark's proximity to slowly Christianizing Germany made it a natural target for missionary activity. One of the first to go there, around 710, was Willibrord, one of the companions of Saint Boniface. But Christianity was slow to catch on. The first Danish king to accept Christianity was Harald Klak in 826, but it was the conversion of King Harald Bluetooth that greatly animated the spread of the faith in Denmark, an episode that allegedly occurred at the sight of a Frisian monk holding a hot coal in his hand without injury. Harald's son, Sweyn Forkbeard, also claimed to have been a Christian, but an insurrection against his own father, as well as his army's persecution of Christians in England, calls that claim into question. In 1086, King Canute IV seemed to have made a sincere embrace of the faith, but his sometimes tyrannical exercise of power, and his insistence on the right to collect tithes from the peasantry, resulted in him suffering a fatal lance to his midsection inside a church, a fate that also befell seventeen of his men.

The first attempts to bring the gospel to Sweden happened around 830, thanks to Anskar, the bishop of Hamburg, sometimes called the "apostle of the North." Anskar was born in 801, and as a young man became a monk. Shortly after he took his vow and accepted the tonsure (the signature monk's haircut of a shaved top and long sides), he had a vision in which God told him, "Go and return to Me crowned with martyrdom."[19] Anskar never did attain martyrdom, a source of disappointment to him, but he did enjoy a long career of evangelizing the Norsemen. Although Anskar was known for his preaching, he also imposed on himself a rigid regimen of self-denial: measuring out his daily intake of food and water, wearing a hair shirt,[20] and performing the mass three times per day. In 829, the German king Ludwig received an emissary from the Swedish king Bjørn, who requested some missionaries on behalf of many people in his land who wished to discover the Christian religion. Anskar "burned with fervour and with love towards God and esteemed it a special joy if he might be allowed to press forward in the work of winning souls," and was sent to Sweden with four companions. On the way, they were robbed by pirates, and lost not only the royal gifts intended for King Bjorn but also forty books useful to their ministry. "But no argument could divert God's servant from the journey which he had undertaken," and Anskar eventually reached Sweden. There he would spend the next thirty years of his life invested in the work of preaching the gospel, despite seeing little fruit from his efforts.[21]

It wasn't until the conversion of King Olof Skötkonung around 1008 that Christianity became a permanent fixture in Sweden. An episcopal see was established in 1000, but an archdiocese did not come until 1164, demonstrating the slow growth of Christianity in the North. Violence between Christians and pagans also disrupted the spread of the faith. In the 1080s, rival kings Sweyn the Sacrificer and Inge the Elder shed copious amounts of blood when Inge decided to ban traditional sacrifices from his kingdom. When Inge decided to ban the ancient practice of sacrificing horses, Sweyn stepped in and told Inge's subjects that if they made him king, he would allow the practice again. Inge's people drove Inge away in a hail of rocks and went back to sacrificing horses, eating their meat, and smearing blood on their sacred trees. But Inge would have his revenge. Some time later, he and his men came upon Sweyn sleeping in his house. They set it ablaze, killing many inside, and slayed the escaping Sweyn. The presence of such senseless violence between competing religions again suggests the weakness of Christianity in Sweden through the 1100s.

NORWAY

Christianity first came to Norway through King Hakkon the Good, who spent his formative years as a hostage in England and was instructed in the faith. In the early tenth century, Hakkon heard of his father the king's death, and returned to Norway to claim the kingdom for himself. Standing in the way was his half brother, Erik Bloodaxe. After several years of fighting Bloodaxe and his clan, Hakkon finally reigned triumphant. Unfortunately, his people refused to adopt his new religion, and any missionary intent he might have had died with him. It wasn't until the conversion of King Olaf I, also known as Olaf Trygvesson, in

995 that Norway became in any sense Christian. Olaf's physical prowess was legendary, and it is said he could juggle five daggers at one time without cutting himself. He was also a merciless raider of the English isles, and was fond of "burning villages, laying waste the lands, putting numbers of people to death by fire and sword, without regard to sex, and sweeping off an immense booty."[22] At some point, a story goes, Olaf heard of a marvelous hermetic fortune-teller who lived off the coast of England. The fortune-teller told him that he would soon suffer a mutiny by his men. But that wasn't all Olaf heard. "Many men wilt thou bring to faith and baptism," the prophet said, "and both to thy own and others' good."[23] With that, Olaf allowed himself to be baptized.

Soon after, he struck an alliance with the king of England and promised to never wage war on him again. In 995, however, Olaf got word from Norway of a notorious king, also named Hakon, who was bringing ruin on the country, committing abuses such as stealing the daughters of the gentry for himself. Moreover, this Hakon was also restoring pagan temples, and had even sacrificed one of his own sons to receive divine favor. This Olaf could not endure, and he sailed back to Norway with a band of men to reclaim his throne. After landing, Olaf made his way inland to confront Earl Hakon. Hakon heard of Olaf's coming and fled to the home of one of his mistresses, who had dug a hole under her pigsty. Hakon climbed in the hole and had it covered with logs and manure. The stench was suffocating, and Hakon lay still, hearing Olaf bark out orders to his men to find and kill him. But one of Hakon's aides, also lying in the pit with him, was terrified of being captured and stuck a knife in Hakon's throat. After presenting Hakon's head to Olaf, he too was beheaded.[24]

Olaf was now the king, and set out on a mission to Christianize Norway, at that time a nation of autonomous fishers and farmers whose population totaled maybe fifty thousand people. Unfortunately, Olaf's preferred method of spreading the faith was through the sword. "I shall make you great and mighty men for doing this work," he told his deputies. "All Norway will be Christian or die."[25] One gruesome episode involved a man named Raud the Strong. Raud was a priest of the indigenous Nordic religion who refused to convert to Christianity and ridiculed Olaf's beliefs in the process. This incensed Olaf, who ordered Raud bound with his face turned upward and a wooden pin keeping his mouth propped open. Olaf and his men tried to force a snake into Raud's mouth, but the snake would not go in. Olaf and company then took a large drinking horn (similar to a funnel), placed the snake inside, and heated it with fire. In an effort to escape the heat, the snake crawled into Raud's mouth and down his throat. Raud would die soon after, when the snake chewed through Raud's side to escape.[26]

In another episode, at a place on the river Gota, Olaf enticed all the local wizards and priests to a longhouse by promising them a great feast. When they arrived, Olaf locked them all inside and burned the hall to the ground. Their leader, who tried to escape through the hall's chimney, was punished by being marooned on a small island off of Norway's coast. In another episode, one victim who refused conversion was killed when a pile of hot coals was placed on his chest.

Such forcible conversions to Christianity seem incomprehensible to us and are of course antithetical to the Christian ethic. But we must remember that these kings had almost zero understanding of the Scriptures, and had probably never had the gospel rightly explained to them. Within the destructive milieu of medieval politics, Christianity was to many of the medieval kings a mere tool that aided their quests for land and treasure. And it took a very long time for Christianity to catch on among the subject peoples of the North, for whom pagan traditions were deeply entrenched. None of the Scandinavian countries were recognized with a permanent archdiocese until the twelfth century.

CYRIL AND METHODIUS

Scandinavia was not the only part of Europe in which the political considerations of local rulers animated efforts to Christianize the population. For a few centuries, the Slavic peoples had inhabited parts of central and eastern Europe in diverse, small kingdoms. In 863, two Slavic princes of Moravia (in today's Czech Republic) wrote to Emperor Michael III and the Patriarch Photius, requesting that he send some missionaries to Christianize their peoples. Earlier European settlers had tried to evangelize the Slavs, but their teaching was unintelligible to them: "Many Christian teachers have reached us from Italy, from Greece and from Germany, who instruct us in different ways. But we Slavs . . . have no one to direct us towards the truth and instruct us in an understandable way."[27] The Slavic motivation for Christianity also centered on a desire to obtain some degree of independence from the German kings with whom they had allied themselves. Starting their own Slavic church would be one way to do this.

The Byzantine emperor appointed two brothers from the Greek town of Salonika (today, Thessaloniki) to serve as missionaries to the Slavs. Cyril (the younger brother) and Methodius (the elder) were the sons of a high-ranking imperial official in the Byzantine Empire who died when the brothers were boys. Methodius (born ca. 815–820) was bound for the same career as his father, and as a young man was appointed a prefect in one of the Slavic provinces. But in 840, he received a spiritual call to embark on the contemplative life, and in that year retired to the Holy Mountain monastery near the shore of the Black Sea. Young Cyril was not too different from his brother. He studied in Constantinople, and was on the path to become a teacher of theology in the great city. His great grasp of theology and multiple languages even afforded him the opportunity to act as an emissary to the Arabic Caliphate, where he tried to explain the idea of the Trinity to the caliph. But Cyril too felt the call to ministry, and became the secretary to the patriarch of Constantinople before begging to go, like his brother, into the monastery.[28]

The two made a formidable duo: Cyril having been through the best institutions of learning in the Byzantine realm, and his brother the contemplative sage. By 863, the brothers had undertaken their historically meaningful mission to Moravia. To aid their work they took along copies of the Bible. But Cyril and Methodius knew that copies of a Latin Bible would not be as useful to the Slavs as one in their own language. The problem was that the Slavs at that time had no written language. To remedy the problem, Cyril and Methodius enlisted a friend named Constantine the Philosopher to help them develop a new alphabet that used a Greek-influenced script to express the phonetic sounds of the Slavic language. Their work produced what is now called the Glagolitic alphabet, the predecessor of the modern Cyrillic alphabet used to write the Russian, Serbian, and Bosnian languages. This written language was perhaps the greatest legacy that Cyril and Methodius bequeathed to Europe, since it also allowed for further conversions of the Slavic peoples. The first books Cyril and Methodius translated were the Psalms and the New Testament. Some rebuked the brothers for establishing a church that made no use of Latin, but Cyril defended their action: "Do not all breathe the air in the same way? And you are not ashamed to decree only three languages (Hebrew, Greek and Latin), deciding that all other peoples and races should remain blind and deaf!"[29]

Despite the brothers being caught in a rivalry between Rome and Constantinople for theological control of the Slavic lands, things continued to go well in Moravia until 869, when Cyril unexpectedly died. On his deathbed, he exhorted his brother Methodius, "Behold, my brother, we have shared the same destiny, ploughing the same furrow; I now fall in the field at the end of my day. I know that you greatly love your Mountain; but do not for the sake of the Mountain give up your work of teaching."[30] Methodius would carry on the work alone for another sixteen years. In 870, he was formally made the bishop of Moravia and Pannonia. This move angered the Catholic Church at Salzburg, which considered Methodius's archdiocese a place that should be under their own control. Moreover, the Germans were repulsed at the idea that Methodius would hold a mass in the native language of the Slavs. Methodius was taken and shut up under house arrest for two years until the pope intervened. Toward the end of his life, Methodius spent a great deal of time translating other parts of the Bible and patristic writings into the first written Slavic language, now referred to as Old Church Slavonic. He died in 885, and to his funeral came "men and women, humble and powerful, rich and poor, free men and slaves, widows and orphans, foreigners and local people, the healthy and the sick."[31] In time, other Slavic populations would slowly be converted. In 966, the first king of independent Poland professed Christianity, as did the Bulgarian *boyar* around the same time. For their work in virtually creating Slavic civilization, Cyril and Methodius are remembered in portions of the Orthodox Church as equal to the apostles. A modern hymn to them expresses this designation:

> *O Cyril and Methodius, inspired by God,*
> *You became equal to the Apostles by your life.*
> *Since you were teachers of the Slavs,*
> *Intercede with the Master of all*
> *That He may strengthen all Orthodox peoples in the True Faith,*
> *And that He may grant peace to the world*
> *And great mercy to our souls.*[32]

THE CHRISTIANIZATION OF THE KIEVAN RUS

The first Christian missions to the area encompassing modern-day Russia may very well have been undertaken by the apostle Andrew; at least this is what Eusebius, citing Origen, claimed in his ordinarily reliable *Church History*.[33] But any efforts made to convert the Scythians (the peoples living in the areas between the northeast shores of the Black Sea and the Caspian Sea) in the centuries after the apostolic age were not lasting. Various scholarly theories dispute when exactly Christianity arrived in Russia in a more permanent iteration. In 867, the patriarch of Constantinople, perhaps inspired by the work of Cyril and Methodius, commissioned a new missionary effort to the area of modern-day Kiev,

Ukraine. Photius even deemed it right to send a bishop to the peoples of the Ukraine, known as the *Rus'*. But Christianity never really caught on in the Russian space until the kingship of Prince Vladimir, which began in the late tenth century.

Russia at the time of the first permanent Christian conversions was as in dismal a condition as any place in Europe. So incapable of any sort of stability were the premodern tribes that, sick of waging useless warfare against one another, they had only one hundred years earlier invited a set of Swedish Viking princes, known as the Varangians, to come rule over their land and establish something of a functioning kingdom. Clustered around the Dnieper river, especially near Kiev, were the first Russian towns. In about 987, their ruler, Prince Vladimir, was the subject of multiple new missionary efforts from both the Western and Eastern churches. In response, he called together the lords and elders of his kingdom and asked them what form of worship they should adopt:

> Behold, the [Volga] Bolgars came before me urging me to accept their religion. Then came the Germans and praised their own faith [Catholicism]; and after them came the Jews. Finally the [Eastern Orthodox] Greeks appeared, criticizing all other faiths but commending their own, and they spoke at length, telling the history of the whole world from its beginning. Their words were artful, and it was wondrous to listen and pleasant to hear them. They preach the existence of another world. "Whoever adopts our religion and then dies shall arise and live forever. But whosoever embraces another faith, shall be consumed with fire in the next world." What is your opinion on this subject, and what do you answer?[34]

To answer the question before them, Vladimir's vassals decided to take a tour of the different faiths. In Bulgaria, they were repulsed at the worship they saw in the mosques, seeing "no happiness among them, but instead only sorrow and a dreadful stench."[35] In Germany, they reported believers "performing many ceremonies in their temples; but we beheld no glory there."[36] They then went to Constantinople, where they were received by the emperor, who ordered that a church service happen that very day. The Hagia Sophia was prepared, and the king dressed in his sacerdotal robes. Incense was burned, and choirs sang. The emperor personally escorted the delegation to the center of the colossal Hagia Sophia and bid them behold the wondrous mystery of Eastern worship. To those unlearned Russians, unaccustomed to such splendor, the experience must have been an overwhelming sensory overload. Upon their return to Kiev, they told Vladimir that the Greeks impressed them most:

> Then we went on to Greece, and the Greeks led us to the edifices where they worship their God, and we knew not whether we were in heaven or on earth. For on earth there is no such splendor or such beauty, and we are at a loss how to describe it. We know only that God dwells there among men, and their service is fairer than the ceremonies of other nations. For we cannot forget that beauty.[37]

Vladimir agreed with them, and decided that all the *Rus'* should be baptized. But the way their en masse conversion came to pass is more a story of political hardball than spiritual change.

The next year Vladimir invaded a Greek city on the Crimean peninsula, called Kherson, and lay siege to it. He claimed he would stay there for three years if he had to. Yet Kherson showed fierce resistance and would not relent. Finally, one of the inhabitants shot an arrow into the Russian camp with a message on it: "There are springs behind you to the east, from which water flows in pipes. Dig down and cut them off."[38] Vladimir lifted his eyes toward heaven and promised he would be baptized if this information proved useful to victory. The inhabitants of Kherson, overcome by thirst, eventually surrendered. Vladimir then sent a message to the Greek emperors Basil and Constantine: "Behold, I have captured your glorious city. I have also heard that you have an unwed sister. Unless you give her to me to wife, I shall deal with your own city as I have with Kherson." The emperors replied, "It is not meet for Christians to give in marriage to pagans. If you are baptized, you shall have her to wife, inherit the kingdom of God, and be our companion in the faith. Unless you do so, however, we cannot give you our sister in marriage." At that, Vladimir agreed to be baptized.[39]

Basil and Constantine cajoled their sister Anna into accepting the marriage. She was less than enthusiastic as she was sent to Russia with a retinue of priests and officials who would conduct Vladimir's baptism. "It is as if I were setting out into captivity," she lamented. "Better were it for me to die here." But they encouraged her to take heart in the missional and civic duty she was performing: "Through your agency God turns the Russian land to repentance, and you will relieve Greece from the danger of grievous war." As Anna and the Greek clergy arrived in Kherson, Vladimir happened to be suffering from an acute eye disease. Immediately as Vladimir was baptized, as the story goes, he regained his eyesight. "I have now perceived the one true God," he said. Vladimir and Anna wed and returned to Kiev. As a wedding gift to Anna, Kherson was returned to the Greeks. Back home, the old idols were torn down, and a band of twelve men beat them with sticks to punish the demon inside them and then threw the gods of wood in the river. Vladimir then sent out an order to the people: "if any inhabitant, rich or poor, did not betake himself to the river [for baptism], he would risk the prince's displeasure." The people there, moved by Vladimir's threats (and miraculous ocular restoration), were brought into the church in one day during an enormous mass baptism ceremony in the Dnieper River. Vladimir capped the whole ceremony with a prayer:

> O God, who hast created heaven and earth, look down, I beseech thee, on this thy new people, and grant them, O Lord, to know thee as the true God, even as the other Christian nations have known thee. Confirm in them the true and unalterable faith, and aid me, O Lord, against the hostile adversary, so that, hoping in thee and in thy might, I may overcome his malice.[40]

Other regions of Russia also followed in converting, but many converts there were also compelled to accept the new faith through threats of physical violence. Still, the introduction of Christianity to the *Rus'* inaugurated Russian civilization (or, perhaps more accurately, Ukrainian civilization). The *Rus'* were brought into lasting contact with the Byzantine church and state, and they, like the Slavs in the West, received their first written alphabet. But as was the case in Scandinavian countries, Christian customs became intertwined with pagan ones, and a purer version of the faith would not become permanently entrenched until the 1100s. We may rightly question whether many, if any, of the first "converts" in these places experienced a true spiritual regeneration. Some probably did, but in the frigid, grim landscapes of the tenth-century Nordic countries and Eurasia, genuine Christianity was scarce.

NINETEEN

THE FACE OF GOD AND SCHISM

Iconoclasm, John of Damascus, Photian Schism, the Great Schism of 1054

By the year 900, the Byzantine Empire had lost a significant amount of power and influence since its peak during the reign of Justinian in the sixth century. It did enjoy a greater degree of material prosperity than the West; its central location along the Silk Road between Europe and Asia meant that commerce was a more robust activity in the great city of Constantinople than elsewhere. And with various missions to the Slavs and Bulgars that culminated in strategic relationships, the influence of the Byzantine church had recently crept into the hinterlands of central and eastern Europe. But the previous centuries had seen an increasing amount of friction between the Byzantine and Roman churches.

Owning to differences in language (Greek in the East and Latin in the West), geographical distance, and power politics, the theological traditions of the East developed differently from those in the West. And in the eighth century, the emergence of the powerful Holy Roman Empire, founded by Charlemagne, meant that the pope, formerly desirous of obeying the Byzantine emperor (with his powerful armies and navies), could now forge an alliance with a set of rulers which acted as a more immediate and reliable bulwark against the violent whims of Western barbarians and misbehaving medieval bully-kings. These new Franco-German kings aligned themselves with Catholic doctrine, ignoring Orthodoxy almost entirely. Lastly, the Byzantine church and state had lost an appreciable amount of territory and influence as it flailed unsuccessfully against the Arab conquests of the Middle East in the seventh and eighth centuries. In 674, the great city of Constantinople had been besieged for four years by Muslim armies, and only the use of the famous "Greek fire," a primitive type of napalm (jellied gasoline), kept the city from submitting entirely. By the time the city had physically and psychologically recovered, key differences in Christian theology between East and West had gone unaddressed for nearly a generation. Near the end of the seventh century, the emperor decided to confront a growing area of disagreement between Christians of all stripes: icon veneration.

JUSTINIAN II AND THE QUINISEXT COUNCIL

The essential theological controversy of the adolescent years of the Byzantine Empire was the policy of iconoclasm. Iconoclasm ("breaking of images") was an East-West and intra-Eastern battle that persisted for several centuries. The essential point of the controversy was whether a Christian could in good conscience incorporate religious paintings or symbols in his worship of God. The basic contours of the controversy were not new. In the Old Testament book of Exodus, God gave to the Israelites the third commandment forbidding the use of "idols" (the Hebrew word suggests a carved object) and "graven images" (NASB) in the worship of God himself. Earthly depictions of God, or objects representing the likeness of God, were not allowed. The earliest generations of the church seemed to follow these precepts; Jesus the man was not usually depicted as a visual object of reverence until roughly the time of Constantine (when Christianity became a means of imperial favor), although he was frequently symbolized in early Christian art as a lamb, and the same art was also filled with biblical scenes that featured him.

Unlike in Islam, the earliest traditions of Christianity did not forbid that art could depict the likeness of any matter at all. In fact, the great purpose of depicting Jesus and biblical scenes was to educate people about the Bible in a time when perhaps only 10 percent of the citizenry was literate. In time, the images of Christ, stories from the Bible, and different saints that adorned the churches began to be depicted on small wooden blocks that could be hung at home. The regular visibility of these images of Christ could help to produce a feeling of reverence for God, and portraits of saints might be an example to the Christian of perseverance, holiness, or some other virtue. Wrote a monk named Leontius the Hierapolian:

> I sketch and paint Christ and the sufferings of Christ in churches, in homes, in public squares . . . and on icons, on linen cloth, in closets, on clothes, and in every place I paint so that men may see them plainly, may remember them and not forget them . . . And as thou, when thou makest thy reverence to the Book of the Law, bowest down not to the substance of skins and ink, but to the sayings of God that are found therein, so I do reverence to the image of Christ. Not to the substance of wood and paint—that shall never happen . . . But, by doing reverence to an inanimate image of Christ, through Him I think to embrace Christ Himself and to do Him reverence . . . We Christians, by bodily kissing an icon of Christ, or of an apostle or martyr, are in spirit kissing Christ Himself or His martyr.[1]

Leontinus's words sounded fine, but over time, some began to question whether an image (in Greek, *eikon*, from which we get *icon* in English) might have a corrupting influence on the worshipper. This

371

line of thinking supposed that worship was directed at the image itself rather than God.

This practice of praying with icons was predominantly found in the East, and the first steps to examine the lawfulness of the practice were taken at a church council at Constantinople in 692, one known as the Quinisext Council. At the behest of the emperor Justinian II, 215 bishops, all of them Eastern, met to resolve a number of matters facing the Byzantine church. Although the last two major councils, in

A twelfth-century mosaic icon of Jesus.

552 and 680, had reaffirmed certain points of doctrine, they had not issued any new guidance on very specific theological matters. Hence, the purpose of the Quinisext council (the "fifth-sixth" council) was to further explicate what had been established in the fifth (553) and sixth (680) ecumenical councils. The bishops issued 102 separate "canons" of church law on multiple areas of theology. Many addressed the minutiae of ecclesiastical office-holding: clergy could not marry if they were not already wed, nor could they enter a tavern, attend horseraces, eat unleavened bread, or teach the Bible in a city other than their own. Monks and nuns who slept overnight in the monastery of the other sex were banned, as were monks who wore their hair long. Those who missed church three weeks in a row without cause were to be denied communion. Cattle were forbidden from being brought into church, unless it was a traveler's only means of conveyance or foul weather threatened the health of the animal. No church was to follow the singularly Armenian tradition of eating eggs and cheese during Lent. A believer was not to enter into marriage with an unbeliever: "for it is not fitting to mingle together what should not be mingled, nor is it right that the sheep be joined with the wolf, nor the lot of sinners with the portion of Christ."[2] There was even some guidance on church music: "We will that those whose office it is to sing in the churches do not use undisciplined vociferations, nor force

nature to shouting, nor adopt any of those modes which are incongruous and unsuitable for the church."[3] And anyone who provided abortion-inducing drugs was to be considered guilty of murder.

But the Quinisext Council was, more importantly, an opportunity for the Byzantine church to define itself anew, in opposition to some practices of the Roman Catholic Church. They decreed a number of canons that agitated Rome. One was a criticism of the Roman practice of fasting on Saturdays during Lent; another was a recommending a greater degree of leniency in allowing married clergy. But much more serious was an imprecation that Christ be depicted in Roman art as a man and not merely as a symbolic lamb:

> We decree that the figure in human form of the Lamb who takes away the sin of the world, Christ our God, be henceforth exhibited in images, instead of the ancient lamb, so that all may understand by means of it the depths of the humiliation of the Word of God, and that we may recall to our memory his conversation in the flesh, his passion and salutary death, and his redemption which was wrought for the whole world.[4]

It is here that the most serious fissures between East and West began to emerge. At the completion of the Quinisext Council, the bishops, believing themselves the true arbiters of orthodoxy, asked Pope Sergius to come to agreement with their conclusions. The request was an insult, and the pontiff recoiled at the Byzantine stance on clerical marriages, as well as the insistence that Christ be depicted in human form only. He wrote that he would prefer "to die rather than to consent to erroneous novelties."[5] The pope did have something of a point; although many of the canons were restatements of the Council of Constantinople in 381 and the Council of Chalcedon in 451, many of them were entirely new and went against the grain of Roman church practice. Moreover, they had been invented without the consultation of the Holy See. Other prominent churchmen in the West, such as the

Venerable Bede and Paul the Deacon, respectively criticized the council as "reprobate" and "erratic."[6]

Pope Sergius therefore took a few steps to agitate Justinian and the Eastern bishops, especially on the question of the visual depiction of Christ. He introduced into the liturgy the phrase "Lamb of God, you take away the sins of the world, have mercy on us," and restored a famous mosaic in Saint Peter's Basilica that depicted Christ as a lamb. This infuriated Justinian II, who arrested papal envoys to Byzantium and dispatched his personal bodyguard, Zacharias, to kidnap the pope himself. When Zacharias and his band of men reached Rome, they gained entrance to the Lateran basilica, and word spread of what was about to happen. A duke from the Italian city of Ravenna sent his troops to aid the pope, and an angry crowd surrounded the papal residence, demanding that they would destroy it if Zacharias did not come out. Zacharias, for his part, was intimidated, and hid under the pope's bed while the pope mercifully defused the situation.

The Quinisext Council also set off an unpleasant reaction in the East. Justinian II was a hard man who used violent tactics in hopes of restoring the past glories of the Byzantine Empire. Persecution and impressment of subject peoples into military service were not uncommon, and he was generally hated by the population. Once when he was caught in a storm on the Black Sea, one of his advisers told him that if he promised to God that he would be merciful to his enemies, he would be spared. Justinian II declined: "If I spare a single one of them, may God drown me here."[7] In obedience to his own synod, Justinian II decided to mint some coins in 695 depicting an image of Christ, an unprecedented action that infuriated the people to the point of riots.

The appearance of these coins helped force Justinian into exile, and the Arabic caliph of the time was so disturbed by it that he redoubled his own campaign of removing images from all art. Before his exile, Justinian had his nose slit, a wound that required him to use a golden prosthetic nose for the rest of his life. Justinian retook his throne in 705 and ruled until 711, when his army mutinied against him. Justinian's madness and cruelty were uncommon even for their time, and it is in no small part due to his avarice that the fissures between East and West were deepened further.

THE FIRST ICONOCLAST ERA (717-775)

Justinian had sown the seeds of controversy over the use of icons in worship, but things did not reach full blast until the reign of the emperor Leo III (nicknamed the Isaurian, from the region in Asia Minor from where he came). Leo, like Justinian II, was a violent and cruel man, but one who managed to recover some degree of imperial stability after a century of conflict with the Islamic armies. Leo reigned from 717 to 741, and his religious policy did not win him much affection. In 722, for example, he ordered the forcible baptism of all Jews in the empire. In the same year, Leo decided to adopt the iconoclast position, which the Byzantine chronicler Theophanes called a "malignant, illegal, and evil doctrine."[8] It is likely that Leo's thinking was shaped by an adviser named Beser, who had converted to Islam after being taken captive in a Syrian prison. Beser was a physically strong man whom Leo probably used as an enforcer. Whatever his role, Theophanes mentioned Beser as one who persuaded Leo toward the iconoclast position (recall that Islam, of course, forbids depictions of any human form). In 723, Leo began to issue edits against the worship of icons. In his estimation, icons were a hindrance to the conversion of Muslims, and the divergent practice of anyone worshipping icons made it harder to centralize power. Leo was also perhaps persuaded further toward a true iconoclast position by the massive eruption of a volcano in the Aegean in 726. This he interpreted as a sign that God was angry with the inhabitants of the empire for their idolatrous worship of icons. In that year, Leo ordered destroyed a huge image of Jesus that rested over the main entrance to the great imperial palace at Constantinople. Like Justinian's decision to mint coins depicting Christ, this move incited a similarly violent reaction among the people; several of Leo's men were killed. Leo exacted his own revenge and punished many iconodules ("icon-servers"), especially the city elites, with "mutilation, lashes, exile, and fines."[9] Many of the iconodules were also monks, and Leo initiated a campaign of shuttering monasteries and imprisoning the men inside.

Leo also sent Pope Gregory II a letter commanding him to accept his anti-iconic edicts, destroy any icons at Rome, and convene a synod that would refute the worship of such idolatry. Gregory replied with a letter of his own that appealed to the tradition of great Eastern theologians such as Basil, Gregory, and John Chrysostom, all of whom permitted icons. More seriously, Gregory insisted that Leo did not have the Holy Spirit, and ought to undergo a period of demonic torment before being restored to the fellowship of the church:

> You persecute us and vex us tyrannically with violent and carnal hand. We, unarmed and defenseless, possessing no earthly armies, call now upon the prince of all the armies of creation, Christ seated in the heavens, commanding all the hosts of celestial beings, to send a demon upon you; as the apostle says: "to deliver such a one unto Satan for the destruction of the flesh, that the spirit may be saved" [1 Cor. 5:5].[10]

Pope Gregory II died in 731, and his successor, Pope Gregory III, continued on his fight. He sent to Leo an envoy named George with papal letters defending the iconodule position, but George, in a bout of cowardice, turned back before he accomplished his mission. Gregory sent him back again, but before George reached Leo he was imprisoned in Sicily, at that time held by the Byzantines. Gregory decided to hold a synod in that same year, which was attended by ninety-nine bishops. Gregory and the bishops effectively recommended excommunication for iconoclasts: "if anyone, for the future, shall take away, destroy, or dishonour the images of Our Lord God and Saviour Jesus Christ, of His Mother, the immaculate and glorious Virgin Mary, or of the Saints, he shall be excluded from the body and blood of Our Lord and the unity of the Church."[11] Leo's response to excommunication was a military one. He sent a fleet to assault Rome, but in a stroke of incredible fortune, it was sunk by a storm in the Adriatic. Undaunted, he seized for his own kingdom papal lands in the south of Italy and Sicily. It is perhaps very fitting that both Gregory and Leo III died in the same year, 741.

JOHN OF DAMASCUS AND CONSTANTINE V

Although Pope Gregory was a relentless thorn in Emperor Leo's flesh, the greatest opponent of Leo's iconoclasm in the East was John of Damascus, also known as John Damascene or John Chrysorrhoas ("golden-speaking" or "streaming with gold"). John, as evinced in his name, was born in Syria, and grew up in a time when the ascendant Islamic and withering Christian culture in Syria competed for prominence. An ethnic Arab, he grew up the son of an official in the Islamic Caliphate. In his youth he sat under the tutelage of a monk named Cosmas, a very learned man whom the Arabs had kidnapped from Sicily. It was through this man's learning that John became something of an authority on subjects such as astronomy, theology, music, and mathematics. John, though a Christian, was himself sometimes said to have served as an administrator to the Islamic caliph at the time when Leo began his persecution of iconodules in 726, though this claim is highly questionable. In 730, John began to write his first rebuttals to Leo's iconoclast campaign, a campaign that infuriated the emperor. But owing to the distance of Damascus from Constantinople (over nine hundred miles), Leo was fairly powerless to confront John, who had become a monk. Whether he enjoyed impunity because of his distance from Constantinople, or because of Muslim protection, John was able to disseminate his anti-iconoclast writings from his monastery in Jerusalem, far beyond Leo's reach to stop him. His works were published in three separate instances over the course of his lifetime. Packed with extensive references to the Bible and theologians from all ages, the writings stand as the crucial pro-icon source of the whole iconoclast controversy. To John, images were tremendously useful for understanding and worshipping God with all the senses: "We proclaim Him also by our senses on all sides, and we sanctify the noblest sense, which is that of sight. The image is a memorial, just what words are to a listening ear. What a book is to the literate, that an image is to the illiterate. The image speaks to the sight as words to the ear; it brings us understanding."[12] John also spent parts of his career criticizing Islam and helping to formulate the doctrine of the assumption of Mary.

John's polemic against iconoclasm continued beyond the death of his nemesis, Leo. In 741, Leo's son Constantine filled his father's position as emperor. Constantine was nicknamed Copronymus, "dung-named" for a story that appears in the chronicle of the historian Theophanes. Theophanes wrote that Constantine was "a forerunner of the Antichrist" for an incident that happened in his boyhood. Constantine V was born in 718 or 719, and while he was being placed into the imperial baptistry, he defecated in the baptismal font.[13] The patriarch who baptized him interpreted the foul act as a harbinger of evil to come: "This is a sign that in the future great evil shall befall the Christians and the church because of him."[14] Theophanes was right: Constantine V was known mostly for his hard stance against icons, one more intolerant than even Leo. He too led a crackdown on the monks, considered the strictest iconodules, and enacted perversions like pulling holy men out of the monasteries and forcing them to marry nuns in a public spectacle in the Hippodrome, all while being cursed and spat upon by the crowd. A famous Stylite (a monk who spent his life sitting on top of a high column) named Peter was forcibly pulled down from his column, beaten, bound, and left to die by being thrown into a mass grave called the "pit of suicides." Theophanes also wrote apopleptically at the wicked treatment of a patriarch who was also named Constantine. Constantine the tyrant had Constantine the patriarch summoned and beaten until he could not walk. He was then placed on a throne inside the Hagia Sophia. A list of his "crimes" was recited to him, and he was struck in the face after every point. Apparently the patriarch was beaten to the point of losing vision and his tormentors mocked him by calling him *Skotiopsis* ("of darkened vision"). The next day he was brought to the public games, and his beard, eyebrows, and head were shaved. As he rode into the arena sitting backward on a donkey, the crowd verbally abused, threw dust at, and spit on him. His nephew, leading the animal, had his nose slit. Partisans of the emperor threw him from the donkey and trampled his neck. Some days later, the patriarch was beheaded and hung by the ears for three days as public entertainment. Finally, his corpse too was thrown "in with the suicides."[15]

Constantine loved to do these impious acts personally, but much of his persecutory agenda was delegated to one of his generals, named Michael Lachanodrakon, often called the Dragon. The Dragon loved to confiscate the personal objects of the monks: things such as amulets, books, animals, and "any anything else under their management." Many monks he whipped to death, others were beheaded, and yet more were blinded. Another of his favorite tactics was to douse a monk's beard with oil and then light it on fire. We can feel Theophanes's frustration and anger as he wrote that Constantine "was a totally destructive bloodsucking wild beast who used his power tyrannically and illegally. First, he sided against our God and Savior Jesus Christ, His altogether immaculate Mother, and all the saints. He was deceived by wizardry, licentiousness, blood sacrifices of horses, dung, and urine. Effeminacy and summoning demons pleased him, and ever since he was a boy he had partaken of absolutely every sort of soul-destroying practice."[16]

In 754, Constantine V sought to formalize his policy of iconoclasm by calling together a synod at the palace of Hieria, located in a suburb of Constantinople (today the neighborhood of Fenerbahce). There, 338 Eastern bishops, whether by threat of force or genuine theological agreement, endorsed the emperor's policy of condemning icons: "If anyone ventures to represent in human figures, by means of material colours, by reason of the incarnation, the substance or person of the Word, which cannot be depicted, and does not rather confess that even after the Incarnation he cannot be depicted, let him be anathema!"[17] Although the Council of Hieria was attended by a large number of bishops, its findings were far from ecumenical. The bishops of important cities such as Jerusalem, Antioch, Alexandria, and Rome were not in attendance, and the church's general opposition to the decisions made there earned it the nickname "the Headless Council" or "the Mock Synod of Constantinople." What did happen in response to the synod was a furtherance of Constantine's ruthless anti-icon campaign.

In 762, a monk who insulted Constantine by calling him "a new Julian"—a reference to the famous pagan Roman emperor Julian the Apostate—was whipped to death in public. In 766, a monk named Stephen the Younger was taken from his monastery and shut up in the prison at Constantinople for a year. Death came when he was dragged through the streets. In the same year, other monks were given one hundred lashes with an ox-hide whip. The end years of Constantine's reign, roughly 762 to 775, were so destructive that the period in time came to be known as the "Decade of Blood."

THE SECOND COUNCIL OF NICAEA

When the emperor Constantine Copronymus died in AD 775, the icon controversy was far from settled, despite decades of persecution of prominent iconodules. Constantine's successor, Leo IV, was a committed iconoclast, but did not share his father's penchant for cruelty. After Leo came his son Constantine VI, who was only all of nine years old when he took the throne in 780. On account of his youth, many of the affairs of state were at this time managed by his mother, the empress Irene (recall it was she whom Charlemagne had unsuccessfully wooed in hopes of unifying two empires). In 787, Irene, an iconophile, decided to call together a new council to help resolve the question of icon veneration. In September, no fewer than three hundred representatives from across the Christian world, including ambassadors of the pope, met at Nicaea, the same spot as the all-important First Council of Nicaea had met nearly five centuries earlier. The Second Council of Nicaea repudiated the decisions of Constantine V's Council of Hieria, which had been held back in 754, and provided for the veneration of icons:

> We, therefore, following the royal pathway and the divinely inspired authority of our Holy Fathers and the traditions of the Catholic Church (for, as we all know, the Holy Spirit indwells her), define with all certitude and accuracy that just as the figure of the precious and life-giving Cross, so also the venerable and holy images, as well in painting and mosaic as of other fit materials, should be set forth in the holy churches of God, and on the sacred vessels and on the vestments and on hangings and in pictures both in houses and by the wayside, to wit, the figure of our Lord God and Saviour Jesus Christ, of our spotless Lady, the Mother of God, of the honourable Angels, of all Saints and of all pious people. For by so much more frequently as they are seen in artistic representation, by so much more readily are men lifted up to the memory of their prototypes, and to a longing after them; and to these should be given due salutation and honourable reverence.[18]

The council was one of the last great instances of agreement between East and West. The pope wrote to Charlemagne at its conclusion, *"Et sic synodum istam, secundum nostram ordinationem, fecerunt"* ("Thus they have held the synod in accordance with our directions"). But the unity that was reached at the time was not to last. When Charlemagne's advisers obtained a copy of the synod's pronouncements, they blanched. In their view, the veneration of icons was an error. In 794, they held their own council, which condemned icons, although unlike Leo III and Constantine V, they did not embark on a destructive campaign against them. Their position contributed to the growing chasm between East and West, a divide that only grew deeper with time.

THE SECOND ICONOCLAST ERA (814–842)

The Second Council of Nicaea attained an unusual degree of unity on the question of icons, but as we have seen with the decrees of other councils, the decisions reached were only binding insofar as the emperor tolerated them. Although Irene protected the right of Christians to worship with icons, Emperor Leo V reinvigorated the iconoclast stance in 814. In that year, Leo called together a conference at his palace to suggest that he was considering imposing an iconoclast policy again. He was boldly confronted by the leader of the new generation of iconophiles, a Greek monk named Theodore of Studium (d. 826). Theodore answered the initial inklings of Leo's persecution by telling him, "I would rather have my tongue cut out than fail to bear testimony to our Faith and defend it with all my might by the power of my speech . . . We will not give our tongue into captivity, no, not for an hour, and we will not deprive the faithful the support of our words."[19] Leo was stayed for a time by Theodore's words. In 811, the patriarch Nikephorus was exiled, and Theodore urged a protest in response. On Palm Sunday, thousands of monks moved through the city in procession, carrying icons as a form of protest, chanting, "We venerate your sacred images, O saints." Later in the year, Theodore himself suffered exile, as imperial officials went from house to house, confiscating icons from ordinary citizens, "with threats and terrorism, so that no single picture may escape the heretics." "The persecution we endure," wrote Theodore, "is beyond any persecution by the barbarians."[20] But in 815,

Leo V decided to raise the placement of icons in churches beyond the height of a human head, thus making them impossible to kiss. But Theodore wouldn't yield, and exhorted the Eastern Church up until his death in 826.

Leo V was assassinated on Christmas Day, 820, as he was approaching the nativity scene in church. But things didn't calm down as much as one could have hoped. The reign of Michael II (reigned 820–829) was relatively peaceful, but under Theophilus (reigned 829–842, sometimes called the Iconoclast), monks were starved, imprisoned, whipped, drowned in sewn-up sacks thrown in the sea, and burned for their beliefs. Two Palestinian monks were banished and then recalled to Constantinople, where they suffered two hundred lashes and had insulting epigrams branded onto their foreheads. An icon painter named Lazarus was imprisoned and had his hands burned, rendering his talents for painting impotent.

Salvation for the Eastern church wouldn't come until the death of Theophilus in 842. The imperial persecution of iconodules was a strange phenomenon in that the imperial policy was endorsed by very few outside their own circles of power. One who did not share Theophilus's sympathies was his wife, the empress Theodora. After Theophilus's death, she, like Irene, became the steward of the empire before Theophilus's son Michael III was ready to assume power. Although Theophilus had on his deathbed forced Theodora to swear to uphold the icnoclast policy, her oath was broken soon after his death. She opened up the prisons, freeing those who had been put in with common criminals for defending icons, and restored the laws on icons to what had been established at the Second Council of Nicaea in 787. On the first Sunday of Lent in 842, the icons were restored to the churches in a muted but reverent ceremony. Today this occasion is commemorated in the Byzantine Church by the Feast of Orthodoxy. As it turned out, Theophilus would be the last Byzantine emperor to oppose icons, a fact that brought peace to the East but heightened tensions with the West.

The Great Schism
(ca. 800–1054)

As previously discussed events make clear, differences between the theology of East and West had snowballed for centuries. Although there was actually a great deal of agreement on the most major theological issues, such as the divinity of Jesus, the reliability of the Bible, and the administration of the sacraments, smaller issues still got in the way. Quarrels erupted on and off for nearly a millennium over issues such as the date of the celebration of Easter (the Quartodecimian controversy), whether clergy should marry (and whether they could stay married), influence in newly Christianized central and eastern Europe, and whether the pope was the final arbiter of church doctrine. The papacy, desperate for military protection, had also reoriented itself toward the strengthening Frankish kingdom in the West around the time that the Byzantine Empire was receding from Muslim attacks. But beginning in the eighth century, a different set of issues emerged that wedged the two Christendoms further apart.

As mentioned previously, icon veneration was accepted in the West until the time of the Frankish kings who founded the Holy Roman Empire. The reasons that many of the early Frankish kings became mild iconoclasts had much to do with the pagan roots of the Germanic culture from which the Frankish kingdoms arose. After the Second of Council of Nicaea in 787, which affirmed icon veneration as an acceptable practice, Pope Adrian I sent to Charlemagne a translation of the council's resolutions. Charlemagne and his bishops were reluctant to endorse it; they knew nothing of the elaborate rituals of the Byzantine church, with its prostrations, prayers, and layers of symbolism. Moreover, the Franks had only been converted out of pagan culture in the past three hundred years, and were suspicious of anything that resembled empty worship of mere objects. Lastly, many renderings of Greek words used to compose the original conclusions of the Second Council of Nicaea could not be adapted into Latin (the reading language of the Franks) in a way that retained the precise meanings of the original Greek. Hence, a word such as *proskynesis* (which meant worship only in the sense of reverence and veneration) was rendered in Latin as *adoratio* (a word conveying a sense of homage due only to God).[21] Hence, confusion and opposition to the council's decrees set in. In 794, Charlemagne demanded that the pope condemn the emperor Constantine IV and his mother, Irene. He declined. In 824, the Franks refused to return to the Byzantine emperor Michael II iconophile monks who had fled to the West. And it wasn't until 872 that a new pope sent a new translation of the Acts of the Council, which helped to allay any confusion. Still, the Frankish response to the Second Council of Nicaea did little to foster rapprochement between East and West.

Another of the most serious fissures also emerged in the 800s, as the result of a conflict known known as the Photian Schism. In 857, the patriarch of Constantinople, Ignatius, was removed by the emperor Michael III ("the Drunkard") for suspicion of treason, although the veracity of that charge is questionable. In his place was installed a statesman-scholar named Photius, who was rushed through the Holy Orders in six days in order to be "qualified" for the office. Such a move was obviously not received favorably, and Michael III wrote a deceitful letter to Pope Nicholas I, contorting the facts of Ignatius's dismissal and Photius's appointment. Nicholas sent envoys to Constantinople to hear the case and told Michael III that the pope's decision would be binding. But the papal representatives accepted bribes in exchange for a favorable report, and Nicholas, growing more suspicious, sent another ambassador to investigate the legates' conclusions. Meanwhile, Ignatius, in exile, sent a letter to Nicholas explaining the whole situation. Now that the pope had both explanations of the same event in hand, he proclaimed that Ignatius must be restored to his see and that Photius (as well as the two lying ambassadors) must be excommunicated unless he resigned his patriarchate.

But Michael and Photius refused to obey Nicholas. Ignatius was kept chained in exile, and Michael threatened that unless the pope removed his order of excommunication, he would come to Rome with his army. In

867, Photius did the unthinkable step of excommunicating Pope Nicholas. The reasons he gave for his decision hardly merited such a decision. The Latin church, he claimed, fasted on Saturday, did not begin Lent till Ash Wednesday (instead of three days earlier, as in the East), did not allow priests to administer confirmation, and had added the *filioque* to the creed (more on this in a minute). Moreover, he added, the Western church was full of "forerunners of apostasy, servants of Antichrist who deserve a thousand deaths, liars, fighters against God."[22] Pope Nicholas was incensed, but he and Michael III both died in 867, leaving the situation unresolved. But as separate councils in both East and West debated Photius's fate, he himself was banished to a monastery, where he spent seven years building an anti-Rome political coalition and doing some impressive scholarship on a number of topics. By the time of his release in 878, after Ignatius's death, he had obtained enough political capital to be named the patriarch of Constantinople. Pope John VIII, hardly desirous of a fresh quarrel over an old incident, decided to honor the appointment, in spite of the fact that Photius had used anti-Roman rhetoric to elevate himself to that station. But Photius would not let his arguments die; he emphasized his *filioque* arguments and insisted on Byzantine influence in newly Christianized Bulgaria. Eventually he was excommunicated again by Rome, and spent his time as patriarch whipping up anti-Roman sentiment in Constantinople until his death in 897. Photius's obdurate personality had poisoned relations between East and West in only one generation, and his divisiveness ultimately sowed the seed for the great schism between East and West that came nearly two hundred years later.

THE CHURCHES SPLIT

The ultimate schism of the Eastern and Western church occurred in the year 1054. There were two great actions animating the rupture. The first, induced by the wily Photius, is discussed above. The others reached back into a set of disagreements that had brewed for some time.

Photius's opposition to the *filioque* portion of the Nicene Creed was not a new sentiment in the East. The term *filioque*, meaning literally "and from the Son," emerged centuries before in western Europe as a way of clarifying that the Holy Spirit proceeded from Jesus *and* God the Father (whereas the Nicene Creed of 325 only stipulated that the Holy Spirit proceeded from the Father). The *filioque* had trickled into Western churches beginning in at least 589, at the Third Council of Toledo, which governed the church in Visigoth Spain. But by what authority, the Eastern church wondered, did the Western churches have to tamper with the one great theological statement of Christendom? The answer wasn't clear. In 867, the Eastern church, probably inspired by the Photian controversy, made sure to clarify in its own creed the idea that the Holy Spirit proceeds "from the Father *alone*."[23] This was just one of many salvos in a centuries-old disagreement, but in the context of the age, it only moved the two churches further apart. In time, the pope began using the Apostles' Creed in the churches, a confessional statement different from the Nicene Creed. In time, its popularity outdid the older, more accepted Nicene Creed.

The last straw before the schism of 1054 had its origins in a conflict in Sicily. Sicily had formerly been a colony of the Byzantine Empire, and many churches there had an Eastern orientation. When a group of Normans (French descendants of Vikings) conquered parts of the island in the 1040s, the Normans replaced Greek bishops with Latin ones and changed long-held church customs. When the Greek patriarch, Michael Cerularius, heard about what was happening, he ordered Latin churches in Constantinople closed and commanded the archbishop of Bulgaria, Leo of Ohrid, to inveigh against the Latin custom of using unleavened bread in communion and keeping clergy unmarried. In response, Pope Leo IX sent a cantankerous ambassador, Cardinal Humbert, to Constantinople, where he railed against Cerularius. But Cerularius, a passionate defender of clerical celibacy, tuned him out completely. Finally, in the summer of 1054, Cerularius burst into the Hagia Sophia just as the Liturgy was being celebrated, and in the name of the pope (who had actually died shortly before), threw an order of excommunication down on the altar. He then stomped out of the church and stomped off, bound for Rome.

Shortly after, Cerularius had the Latin church declared excommunicate from the Greek. The definitive break was much more theological than it was relational. Despite uneasy, intermittent times of communication and cooperation (such as during parts of the Crusades, which began in 1095), the two churches had become strained to the point that they could not accept one another as following the same headship of Christ. The mutual decrees of excommunication were not revoked until 1965, and no pope visited Constantinople until 1967. Though some rapprochement has occurred in many ways, it was at the time the deepest depression of church history—a darkness which at the time broached no hint of dawn.

CONCLUSION

You might be shocked to see that this book ends at a rather gloomy spot in the story of the Christian church. Shortly after the turn of the millennium, few embers of good hope seemed to glow. The church around the year 1000 looked unpleasantly preoccupied with anything but the ministration of the gospel: popes and patriarchs zealous for dishonest gain and political power, internal fighting over theological creeds and icons, and vicious persecution of those who disagreed on comparatively minor theological issues. In the eleventh and twelfth centuries, more controversies would simmer. The pope and the German kings would feud over who had the ultimate authority to appoint church officials, such as bishops and abbots. During the Crusades (1095–1291), Western inhabitants of Constantinople would be murdered, and Western crusaders would sack and plunder the town. The practice of simony—the selling of ecclesiastical offices—would persist through the Reformation. The Byzantine Empire itself, once the ballast of power in the Mediterranean after the ruin of the Western Roman Empire, would disintegrate by 1453, a victim of the Ottoman Turks. The Hagia Sophia was turned into a mosque, which it remains today (though we must credit the Turkish ruler Ataturk's decision to turn it into a museum in the 1930s). Centuries of discord between East and West eventually produced a great schism, which has never been fully healed. In spite of more dialogue than ever before between the Catholic and Orthodox churches, the two bodies have never been fully reconciled to one another, at least in a theological sense.

But things would not remain completely hopeless forever. In the twelfth and thirteenth centuries, the Western church experienced something of an intellectual renaissance. Powerful thinkers such as Thomas Aquinas, Bernard of Clairvaux, and Peter Abelard provided some sunlight into a long-darkened room of thought. Aquinas especially functioned like an Aristotle for the church: a systematic examiner of almost every point of doctrine that could be known, and a developer of ideas about the natural law not considered since Cicero. But by 1500, the great challenge to Catholicism, the Protestant Reformation, was nigh. The growth of Protestantism, fueled primarily by the German Martin Luther and Frenchman John Calvin, as well as some English reformers, shaped the continent's history in monumental ways. The great age of European exploration in the sixteenth and seventeenth centuries opened up new areas around the world for missionary activity.

It has been a joy to tell the stories of Irenaeus, Augustine, Ambrose, John Chrysostom, and many other churchmen who serve as examples of faithful persistence in Christ. Though they are in many ways much more gifted than we are, in the light of the gospel they are not so different spiritually. In reading their writings, we see them self-reduced to the same sort of people we very often know ourselves to be: riven with imperfections and dependent on the daily bread of God. This book is also dotted with stories of many ecclesiastics who seemed to bear more thorns than fruit. As much as the story of the church is an encouragement to the church today to see Christians of old continue in faithfulness in the face of burnings, beheadings, whippings, and robbery, it is also a cautionary reminder of Lord Acton's words that "power tends to corrupt, and absolute power corrupts absolutely." As the Roman

Empire collapsed, ambitious men filled the church, very often seeking to be served more than live as servants. Some of the abuses there were so grave, and so uncharacteristic of inward repentance, that we cannot in all probability call these men Christians. Many of their abuses went unpunished, especially as the church became allied with the state in the age of Constantine and beyond. God will judge these things too.

But this is only part of the story. The earliest Christians had no such refuge in the state. The spread of the faith (which was, let us remember, an Eastern phenomenon) occurred *despite* the culture's opposition, not because of it. The spread of Christianity was certainly not, as some sensationalist scholars have suggested, a hoax useful for the suppression of humanity, invented by a small band of clever writers. The historical support is not just in the sheer unbelievability of grand conspiracies, but in the lack of earthly benefits the early Christians enjoyed. The first Christians were not as a group particularly powerful, wealthy, or influential. In fact, they suffered under sporadic bouts of capital punishment, confiscation, and mockery. Would any man be crucified upside down (as Peter was) for such a concoction?

The essential motivation behind the slow adoption of Christianity in the first few centuries of the millennium was captured in one of Augustine's most famous sentiments: "You have made us for yourself, O Lord, and our hearts are restless until they rest in you."[1] The great Author of life has made us for himself, and the full revelation of God in Christ to the first-century Jews and Gentiles was—and still is—a reality too overwhelming to the soul to be less than completely true. If you look closely, Christianity wasn't confined to geography, class, or race. Irish, Syrians, Romans, Norwegians, Jews, Armenians, Russians, Indians, and Egyptians are all mentioned in this book.

It is tempting for us to look today at mass killings in Nigeria, imprisonment of pastors in places such as Iran, the functional collapse of the church in Europe, and the proliferation of speech codes on American college campuses and wonder if the church is about to enter a new dark age of unbelief or persecution. Part of the answer must be based upon regional variance: in Africa and Asia, Christianity is growing as never before, while in the West it appears to be shriveling, at least as a cultural fixture. Whatever the case, the experience of the church's first one thousand years reminds us of something that is important for any Christian to remember in our time: the early Christians depended on the promise of heaven to get them through what was probably for the most part a miserable existence of hunger, poverty, illness, and early death. The same hope of a truly better life that allowed Polycarp to suffer burning at the stake also led the twenty-one Egyptian Christians beheaded by the Islamic State to confess Christ to the last.[2] It fuels the Christians running AIDS orphanages in Kenya and Thailand and Brazil to reach out to those whom Jesus called "the least of these" (Matt. 25:40). Would that we too be so eternally minded.

Glossary of Biographical, Geographical, and Theological References

Alcuin of York (ca. 735–804): A British-born scholar of grammar, logic, rhetoric, math, music, and more at the court of Charlemagne. His influence helped fuel the Carolingian Renaissance, a brief time of cultural renewal in Charlemagne's Europe.

Alfred the Great (849–899): The most successful and learned king of Anglo-Saxon England, who for a time managed to reform the country's military organization and unify great portions of the country against the Viking threat. He placed great worth on learning the liberal arts and generally seems to have been a pious man.

Ambrose of Milan (ca. 339–397): The bishop of Milan whose confrontation of the emperor Theodosius over his slaughter of innocents proved his mettle in guarding the church from heresy. A staunch opponent of Arianism, he also made significant contributions to church music.

Athanaric (d. 381): A Gothic leader of the fourth century who, fearing that Christianity would destroy Gothic culture, persecuted those of his tribe who converted, even down to women with young babies. In one episode, he burned alive hundreds of his own people who used a tent as a church.

Anthony of the Desert (ca. 251–356): The most prominent of the Desert Fathers, Anthony renounced the world at twenty and fled into the desert of Egypt, so popularizing ascetic monasticism during the late third century. He was renowned for his abstention from worldly behaviors, even to the point of eating and drinking almost next to nothing. Hagiographical tales of his battles with demons became a very popular inspiration for medieval and Renaissance artists.

Arianism: A theological belief concocted by an Alexandrian presbyter, Arius, in the early fourth century. Its core tenet denied that Jesus and God were of the same essence (*"homoousios"*), a position that was, in the eyes of Arius's opponents, tantamount to a denial of Jesus' divinity. Arianism was extremely controversial and it was the central topic of the Council of Nicaea in AD 325, where it was condemned. This heresy flourished mostly in the East and among barbarian tribes, and its defeat did not come until the end of the century.

Athanasius (ca. 293–373): Gained his first fame at the Council of Nicaea for his opposition to the Arian heresy, and would remain the most vocal and high-profile opponent of Arianism during its heyday in the fourth century. Athanasius was exiled many times for his beliefs and was greatly influenced by the monastic traditions of Egypt, his homeland. His biography of Saint Anthony of the Desert helped trigger a fanaticism for monastic living in the fourth century. He wrote down the earliest version of the current Protestant version of the canon of Scripture in 367, and his other theological works still hold great value.

Attila the Hun (d. 453): Nicknamed "the Scourge of God" for his brutal campaigns, Attila the Hun terrorized Europe for years before Pope

Leo I persuaded him not to attack Rome in 452. It is ironic that such a mighty ruler died some time afterward as the victim of, as some suggest, either a nosebleed or alcohol poisoning.

Augustine of Hippo (354–430): The greatest theologian of the ancient church. A hedonistic professor of philosophy and rhetoric before his conversion at the age of thirty-two, Augustine gave his dramatic testimony in his spiritual autobiography, the *Confessions.* His *City of God* helped assuage anxious Christians that their true "city" was not Rome, but in heaven. Augustine wrote exhaustively on other theological topics, especially the nature of sin and divine grace, just war, free will versus predestination, baptism, and the wrongness of Pelagianism. He was a major influence on Thomas Aquinas and countless other generations of Catholic scholars.

Basil the Great (Basil of Caesarea) (ca. 330–379): One of the fathers of communal monasticism and a major influence in the development of Eastern Orthodox theology. Along with Gregory of Nazianzus (an intimate friend) and Gregory of Nyssa (his brother), the charismatic Basil is known as one of the "Cappadocian Fathers," so named from the rocky region of Turkey from whence they all came. He wrote prodigiously to combat Arianism, but from his letters we also see a man with a sensitive pastoral heart.

Pope Benedict IX (reigned 1032–1048): He was only about twenty when he became pope, but had already established a reputation for hedonistic living. His entry into the papal office only increased his appetite. One historian wrote, "It seemed as if a demon from hell, in the disguise of a priest, occupied the chair of Peter and profaned the sacred mysteries of religion by his insolent courses."[1] Benedict too had a rapacious sexual appetite, which, it was said, extended to both men and women. Other accusations included organizing bands of priests to dress up as robbers, regular applications of burns and tortures on his enemies, and bestiality. Benedict's low point was his decision to sell the papacy to his godfather, and his subsequent decision to use his own army to take it back. Benedict's actions ultimately led to his dismissal for the charge of simony (selling ecclesiastical offices).

Benedict of Nursia (ca. 480–540s): The greatest influence on Western communal monasticism. "Benedictine" monasticism became virtually the only form of monasticism in western Europe from roughly the sixth to the twelfth centuries. The Rule of Saint Benedict is still the most commonly used in the world. His most famous abbey, Monte Cassino, was bombed badly by the Allies during World War II.

Boethius (ca. 480–524): Initially a high-ranking adviser to the post-Roman barbarian king in Italy, Theodoric, Boethius was put to death by the king in 524 for suspicion of treason. Before he died, he wrote *The Consolation of Philosophy*, a philosophical work in which he ruminates on concepts like why the good suffer and the evil thrive, the nature of justice, and predestination versus free will. The *Consolation* is often considered the last great piece of classical literature.

The Cadaver Synod: In 897, Pope Stephen VII, who ultimately ruled only fifteen days as pope, desired to humiliate his deceased predecessor, Formosus, as a heretic. When Stephen took the papal throne, he ordered the body of Formosus exhumed. The corpse was then brought into the papal palace for a synod, and Stephen commanded the deceased Formosus to testify in his own defense. Because the disinterred body could produce no testimony but silence, a guilty verdict was pronounced against Boniface, and his rotting body was stripped naked. Stephen ordered the three fingers used for blessings cut off from the hand of the corpse, which was then thrown in the Tiber river. Stephen's actions so shocked the church that a synod promptly removed him from the papal throne.

Caesarea: A town in modern-day Israel between Tel Aviv and Haifa that was a major city of the ancient and medieval Near East.

Cassiodorus (ca. 485–ca. 580): Boethius's successor, Cassiodorus served as Theodoric's able prime minister before retiring to a life of monasticism. He had a deep appreciation for the liberal arts, and his great mission was to preserve many of the great Greek and Latin texts of antiquity. The copy house at his monastery, Vivarium, served as a model for generations of monastic scribes in Europe.

Charlemagne (ca. 740s–814): King of the Franks, the son of Pepin the Short, and the greatest European ruler between the end of the Roman Empire and the Renaissance. For an uneducated man, he showed a great interest in the life of the mind and administering his kingdom in fairness and justice. He solidified the relationship of the Holy Roman Empire, which he inaugurated, with the blessing of the papacy. This bond of church and state helped define the international relations of the Middle Ages. His great dream was to revive the Roman Empire in a Christian form. His passion for the liberal arts helped trigger the Carolingian Renaissance of his era.

Charles Martel (ca. 688–741): A survivor of the bloody intra-family rivalries common to his age, Charles was one of the first kings of the Franks and best known for commanding the forces who stopped the advance of Muslim armies into mainland Europe at the Battle of Tours in 732. Also took great pains to support missionary efforts throughout his kingdom, including those of Saint Boniface.

Circumcellions: An extreme, if small group of the breakaway Donatist sect, which craved martyrdom and provoked fights with other Christians to try and obtain it (usually unsuccessfully). Circumcellions took a number of other bizarre positions, including a sometime philosophy of totally communal property and sexual behavior.

Clement of Alexandria (150–215): Like Justin Martyr, Clement explored Christianity as a philosophical system. He was heavily influenced by the philosophy of Plato. Clement believed that the soul went through a process of purification before entering heaven, and it is to him we can trace the idea of purgatory. He was decanonized in the seventeenth century after a review of his theology showed some erroneous beliefs.

Clement of Rome (d. ca. 99): Said to have been appointed by Saint Peter, Clement was one of the first leaders of the church at Rome in the first century AD. Virtually nothing is known about his life. His most notable work, a letter entitled 1 Clement, is notable for its calls for Christians to respect their leaders and for its early definition of the canon of Scripture. His letter 2 Clement is of dubious authorship.

Clovis I (ca. 466–511): Purportedly the first Frankish king to convert to Christianity, at the urging of his wife, Clotilde. Clovis embodied more the brutal methods of post-Roman barbarian tribes than Christian piety. As was the case with many barbarian tribes, Clovis's "conversion" helped trigger the conversion of his people.

Cluny (Monastery): A monastery founded in the eleventh century whose governance was free from the patronage of the era that resulted in monasteries filled with unconcerned or unqualified monks. The Cluniac program of autonomy was quickly adopted across Europe, and its founding led to something of a reform in European monastic life.

Constantine ("the Great") (ca. 280–337): Emerged as sole ruler of the Roman Empire after a factious political arrangement among co-rulers crumbled in the early 300s. Constantine became the first Christian emperor of Rome after a somewhat mythical battlefield conversion experience, and in 313 issued the Edict of Milan, making the faith officially tolerated in Roman lands. In 325, he presided over the Council of Nicaea, in which he gave the bishops of the empire room to rule on the

Arian heresy. He also was responsible for often ruthless campaigns of oppressions against paganism and political opponents. Questions still linger as to whether he was truly a Christian or an opportunist who used Christianity for political ends.

Constantinople: Now Istanbul, Turkey, Constantinople quickly rose to become the most prominent city in the Roman world after its founding in 324 by the emperor Constantine. As the new capital of the empire, Constantinople was immediately adorned with statues, marbles, gold, and other objects of splendor taken from elsewhere. Its fame and wealth allowed it to endure as the capital of the Byzantine and later Ottoman eras in the Middle Ages.

Council of Nicaea: An assemblage of bishops called together in AD 325 to consider the novel Arian heresy: whether Jesus and God the Father were both eternally coequal and cosubstantial as God. The bishops, after some dispute, reaffirmed that they were. Their theological conclusions were codified in the Nicene Creed, which is still recited today. To an extent, their decision was enforceable by the emperor, and set a precedent that the conclusions of church councils were only as binding as the emperor decided they were.

Cyprian of Carthage (ca. 200–258): One of the key figures in the Novationist controversy, Cyprian was the bishop of Carthage, who argued that Christians who had made pagan sacrifices (the lapsed) should not be readmitted to the church. A schism broke out over this question, and Cyprian was overruled by other bishops. Cyprian was also criticized for fleeing during a persecution, a charge he defended himself against by insisting that his flock could not be without a pastor. Ultimately his protestations seem sincere; he was martyred in 258.

Damasus I (ca. 305–384): Perhaps can without contention be called the first pope after being formally invested with ultimate authority over church matters by the emperor Theodosius. Damasus defended the church from the Monophysite heresy and recruited Jerome to produce his new, improved version of the Bible, the Vulgate.

Decius (ca. 201–251): Roman emperor from 251–253 who demanded that Roman citizens make a sacrifice to the emperor or face punishment. The Christian refusal to obey his commands meant that he inaugurated a brutal campaign of persecution. Decius died soon after becoming emperor.

Diocletian (ca. 245–316): Roman emperor who did a great deal to preserve the empire in a time of political and social disintegration. He is more remembered for an exhaustive campaign of persecutions of Christians from 303 to 311, often called the "Great Persecution," which he conducted in tandem with another of his co-emperors, Galerius.

Donatists: A group of North African Christians, not in communion with the rest of Christianity, who refused Christians who had surrendered to persecution readmission into the churches. Donatists believed that sacraments issued by lapsed clergy were ineffectual. The persistence of the sect continued well after Christianity became tolerated by Roman society, and they did not disappear until the Muslims overran North Africa in the seventh century.

Ephrem the Syrian (306–373): A hermit in the desert of Syria for most of his adult life, Ephrem was also a prolific theologian and the dominant Orthodox literary voice of the fourth century. An abundance of his hymns, sermons, and exegetical works survive.

Eusebius of Caesarea (ca. 260s–ca. 340): One of the most important historians of the early church. Our knowledge of the first three hundred years of the church would be greatly diminished without Eusebius's work. He was a bishop of the town of Caesarea and a close associate of Constantine, of whom he wrote an overly laudatory biography.

filioque: In Latin, "and from the Son," a phrase that was inserted into Western church creeds over time to make clear that the Holy Spirit proceeded from the Father and the Son. Intended as an affirmation of Jesus' deity in the face of the many heresies of the East, it produced consternation between East and West, as the East accused Western clergy of tampering with creeds that were long agreed-upon.

Gaul: The Roman name for the area that we today understand to be France, as well as parts of Germany, Belgium, and Italy.

George the Cappadocian (d. 361): The hated Arian bishop of Alexandria in the fourth century, George displayed a level of cruelty unusual even for his time. Bishops were imprisoned, young girls were burned at the stake, and grown men were whipped with thorny palm branches until they died. In the end, it was George's maltreatment of the Alexandrian pagan population that got him killed: he was imprisoned, kicked to death, and then paraded around town on a camel.

Gnostics: From the Greek word meaning "to know," the Gnostics were a group of people who existed mostly outside of the church, and who claimed special revelations, unknowable to others, as the basis for their beliefs. Predictably, many aspects of their theology were regarded as heretical.

Pope Gregory the Great (ca. 540–604): One of the most influential figures of the early church age, Gregory won great acclaim in his own life for his highly popular disposition and extensive missionary efforts. Gregory commissioned many missionary trips around the continent and himself made tours around Europe as a way of making the church visible in underpopulated and pagan areas. He had a very tender spot for hands-on ministry, judging from his *Pastoral Rule*. Only two popes have the title "the Great," and he is one of them (the other is Pope Leo I).

Gregory Nazianzus (ca. 329–390): One of the Cappadocian Fathers, Gregory teamed up with Basil of Caesarea to fight for orthodoxy in the fourth century, before the two had a falling out. His funeral oration for Basil solidified his reputation as the greatest orator of the Patristic era, and he is also renowned for his defense of the Trinity.

Gregory of Nyssa (ca. 335–ca. 395): Another of the Cappadocian Fathers who labored quietly in defense of the Trinity. Very little is known about his life, but his writing is heavily influenced by Origen and Athanasius, as well as his brother, Basil of Caesarea.

Hagia Sophia: Started and completed during the reign of the Byzantine emperor Justinian, the Hagia Sophia was immediately considered the most wondrous structure of its day when it opened in 537. The purpose of its erection was to replace a previous church on the site that burned during the famous Nika Riots of 532. It was very much a display of Byzantine power until the Ottoman conquest of 1453, when it became a mosque. In the 1930s, it was converted into a museum, which it remains today.

hagiography: The written records of the lives of the saints, often enlivened with exaggerated or entirely fabricated details.

Iconoclasm Controversy: A debate that persisted for several hundred years, almost entirely within the Eastern church, as to whether depictions of Jesus, Mary, or the saints could be incorporated into worship. Permission on the matter ebbed and flowed according to who was emperor. Ultimately the pro-icon party prevailed.

Ignatius of Antioch (d. ca. 110): The bishop of Antioch, Syria, who wrote profuse calls for Christian unity and rejection of heresies in the early second century. In his letters is a litany of exhortations to Christian unity, orders for right obedience to bishops and presbyters, and a passion for a bloody martyrdom. His wish was obtained: Ignatius was martyred at Rome by wild beasts, perhaps wolves, after a personal interview with the emperor Trajan. He was a very important source for the immediate period after the New Testament.

Irenaeus of Lyon (ca. early second century–202): The bishop of Lyon, in France, whose mission was to refute the heresies of Marcion. Irenaeus also laid foundational arguments for the supremacy of the Roman church over others. He played a peacemaker role in the Quartodeciman controversy, a dispute over the date of celebrating Easter that stands as one of the first disagreements between the Eastern and Western church.

Isidore of Seville (ca. 560–636): The archbishop of Seville, in Spain, and the only true noteworthy intellectual of the Visigoth period in Spain. His magisterial *Etymologies* was the great encyclopedia of the Middle Ages, and he was also instrumental in helping convert the Arian Visigothic leaders to Catholicism.

Ivar the Boneless (d. ca. 870?): A Viking leader of multiple invasions of England in the 800s. A favorite method of execution that he performed on certain rivals was the "blood eagle," in which the rib cage is opened from behind and the lungs are pulled out, seemingly representing a pair of wings. The source of his nickname is the subject of debate: he may have been lame and unable to walk, but it is more likely that his fighting prowess made it seem as if he had no limbs at all.

Jerome (347–ca. 420): A multifaceted, genius scholar who made many enemies for his frank views and suspicious relationships with female benefactors. Jerome was a priest and monk who served Pope Damasus as secretary, and under his direction, completed the Vulgate translation of the Bible, a new edition of the Hebrew and Greek Scriptures translated into Latin. Jerome also wrote voluminous commentaries on many books of the Bible. He is remembered as one of the four Doctors of the Latin Church (with Ambrose, Augustine, and Pope Gregory).

John Chrysostom (ca. 347–407): A fearless and eloquent preacher at Antioch, and later Constantinople, who attacked lay Christians, clergy, and royals alike for lifestyles incongruent with Christianity. Eventually he became the archbishop of Constantinople, from which he was later exiled because of his preaching. His homilies are still worth reading and studying.

Julian the Apostate (ca. 331/332–363): Emperor from 361 to 363, Julian gained his nickname by turning away from Christianity. Unlike his predecessors, who used more brutal and gruesome means of persecutions, Julian set up a number of legal barriers to Christianity and attempted to play rival Christian leaders against one another. He had little success, and died on campaign after only two years on the throne as the last pagan emperor of Rome.

Justin Martyr (ca. 100–ca. 165): One of the very first Christian philosophers, who made great strides in interpreting the Bible. He was a ferocious apologist for Christianity who realized that Christianity could be a religious and philosophical system; his two-part *Apology* is his masterwork in this regard. Justin earned the name "Martyr" when he was beheaded sometime in the second century.

Justinian I (482–565): An altogether ruthless man, Justinian nevertheless was a skillful king in a moment of great historical change. He won back a great deal of Roman territory for the Byzantine Empire, and it is under him the Byzantines began to carve out a distinct identity. Justinian commissioned the construction of the magnificent Hagia Sophia church. He was simultaneously aided and confounded by his wife, the empress

Theodora, who added her own layer of political intrigue to the politics of the day.

Pope Leo I (ca. 400–461): One of two popes with the honorific "the Great" (the other is Gregory), Leo's most famous accomplishment was convincing Attila the Hun to stay his planned assault on the city of Rome in 452. He also famously issued "The Tome," which affirmed that Christ had two natures, human and divine, a proposition that was hotly contested during the Monophysite controversy of the fifth century. Leo also unambiguously asserted the church at Rome's authority over churches everywhere, citing its Petrine lineage.

Pope Leo IX (1002–1054): Something of a reformer who helped end a period of corruption in the papacy in particular and the church in general in the form of a campaign against simony. As a German by birth, Leo was insulated from much of the local factionalism that had for several generations used the papacy as a bargaining chip. His invocation of the *Donation of Constantine*, which purported to give the Roman church authority over imperial government, helped incite the great Schism of 1054.

Martin of Tours (316–397): A Roman soldier of the fourth century who became a Christian (at the time, a controversial act), and later, a monk and bishop of Tours. His reputation for poverty was legendary, and his mode of life made him the great inspiration for many Europeans to adopt the monastic lifestyle. Even today he remains one of the most notable saints.

Maximus the Confessor (ca. 580–662): Formerly an adviser to the emperor Heraclius, Maximus was a theologian and scholar whose tongue was cut out for his theological views during the arcane Monothelite controversy of the seventh century.

Michael Lachanodrakon (d. 792): Nicknamed "the Dragon," Lachanodrakon was a general in the employment of the rabidly iconoclast Byzantine Emperor Constantine V. He whipped, blinded, and beheaded many monks, but his favorite tactic was to douse a monk's beard with oil and then light it on fire. The Dragon lived by the sword and died by it: he fell during a battle against the Bulgars in 792.

Montanism: A movement of the early second century so named after its founder, Montanus. Montanism was probably similar to the modern Pentecostal movement in that its adherents were distinguished by sudden, frenzied utterances that they claimed were inspired by the Holy Spirit. There was disagreement within the church on how they should be dealt with; they were sometimes regarded as heretical, and sometimes not.

Moses the Black (ca. 330–ca. 400): Also known as Moses the Robber, the Abyssinian, the Ethiopian, and the Strong, Moses was an escaped slave, bandit, and murderer who reformed his ways and became a desert monk in the fourth century. Though a giant man, Moses often only ate a little bread each day and prayed up to fifty times per day. When raiders attacked his monastery in 405, Moses refused to fight back and was killed, seeing his death as a kind of atonement for his past transgressions.

Muhammad (570–632): A self-regarded prophet of God, Muhammad claimed to have received divine revelation from the God of Abraham in the year 610, and quickly gained a following from among the various tribes of the Arabian peninsula, sometimes by force. By the end of his life he had conquered an astounding amount of territory in the Middle East. His purported sayings were recorded by Islamic scholars as the *Hadith*.

Olaf Tryggvason (ca. 960s–ca. 1000): The first Christian king of Norway of any consequence, Olaf was said to juggle five daggers at one time without cutting himself, and was fond of burning, looting, and slaughtering until his conversion. His evangelistic method of choice was the threat of brute force; in one episode, he forced a live snake down the throat of one dissenter, and piled hot coals atop the chest of another.

Origen (ca. 184/185–ca. 253/254): Tremendously influential theologian from Alexandria whose scholarly output was unmatched for his time. Unfortunately, very little of his commentaries, sermons, and textual criticism survive. Questions abound about how faithful of an interpreter of Scripture he was; some accuse him of being overly allegorical to the point of error, perhaps a consequence of the Platonic philosophy that was very popular in his day. His passion for the Word is undeniable; he performed self-castration in a literal interpretation of Matthew 5:29.

Pachomius (ca. 290–346): A Egyptian monk who founded perhaps the first communal (cenobitic) monastery in Egypt, and his Rule for the practice became very popular. He was referred to as *Abba* ("father") by his fellow monks, from which the monastic term *Abbot* comes.

Paschal controversy: One of the earliest theological differences between East and West, concerning the celebration of Easter. It is also called the Quartodeciman (pertaining to the number fourteen) controversy, so called for the date of the month. Pope Victor I excommunicated members of the Eastern church for celebrating the holiday on a different date, but cooler heads prevailed, and he was rebuked. The matter would not be completely set to rest in successive centuries.

Polycarp of Smyrna (ca. 70–ca. 155): The bishop of Smyrna, in Turkey, and contemporary of Ignatius, who at the age of eighty-six was burned to death for being a Christian. The very detailed and moving account of his death is one of the best pieces of early Christian literature. He was supposedly a disciple of the apostle John. His *Letter to the Philippians* survives.

Simeon the Stylite (ca. 390–459): A sincere, if eccentric ascetic in the desert of Syria who spent the great majority of his life living on a platform set atop a column that eventually rose to be fifty feet or higher. Despite his seclusion, he welcomed visitors up his ladder and gave sermons to his admirers below. His example made him one of the most famous men in the world at the time of his death, and spawned many imitators.

Tertullian (ca. 160–ca. 225): An early Christian writer from Carthage. An important source for early Christian theology and practice, Tertullian's precise and stern writing, informed by a law background, indicates that intellectuals were also taking Christianity seriously by the third century AD. He inexplicably adopted some heretical positions later in life, which has prevented his sainthood in later times. Tertullian covered much ground in his works, including repentance, prayer, baptism, women, and sundry other topics. He is famous for his rejection of philosophy in the life of the Christian: "What hath Athens to do with Jerusalem?"

Theodosius (347–395): The last emperor of Rome of real consequence, he issued a decree that made Christianity the state religion of Rome, an unthinkable act one hundred years before. Theodosius was confronted and subsequently excommunicated by the bishop Ambrose of Milan over a massacre of innocents at the town of Thessalonica. He eventually was restored to the church after expressing seemingly genuine repentance.

Valerian (ca. 200–260): Emperor from 253 to 260 who continued the campaigns of persecution started by the emperor Decius in 251. He was captured by Persians in battle and died shortly after in their hands.

The Venerable Bede (672/673–735): A monk from England whose *Ecclesiastical History of the English People* is critical for understanding the period. The work is also notable for being one of the first to date history from the time of Christ using the AD chronology. Bede was also a major preservationist of all kinds of writings from antiquity and the early Middle Ages.

ACKNOWLEDGMENTS

This book would not have been possible without the help of many family members, friends, and trusted colleagues. I submit to the reader the names of those who helped me persevere through a long, valuable, and absorbing project.

My wife, Elayne, and my sons, John and Joe: I love you all very much. Your support lies behind everything I do.

My assistant, Noreen Burns: Thank you for helping me in matters large and small for almost thirty years.

Joel Miller: A fine editor at Thomas Nelson, who first proposed this book, and who knows his craft well.

Webster Younce: Another top-notch editor at Thomas Nelson, who has read every word.

Renee Chavez, Jennifer McNeil, and Heather Skelton: Tireless copy editors who labored over the manuscript to ensure accuracy in all facts, citations, and usages of grammar and style.

Kevin Knight and New Advent.org, the Christian Classics Ethereal Library (CCEL), the Fordham University *Medieval Sourcebook*, and Google Books: Thank you for compiling so many early church writings in one place. This book would have taken twice the time to write and edit were it not for your digitization of important works of and about church history.

Dr. Tim Furnish: Thank you for your helpful comments and corrections in chapter 15.

James Rich: A loyal *Morning in America* listener and church historian who patiently and thoughtfully reviewed the manuscript.

David Wilezol: A friend, colleague, and gifted writer, whose diligence and perseverance made this book a reality.

NOTES

INTRODUCTION

1. Raymond Ibrahim, "Christmas Slaughter: Muslim Persecution of Christians, December 2014," The Gatestone Institute, February 1, 2015, http://www.gatestoneinstitute.org/5169/christmas-slaughter-muslim-persecution.
2. Anugrah Kumar, "Pope Francis 'Deeply Concerned' About Christian Persecution, Says Stronger Than First Century Church," *Christian Post*, June 15, 2014, http://www.christianpost.com/news/pope-francis-deeply-concerned-about-christian-persecution-says-stronger-than-1st-century-church-121562/.
3. Barbara Boland, "Pew Study: Christians Are the World's Most Oppressed Religious Group," CNSNews.com, February 6, 2014, http://cnsnews.com/news/article/barbara-boland/pew-study-christians-are-world-s-most-oppressed-religious-group.
4. CNN Staff, "ISIS video appears to show beheadings of Egyptian Coptic Christians in Libya," CNN Online, February 16, 2015, http://www.cnn.com/2015/02/15/middleeast/isis-video-beheadings-christians/.
5. Tertullian, *Apologeticus* 50.13, author's translation.

PART 1: SCATTERED SHEEP

1. Tacitus, *Annals* 15.33, trans. Alfred John Church and William Jackson Brodribb (London: Macmillan, 1876).

2. Suetonius, "VI. Nero" in *Lives of the Caesars*, vol. 2, trans. J. C. Rolfe, Loeb Classical Library 38 (Cambridge, MA: Harvard University Press, 1913–1914).
3. Ibid., 16.2.
4. Eusebius, *Church History* 1.25, trans. Arthur Cushman McGiffert, in *Nicene and Post-Nicene Fathers*, 2nd series, vol. 1, eds. Philip Schaff and Henry Wace (Buffalo: Christian Literature, 1890), accessed January 25, 2015, http://www.newadvent.org/fathers/250102.htm.
5. Tacitus, *Annals* 15.44. Those Christians who pled guilty did so under threat of torture.
6. Tertullian, quoted in Eusebius, *Church History* 25.4.
7. Clement, *The First Epistle of Clement to the Corinthians* 5:5–6, trans. J. B. Lightfoot, in J. B. Lightfoot and Joseph Barber, eds., *The Apostolic Fathers: A Revised Text with Introductions, Notes, Dissertations, and Translations* (London: Macmillan, 1890), 274. Ignatius of Antioch's *Epistle to the Ephesians* 12, written about 110, and Eusebius's *Church History* 2.25, from the fourth century, also confirm Paul's martyrdom at Rome.
8. "Remains of St. Paul Confirmed," *Washington Times*, June 29, 2009, http://www.washingtontimes.com/news/2009/jun/29/remains-confirmed-to-belong-to-st-paul/.
9. Niall Ferguson, *Civilization* (New York: Penguin, 2011), 287.
10. Eusebius, *Church History* 2.9.
11. "The Acts of Philip" in M. R. James, *The Apocryphal New Testament* (Oxford: Clarendon Press, 1924), accessed January 25, 2015, http://gnosis.org/library/actphil.htm.
12. Ibid.
13. Renzo Allegri, "How I Discovered the Tomb of the Apostle Philip," Zenit Online, accessed January 25, 2015, http://www.zenit.org/en/articles/how-i-discovered-the-tomb-of-the-apostle-philip.
14. Ibid.
15. Jerome, *Lives of Illustrious Men—James*, trans. Ernest Cushing Richardson, in *Nicene and Post-Nicene Fathers*, 2nd series, vol. 3, eds. Philip Schaff and Henry Wace (Buffalo: Christian Literature, 1892).
16. Eusebius, *Church History* 2.23.
17. For these references and extensive scholarship on the subject, see Adolphus E. Medlycott, *India and the Apostle Thomas, an Inquiry* (London: David Nutt, 1905).

18. Ephrem the Syrian, "Hymn," ed. Msr. Lamy, col. 706, vol. 4, 1866, translated by Medlycott in *India*, 29.

19. Justo González, *The Story of Christianity*, vol. 1 (New York: HarperCollins, 1984), 30.

Part 2: The First Saints

1. Suetonius, *The Lives of the Caesars*, vol. 2, bk. 8, "Domitian" 3.1, trans. J. C. Rolfe, Loeb Classical Library 38 (Cambridge, MA: Harvard University Press, 1913–1914).

2. Ibid., 14.1.

3. Clement of Rome, *Letter to the Corinthians* I, trans. Maxwell Staniforth in *Early Christian Writings* (New York: Penguin Books, 1972), 23.

4. Tertullian, *The Prescription Against Heretics* 36, trans. Peter Holmes, in *Ante-Nicene Fathers*, vol. 3, eds. Alexander Roberts, James Donaldson, and A. Cleveland Coxe (Buffalo, NY: Christian Literature Publishing Co., 1885).

5. The Orthodox Church in America, "The Apostle Timothy of the Seventy," accessed February 7, 2014, http://oca.org/saints/lives/2013/01/22/100262-apostle-timothy-of-the-seventy.

6. Eventually the council ruled that Gentiles did not have to keep elements of the Jewish law, except for some prohibitions on eating meat containing blood or meat of animals not properly slain (Acts 15:22–29).

7. Irenaeus, *Against Heresies* 3.3., trans. Alexander Roberts and William Rambaut, in *Ante-Nicene Fathers*, vol. 1, eds. Alexander Roberts, James Donaldson, and A. Cleveland Coxe (Buffalo: Christian Literature, 1885).

8. See, for instance, 1 Timothy 3 and Titus 1.

9. Clement of Rome, *Letter to the Corinthians* 44, in Staniforth, *Early Christian Writings*, 46.

10. Ibid., 45–46.

11. Theodoret of Cyrus, *Dial. Immutabile* 1.4.33a.

12. *The Catholic Encyclopedia*, s.v. "Saint Ignatius of Antioch," accessed February 4, 2014, http://www.newadvent.org/cathen/07644a.htm.

13. Ignatius of Antioch, *Epistle to the Trallians* 6, trans. Maxwell Staniforth in *Early Christian Writings* (New York: Penguin, 1972), 96.

14. Ibid., 77.

15. Ignatius of Antioch, *Epistle to the Trallians* 20, 82.

16. Ibid., 7, 97.

17. Ignatius, *Epistle to the Ephesians* 13, 79.

18. Ibid., 7, 77.

19. Ignatius, *Epistle to the Smyrnaeans* 8, trans. Maxwell Staniforth in *Early Christian Writings* (New York: Penguin, 1972), 121.

20. Ignatius, *Epistle to the Romans* 5, trans. Maxwell Staniforth in *Early Christian Writings* (New York: Penguin, 1972), 105.

21. *The Catholic Encyclopedia*, s.v. "St. Ignatius of Antioch," http://www .newadvent.org/cathen/07644a.htm.

22. Pliny the Younger, *Letters to Trajan* 97, *The Harvard Classics*, vol. 9, pt. 4 (Cambridge: MA, Harvard University Press, 1909–1914).

23. Ibid.

24. Ibid.

25. Pliny the Younger, *Letters to Trajan* 98.

26. Irenaeus, *Against Heresies* 3.3.

27. Marcion of Smyrna, *Epistle to the Church at Philomelium* 5, trans. Maxwell Staniforth in *Early Christian Writings* (New York: Penguin, 1968), 157.

28. Ibid.

29. Ibid.

30. Burning incense at shrines was a common form of worship of the Roman gods.

31. Marcion of Smyrna, *Epistle to the Church at Philomelium* 8, 158.

32. Ibid.

33. Ibid., 9, 159.

34. Ibid., 11, 159.

35. Ibid., 12, 159.

36. Ibid., 13, 160.

37. Ibid., 14, 161.

Part 3: Defining Doctrine

1. International Christian Concern, "Christian Worship Thrives in Northern Nigeria, Despite Dangers," Persecution.org, accessed September 30, 2013, http://www.persecution.org/2013/09/30 /christian-worship-thrives-in-northern-nigeria-despite-dangers/.

2. Tertullian, *Against the Valentinians* 4, trans. Alexander Roberts in *Ante-Nicene Fathers*, vol. 3 (Buffalo: Christian Literature, 1885), accessed January 28, 2015, http://earlychristianwritings.com/text/tertullian14 .html.

3. A newlywed couple's bed.

4. Eusebius, *Church History* 4.11, trans. Arthur Cushman McGiffert, in *Nicene and Post-Nicene Fathers,* 2nd series, vol. 1, eds. Philip Schaff and Henry Wace (Buffalo: Christian Literature, 1890), accessed January 25, 2015, http://www.newadvent.org/fathers/250104.htm.

5. Eusebius, *Church History* 5.13, http://www.newadvent.org/fathers /250105.htm. Pontus is the region of Turkey from which Marcion came.

6. Marcion could not accept the Gospels of Matthew, Mark, and John because they were written by Jews, who, he believed, had incorrectly interpreted Jesus' life and teachings.

7. Eusebius, *Church History* 4.11.

8. Irenaeus, *Against Heresies* 2.11.

9. Ibid.

10. Eusebius, *Church History* 7.3, http://www.newadvent.org/fathers/250107 .htm.

11. Ibid., 7.25.

12. Eusebius, *Church History* 5.20, http://www.newadvent.org/fathers /250105.htm.

13. Irenaeus, *Against Heresies* 1.8.

14. Ibid., 4.28.

15. Ibid., 3.3.

16. Justin Martyr, *Dialogue with Trypho* 2, trans. Marcus Dods and George Reith, in *Ante-Nicene Fathers,* vol. 1, eds. Alexander Roberts, James Donaldson, and A. Cleveland Coxe (Buffalo: Christian Literature, 1885), http://www.newadvent.org/fathers/01281.htm.

17. Justin Martyr, *Dialogue* 8.

18. Ibid., 138.

19. Justin Martyr, quoted in Eusebius, *Church History* 4.9, http://www .newadvent.org/fathers/250104.htm.

20. Justin Martyr, *First Apology* 3, trans. Marcus Dods and George Reith, in *Ante-Nicene Fathers*, vol. 1, eds. Alexander Robert, James Donaldson, and A. Cleveland Coxe (Buffalo: Christian Literature, 1885), accessed January 27, 2015, http://www.newadvent.org/fathers/0126.htm.

21. Matthew 22:20–22.

22. Justin Martyr, *First Apology*, 17.

23. Ibid., 27.

24. Ibid., 11.

25. Justin Martyr, *Second Apology* 2, trans. Marcus Dods and George Reith, in *Ante-Nicene Fathers*, vol. 1, eds. Alexander Roberts, James Donaldson, and A. Cleveland Coxe (Buffalo: Christian Literature, 1885), rev. and ed. for New Advent by Kevin Knight, http://www.newadvent.org/fathers/0127.htm.
26. Ibid.
27. Ibid., 3.
28. Adapted from "The Account of the Martyrdom of Saint Justin," posted on the Crossroads Initiative website, accessed February 18, 2014, http://crossroadsinitiative.com/library_article/622/Martyrdom_of_St._Justin.html.
29. Justin Martyr, *First Apology* 67.
30. Excepting the missionary campaigns of Paul and the other apostles.
31. Eusebius, *Church History* 5.1, http://www.newadvent.org/fathers/250105.htm.
32. Ibid.
33. Ibid.
34. Ibid.
35. Ibid.
36. *Foxe's Book of Martyrs* (Philadelphia: Claxton, 1881), 65.
37. Eusebius, *Church History* 5.21.
38. Ibid.
39. St. Patrick Catholic Church, "Apollonius the Apologist," accessed February 18, 2014, http://www.saintpatrickdc.org/ss/0418.shtml#apol.
40. Candida Moss, *The Myth of Persecution: How Early Christians Invented a Story of Martyrdom* (New York: HarperOne, 2013).

PART 4: BRUTAL OPPOSITION

1. This is an example of syncretism, or the combining of different belief systems.
2. Eusebius, *Church History* 6.1, trans. Arthur Cushman McGiffert, in *Nicene and Post-Nicene Fathers*, 2nd series, vol. 1, eds. Philip Schaff and Henry Wace (Buffalo: Christian Literature, 1890), accessed January 25, 2015, http://www.newadvent.org/fathers/250102.htm.
3. Ibid., 6.7.
4. W. H. Shewring, trans., "The Passion of Saints Perpetua and Felicity" (London: 1931), as updated by and posted in the Fordham University *Medieval Sourcebook*, accessed March 7, 2014, http://www.fordham.edu/halsall/source/perpetua.asp.

5. Ibid.

6. Ibid.

7. Ibid.

8. Ibid.

9. Tertullian, *Apologeticus* 50.13, author's translation.

10. Tertullian, *To the Martyrs* 2, trans. S. Thelwall, in *Ante-Nicene Fathers*, vol. 3, eds. Alexander Roberts, James Donaldson, and A. Cleveland Coxe (Buffalo: Christian Literature, 1885), accessed March 7, 2014, http://www.newadvent.org/fathers/0323.htm.

11. Tertullian, *Apology* 2, trans. S. Thelwall, in *Ante-Nicene Fathers*, vol. 3, eds. Alexander Roberts, James Donaldson, and A. Cleveland Coxe (Buffalo: Christian Literature, 1885), accessed March 7, 2014, http://www.newadvent.org/fathers/0301.htm.

12. Henry Chadwick, *The Early Church*, vol. 1 (New York: Penguin, 1993), 29.

13. Tertullian, *Apology* 10.

14. Ibid., 25.

15. Tertullian, *Against Heresies* 7, trans. S. Thelwall, in *Ante-Nicene Fathers*, vol. 3, eds. Alexander Roberts, James Donaldson, and A. Cleveland Coxe (Buffalo: Christian Literature, 1885), accessed January 28, 2014, http://www.newadvent.org/fathers/0311.htm.

16. Tertullian, *Apology* 30–31.

17. Eusebius, *Church History* 5.21, http://www.newadvent.org/fathers/250105.htm.

18. Tertullian, *Apology* 1.

19. E.g., the deaconess Phoebe in Romans 16:1.

20. Tertullian, *Apology* 9.

21. Tertullian, *Against Marcion* 2, trans. Peter Holmes, in *Ante-Nicene Fathers*, vol. 3, eds. Alexander Roberts, James Donaldson, and A. Cleveland Coxe (Buffalo: Christian Literature, 1885), accessed March 7, 2014, http://www.newadvent.org/fathers/03121.htm.

22. Ibid., 1.

23. Tertullian, *Against Heresies* 21.

24. Ibid., 36.

25. Tertullian, *De Fuga* 9, trans. S. Thelwall, in *Ante-Nicene Fathers*, vol. 4, eds. Alexander Roberts, James Donaldson, and A. Cleveland Coxe (Buffalo: Christian Literature, 1885), accessed March 7, 2014, http://www.newadvent.org/fathers/0409.htm.

26. Eusebius, *Church History* 5.17.

27. Much of the Montanist practice probably resembled modern-day charismatic and Pentecostal movements. The question of whether prophetic gifts continued after the apostolic age is still a point of disagreement among theologians, with the two camps generally divided into "continuationists" and "secessionists."

28. Eusebius, *Church History* 5.23.

29. Ibid., 5.24.

30. Ibid.

31. It has been suggested that Irenaeus's conspicuous role in the controversy brought him to Severus's attention, and that this was the impetus for his martyrdom circa 202.

32. Eusebius, *Church History* 5.24.

33. Ibid., 5.25.

34. Hippolytus, *Refutation of All Heresies* 9.7, trans. J. H. MacMahon, in *Ante-Nicene Fathers*, vol. 5, eds. Alexander Roberts, James Donaldson, and A. Cleveland Coxe (Buffalo: Christian Literature, 1886), accessed March 7, 2014, http://www.newadvent.org/fathers/050109.htm.

35. *Foxe's Book of Martyrs*, 29.

36. Ibid.

37. Ibid.

38. Ibid., 30.

39. Ibid.

40. Ibid., 34–35.

41. Alban Butler, *The Lives of the Fathers, Martyrs, and Other Principal Saints*, vol. 8 (Dublin: James Duffy, 1866), accessed March 7, 2014, http://www.bartleby.com/210/8/101.html.

42. See, for example, Ambrose of Milan, *De Officiis Ministrorum* 204.

43. Eusebius, *Church History* 5.1.

44. Tertullian, *De Fuga* 4, trans. S. Thelwall, in *Ante-Nicene Fathers*, vol. 4, eds. Alexander Roberts, James Donaldson, and A. Cleveland Coxe (Buffalo: Christian Literature, 1885), accessed March 7, 2014, http://www.newadvent.org/fathers/0409.htm.

45. Eusebius, *Church History* 7.8, http://www.newadvent.org/fathers/250107.htm.

46. Justo González, *The Story of Christianity*, vol. 1 (New York: Harper and Row, 1984), 90.

PART 5: EGYPT AND THE GREAT PERSECUTION

1. Eusebius, *Church History* 2.16, trans. Arthur Cushman McGiffert, in *Nicene and Post-Nicene Fathers,* 2nd series, vol. 1, eds. Philip Schaff and Henry Wace (Buffalo: Christian Literature, 1890), accessed January 25, 2015, http://www.newadvent.org/fathers/250102.htm.

2. Clement of Alexandria, *The Stromata* 1.1, trans. William Wilson, in *Ante-Nicene Fathers*, vol. 2, eds. Alexander Roberts, James Donaldson, and A. Cleveland Coxe (Buffalo: Christian Literature, 1885), accessed January 28, 2015, http://www.newadvent.org/fathers/0210.htm.

3. Clement of Alexandria, *Exhortation to the Heathen* 12, trans. William Wilson in *Ante-Nicene Fathers*, vol. 2, eds. Alexander Roberts, James Donaldson, and A. Cleveland Coxe (Buffalo: Christian Literature, 1885), rev. and ed. for New Advent by Kevin Knight, http://www.newadvent.org/fathers/0208.htm.

4. Clement of Alexandria, *Stromata* 6.8.

5. Ibid., 7.

6. Clement of Alexandria, *The Instructor* 2.1, trans. William Wilson, in *Ante-Nicene Fathers*, vol. 2, eds. Alexander Roberts, James Donaldson, and A. Cleveland Coxe (Buffalo: Christian Literature, 1885), rev. and ed. for New Advent by Kevin Knight, http://www.newadvent.org/fathers/02092.htm.

7. Ibid., 2.2.

8. Ibid., 2.7.

9. This figure includes everything from the most minor personal letters to the lengthiest biblical commentaries.

10. Robert J. Daly, "Origen," in Everett Ferguson, ed., *The Encyclopedia of Early Christianity* (New York: Routledge, 1990), 836.

11. Eusebius, *Church History* 6.3.

12. Ibid.

13. Ibid.

14. Ibid.

15. Ibid.

16. Ibid., 6.8.

17. Or he severed the testicles from the body.

18. Eusebius, *Church History* 6.8. Modern historians such as Edward Gibbon (*The History of the Decline and Fall of the Roman Empire*, chap. 15, n. 97) and Peter Brown (*The Body and Society*, London: Columbia University Press, 1988) see no reason to doubt the veracity of this story.

19. Eusebius, *Church History* 6.24.
20. Ibid., 6.39.
21. Justo González, *The Story of Christianity*, vol. 1 (New York: Harper and Row, 1984), 78.
22. Eusebius, *Church History* 6.19.
23. Origen, *Letter to Africanus*, trans. Frederick Crombie, in *Ante-Nicene Fathers*, vol. 4, eds. Alexander Roberts, James Donaldson, and A. Cleveland Coxe (Buffalo: Christian Literature, 1885), accessed January 28, 2015, http://www.newadvent.org/fathers/0414.htm.
24. Bruce M. Metzger, *Manuscripts of the Greek Bible: An Introduction to Palaeography* (Oxford: Oxford University Press, 1991), 76.
25. Eusebius, *Church History* 8.1.
26. Keith Hopkins, "Christian Number and Its Implications," *Journal of Early Christian Studies* 6, no. 2 (1998): 191.
27. Porphyry of Tyre, *Fragment* 1, trans. Elizabeth Digeser in *The Making of a Christian Empire* (Ithaca, NY: Cornell University Press, 2000), 6.
28. Graeme Clarke, "Third-Century Christianity," in *The Crisis of Empire*, vol. 12 of *The Cambridge Ancient History*, eds. Alan Bowman, Averil Cameron, and Peter Garnsey (New York: Cambridge University Press, 2005), 648.
29. Lactantius, *De Mortibus Persecutorum* 11.1–2.
30. Lactantius, *Of the Manner in Which the Persecutors Died*, ch. 12, trans. William Fletcher, in *Ante-Nicene Fathers*, vol. 7, eds. Alexander Roberts, James Donaldson, and A. Cleveland Coxe (Buffalo: Christian Literature, 1886), rev. and ed. for New Advent by Kevin Knight, http://www.newadvent.org/fathers/0705.htm.
31. Ibid., 11.8.
32. Ibid., ch. 13.
33. Ibid., ch. 14.
34. Eusebius, *Church History* 8.4.
35. Lactantius, *Of the Manner in Which the Persecutors Died* 6.15.
36. Eusebius, *Church History* 8.6.
37. Ibid., 8.4, appendix.
38. Ibid., 8.12.
39. *Foxe's Book of Martyrs*, 42.
40. Ibid.
41. Eusebius, *Church History* 8.5.

42. Ibid., 8.15.

43. Aurelius Victor, *Liber de Caesaribus* 39.6, ed. and trans. H. W. Bird (Liverpool: Liverpool University Press, 1994).

44. Eusebius, *Church History* 8.17.

45. Ibid., 8.9, appendix.

PART 6: CHURCH, STATE, AND EMPEROR

1. Peter Leithart, *Defending Constantine* (Downer's Grove, IL: Intervarsity Press, 2010), 55–56.

2. Lactantius, *Of the Manner in Which the Persecutors Died*, 24.

3. Ibid., 24–25.

4. Ibid., 24.

5. Ibid., 44.

6. Eusebius, *Church History* 9.9, trans. Arthur Cushman McGiffert, in *Nicene and Post-Nicene Fathers*, 2nd series, vol. 1, eds. Philip Schaff and Henry Wace (Buffalo: Christian Literature, 1890), accessed January 25, 2015, http://www.newadvent.org/fathers/250109.htm. In reality, Maxentius had a superior number of troops. This was probably a more likely reason for Constantine's prayer for help, if one ever took place.

7. Eusebius, *Life of Constantine* 1.27, trans. Ernest Cushing Richardson, in *Nicene and Post-Nicene Fathers*, 2nd series, vol. 1, eds. Philip Schaff and Henry Wace (Buffalo: Christian Literature, 1890), rev. and ed. for New Advent by Kevin Knight, http://www.newadvent.org/fathers/2502.htm.

8. Banners carried by armies indicating various pieces of tactical and unit information.

9. Lactantius, *Of the Manner*, 44.

10. Ibid., 48.

11. Eusebius, *Church History* 10.9, http://www.newadvent.org/fathers/250110.htm.

12. Eusebius, *Life of Constantine* 2.2.

13. In Latin, "Holy."

14. In Latin, "Blessed."

15. Inscription from the Arch of Constantine, trans. Bill Thayer, University of Chicago, hosted at LacusCurtius, accessed June 3, 2015, http://penelope.uchicago.edu/Thayer/E/Gazetteer/Places/Europe/Italy/Lazio/Roma/Rome/Arch_of_Constantine/inscriptions.html.

16. Peter Leithart, *Defending Constantine* (Downers Grove, IL: IVP Academic, 2010), 125.

17. Eusebius, *Church History* 10.7.

18. Eusebius, *Life of Constantine* 4.18–20.

19. Ibid., 4.

20. Ibid., 4.6.

21. Sozomen, *Ecclesiastical History* 2.3, trans. Chester D. Hartranft, in *Post-Nicene Fathers*, 2nd series, vol. 2, eds. Philip Schaff and Henry Wace (Buffalo: Christian Literature, 1890), http://www.newadvent.org /fathers/26022.htm.

22. See Jerome, *Chronicle* 330.

23. Eusebius, *Life of Constantine* 3.49.

24. Ibid., 3.48.

25. Ferguson, *Encyclopedia of Early Christianity*, 172.

26. Gregory T. Armstrong, "Basilica," in Ferguson, ed., *Encyclopedia of Early Christianity*, 173.

27. Armstrong, "Church of the Holy Sepulchre," in Ferguson, ed., *Encyclopedia of Early Christianity*, 535.

28. Eusebius, *Life of Constantine* 3.27.

29. Sozomen, *Ecclesiastical History* 2.1.

30. Armstrong, "Church of the Holy Sepulchre," 535.

31. Sozomen, *Ecclesiastical History* 2.2.

32. Eusebius, *Life of Constantine* 3.35.

33. Eusebius, *Church History* 10.5.

34. Michael Gaddis, *There Is No Crime for Those Who Have Christ: Religious Violence in the Christian Roman Empire* (Berkeley: University of California Press, 2005), 54.

35. Frederick W. Norris, "Circumcellions," in Ferguson, ed., *Encyclopedia of Early Christianity*, 260.

36. Optatus, *Against the Donatists*, trans. and ed. Mark Edwards (Liverpool: Liverpool University Press, 1998), as quoted in Leithart, *Defending Constantine*, 160–61.

37. Ibid., 162.

38. Robert M. Grant, "Constantine the Great," in Ferguson, ed., *Encyclopedia of Early Christianity*, 281.

39. Zosimus, *New History*, bk. 2 (London: Green and Chaplin, 1814), accessed May 3, 2015, http://www.tertullian.org/fathers/zosimus02 _book2.htm.

40. Sozomen, *Ecclesiastical History* 2.34.

PART 7: TARES AMONG WHEAT

1. Eusebius, *Life of Constantine*, trans. Ernest Cushing Richardson, in *Nicene and Post-Nicene Fathers*, 2nd series, vol. 1, eds. Philip Schaff and Henry Wace (Buffalo: Christian Literature, 1890), 2.61, rev. and ed. for New Advent by Kevin Knight, http://www.newadvent.org/fathers/2502.htm.

2. Theodoret of Cyrus, *Ecclesiastical History* 1.1, trans. Blomfield Jackson, in *Post-Nicene Fathers*, 2nd series, vol. 3, eds. Philip Schaff and Henry Wace (Buffalo: Christian Literature, 1892), http://www.newadvent.org/fathers/27021.htm.

3. Eusebius, *Life of Constantine* 2.61.

4. Theodoret of Cyrus, *Ecclesiastical History* 1.1.

5. Eusebius, *Life of Constantine* 2.61–62.

6. Ibid.

7. Sozomen, *Ecclesiastical History* 1.15, trans. Chester D. Hartranft, in *Post-Nicene Fathers*, 2nd series, vol. 2, eds. Philip Schaff and Henry Wace (Buffalo: Christian Literature, 1890), http://www.newadvent.org/fathers/26021.htm.

8. Theodoret, *Ecclesiastical History* 1.1.

9. Eusebius, *Life of Constantine* 2.61.

10. Theodoret, *Ecclesiastical History* 1.1.

11. Ibid., 1.2.

12. Ibid., 1.3.

13. Ibid., 1.4.

14. Ibid., 1.5.

15. Eusebius, *Life of Constantine* 2.63.

16. Ibid.

17. Ibid., 2.68.

18. Ibid., 2.66.

19. The exact figures differ between historical sources, but all put the tally around three hundred.

20. Sozomen, *Ecclesiastical History* 2.17.

21. Theodoret, *Ecclesiastical History* 1.6.

22. Sozomen, *Ecclesiastical History* 2.17.

23. Zosimus, *New History*, in Arthur Penrhyn Stanley, *Lectures on the History of the Eastern Church* (New York: Scribner, 1872), 140.

24. Stanley, *Lectures*, 204.

25. Sozomen, *Ecclesiastical History* 2.17.

26. Stanley, *Lectures*, 198.

27. The St. Nicholas Center, "Anatomical Examination of the Bari Relics," accessed June 4, 2015, http://www.stnicholascenter.org/pages/anatomical -examination/.

28. Theodoret, *Ecclesiastical History* 1.6.

29. Eusebius, *Life of Constantine* 3.10.

30. Ibid., 3.11.

31. Ibid., 3.12.

32. Ibid., 3.13.

33. Sozomen, *Ecclesiastical History* 1.20.

34. Theodoret, *Ecclesiastical History* 1.6.

35. Stanley, *Lectures*, 230.

36. The Nicene Creed, ed. and trans. Philip Schaff, in *The Creeds of Christendom*, vol. 1 (New York: Harper, 1877). Reprinted online by the Christian Classics Ethereal Library (CCEL), accessed June 5, 2015, http://www.ccel.org/ccel/schaff/creeds1.iv.iii.html.

37. Athanasius, *Defense of the Nicene Definition* 39, trans. AJW, on Fourth-Century Christianity (website), accessed April 30, 2014, http://www .fourthcentury.com/index.php/urkunde-33.

38. A. W. Tozer, *Knowledge of the Holy* (New York: HarperOne, 2009), 14.

39. Marius Victorinus, quoted in James Bridge, "Homoousion," in *The Catholic Encyclopedia*, vol. 7 (New York: Robert Appleton Company, 1910), accessed April 30, 2014, http://www.newadvent.org/cathen /07449a.htm.

40. One prominent misconception about the council is that it defined the canon of Scripture. It did not—this would come later in the fourth century at the Councils of Hippo (393) and Carthage (397 and 419). The Muratorian Fragment of the second century contains almost the entire New Testament, and Athanasius also produced in 367 a list of the New Testament books as they appear in the Protestant Bible today.

41. *The Nicene Creed*, trans. Henry Percival, in *Nicene and Post-Nicene Fathers*, 2nd series, vol. 14, eds. Philip Schaff and Henry Wace (Buffalo: Christian Literature, 1900), accessed May 4, 2015, http://www.newadvent.org /fathers/3801.htm.

42. Stanley, *Lectures*, 269.

43. Ibid., 270.

44. Eusebius, *Life of Constantine* 2.21.

45. Socrates Scholasticus, *Ecclesiastical History* 1.38, trans. A. C. Zenos, in *Nicene and Post-Nicene Fathers*, 2nd series, vol. 2, eds. Philip Schaff and Henry Wace (Buffalo: Christian Literature, 1890), rev. and ed. for New Advent by Kevin Knight, http://www.newadvent.org/fathers/26011.htm.
46. Sozomen, *Ecclesiastical History* 2.17.
47. Theodoret, *Ecclesiastical History* 1.25.
48. Ibid., 1.26.
49. Ibid., 1.28.
50. Ibid.
51. Ibid., 1.32.

PART 8: SAVING WASTELANDS

1. Though, as far as we know, the practice of self-castration did not continue after Origen.
2. Jerome, *The Life of Paulus the First Hermit*, trans. W. H. Fremantle, G. Lewis, and W. G. Martley, in *Nicene and Post-Nicene Fathers*, 2nd series, vol. 6, eds. Philip Schaff and Henry Wace (Buffalo: Christian Literature, 1893), rev. and ed. for New Advent by Kevin Knight, http://www.newadvent.org/fathers/3008.htm.
3. Athanasius, *Life of Saint Anthony* 4, trans. H. Ellershaw, in *Nicene and Post-Nicene Fathers*, 2nd series, vol. 4, eds. Philip Schaff and Henry Wace (Buffalo: Christian Literature, 1892), http://www.newadvent.org/fathers/2811.htm.
4. Athanasius, *Life of Saint Anthony* 5.
5. Ibid., 14.
6. Sozomen, *Ecclesiastical History* 2.13, trans. Chester D. Hartranft, in *Post-Nicene Fathers*, 2nd series, vol. 2, eds. Philip Schaff and Henry Wace (Buffalo: Christian Literature, 1890), http://www.newadvent.org/fathers/26022.htm.
7. Athanasius, *Life of Anthony* 81.
8. Athanasius, *Life of Saint Anthony* 14, in Claudia Rapp and H. A. Drake, *The City in the Classical and Post-Classical World* (Cambridge: Cambridge University Press, 2014), 164.
9. Sozomen, *Ecclesiastical History* 3.14.
10. *The Rule of Pachomius*, pt. 1, trans. Esmerelda de Jennings Ramirez, ed. Rev. Daniel R. Jennings, Patristics in English Project (website), accessed May 16, 2014, http://www.seanmultimedia.com/Pie_Pachomius_Rule_1.html.
11. Ibid.

12. Peter Dykhorst, "St. Moses the Black, A Patron Saint of Non-Violence," In Communion, October 2011, http://www.incommunion.org/2011/12/07 /st-moses-the-black-a-patron-saint-of-non-violence-by-pieter-dykhorst/.

13. Sozomen, *Ecclesiastical History* 6.30.

14. Palladius, *The Lausiac History* 38, ed. and trans. W. K. Lowther Clarke (London: Macmillan, 1918), http://www.tertullian.org/fathers /palladius_lausiac_02_text.htm#C38.

15. Evagrius Ponticus, *The Praktikos* 12–19, in William Harmless, *Desert Christians: An Introduction to the Literature of Early Monasticism* (New York: Oxford University Press, 2004), 325.

16. Evagrius Ponticus, *Instructions* 41–44, ed. and trans. Luke Dysinger (public domain), accessed June 6, 2015, http://www.ldysinger.com /Evagrius/01_Prak/02_Prk_40–100.htm.

17. "The Life of Saint Pelagia the Harlot," trans. Benedicta Ward, from "Pelagia, Beauty Riding By" in *Harlots of the Desert, a Study of Repentance in Early Monastic Sources* (Kalamazoo: Cistercian Publications, 1986), https://facultystaff.richmond.edu/~wstevens/FYStexts/biospelagias.pdf.

18. Ibid.

19. *The Life of St. Pelagia the Harlot* 4–7, 18, 20–26, 53, in Helen Waddell, *The Desert Fathers* (Ann Arbor: University of Michigan Press, 1971), 178–88.

20. Sozomen, *Ecclesiastical History* 3.16.

21. Ibid.

22. Ephrem the Syrian, Hymn VI, trans. John Gwynn, in *Selections Translated into English from the Hymns and Homilies of Ephraim the Syrian*, 1898, in Christian Classics Ethereal Library, accessed June 6, 2015, http://www.ccel.org/ccel/schaff/npnf213.iii.iv.vii.html.

23. Ibid., http://www.ccel.org/ccel/schaff/npnf213.iii.iv.xxxii.html?highlight =concerning,satan,and,death#highlight

24. Bedjan, *The Heroic Deeds of Mar Simeon, the Chief of the Anchorites (Acts of Martyrs and Saints)*, eds. Charles C. Torrey and Hanns Oertel, in Michael Maas, *Readings in Late Antiquity: A Sourcebook* (New York: Routledge, 2010), 148.

25. Ibid.

26. Benedicta Ward, *Sayings of the Desert Fathers: The Alphabetical Collection* (London: Mowbrays, 1975), 69.

27. Ibid., 10.

28. Evagrius Ponticus, *Praktikos,* 95, trans. Dysinger.

29. Sulpitius Severus, *The Life of Saint Martin* 4, ed. and trans. Alexander Roberts in *Nicene and Post-Nicene Fathers,* 2nd series, vol. 11 (New York, 1894), http://www.users.csbsju.edu/~eknuth/npnf2–11/sulpitiu/lifeofst.html#2.

30. Ibid.

31. Ibid.

32. Ibid., 26.

33. John Cassian, *Institutes* 4.16, trans. C. S. Gibson, in *Nicene and Post-Nicene Fathers,* 2nd series, vol. 11, eds. Philip Schaff and Henry Wace (Buffalo: Christian Literature, 1894), http://www.newadvent.org/fathers/350704.htm.

34. Ibid., 5.6.

35. John Cassian, *Conferences* 14.9, trans. C. S. Gibson, in *Nicene and Post-Nicene Fathers,* 2nd series, vol. 11, eds. Philip Schaff and Henry Wace (Buffalo: Christian Literature, 1894), http://www.newadvent.org/fathers/350814.htm.

PART 9: FATHERS KNOW BEST

1. Justo González, *The Story of Christianity,* vol. 1 (New York: Harper and Row, 1984), 178.

2. Sozomen, *Ecclesiastical History* 3.5, trans. Chester D. Hartranft, in *Post-Nicene Fathers,* 2nd series, vol. 2, eds. Philip Schaff and Henry Wace (Buffalo: Christian Literature, 1890), http://www.newadvent.org/fathers/26023.htm.

3. Ibid., 4.30, http://www.newadvent.org/fathers/26024.htm.

4. Socrates Scholasticus, *Ecclesiastical History* 2.28, http://www.newadvent.org/fathers/26012.htm.

5. Ibid., 2.38.

6. Ibid.

7. Ibid.

8. Sozomen, *Ecclesiastical History* 3.8.

9. Ibid., 3.12.

10. Johann Peter Kirsch, "Pope St. Julius I," in *The Catholic Encyclopedia,* vol. 8 (New York: Robert Appleton, 1910), accessed June 2, 2014, http://www.newadvent.org/cathen/08561a.htm.

11. Sozomen, *Ecclesiastical History* 3.13.

12. Jerome, *Dialogue Against the Luciferians* 19, trans. W. H. Fremantle,

G. Lewis, and W. G. Martley, in *Nicene and Post-Nicene Fathers*, 2nd Series, vol. 6, eds. Philip Schaff and Henry Wace (Buffalo: Christian Literature, 1893), http://www.newadvent.org/fathers/3005.htm.

13. Sozomen, *Ecclesiastical History* 5.5.

14. Julian, quoted in Peter Brown, *The World of Late Antiquity* (New York: W. W. Norton, 1989), 93.

15. Sozomen, *Ecclesiastical History* 5.18.

16. Ibid., 5.10.

17. Theodoret, *Ecclesiastical History* 3.18–19.

18. Ibid., 3.20.

19. Sozomen, *Ecclesiastical History* 6.4.

20. Ibid., 6.6.

21. Ibid., 6.7.

22. Gregory Nazianzus, *Oratio* 43.30, trans. Charles Gordon Browne and James Edward Swallow, in *Nicene and Post-Nicene Fathers*, 2nd series, vol. 7, eds. Philip Schaff and Henry Wace (Buffalo: Christian Literature, 1894), rev. and ed. for New Advent by Kevin Knight, http://www.newadvent.org/fathers/310243.htm.

23. Theodoret, *Ecclesiastical History* 4.21.

24. Sozomen, *Ecclesiastical History* 6.18.

25. Theodoret, *Ecclesiastical History* 4.19.

26. Ibid., 4.18.

27. Ibid., 4.19.

28. Ibid.

29. Sozomen, *Ecclesiastical History* 6.20.

30. Thodoret, *Ecclesiastical History* 4.17.

31. Gregory Nazianzus, *Oratio* 43.24.

32. Basil of Caesarea, *Epistle* 223.2, trans. Blomfield Jackson, in *Nicene and Post-Nicene Fathers*, 2nd series, vol. 8, eds. Philip Schaff and Henry Wace (Buffalo: Christian Literature, 1895), rev. and ed. for New Advent by Kevin Knight, http://www.newadvent.org/fathers/3202223.htm.

33. Gregory Nazianzus, *Oration* 43.40.

34. Basil, *Epistle* 46.6.

35. Ibid., 106.

36. Sozomen, *Ecclesiastical History* 6.16.

37. Ibid., 5.18.

38. Theodoret, *Ecclesiastical History* 4.16.

39. Sozomen, *Ecclesiastical History* 6.16.

40. See Gregory of Nazianzus, *Oratio* 43.

41. Socrates Scholasticus, *Ecclesiastical History* 4.26, http://www.newadvent .org/fathers/26014.htm.

42. Ibid.

43. Gregory Nazianzus, *Letter* 2.71, trans. Charles Gordon Browne and James Edward Swallow, in *Nicene and Post-Nicene Fathers*, 2nd series, vol. 7, eds. Philip Schaff and Henry Wace (Buffalo: Christian Literature, 1894), rev. and ed. for New Advent by Kevin Knight, http://www.newadvent.org /fathers/310202.htm.

44. Gregory Nazianzus, *Oration* 43.43.

45. Theodoret, *Ecclesiastical History* 4.31.

46. Ibid.

PART 10: DOCTORS' ORDERS

1. Jerome, preface to his *Commentary on Ezekiel*, bk. 3, trans. James Harvey Robinson, *Readings in European History*, vol. 1 (Boston: Ginn, 1904), 45. Accessed via Internet Archive, June 6, 2015, https://archive.org/details /readingsineurope005820mbp.

2. Theodoret, *Ecclesiastical History* 5.6.

3. Socrates Scholasticus, *Ecclesiastical History* 5.2, trans. A. C. Zenos, in *Nicene and Post-Nicene Fathers*, 2nd series, vol. 2, eds. Philip Schaff and Henry Wace (Buffalo: Christian Literature, 1890), rev. and ed. for New Advent by Kevin Knight, http://www.newadvent.org/fathers/26015.htm.

4. *The Edict of Thessalonica*, trans. Sidney Z. Ehler and John B. Morrall, in *Church and State Through the Centuries, A Collection of Historic Documents* (New York: Biblo and Tannen, 1967), 7.

5. Sozomen, *Ecclesiastical History* 7.6, trans. Chester D. Hartranft, in *Post-Nicene Fathers*, 2nd series, vol. 2, eds. Philip Schaff and Henry Wace (Buffalo: Christian Literature, 1890), http://www.newadvent.org/fathers /26027.htm.

6. Ibid.

7. Theodoret, *Ecclesiastical History* 5.8.

8. Gregory Nazianzus, *Oration* 42.

9. Sozomen, *Ecclesiastical History* 7.9.

10. Socrates Scholasticus, *Ecclesiastical History* 5.8.

11. Sozomen, *Ecclesiastical History* 7.12.

12. Socrates Scholasticus, *Ecclesiastical History* 5.16.

13. Theodoret, *Ecclesiastical History* 5.22.

14. It appears that Milan was one of the very few exceptions to the relative absence of Arianism in the West at the time. Sozomen (6.24) claimed that "with the solitary exception of Auxentius and his partisans, there were no individuals among them who entertained heterodox opinions."

15. Paulinus, *Life of Ambrose*, ch. 3, unknown translation hosted by Professor Christopher Haas, Villanova University, accessed June 20, 2014, http://www29 .homepage.villanova.edu/christopher.haas/Life%20of%20Ambrose.html.

16. Augustine, *Confessions* 6.3, trans. J. G. Pilkington, in *Nicene and Post-Nicene Fathers*, 1st series, vol. 1., ed. Philip Schaff (Buffalo: Christian Literature, 1887), http://www.newadvent.org/fathers/110106.htm, rev. and ed. for New Advent by Kevin Knight.

17. Ambrose, *On the Duties of Clergy* 2.28.131, trans. H. de Romestin, E. de Romestin, and H. T. F. Duckworth, in *Nicene and Post-Nicene Fathers*, 2nd series, vol. 10, eds. Philip Schaff and Henry Wace (Buffalo: Christian Literature, 1896), rev. and ed. for New Advent by Kevin Knight, http://www.newadvent.org/fathers/3401.htm.

18. Ambrose, in Justo González, *The Story of Christianity*, vol. 1 (New York: Harper and Row, 1984), 191.

19. Ambrose, *Concerning Virginity* 2.1, trans. H. de Romestin, E. de Romestin, and H. T. F. Duckworth, in *Nicene and Post-Nicene Fathers*, 2nd series, vol. 10, eds. Philip Schaff and Henry Wace (Buffalo: Christian Literature, 1896), rev. and ed. for New Advent by Kevin Knight, http://www.newadvent.org/fathers/34072.htm.

20. Vincent A. Lenti, "Saint Ambrose, the Father of Western Hymnody," *The Hymn* 48, no. 4 (October 1997), 47, http://www.hymnary.org/files /articles/Lenti,%20Saint%20Ambrose,%20the%20Father%20of%20 Western%20Hymnody.pdf.

21. William Morton Reynolds, "Come Thou Savior of Our Race," in *Hymns, Original and Selected, for Public and Private Worship, in the Evangelical Church* (General Synod of the Lutheran Church, 1852).

22. Ambrose, *The Proceedings of the Council of Aquileia Against the Heretics Palladius and Secundianus*, in Saint Ambrose of Milan, *Letters*, ed. and trans. James Parker et al. (London: Oxford University Press, 1881), accessed June 20, 2014, http://www.tertullian.org/fathers/ambrose _letters_01_letters01_10.htm.

23. Theodoret, *Ecclesiastical History* 5.13.

24. As quoted in Ruth A. Tucker, *Parade of Faith: A Biographical History of the Christian Church* (Grand Rapids: Zondervan, 2011), 77.

25. Ambrose, *Against Auxentius* 36, in Louis J. Swift, "Ambrose," in Ferguson, ed., *Encyclopedia*, 43.

26. Theodoret, *Ecclesiastical History* 5.17.

27. Ibid.

28. Sozomen, *Ecclesiastical History* 7.25.

29. Theodoret, *Ecclesiastical History* 5.17.

30. Ibid.

31. Ambrose, *Letter* 51.3.

32. Theodoret, *Ecclesiastical History*, 5.17.

33. Ibid.

34. Ibid.

35. Jerome, *Letters*, 22.30, 22.28, trans. W. H. Fremantle, G. Lewis, and W. G. Martley, in *Nicene and Post-Nicene Fathers*, 2nd series, vol. 6, eds. Philip Schaff and Henry Wace (Buffalo: Christian Literature, 1893), rev. and ed. for New Advent by Kevin Knight, http://www.newadvent.org/fathers/3001022.htm.

36. Ibid., 22.30.

37. Ibid., 22.7.

38. Jerome, *Letters* 61.2, http://www.newadvent.org/fathers/3001061.htm.

39. See Michael P. McHugh, "Damasus I," in Ferguson, ed., *Encyclopedia of Early Christianity*, 316.

40. Ibid. An Apostolic See denotes a bishopric whose foundation purports to be traced back to an apostle of Jesus.

41. Unfortunately, Auxentius refused to resign, and actually held the episcopate until he died in 374, at which point Ambrose obtained it.

42. Theodoret, *Ecclesiastical History* 5.10.

43. Jerome, *Letters* 15.

44. Jerome, *Letter to Pope Damasus: Preface to the Gospels*, trans. Kevin P. Edgecomb, accessed June 20, 2014, http://www.tertullian.org/fathers/jerome_preface_gospels.htm#1.

45. Jerome, *Letters* 39.5.

46. Ibid., 71.5.

47. Jerome, *Preface to the Chronicle of Eusebius* 1.1, trans. W. H. Fremantle, G. Lewis, and W. G. Martley, in *Nicene and Post-Nicene Fathers*, 2nd series,

vol. 6, eds. Philip Schaff and Henry Wace (Buffalo: Christian Literature, 1893), rev. and ed. for New Advent by Kevin Knight, http://www .newadvent.org/fathers/3002.htm.

48. C. G. Richards, ed., *A Concise Dictionary to the Vulgate New Testament* (London: Bigster and Sons, 1934), viii, accessed June 29, 2015, http:// www.bible-researcher.com/vulgate.diction.pdf.

49. "Canons and Decrees of the Council of Trent, The Fourth Session Celebrated on the eighth day of the month of April, in the year 1546," trans. James Waterworth (London: 1848), http://www.bible-researcher .com/trent1.html.

50. Joseph Pohle, "Pelagius and Pelagianism" in *The Catholic Encyclopedia*, vol. 11 (New York: Robert Appleton, 1911), accessed June 20, 2014. http://www.newadvent.org/cathen/11604a.htm.

PART 11: TWO GIANTS

1. Sozomen, *Ecclesiastical History* 8.1, trans. Chester D. Hartranft, in *Post-Nicene Fathers*, 2nd series, vol. 2, eds. Philip Schaff and Henry Wace (Buffalo: Christian Literature, 1890), rev. and ed. for New Advent by Kevin Knight, http://www.newadvent.org/fathers/26028.htm.

2. Ibid., 8.2.

3. Ibid.

4. Palladius, *Dialogue of John Chrysostom*, chap. 5, trans. Herbert Moore, 1921 (public domain), accessed February 5, 2015, http://www.tertullian .org/fathers/palladius_dialogus_02_text.htm#C5.

5. See John Chrysostom, *Homilies on the Statues*.

6. Sozomen, *Ecclesiastical History* 8.2.

7. John Chrysostom, *On the Gospel of Saint Matthew*, 50.3–4, trans. George Prevost, rev. M. B. Riddle, in *Nicene and Post-Nicene Fathers*, 1st series, vol. 10, ed. Philip Schaff (Buffalo: Christian Literature, 1888), rev. and ed. for New Advent by Kevin Knight, http://www.newadvent.org/fathers /200150.htm.

8. Palladius, *Dialogue*, 5.

9. Sozomen, *Ecclesiastical History* 8.2.

10. Palladius, *Dialogue*, 5.

11. Ibid.

12. Ibid.

13. A kind of white sash worn draped over the shoulders.

14. Palladius, *Dialogue*, 6.

15. Sozomen, *Ecclesiastical History* 8.13.

16. Palladius, *Dialogue* 8.

17. Ibid.

18. Ibid.

19. Sozomen, *Ecclesiastical History* 8.20.

20. Ibid., 8.22.

21. Palladius, *Dialogue* 10.

22. Sozomen, *Ecclesiastical History* 8.22.

23. Palladius, *Dialogue* 11.

24. Augustine, *Confessions* 1.11, http://www.newadvent.org/fathers/110101
.htm.

25. Ibid., 12.33.

26. Ibid., 2.6.

27. Ibid.

28. Ibid., 3.1.

29. Ibid., 3.5.

30. Ibid., 3.6.

31. Ibid., 3.12.

32. Ibid., 4.1.

33. Ibid., 4.4.

34. Ibid., 5.8.

35. Ibid., 5.8.

36. Ibid., 5.13.

37. Ibid.

38. Ibid., 8.7.

39. Ibid., 8.8.

40. Ibid., 8.12.

41. Ibid., 9.12.

42. Possidius, *Life of Augustine* 22, trans. Herbert Theberath Weiskotten,
1919, accessed February 5, 2015, http://www.tertullian.org/fathers
/possidius_life_of_augustine_02_text.htm#C18.

43. Ibid., 24.

44. Ibid., 22.

45. Ibid., 24.

46. Ibid., 27.

47. Margaret R. Miles, "Augustine," in Ferguson, ed., *Encyclopedia of Early Christianity*, 150.

48. Augustine, *City of God* 18.53, trans. Henry Bettenson (New York: Penguin, 1981), 838.

49. Ibid., 3.2.

50. Ibid., 5.10.

51. See, for instance, *On the Proceedings of Pelagius*, trans. Peter Holmes and Robert Ernest Wallis, rev. by Benjamin B. Warfield, in *Nicene and Post-Nicene Fathers*, 1st series, vol. 5, ed. Philip Schaff (Buffalo: Christian Literature, 1887), rev. and ed. for New Advent by Kevin Knight, http://www.newadvent .org/fathers/1505.htm; and *Against Two Letters of the Pelagians*, http://www .freecatholicbooks.com/books/AgainstTwoLettersothePelagians.pdf.

52. See Augustine, *On Baptism, Against the Donatists*, trans. J. R. King and rev. by Chester D. Hartranft, in *Nicene and Post-Nicene Fathers*, 1st series, vol. 4, ed. Philip Schaff (Buffalo: Christian Literature, 1887), rev. and ed. for New Advent by Kevin Knight, http://www.newadvent.org/fathers /1408.htm.

53. Miles, "Augustine," in Ferguson, ed., *Encyclopedia*, 152.

54. Ibid., 153.

PART 12: FROM ANCIENT TO MEDIEVAL

1. *The Gallic Chronicle*, 408.13–16, ed. and trans. A. C. Murray in A. C. Murray, *From Roman to Merovingian Gaul* (Toronto: Broadview Press, 2000), 76.

2. Procopius of Caesaria, *History of the Wars* 3.2.7–39, trans. H. B. Dewing (Cambridge, MA, and London: Harvard University Press and Wm. Heinemann, 1914), accessed June 15, 2015 via Project Gutenberg, http://www.gutenberg.org/files/16765/16765-h/16765-h.htm.

3. Socrates Scholasticus, *Ecclesiastical History* 7.10, trans. A.C. Zenos, in *Nicene and Post-Nicene Fathers*, 2nd series, vol. 2, eds. Philip Schaff and Henry Wace (Buffalo: Christian Literature, 1890), rev. and ed. for New Advent by Kevin Knight, http://www.newadvent.org/fathers/26017.htm.

4. Ammianus Marcellinus, *Res Gestae* 14.16, in ed. William Stearns Davis, *Readings in Ancient History: Illustrative Extracts from the Sources*, vol. 2 (Boston: Allyn and Bacon, 1912–13), 306.

5. Hydatius, *Chronicle*, Olympiad 297ff., ed. and trans. R. W. Burgess, in *The Chronicle of Hydatius and the Consularia Constantinopolitana* (Oxford: Oxford University Press, 1994), 83.

6. Socrates Scholasticus, *Ecclesiastical History* 7.22.

7. Ibid.

8. Ibid., 7.18.

9. Ibid., 7.21.

10. See the *Code of Justinian* 1.2.4.

11. See the *Code of Theodosius* 15.5.5.

12. Ibid., 16.2.47.

13. Ibid., 9.16.12.

14. Socrates Scholasticus, *Ecclesiastical History* 7.29.

15. Ibid.

16. Ibid., 7.32.

17. Ibid.

18. Ibid., 7.31.

19. Ibid.

20. James Craigie Robertson, *History of the Christian Church* (London: J. Murray, 1854), 405.

21. Cyril of Jerusalem, *Letter to Celestine*, eds. P. E. and E. B. Busey (Oxford: James Parker, 1881), accessed July 22, 2014, http://www.tertullian.org /fathers/cyril_against_nestorius_00_intro.htm.

22. "Decree of the Council against Nestorius," at CCEL, accessed July 21, 2014, http://www.ccel.org/ccel/schaff/npnf214.x.xi.html.

23. Council of Ephesus, canon 7, trans. Henry Percival, in *Nicene and Post-Nicene Fathers*, 2nd series, vol. 14, eds. Philip Schaff and Henry Wace (Buffalo: Christian Literature, 1900), rev. and ed. for New Advent by Kevin Knight, http://www.newadvent.org/fathers/3810.htm.

24. Pope John Paul II, "Common Christological Declaration Between the Catholic Church and the Assyrian Church of the East" address delivered at Saint Peter's Basilica, Rome, November 11, 1994, accessed June 29, 2015. http://www.vatican.va/roman_curia/pontifical_councils/chrstuni /documents/rc_pc_chrstuni_doc_11111994_assyrian-church_en.html.

25. Socrates Scholasticus, *Ecclesiastical History* 7.15.

26. Ibid.

27. Ibid., 7.14.

28. Ibid.

29. Ibid., 7.15.

30. Jordanes, *An Account of the Person of Attila*, in Davis, ed., *Readings*, 322.

31. Callinicus, *Life of Saint Hypatius*, in Patrick Howarth, *Attila: King of the Huns: The Man and the Myth* (New York, Basic Books, 2001), 49.

32. *Leo I and Attila*, from accounts translated in J. H. Robinson, *Readings in European History* (Boston: Ginn, 1905), 50.

33. Ibid.

34. Jordanes, *An Account of the Life of Attila*, in Sterns, *Readings in Ancient History*, 324.

35. Johann Peter Kirsch, "Pope St. Leo I (the Great)," in *The Catholic Encyclopedia*, vol. 9 (New York: Robert Appleton, 1910), http://www.newadvent.org/cathen/09154b.htm.

36. Leo I, *Letter* 4, trans. Charles Lett Feltoe, in *Nicene and Post-Nicene Fathers*, 2nd series, vol. 12, eds. Philip Schaff and Henry Wace (Buffalo: Christian Literature, 1895), rev. and ed. for New Advent by Kevin Knight, http://www.newadvent.org/fathers/3604004.htm.

37. Ibid., 7.1.

38. Leo the Great, *Sermon* 82, trans. Charles Lett Feltoe, in *Nicene and Post-Nicene Fathers*, 2nd series, vol. 12, eds. Philip Schaff and Henry Wace (Buffalo: Christian Literature, 1895), rev. and ed. for New Advent by Kevin Knight, http://www.newadvent.org/fathers/360382.htm.

39. Pope Leo I, *Letter* 9.

40. Ibid., 28, "The Tome."

41. Ibid.

Part 13: Christianity in the Early Barbarian Kingdoms: The Barbarians Become Arians

1. Orosius, *History Against the Pagans*, as quoted in Justo González, *The Story of Christianity*, vol. 1 (New York: Harper and Row, 2010), 232.

2. Sozomen, *Ecclesiastical History* 6.38, trans. Chester D. Hartranft, in *Post-Nicene Fathers*, 2nd series, vol. 2, eds. Philip Schaff and Henry Wace (Buffalo: Christian Literature, 1890), http://www.newadvent.org/fathers/26026.htm.

3. Victor of Vita, *History of the Vandal Persecution* 22, ed. and trans. John Moorhead (Liverpool: Liverpool University Press, 1992), 11.

4. Ibid., 24–26.

5. González, *The Story of Christianity*, 232–33.

6. Jacob Marcus, *The Jew in the Medieval World: A Sourcebook, 315–1791* (New York: JPS, 1938), 20–23, in Fordham University *Medieval*

Sourcebook, accessed August 25, 2014, http://www.fordham.edu/halsall/jewish/jews-visigothic1.asp.

7. Clifford Backman, *The Worlds of Medieval Europe* (New York: Oxford University Press, 2003), 64.

8. Steven A. Barney, W. J. Lewis, et al., *The Etymologies of Isidore of Seville* (Cambridge: Cambridge University Press, 2006), 109.

9. John Bonaventure O'Connor, "St. Isidore of Seville" in *The Catholic Encyclopedia*, vol. 8 (New York: Robert Appleton, 1910), accessed August 26, 2014, http://www.newadvent.org/cathen/08186a.htm.

10. King Theodoric, *Letter* 2.7, ed. and trans. Thomas Hodgkin, in *Letters of Cassiodorus* (London: H. Frowde, 1886), accessed July 1, 2015 via Project Gutenberg, http://www.gutenberg.org/files/18590/18590-h/18590-h.htm.

11. King Theodoric, *Letter to the Senate of the City of Rome*, 2.22, ed. Hodgkin, accessed August 26, 2014.

12. Boethius, *The Consolation of Philosophy*, bk. 5, song 3, trans. Henry Rosher James (London: Elliot Stock, 1897), 241.

13. Cassiodorus, *Letters* 1.2.

14. Ibid., 2.9.

15. Ibid., 4.7.

16. Cassiodorus, *Institutes* 1.1, trans. James W. and Barbara Halporn, accessed August 26, 2014, http://faculty.georgetown.edu/jod/inst-trans.html.

17. Ibid.

18. Ibid., 1.2.

19. Cassiodorus, *Variae* 9.7, ed. Thomas Hodgkin, in *The Letters of Cassiodorus* (London: Henry Frowde, 1886), accessed August 26, 2014, http://www.gutenberg.org/files/18590/18590-h/18590-h.htm.

20. Gregory of Tours, *History of the Franks*, in J. H. Robinson, *Readings in European History*, vol. 1 (Boston: Ginn, 1905).

21. Ibid., 53. Text modernized by the author.

22. Ibid., 53–54. Text has been modernized by the author.

23. Ibid., 54.

24. This mass baptism happened without any theological instruction, and it is highly doubtful that many of these men were truly converted.

25. Jonas the Monk, *Life of St. Columban* 7, ed. Dana C. Munro, *Translations and Reprints from the Original Sources of European History*, vol. 2, no. 7 (Philadelphia: University of Pennsylvania Press, 1897–1907), in Fordham University *Medieval Sourcebook*, accessed August 26, 2014, http://www.fordham.edu/Halsall/basis/columban.asp.

26. Ibid., 8.

27. Ibid., 9.

28. Ibid., 49.

29. John Calvin, *Institutes of the Christian Religion*, bk. 4, ed. F. L. Cross (New York: Oxford University Press, n.d.).

30. The other being Leo the Great, who is profiled in chapter 12.

31. Bede, *Ecclesiastical History of the English People*, 2.1, ed. D. Farmer, trans. Leo Sherley-Price (London: Penguin UK, 2003).

32. Pope Gregory the Great, *Letter* 1.5, in Jeffrey Richards, *Consul of God: The Life and Times of Gregory the Great* (London/Boston: Routledge and Kegan Paul, 1980), 42–43.

33. Bede, *Ecclesiastical History* 2.1.

34. Paul the Deacon, *History of the Lombards* 4.5–9, in William Stearns Davis, ed., *Readings in Ancient History: Illustrative Extracts from the Sources*, vol. 2 (Boston: Allyn and Bacon, 1912–1913), 369.

35. Gregory the Great, *Letter* 9.76, trans. James Barmby, in *Nicene and Post-Nicene Fathers*, 2nd series, vol. 13, eds. Philip Schaff and Henry Wace (Buffalo: Christian Literature, 1898), http://www.newadvent.org/fathers/360211076.htm.

36. Gregory, *Letter* 76, in Clifford Backman, *The Worlds of Medieval Europe* (New York: Oxford University Press, 2003), 66.

37. Bede, *Ecclesiastical History* 2.1.

38. Gildas, *Works* 9, in J. A. Giles *Six Old English Chronicles* (London: G. Bell & Sons, 1891), 302.

39. Bede, *Ecclesiastical History* 2.1.

40. Ibid.

41. Ibid.

42. Gildas, *History* 12.

43. Ibid.

44. Ibid., 1.19.

45. Ibid., 1.20.

46. Backman, *Worlds of Medieval Europe*, 91.

47. Bede, *Ecclesiastical History* 2.1.

48. Not to be confused with the great Saint Augustine of Hippo.

49. Bede, *Ecclesiastical History* 1.23.

50. Ibid.

51. Ibid., 1.25.

52. Ibid.

53. Ibid., 1.26.

54. Ibid., 1.29.

55. Saint Patrick, *Confessions* 16, posted in Christian Classics Ethereal Library, accessed August 26, 2014, http://www.ccel.org/ccel/patrick/confession.iv.html.

56. Ibid., 17, in CCEL, http://www.ccel.org/ccel/patrick/confession.v.html.

57. Ibid., 23, in CCEL, http://www.ccel.org/ccel/patrick/confession.vi.html.

58. Ibid., 50, in CCEL, http://www.ccel.org/ccel/patrick/confession.x.html.

59. For these references and Columba generally, see Edward Alexander Cooke, *Saint Columba: His Life and Work* (Edinburgh: St. Giles, 1893).

PART 14: THE BYZANTINE EMPIRE

1. Byzantium was the original Greek name for the city founded on the Bosphorus strait, a city now called Istanbul. Additionally, though many think *Istanbul* is a Turkish or Arabic word, in reality it is a portmanteau (combination) of the Greek words *eis ton polon*: "toward the city." Such was the fame of the great city of Constantinople that it simply became known as "the city." The Eastern Roman Empire was not remembered in the West as the Byzantine Empire until 1557.

2. Procopius, *The Secret History* 8.22, trans. H. B. Dewing (Cambridge, MA: Harvard University Press, 1935), accessed via LacusCurtius, June 12, 2015, http://penelope.uchicago.edu/Thayer/E/Roman/Texts /Procopius/Anecdota/home.html.

3. Ibid., 18.20.

4. Procopius, *History of the Wars* 1.22.7, trans. H. B. Dewing in *Loeb Library of the Greek and Roman Classics* (Cambridge, MA: Harvard University Press, 1914), 451–73, accessed via Project Gutenberg, June 12, 2015, http://www.gutenberg.org/files/16764/16764-h/16764-h.htm.

5. Evagrius Scholasticus, *Ecclesiastical History* 4.29, trans. E. Walford, 1846, available at Tertullian.org, accessed September 13, 2014, http://www .tertullian.org/fathers/evagrius_4_book4.htm.

6. Procopius, *History of the Wars* 1.23.4.

7. Ibid., 2.22.10–15.

8. Procopius, *Secret History* 19.10.

9. Public horseracing track and all-around arena. *Hippos* is the Greek word for horse; *dromos* means "course." A "hippopotamus," then, is a "river-horse."

10. Procopius, *Secret History* 9.

11. Procopius, *Wars* 1.24.
12. Procopius, *Buildings* 1.1.22, trans. H. B. Dewing (Cambridge, MA: Loeb Classical Library, 1940), accessed via LacusCurtius, June 16, 2015, http://penelope.uchicago.edu/Thayer/E/Roman/Texts/Procopius /Buildings/home.html.
13. Ibid., 1.1.23.
14. Ibid., 1.1.48.
15. Ibid., 1.1.29.
16. Ibid., 1.1.61.
17. *The Institutes of Justinian*, trans. B. Moyle, 3rd ed. (Oxford: Oxford University Press, 1896), 3–5, in Fordham University *Medieval Sourcebook*, accessed September 13, 2014, http://www.fordham.edu/Halsall/source /corpus1.asp.
18. Justinian, *Novel* 137, trans. S. P. Scott in *The Civil Law*, vol. 17 (Cincinnati: 1932), 152–56, in Fordham University *Medieval Sourcebook*, accessed September 13, 2014, http://www.fordham.edu/Halsall/source /justinian-nov137.asp.
19. Facundus of Hermione, *In Defense of the Three Chapters* 12.3, trans. Francis Dvornik, *Early Christian and Byzantine Political Philosophy: Origins and Background II* (Washington, D.C.: Dumbarton Oaks Press, 1966), 826.
20. *The Code of Justinian* I.11.1–2, trans. S. P. Scott, in *The Civil Law* (Cincinnati: Central Trust, 1932), 79.
21. John of Ephesus, *Ecclesiastical History,* fragment, trans. Maas, in Michael Maas, *Readings in Late Antiquity: A Sourcebook* (New York: Routledge, 2010), 186.
22. Evagrius Scholasticus, *Ecclesiastical History* 4.39.
23. Ibid., 5.1.
24. Antiochus Strategos, *The Capture of Jerusalem by the Persians in 614 AD,* trans. F. C. Conybeare, *English Historical Review* 25 (1910): 502–17, accessed September 13, 2014, http://www.tertullian.org/fathers/antiochus _strategos_capture.htm.
25. Sebeos, *History* 29.99, trans. Robert Bedrosian, in *Sebeos' History* (New York: Sources of the Armenian Tradition, 1985), 115–16.
26. John Chapman, "St. Maximus of Constantinople," in *The Catholic Encyclopedia*, vol. 10 (New York: Robert Appleton, 1911), accessed September 13, 2014, http://www.newadvent.org/cathen/10078b.htm.

Part 15: Crescent and Cross

1. Nadia Maria El-Cheikh, "Muhammad and Heraclius: A Study in Legitimacy," *Studia Islamica* no. 89 (1999): 5–21, accessed October 18, 2014, http://www.jstor.org/stable/1596083.

2. Ibid.

3. Theophanes the Confessor, *Chronicle* AM6122, trans. Cyril Mango and Roger Scott (Oxford: Clarendon Press, 1997), 464–65.

4. E.g., Qu'ran, Sura 4.171.

5. E.g., Qu'ran, Sura 112.1–4.

6. See, for example, the tenth-century history *Tarikh al-Tabari*.

7. Abu Huraira, *Sahih Al-Bukhari*, vol. 5, bk. 58, no. 234, in Sam Shamoun and Jochen Katz, "Muhammad and the Issue of Plagiarism," Answering-Islam.org, accessed October 18, 2014, http://www.answering-islam.org /Responses/Menj/mhd_plagiarizing.htm.

8. Translation of the Qu'ran accessed via Quran.com, accessed June 16, 2015, http://quran.com/about.

9. Abu Huraira, *Sahih Al-Bukhari*, vol. 9, bk. 93, no. 589, in Sam Shamoun and Jochen Katz, "Muhammad and the Issue of Plagiarism," Answering-Islam.org, accessed October 18, 2014, http://www.answering-islam.org /Responses/Menj/mhd_plagiarizing.htm.

10. Robert Spencer, "Scholar Researches the Koran, Fears for His Life," Jihad Watch, March 18, 2004, http://www.jihadwatch.org/2004/03 /scholar-researches-origins-of-the-quran-fears-for-his-life.

11. The succession crisis of early Islam revolved around whether the heir to Muhammad should be chosen from the Qur'ayash tribe by the whole community (the Sunni belief), or whether he should be a direct descendant of Muhammad (Shi'i).

12. Fred Donner, *The Early Islamic Conquests* (Princeton: Princeton University Press, 1981), 251.

13. Qu'ran, Sura 47, in Demetrios Constantelos, "Greek Christian and Other Accounts of the Muslim Conquest of the Near East," in Andrew Bostom, ed., *The Legacy of Jihad* (Amherst, New York: Prometheus Books), 399.

14. *Homily on the Child Saints of Babylon* 36, trans. DeVis, 99–100, in Robert Hoyland, *Seeing Islam as Others Saw It: A Survey and Evaluation of Christian, Jewish and Zoroastrian Writings on Early Islam* (Princeton, NJ: Darwin Press, 1998), 121.

15. Constantelos, "Greek Christian" in Bostom, *The Legacy of Jihad*, 387.

16. Many early Christians (and Islamic tradition) believed that Muslims were the direct descendants of Ishmael, the son of Abraham conceived by Hagar.

17. John of Nikiu, *Chronicle* 111.9, ed. and trans. R. H. Charles (London: Williams and Northgate, 1916), accessed October 18, 2014, http://www.tertullian.org/fathers/nikiu2_chronicle.htm.

18. Theophanes, *Chronicle*, 416.

19. Constantelos, "Greek Christian" in Bostam, *The Legacy of Jihad*, 392.

20. Ibid., 388.

21. Primary and secondary sources vary wildly in their estimation of the size of Heraclius's force, but it seems likely Heraclius commanded an unusually huge number. He may have commanded up to 200,000 troops, according to Islamic sources, but that count seems inflated.

22. *Kitab Futuh al-Buldha* of Ahmad ibn Jabir al-Baladhuri, trans. P. K. Hitti and F. C. Murgotten, *Studies in History, Economics and Public Law* 68 (New York: Columbia University Press, 1916, 1924), 207–11, hosted at Fordham University *Medieval Sourcebook*, accessed October 18, 2014, http://www.fordham.edu/Halsall/source/Yarmouk.asp.

23. Nadia Maria El-Cheikh, *Byzantium Viewed by the Arabs* (Cambridge, MA: Harvard University Press, 2004), 42.

24. The traditional Greek name for Arabs from the Arabian Peninsula.

25. Sophronius, *Ep. Synodica, Patrologica Greca* 87, 3197D–3200A, in Hoyland, *Seeing Islam*, 69.

26. Sophronius, *Holy Baptism* 162, in Hoyland, *Seeing Islam*, 72–73.

27. The Pact of Umar, no source of text or translation given. Hosted at Fordham University *Medieval Sourcebook*, accessed October 18, 2014, http://www.fordham.edu/halsall/source/pact-umar.asp.

28. John Monachos, *Narratio*, PG 109, col. 517.2, in Constantelos, "Greek Christian."

29. Constantelos, "Greek Christian," in Bostom, *The Legacy of Jihad*, 392. Today, the Islamic State in Iraq and Syria (ISIS) gives religious minorities the choice of converting to Islam, going into exile, or paying the *jizya* tax. The alternative is to be killed.

30. Theophanes, *Chronicle*, cited in Constantelos, "Greek Christian," in Bostom, *Legacy*, 390.

31. Constantelos, "Greek Christian," in Bostom, *Legacy*, 392.

32. Timothy, in Samuel Hugh Moffett, *A History of Christianity in Asia*, vol. 1 (Maryknoll, NY: Orbis Books, 1992), 352.

33. Ibid., 353.

34. Ibid., 349.

35. Ibid., 350–51.

36. Ibn Abd-el-Hakem, *History of the Conquest of Spain*, trans. John Harris Jones (Gottingen, W. Fr. Kaestner, 1858), 18–22.

37. Isidore of Beja, *Chronicle*, in William Stearns Davis, ed., *Readings in Ancient History: Illustrative Extracts from the Sources*, vol. 2 (Boston: Allyn and Bacon, 1912–13), 363.

38. Scimitars, or swords.

39. Anonymous Chronicle in Edward Creasy, *Fifteen Decisive Battles of the World* (New York: E. P. Dutton, 1852), 168–69.

40. Musa the Arab Chronicler of Spain, in Stearns Davis, ed., *Readings in Ancient History*, 362.

41. Isidore of Beja, *Chronicle*, in Davis, ed., *Readings in Ancient History*, 363.

42. St. Denis, *Chronicle*, in Davis, ed., *Readings in Ancient History*, 364.

Part 16: Europe Is Born

1. Pope Gregory II, *Letter* to Charles Martel, in Oliver J. Thatcher and Edgar Holmes McNeal, eds., *A Source Book for Medieval History* (New York: Scribners, 1905), 102, accessed October 18, 2014 at Project Gutenberg, http://www.gutenberg.org/files/42707/42707-h/42707-h.htm.

2. Pope Gregory II, Letter 9, ed. Tangl, translator unknown. Hosted at the Catholic University of America, accessed June 18, 2015, http://faculty.cua.edu/pennington/churchhistory220/LectureTwo /BonifaceLetters.html.

3. Willibald, *The Life of St. Boniface* 1, in C. H. Talbot, *The Anglo-Saxon Missionaries in Germany* (London and New York: Sheed and Ward, 1954).

4. Ibid., 3.

5. Ibid., 4.

6. Ibid., 5.

7. Ibid., 6.

8. Boniface, *Letters*, 10, in Talbot, *The Anglo-Saxon Missionaries in Germany*.

9. Ibid., 30.

10. Ibid.

11. Willibald, *Life of Boniface*, 8.

12. Scholars are conflicted on whether Pepin was actually shorter than the average man. There is a good possibility that the man we know as Pepin the Short was confused with another Pepin from the period, and wrongly was assigned his nickname by an eleventh-century writer.

13. *Encyclopedia Britannica Online*, s.v. "Pippin III," accessed October 18, 2014, http://www.britannica.com/EBchecked/topic/450778/Pippin-III.

14. Ibid.

15. *The Donation of Constantine*, trans. Ernest F. Henderson, in *Select Historical Documents of the Middle Ages* (London: George Bell, 1892), 319–29.

16. Einhard, *Life of Charlemagne* 25, trans. Samuel Epes Turner (New York: Harper & Brothers, 1880).

17. Ibid., 25.

18. Ibid., 24.

19. Ibid., 7.

20. Clifford Backman, *The Worlds of Medieval Europe* (New York: Oxford University Press, 2003), 117.

21. Einhard, *Life of Charlemagne*, 26.

22. Ibid., 27.

23. Backman, *The Worlds of Medieval Europe*, 130.

24. Ibid.

25. Einhard, *Life of Charlemagne*, 25.

26. J. J. O'Connor and E. F. Robertson, "Propositiones ad acuendos iuvenes by Alcuin," accessed October 18, 2014, http://www-history.mcs.st-and.ac.uk/HistTopics/Alcuin_book.html. Answer: "Suppose there are x men, y women, and z children. Then $x + y + z = 30$ and $6x + 4y + z = 60$. Then $x = 3$ and $z = 22$ so there are 3 men, 5 women and 22 children who are servants in the household."

27. Ibid. Answer: "Of course the problem has no solution since the sum of three odd numbers can never be even." Alcuin suggested giving this problem to children who have misbehaved!

28. Andrew Fleming West, *Alcuin and the Rise of Christian Schools* (New York: Charles Scribner's Sons, 1899), 48.

29. Ibid., 46.

30. Bobbio the Monk, in Ruth A. Tucker, *Parade of Faith: A Biographical History of the Christian Church* (Grand Rapids: Zondervan, 2011), 211.

31. J. J. O'Connor and E. F. Robertson, "Alcuin of York," accessed October 18, 2014, http://www-history.mcs.st-and.ac.uk/Biographies/Alcuin.html.

PART 17: DECLINE AND REFORM

1. Clifford Backman, *The Worlds of Medieval Europe* (New York: Oxford University Press, 2003), 143.
2. Ibid., 139. Original source unknown.
3. The reckoning of the calendar varied by place, and so there might be a legitimate difference of computation of the year in different kingdoms.
4. Raoul Glaber, *On the First Millennium*, from C. G. Coulton, ed., *Life in the Middle Ages*, vol. 1 (New York: Macmillan, c.1910), at Fordham University *Medieval Sourcebook*, January 3, 2015, http://legacy.fordham.edu/halsall/source/glaber-1000.asp.
5. Ibid.
6. Ralph Waldo Emerson, "Essay on Self-Reliance."
7. Glaber, *On the First Millennium*.
8. See the relationship between Pope Symmachus (489–514) and Antipope Laurentius.
9. *The Catholic Encyclopedia*, s.v. "Pope John VIII" (New York: Robert Appleton, 1910), accessed January 3, 2015, http://www.newadvent.org/cathen/08423c.htm.
10. Horace K. Mann, *The Lives of the Popes in the Early Middle Ages*, vol. 4, *The Popes in the Days of Feudal Anarchy, 891–999* (London: K. Paul, Trench, Trubner, 1902), accessed via Internet Archive, June 19, 2015, https://archive.org/details/popesearlymid04mannuoft.
11. Ferdinand Gregovarius, *The History of the City of Rome in the Middle Ages*, trans. Annie Hamilton (London: George Bell and Sons, 1896), 47.
12. Backman, *The Worlds of Medieval Europe*, 215–16.
13. Ibid., 210.
14. Lucy Margaret Smith, *The Early History of the Monastery of Cluny* (London: Oxford University Press, 1920), 27.
15. Thomas Oestereich, "Pope St. Boniface IV," in *The Catholic Encyclopedia*, vol. 2 (New York: Robert Appleton, 1907), accessed July 1, 2015, http://www.newadvent.org/cathen/02660c.htm.
16. Bede, *Ecclesiastical History of the English People* 4.2, ed. D. Farmer, trans. Leo Sherley-Price (London: Penguin UK, 2003).

17. Peter Brown, *The Rise of Western Christendom*, rev. ed. (Chichester, UK: Wiley & Sons, 2013), 370.

18. Ibid., 362.

Part 18: Northern Lights

1. *The Anglo-Saxon Chronicle, AD 793*, unknown edition and translation, posted on the Online Medieval and Classical Library, accessed December 4, 2014, http://omacl.org/Anglo/part2.html.

2. Clifford Backman, *The Worlds of Medieval Europe* (New York: Oxford University Press, 2003), 141.

3. Asser, *Life of Alfred*, trans. L. C. Jane (London: Chatto and Windus, 1908), 18.

4. Ibid., 20.

5. It is unclear why Ivar was named "the boneless." One supposition is that he was impotent. Another, more likely explanation is his physical flexibility, which proved an asset on the field of battle. Another suggestion is that he could not walk and had to be carried from place to place on his shield.

6. Asser, *Life of Alfred*, 30.

7. Ibid., 31.

8. See G. Craig, "Alfred the Great: A Diagnosis," *Journal of the Royal Society of Medicine* 84, no. 5 (May 1991): 303–5, http://www.ncbi.nlm.nih.gov/pmc/articles/PMC1293232/

9. Asser, *Life of Alfred*, 51.

10. Ibid., 55–56.

11. Ibid., 57.

12. Ibid., 71.

13. Ibid., 65.

14. Ibid., 88.

15. Alcuin of York, *Letter to Ethelred, King of Northumbria*, hosted at the website of the University of Chicago, accessed December 4, 2014, http://penelope.uchicago.edu/~grout/encyclopaedia_romana/britannia/anglo-saxon/lindisfarne/lindisfarne.html.

16. Gerald of Wales, *Topography of Ireland* 2.71, trans. J. O'Meara, in Brown, *Rise of Western Christendom*, 373.

17. *Beowulf* 1.786, trans. James Garnett (Boston: Ginn, 1892), 24.

18. Windukind of Covey, *Rerum Gestarum Saxonicarum Libri Tres*, in Richard

Fletcher, *The Barbarian Conversions* (Berkeley: University of California Press, 1999), 373.

19. Charles H. Robinson, *Anskar, the Apostle of the North, 801–865* (London, 1921), hosted at Fordham University *Medieval Sourcebook*, accessed February 17, 2015, http://legacy.fordham.edu/halsall/basis/anskar.asp#lifeans.

20. A coarse garment worn directly on the skin that induces discomfort. The hair shirt was used to mortify the body as a form of repentance.

21. Robinson, *Anskar*.

22. James Reston, Jr., "Be Christian or Die." *Christian History Institute*, no. 63, accessed December 4, 2014, https://www.christianhistoryinstitute.org/magazine/article/norway-part-1-be-christian-or-die/.

23. Ibid.

24. Ibid.

25. Ibid.

26. Ibid.

27. *Life of Methodius* 5.2, in John Paul II, *Slavorum Apostoli* 9, address given at Rome, 1985, accessed December 4, 2014, http://www.vatican.va/holy_father/john_paul_ii/encyclicals/documents/hf_jp-ii_enc_19850602_slavorum-apostoli_en.html.

28. Ibid.

29. Ibid., 5.

30. Ibid., 2.6.

31. Ibid., 2.7.

32. Troparion Hymn to Sts. Cyril and Methodus, found at the American Orthodox Institute website, accessed June 26, 2015, http://www.aoiusa.org/sts-cyril-and-methodius/.

33. Eusebius, *Church History* 3.1, trans. Arthur Cushman McGiffert, in *Nicene and Post-Nicene Fathers*, 2nd series, vol. 1, eds. Philip Schaff and Henry Wace (Buffalo: Christian Literature, 1890), accessed January 25, 2015, http://www.newadvent.org/fathers/250103.htm.

34. *The Primary Chronicle*, trans. unknown, hosted by Professor Alan Kimball at the University of Oregon, accessed December 4, 2014, http://pages.uoregon.edu/kimball/chronicle.htm.

35. Ibid.

36. Ibid.

37. Ibid.

38. Ibid.

39. Ibid.

40. Ibid.

PART 19: THE FACE OF GOD AND SCHISM

1. Leontius, quoted in Protopresbyter Alexander Schmemann, "Byzantium, Iconoclasm and the Monks," *St. Vladimir's Seminary Quarterly* 3, no. 3 (Fall 1959): 18–34, accessed January 2, 2014, http://www.schmemann .org/byhim/byzantiumiconoclasm.html.

2. *Council in Trullo*, canon 55, trans. Henry Percival, in Philip Schaff and Wace eds., *Nicene and Post-Nicene Fathers*, vol. 14 (Buffalo: Christian Literature, 1900), accessed January 2, 2015, http://www.newadvent.org /fathers/3814.htm.

3. Ibid., canon 75.

4. Ibid., canon 82.

5. Andrew J. Ekonomou, *Byzantine Rome and the Greek Popes* (New York: Lexington Books, 2007), 222.

6. *The Catholic Encyclopedia*, s.v. "Council in Trullo" (New York: Robert Appleton, 1908), accessed online at New Advent, January 2, 2015, http:// www.newadvent.org/cathen/04311b.htm.

7. J. B. Bury, *A History of the Later Roman Empire* (New York: MacMillan, 1923), 359, accessed via LacusCurtius, June 25, 2015, http://penelope .uchicago.edu/Thayer/E/Roman/Texts/secondary/BURLAT/home.html.

8. Theophanes, *Anni Mundi* 402, trans. Harry Turtledove in *The Chronicle of Theophanes* (Philadelphia: University of Pennsylvania Press, 1982), 93.

9. Ibid., 405, 97.

10. "Letter from Pope Gregory II to Emperor Leo III," Oliver J. Thatcher and Edgar Holmes McNeal, eds., *Source Book for Mediæval History* (New York: Scribners, 1905), accessed January 2, 2015, http://rbsche.people .wm.edu/H111_doc_gregoryiitoleoiii.html.

11. Horace K. Mann, *The Lives of the Popes in the Early Middle Ages*, vol. I: *The Popes Under the Lombard Rule, Part 2, 657–795* (London: Trubner, 1903), 205–6.

12. John Damascene, *On Holy Images*, trans. Mary H. Allies (London: Thomas Baker, 1898), 19.

13. Theophanes, *Anni Mundi* 400, trans. Harry Turtledove in *The Chronicle of Theophanes* (Philadelphia: University of Pennsylvania Press, 1982), 91.

14. Ibid.

15. Ibid., 442, 130.
16. Ibid., 443, 131.
17. "Epitome of the Definition of the Iconoclastic Conciliabulum, Held in Constantinople, AD 754," in Fordham University *Medieval Sourcebook*, accessed January 2, 2015, http://legacy.fordham.edu/halsall/source/icono-cncl754.asp.
18. "Excerpts from the Acts of the Second Council of Nicea," session 4, trans. Henry Percival., in *Nicene and Post-Nicene Fathers,* 2nd series, vol. 14, eds. Philip Schaff and Henry Wace (Buffalo: Christian Literature, 1900), accessed January 2, 2015, http://www.newadvent.org/fathers/3819.htm.
19. J. B. Bury, *The Cambridge Medieval History,* vol. 4 (Cambridge: Cambridge University Press, 1923), 30.
20. Ibid., 31–32.
21. *The Catholic Encyclopedia*, s.v. "Iconoclasm," accessed June 25, 2015, http://www.newadvent.org/cathen/07620a.htm.
22. *The Catholic Encyclopedia*, s.v. "Photius of Constantinople," accessed January 2, 2015, http://www.newadvent.org/cathen/12043b.htm.
23. Sergeï Nikolaevich Bulgakov, *The Comforter* (Grand Rapids: Eerdmans, 2004), 95.

CONCLUSION

1. Augustine, *Confessions* 1.1.
2. Dan Murphy, "Islamic State Beheads 21 Christians in Libya on film, signaling major expansion," *Christian Science Monitor,* February 15, 2015, http://www.csmonitor.com/World/Security-Watch/Backchannels/2015/0215/Islamic-State-beheads-21-Christians-in-Libya-on-film-signaling-major-expansion.

GLOSSARY OF BIOGRAPHICAL, GEOGRAPHICAL, AND THEOLOGICAL REFERENCES

1. Ferdinand Gregovarius, *The History of the City of Rome in the Middle Ages,* trans. Annie Hamilton (London: George Bell and Sons, 1896), 47.

IMAGE CREDITS

PART 1

1. https://upload.wikimedia.org/wikipedia/commons/a/af/Nero_pushkin
   .jpg. Image uploaded to Wikimedia Commons by user Shakko. Licensed
   under the terms of Creative Commons Attribution-Share Alike 3.0
   Unported. http://creativecommons.org/licenses/by-sa/3.0/legalcode.
2. https://upload.wikimedia.org/wikipedia/commons/9/94/Michelangelo
   _Merisi_da_Caravaggio_-_The_Conversion_of_St._Paul_-_WGA04135
   .jpg. Uploaded to Wikimedia Commons by user JarektUploadBot. This
   work is in the public domain.
3. https://upload.wikimedia.org/wikipedia/commons/f/f9/Paolo
   Uccello-_Stoning_of_St_Stephen_-_WGA23196.jpg. Uploaded to
   Wikimedia Commons by user JarektUploadBot. This work is in the
   public domain.

PART 2

1. https://upload.wikimedia.org/wikipedia/commons/b/ba/Ignatius_of
   _Antioch.jpg. Image uploaded to Wikimedia Commons by user Shakko.
   This work is in the public domain.

PART 3

1. https://upload.wikimedia.org/wikipedia/commons/1/13/Saint_Irenaeus
   .jpg. Image uploaded to Wikimedia Commons by user Mattes. This
   work is in the public domain.
2. https://upload.wikimedia.org/wikipedia/commons/8/8d/Justin_Martyr
   .jpg. Image uploaded to Wikimedia Commons by user Tomisti. This
   work is in the public domain.
3. https://upload.wikimedia.org/wikipedia/commons/e/ea/Bust_of_Marcus
   _Aurelius.jpg. Image uploaded to Wikimedia Commons by user Shakko.
   This image is licensed under Creative Commons license 3.0, http://
   creativecommons.org/licenses/by-sa/3.0/legalcode.

PART 4

1. https://upload.wikimedia.org/wikipedia/commons/6/6b/Perpetua.jpg.
   Uploaded to Wikimedia Commons by user Canoe1967. This work is in
   the public domain.
2. https://upload.wikimedia.org/wikipedia/commons/e/e9/Tertullian.jpg.
   Image uploaded to Wikimedia Commons by user Sergei Lachinov. This
   work is in the public domain.
3. http://upload.wikimedia.org/wikipedia/commons/0/0e/Herbert
   _schmalz28.jpg. Uploaded to Wikimedia Commons by user Pimbrils.
   This work is in the public domain.

PART 5

1. http://upload.wikimedia.org/wikipedia/commons/2/20/Origen.jpg.
   This work is in the public domain, uploaded to Wikimedia Commons by
   unknown user.
2. https://upload.wikimedia.org/wikipedia/commons/b/b8/Codex
   _Sinaiticus_Matthew_6%2C32–7%2C27.JPG. This work is in the
   public domain, uploaded to Wikimedia Commons by unknown user.
3. https://upload.wikimedia.org/wikipedia/commons/7/73/Jean
   -L%C3%A9on_G%C3%A9r%C3%B4me_-_The_Christian
   _Martyrs%27_Last_Prayer_-_Walters_37113.jpg. This work is in the
   public domain, uploaded to Wikimedia Commons by user Soerfm.
4. http://commons.wikimedia.org/wiki/File:The_Martyrdom_of
   _St_Sebastian.jpg. This work is in the public domain, uploaded to
   Wikimedia Commons by user Gun Powder Ma.

452

PART 6

1. http://commons.wikimedia.org/wiki/Category:Chi_Rho_symbols#
   /media/File:Chi_rho_3_a_wiki.jpg. This work is in the public domain,
   uploaded to Wikimedia Commons by user Mich Taylor.
2. https://upload.wikimedia.org/wikipedia/commons/3/3a/Battle_of_the
   _Milvian_Bridge_by_Giulio_Romano%2C_1520–24.jpg. This work is
   in the public domain, uploaded to Wikimedia Commons.
3. https://upload.wikimedia.org/wikipedia/commons/c/ce/Rome-Capitole
   -StatueConstantin.jpg. This work is licensed under Creative Commons
   Attribution-Share Alike 3.0 Unported, uploaded to Wikimedia
   Commons by user Jean-Christophe BENOIST.
4. https://upload.wikimedia.org/wikipedia/commons/f/f9/Trier_basilica
   _DSC02373.jpg. This work is licensed under Creative Commons
   Attribution-Share Alike 3.0 Unported, uploaded by user David Monniaux.

PART 7

1. http://commons.wikimedia.org/wiki/File:THE_FIRST_COUNCIL
   _OF_NICEA.jpg. This work is licensed under Creative Commons
   Attribution-Share Alike 3.0 Unported, uploaded by user Coemgenus.
2. https://upload.wikimedia.org/wikipedia/commons/6/6a/Mar_Jacob
   _Church%2C_Nisibis.jpg. Photograph by Gareth Hughes, uploaded
   to Wikimedia Commons by user Garzo. This work is licensed under
   Creative Commons Attribution-Share Alike 3.0 Unported.

PART 8

1. https://upload.wikimedia.org/wikipedia/commons/1/16/The_Torment
   _of_Saint_Anthony_%28Michelangelo%29.jpg. Uploaded to
   Wikimedia Commons by the Kimball Art Museum, Dallas, TX. This
   image is in the public domain.
2. https://upload.wikimedia.org/wikipedia/commons/2/25/Assuan
   _Simeonskloster_15.jpg. Photograph by Olaf Tausch. Uploaded to
   Wikimedia Commons by user Oltau. This image is licensed under
   Creative Commons Attribution 3.0 Unported.
3. http://commons.wikimedia.org/wiki/File:Ephrem_the_Syrian
   _(mosaic_in_Nea_Moni).jpg. Uploaded to Wikimedia Commons by
   unknown user. This image is in the public domain.

4. http://commons.wikimedia.org/wiki/File:Column_of_St_Simeon_The
_Stylite.jpg. Photograph taken and uploaded to Wikimedia Commons by
user Bo-deh~commonswiki. This work is in the public domain.

PART 9

1. https://upload.wikimedia.org/wikipedia/commons/0/0a/Giuliano
_l%27Apostata%2C_IV_secolo%2C_Museo_archeologico
_nazionale%2C_Atene.jpg. Uploaded to Wikimedia Commons by
user MICHI abba. This work is licensed under the Creative Commons
Attribution-Share Alike 4.0 International.
2. https://upload.wikimedia.org/wikipedia/commons/b/b1/U%C3%A7hisar
_Castle_01.jpg. Photograph taken and uploaded to Wikimedia Commons
by Bernard Gagnon. This work is licensed under the Creative Commons
Attribution-Share Alike 3.0 Unported, 2.5 Generic, 2.0 Generic and 1.0
Generic license.
3. http://commons.wikimedia.org/wiki/File:St._Basil_the_Great,_lower
_register_of_sanctuary.jpg. Image uploaded by user Raso mk. This work
is in the public domain.

PART 10

1. https://upload.wikimedia.org/wikipedia/commons/0/05/Theodosius
.jpg. Uploaded to Wikimedia Commons by user Henryart. This work
is licensed under the Creative Commons Attribution-Share Alike 2.0
Generic license.
2. https://upload.wikimedia.org/wikipedia/commons/d/dd/Council_of
_Constantinople_381-stavropoleos_church.jpg. Uploaded to Wikimedia
Commons by user Igna. This work is in the public domain.
3. https://upload.wikimedia.org/wikipedia/commons/9/9a
/AmbroseOfMilan.jpg. Uploaded to Wikimedia Commons by user
Irmgard. This work is in the public domain.
4. https://upload.wikimedia.org/wikipedia/commons/d/df/Camillo
Procaccini-_St_Ambrose_Stopping_Theodosius_-_WGA18422.jpg.
Uploaded to Wikimedia Commons by user JarektUploadBot. This work
is in the public domain.
5. https://upload.wikimedia.org/wikipedia/commons/0/07/Artus
Wolffort-_St_Jerome.jpg. Uploaded to Wikimedia Commons by user
FRAYKT. This work is in the public domain.

PART 11

1. https://upload.wikimedia.org/wikipedia/commons/0/0e/Hosios
   Loukas%28nave%2C_south_east_conch%29_-_John_Chrysostom
   _-_detail.jpg. Uploaded to Wikimedia Commons by user Shakko. This
   work is in the public domain.
2. https://upload.wikimedia.org/wikipedia/commons/6/6c/John
   _Chrysostom_and_Aelia_Eudoxia.jpg. Uploaded to Wikimedia
   Commons by user Testus. This work is in the public domain.
3. https://upload.wikimedia.org/wikipedia/commons/d/df/Fra_angelico
   _-_conversion_de_saint_augustin.jpg. Uploaded to Wikimedia
   Commons by user Drolexandre. This work is in the public domain.
4. https://upload.wikimedia.org/wikipedia/commons/4/44/Augustine
   _Lateran.jpg. Uploaded to Wikimedia Commons by user Mladifilozof.
   This work is in the public domain.

PART 13

1. https://upload.wikimedia.org/wikipedia/commons/f/f9/Concil_Toled
   .jpg. Uploaded to Wikimedia Commons by user Ancoma. This image is
   in the public domain.
2. https://upload.wikimedia.org/wikipedia/commons/6/6b/Clovis_I%2C
   _King_of_the_Franks.jpg. Uploaded to Wikimedia Commons by user
   JoJan. This image is in the public domain.
3. https://upload.wikimedia.org/wikipedia/commons/c/cf/Bust_of_St.
   _Patrick_at_Dublin_Castle_%288339101774%29.jpg. Photograph by
   Frank Kovalchek, uploaded to Wikimedia Commons by user Magnus
   Manske. This file is licensed under the Creative Commons Attribution
   2.0 Generic license.

PART 14

1. https://upload.wikimedia.org/wikipedia/commons/8/89/Meister_von
   _San_Vitale_in_Ravenna.jpg. Uploaded to Wikimedia Commons by
   user Trajan 117. The reproduction is part of a collection of reproductions
   compiled by the Yorck Project. The compilation copyright is held by
   Zenodot Verlagsgesellschaft mbH and licensed under the GNU Free
   Documentation License.
2. https://upload.wikimedia.org/wikipedia/commons/7/79/Teodora1.jpg.
   Uploaded to Wikimedia Commons by user Aranzuisor. This image is in
   the public domain.

3. https://upload.wikimedia.org/wikipedia/commons/c/c2
/LocationByzantineEmpire.png. Map made by Zakuragi. Image
uploaded to Wikimedia Commons by user Tonym88. This file is
licensed under the Creative Commons Attribution-Share Alike 3.0
Unported license.

4. https://upload.wikimedia.org/wikipedia/commons/9/9c/Interior
_of_Hagia_Sofia.JPG. Photograph by Philip Romanski, uploaded to
Wikimedia Commons by user Mr. Seafall. This file is licensed under the
Creative Commons Attribution-Share Alike 3.0 Unported license.

5. https://upload.wikimedia.org/wikipedia/commons/4/49/Hagia
_Sophia_09.JPG. Photograph by Osvaldo Gago, uploaded to Wikimedia
Commons by the photographer. This file is licensed under the Creative
Commons Attribution-Share Alike 3.0 Unported license.

Part 15

1. https://upload.wikimedia.org/wikipedia/commons/2/20/Mohammed
_receiving_revelation_from_the_angel_Gabriel.jpg. Uploaded to Wikimedia
Commons by user Mladifilozof. This work is in the public domain.

2. https://upload.wikimedia.org/wikipedia/commons/3/31/Banu
_Qurayza.png. Image uploaded to Wikimedia Commons by user
Magnus Manske. This work is in the public domain.

3. https://upload.wikimedia.org/wikipedia/commons/f/f7/Greekfire
-madridskylitzes1.jpg. Image uploaded to Wikimedia Commons by user
Amandajm. This work is in the public domain.

4. https://upload.wikimedia.org/wikipedia/commons/1/15/Abbasid
_Caliphate_900.png. Image uploaded to Wikimedia Commons by user
Ro 4444. This file is licensed under the Creative Commons Attribution-
Share Alike 3.0 Unported license. Background topography taken from
DEMIS Mapserver, which are public domain.

5. https://upload.wikimedia.org/wikipedia/commons/e/e7/Steuben
_-_Bataille_de_Poitiers.png. Uploaded to Wikimedia Commons by user
Bender235. This image is in the public domain.

Part 16

1. https://upload.wikimedia.org/wikipedia/commons/6/6f/Charlemagne
_coronation.jpg. Image uploaded to Wikimedia Commons by user
Albedo-ukr. This image is in the public domain.

2. https://upload.wikimedia.org/wikipedia/commons/6/61/Reeve_and_Serfs.jpg. Image uploaded to Wikimedia Commons. This work is in the public domain.

3. https://upload.wikimedia.org/wikipedia/commons/b/b5/Aachen _Domschatz_Bueste1.jpg. Photograph by Beckstet, uploaded to Wikimedia Commons by user CsvBibra. This file is licensed under the Creative Commons Attribution-Share Alike 3.0 Unported license.

4. https://upload.wikimedia.org/wikipedia/commons/3/3a/Raban-Maur _Alcuin_Otgar.jpg. Image uploaded to Wikimedia Commons by user Thomas Gun. This work is in the public domain.

PART 17

1. https://upload.wikimedia.org/wikipedia/commons/8/8f/Dehio_212 _Cluny.jpg. Image uploaded to Wikimedia Commons by user Fb78. This work is in the public domain.

PART 18

1. https://upload.wikimedia.org/wikipedia/commons/7/7e/Kulturhistorisk _museum%2C_Oslo_-_IMG_9159.jpg. Photograph taken and uploaded to Wikimedia Commons by user Daderot. This image is in the public domain.

2. https://upload.wikimedia.org/wikipedia/commons/5/50/Viking _Expansion.svg. Map created by Max Naylor and uploaded to Wikimedia Commons by user Wereldberger578. This image is in the public domain.

3. https://upload.wikimedia.org/wikipedia/commons/6/6d/Alfred_-_MS _Royal_14_B_VI.jpg. Image uploaded to Wikimedia Commons by user Aelfgar. This image is in the public domain.

4. https://commons.wikimedia.org/wiki/File:Lindisfarne_Castle_,_Holy _Island_(7272362210).jpg. Photograph by Phil Sangwell, and uploaded to Wikimedia Commons by user Ultra7. This file is licensed under the Creative Commons Attribution 2.0 Generic license.

5. https://upload.wikimedia.org/wikipedia/commons/d/d2 /LindisfarneFol27rIncipitMatt.jpg. Image uploaded to Wikimedia Commons by user Airunp. This image is in the public domain.

PART 19

1. https://upload.wikimedia.org/wikipedia/commons/8/8a/Mosaik-Ikone _Christus_der_Barmherzige.jpg. Photograph taken and uploaded to Wikimedia Commons by user Andreas Praefcke. This image is in the public domain.

Index

Libanius, 200

Liber iudiciorum (Visigothic law code), 241

librarians, patron saint of, 197

Licinius, 95–96, 97–98
  reports of persecutions, 98–99

The Life of Saint Anthony (Athanasius), 139

Lindisfarne Gospels, 354

Lindisfarne monastery
  attack on, 347
  destruction of, 353–354

lions, Ignatius death by, 23

Lombards, 253

London, 352

Lord's Supper. *See* Eucharist

Louis the Pious, 324

Lucina, 88

Lucius, 41–42

Lucius of Alexandria, 167

Ludwig (German king), 357

lust, Evagrius and, 145

Luther, Martin, 215, 390

Luxenberg, Christophe, 290

Lyon, 67
  persecution in, 48

M

Macarius (bishop of Jerusalem), 106–107, 142

Maccabees, 197

Macedonians, 222

Macedonius, 160

magic rites, 33

al-Mahdi (caliph), 297
  Timothy I and, 298–300

Maimonides (rabbi), 301

Manichaeans, 83–84, 178, 221
  Augustine and, 207

Manichaeism, Augustine and, 208

Marcion, 28, 33–34, 57
  Justin on, 40

Marcus, 33

Marcus Aurelius, and martyrdom, 45–49

Mariamne (sister of Philip), 12

Marinus (pope), 351

Mark of Arethusa (bishop), persecution, 164–165

Mark the Evangelist, and Alexandrian church founding, 231

Marozia (Theophylact's daughter), 332

marriage, 372
  Christian teachings, 56

Martin of Tours, 152–154, 336, 405

Martina, 63

martyrdom
  Ignatius on, 25–26
  Marcus Aurelius and, 45–49
  of Origen's father, 73

martyrion, 107

Mary (mother of Jesus)
  Ambrose on, 185
  doctrine of the assumption, 378
  as *Theotocos*, 222

Mary (Pachomius's sister), 146

Matthew (apostle), 11–12

Maturus, 46

Maurice (Byzantine emperor), 280

Maxentius, 96

Maximinus Daia, 96
  Constantine and Licinius against, 98

Maximinus (emperor), 62–63, 90–91
  resignation from power, 89

Maximus (bishop), 180

Maximus the Confessor, xiv, 283–284, 405

Mecca, 288